CW00832471

Three Cheers for the CHESAPEAKE!

History of the 4th Maryland Light Artillery Battery in the Civil War

RICK RICHTER

Schiffer Publishing Ltd

4880 Lower Valley Road • Atglen, PA 19310

Other Schiffer Books on Related Subjects:
Their Horses Climbed Trees: A Chronicle of the California 100 and Battalion in the Civil War, from San Francisco to Appomattox, ISBN: 978-0-7643-1391-2
Chesapeake Bay in the Civil War, ISBN: 978-0-7643-3592-1

Library of Congress Control Number: 2016963697

Copy edit by Sunah Cherwin
Type set in Aldine721 BT/Times New Roman

ISBN: 978-0-7643-5262-1
Printed in China

Published by Schiffer Publishing, Ltd.
4880 Lower Valley Road
Atglen, PA 19310
Phone: (610) 593-1777; Fax: (610) 593-2002
E-mail: Info@schifferbooks.com
Web: www.schifferbooks.com

For Philip, who introduced me to the Chesapeake.

MARYLAND LINE CONFEDERATE SOLDIERS HOME
VISITORS ALWAYS WELCOME
ENTRANCE TO CONFEDERATE SOLDIER'S HOME, PIKESVILLE, BALTIMORE, MD.

CONTENTS

FOREWORD

In the years following the Civil War many memoirs were written by prominent Maryland Confederate soldiers. Most of these recounted service in the infantry or cavalry branches of the Confederate Army. Only two focused on the "Long Arm of Lee": a memoir by Lt. Col. Richard Snowden Andrews of the 1st Maryland Artillery, and Capt. William L. Ritter's diary of service in the 3rd Maryland Artillery, which was published serially in *The Southern Historical Society Papers*. Although it was written during the war, Maryland historian Jonathan Thomas Scharf's account of service in the 1st Maryland Artillery was not published until 1992. A renewed interest in Maryland Confederate soldiers during the last two decades has yielded a number of excellent books on the infantry, the cavalry, and their associations with the Stuart Horse Artillery. Until now, the only reference to the Chesapeake Artillery has been a mere twenty pages in Goldsborough's *The Maryland Line*. Rick Richter's *Three Cheers for the Chesapeake!* is a major contribution to the history of the Maryland Confederate soldier and the artillery corps of the Army of Northern Virginia.

One cannot help but appreciate the courage and devotion shown by the men of Maryland who enlisted in the Confederate Army. During the war two infantry units, two battalions of cavalry, and four batteries of artillery carried the banner of the Old Line State. Thousands of other recruits served in non-Maryland units, as well as in the Confederate Navy, the US Marine Corps, and the US Secret Service. They were all true volunteers, risking their lives and fortunes to serve the cause they believed in. The least known of all of these were the men of the Chesapeake Artillery.

Most of the men made their way south across the lower Potomac River. When the battery organized at Machodoc, Virginia, on January 1, 1862, it consisted of only three officers and forty-seven enlisted men. The author goes deep into the makeup of the unit to bring to life each man who served in the battery. For instance, he notes the first commanding officer in the battery was the only slave owner and gives the prewar occupation of many of the men who served in the battery. The one common denominator was that "Maryland, and home, was behind Federal lines." As a result of an act passed by the Confederate Congress recognizing Maryland units as officially part of the Confederate Army, the Chesapeake Artillery became the 4th Maryland Light Artillery on May 15, 1862.

The battery would see its first action and suffer its first combat losses at Cedar

Mountain. Six weeks of constant campaigning rendered horses and equipment unserviceable. The Chesapeake Artillery was one of three batteries left behind at Harper's Ferry to refit from the captured stores there. The battery's success throughout the summer campaigns resulted in a great deal of notoriety. Its banner would be heavily laden with battle honors by the end of the war. This came at a heavy price. Counter-battery fire usually resulted in the loss of limbs and other ghastly wounds, if not outright death. At both First and Second Fredericksburg, the battery was subjected to intense counter-battery fire. At Gettysburg, the battalion was positioned on Benner's Hill to supply fire support for the Confederate attack on Culp's Hill. A highlight of this book is the description by the author of the destruction of the Chesapeake Battery during the battle there.

After a long period of recuperation, the Fourth Maryland Artillery fought from Cold Harbor to Petersburg. The Chesapeake Artillery died a glorious death on April 2, 1865, as part of the valiant defense of Fort Gregg. A remnant of the battery marched to Appomattox with Lee's army, where Sgt. John Richardson surrendered the last of the Chesapeake—one gun and thirteen men. It is time for the story of the Chesapeake to be told.

Daniel Carroll Toomey
Author, *The Civil War in Maryland*
Baltimore, Maryland

PREFACE

Comprising chiefly of men who lived near the shores of its namesake bay, the Chesapeake Artillery was the last Confederate battery organized from the state of Maryland. It was also by far the smallest, with only 135 men serving in its ranks during the course of the Civil War—barely more than half the average enrollment of the 1st, 2nd, and 3rd Maryland batteries of the Confederate Army. In spite of its size, the unit was frequently cited for its bravery and efficiency by its superior officers and commanding generals, including even Stonewall Jackson.

The motivations of its members to join the battery—like those of all Confederate soldiers, and soldiers from Maryland in particular—were varied and complex. Some joined because of Southern sympathy, or to protect their wealth and property, and some to seek adventure. Still others sought to escape persecution in Federally occupied Maryland, or to avoid service in the Union Army after being drafted.

Formed on January 1, 1862, from elements of companies that had tried unsuccessfully to organize a second Confederate infantry regiment in Maryland, the Chesapeake Artillery was not accepted into Confederate service until May, and did not see its first action until the Battle of Cedar Mountain that August. As part of Stonewall Jackson's command, it performed with distinction at Cedar Mountain, Second Manassas, Harper's Ferry, and 1st and 2nd Fredericksburg, until incurring devastating losses during the Pennsylvania campaign (see appendix B for an outline of the unit's operations at Second Manassas and appendix C for complete details on the unit's losses at Gettysburg). Consequently, for the next nine months it served only as a two-gun section during the Bristoe and Mine Run campaigns until brought back to battery strength at the formation of the Maryland Line in spring 1864 (see appendix G for an outline of the company's armament during the war). In this capacity the company fought at Cold Harbor and in the Petersburg campaign. In 1865, discharges, transfers, illness, and detail assignments resulted in the reduction of the battery's strength to fewer than thirty men by March, and it was ordered that the battery be consolidated with the 2nd Maryland Artillery, although this order was never carried out (see appendix D for a discussion of the unit's strength during the war). Even thus limited in effectiveness, a portion of the unit performed heroically in the Petersburg defenses at Fort Gregg—the "Confederate Thermopylae"—as part of a 350-man force that resisted 4,000 Federal attackers for several hours just a week before the end of the war. Only thirteen members of the company were present at the final surrender at Appomattox.

The need for horses would also limit the battery's effectiveness and shape the nature of its service. Even just a few weeks after its organization men were detailed from the company to procure additional horses. During the Maryland campaign the battery was detained at Harper's Ferry because of the condition of its horses, and as a result did not participate in the Battle of Sharpsburg. Severe losses in horses occurred in both battles at Fredericksburg, as well as Gettysburg, and by July 1864, while at Petersburg, the battery had fewer horses than required to take active operations in the field. This situation was not ameliorated until the disbandment of the 1st Maryland Artillery in October, when the horses of that unit were given to the Chesapeake. In spite of their difficulties, the 4th Maryland Artillery consistently demonstrated a high level of unit cohesion and esprit de corps (see appendix F on desertions).

No comprehensive modern history of the unit has been written. As might be expected from its limited enrollment, there are few primary sources of the battery's history. The earliest and most extensive of these is a series of articles published in the *Baltimore Telegram* in the postwar years before 1879 by Pvt. Jacob F. Cook. Cook's highly readable and frequently humorous anecdotes also provide some of the few battle descriptions extant for the company. Although he is the progenitor of a couple of incorrect stories about the battery, Cook's history provides many details of the company's service that are supported by other sources (see appendix A on a discussion of these myths). His accounts are disordered in time and sequence, but since he frequently referred to weather conditions and the company's position relative to other units, these are readily unraveled.

The best-known and frequently cited primary source on the company's history is the chapter on the 4th Maryland Artillery in William W. Goldsborough's *The Maryland Line in the Confederate Army*, published in 1900.

Goldsborough obtained his material from printed sources, as well as conversations and correspondence with members of Confederate Maryland units, some of whom also wrote portions of his book. Many of Goldsborough's descriptions of the 4th Maryland Artillery's service are supported by other sources, although he repeated some of Cook's errors from the *Baltimore Telegram* articles. It is apparent that the latter half of Goldsborough's chapter on the company was written by Pvt. Christopher Goodhand Lynch. Lynch was one of only six soldiers of the battery present at Gettysburg and Fort Gregg, and in a position to describe the action in both battles, and the only one who wrote about the battery postwar. Further, the roster and casualty list in Goldsborough's book conforms nearly exactly in content and structure with Lynch's handwritten lists in the collections of the US Army Heritage and Education Center in Carlisle, Pennsylvania. Lynch also wrote additional accounts of the battery's experiences at Gettysburg and Fort Gregg for his hometown newspaper, the *Centreville Record*.

There are three principal sources of contemporary primary accounts by members of the company. The largest is the collection of letters by Sgt. James Peter Williams in the Albert and Shirley Small Special Collections Library at the University of Virginia. Williams originally enlisted in the Richmond Howitzers, but served with the Chesapeake Artillery for a year from June 1862 until just before the Battle of Gettysburg. Williams' extensive writing provides numerous insights into the lives of the men of the battery, battle accounts, and details of its movements.

Another important cache of letters is contained within the Ward Family Papers at the Library of Congress. Although few in number, letters from Capt. William D. Brown and Pvt. John J. Hooff provide important details of the company's experiences not found in other sources. Lastly, a surprisingly rich source of contemporary material is contained in the Compiled Service Records of the soldiers of the Chesapeake Artillery in the National Archives. Because of the unique situation whereby Maryland Confederate soldiers could apply for a discharge after three years' service, there are a number of letters in these records written by the men themselves and their character references as part of the application process. These letters not only provide many details of the men's service and their reasons for serving, but also helped contribute additional information on casualties not available elsewhere.

The information included in the Compiled Service Records has also been combined with that of the 1860 Census to create a statistical profile of the unit that was previously unknown. Using Joseph T. Glatthaar's work in applying statistical analysis to this data for soldiers of the Army of Northern Virginia as a basis of comparison, some of the 4th Artillery's salient characteristics become evident. Compared to their counterparts in the Army of Northern Virginia, the men of the Chesapeake were much younger, had a much higher literacy rate, and were far more likely to have been in occupations of skilled labor, or white-collar or professional work, and to come from lower- or middle-class households. They were also only half as likely to come from slaveholding households as the other soldiers of the Army of Northern Virginia.

The watershed for primary accounts of the unit occurred around the time of the Battle of Gettysburg. Cook left the unit, Williams transferred out, Brown was killed, and there are no further letters of Hooff extant. Even Lynch provided no details about the unit's service for the nearly two-year interval between Gettysburg and Fort Gregg, creating a distinct paucity of information about the battery during this period. To supplement the few mentions of the unit in the official records during this time, the accounts of soldiers in other units serving in proximity to the 4th Maryland Artillery have been used to complete the picture of their operations. Notably these include the memoir of Pvt. John Ford Hatton of the 1st Maryland Artillery, as well as the diary of Pvt. Samuel Thomas McCullough of the 2nd Maryland Infantry Battalion, both in the Library of Congress.

Fortunately, there is considerable source material about the unit's operations during the last weeks of the war. These include first-hand accounts of the attack on Fort Gregg by Lynch, Pvt. Edward Cottrell, and men in other units, as well as a second-hand account by Cook. The diary of Col. David G. McIntosh in the Virginia Historical Society collections, as well as a published memoir based on diary entries by Lt. Col. William Owen—the battery's battalion commanders at the time—provide extensive details on its movements during the Appomattox Campaign.

Further postwar material on veterans of the unit and their experiences are contained in the records of the Society of the Army & Navy of the Confederate States in Maryland, as well as those of the Maryland Line Confederate Soldiers' Home (see appendix G for a discussion of reminiscences by members of the home after the war). Both reside in the collections of the Maryland Historical Society in Baltimore.

Finally, a few comments on nomenclature. As with nearly all organizations that joined the Confederate Army, the company chose its own moniker. Designated the 4th Maryland Artillery when it was accepted into Confederate service, the unit continued to be almost universally referred to as the Chesapeake Artillery, even in official correspondence. At the formation of the Maryland Line in April 1864, the 4th Maryland Artillery designation took on consistent use in official records, but the men of the company, as well as others in the Army of Northern Virginia, continued to call the battery the Chesapeake Artillery, or simply the Chesapeake, and the men referred to themselves as the Chesapeakes. This is also how they are referred to here, with usage of the 4th Maryland Artillery in the text more prevalent after April 1864. Original spelling and punctuation have been retained in contemporary accounts. In addition, the individual men are referred to by their usual given names and nicknames, if known, as they would have been at the time, and the rank they held at the time they are mentioned.

In many ways, the composition and the record of the Chesapeake Artillery, 4th Maryland Light Artillery Battery, are unique. That its members bravely stood to their guns is reflected in their killed and captured casualty rates that, when combined, were double the average of an artillery unit in the Army of Northern Virginia (see appendix E for a discussion of the battery's losses during the war). They provide further insight not only into the service of Maryland Confederate soldiers, but that of the artillery arm of the Army of Northern Virginia.

ACKNOWLEDGMENTS

Authors consistently write that they could not have completed their book without the help of others. I certainly have found that to be true to a far greater extent than I expected, and as this book is the culmination of a quarter century of research, I am grateful for the help of a great many people.

Dan Toomey is the leading authority on the Civil War in Maryland and has been of vital help in his support and participation. From pitching the idea of writing this book, to identifying sources, proofreading, and making comments and suggestions, and writing the foreword, he has been instrumental in making this project happen. I can never thank him enough and am pleased to call him a friend.

John Hennessy, chief historian at the Fredericksburg and Spotsylvania National Military Park, cheerfully lent his help in providing and pinpointing sources. John is the acknowledged expert on the Second Manassas campaign; he reviewed the part of the narrative on that campaign and made several helpful suggestions that clarified the text. He also helped test and hone the conclusions in the appendix regarding the Chesapeake's movements and actions during the battle.

John Heiser, chief historian at the Gettysburg National Military Park, has frequently lent his expertise as a historian, cartographer, and master of the Gettysburg NMP Library's considerable holdings. I have been seeking John's assistance for years, and he has always been able to point out sources of interest; I owe him many thanks.

Dr. Kerry Richter of Mahidol University in Bangkok helped structure the statistical analyses and reviewed the portions of the text on the results. She was enormously helpful in bringing this part of the study to life.

George Brigham, president of the Central Maryland Heritage League, generously lent his time, expertise, and research. George is the leading expert on the Civil War in Frederick County, and his research on Civil War soldiers from that area is staggering. He helped clarify the background of a number of soldiers of the Chesapeake.

Two gentlemen who are no longer with us contributed to unraveling conflicting information about the Chesapeake's actions and the disposition of its wounded and dead at Gettysburg. Greg Coco and Ron Waddell lent their time in conducting me through the area around Benner's Hill and sharing their knowledge of now-vanished farm lanes and sightlines, as well as their expertise and research on aid stations and field hospitals. They are missed.

Courtney Wilson, executive director of the Baltimore & Ohio Railroad Museum, also encouraged me to take on this project and provided some helpful suggestions on its scope that were adopted.

I am thankful for the enthusiasm and technical expertise of Jean and Cindy Buchen and the members of the Fourth Maryland Light Artillery living history group. Becky Plummer shared her wealth of sources and research into burial sites of members of the battery.

Dave Mark generously supplied the illustration of Capt. William D. Brown in uniform. W. W. Goldsborough's article on the Chesapeake Artillery's participation at Gettysburg is courtesy of the New York Historical Society, with thanks to Tammy Kiter. The picture of Goldsborough is courtesy of "Company D," 2nd Maryland Infantry, CSA, Living History Group, with thanks to Jake Duda. The picture of Lt. Col. William Miller Owen is courtesy of Glen C. Cangelosi, MD, and his excellent website on the Washington Artillery of New Orleans. Debi Burt, a descendent of Capt. Joseph Forrest, shared much family information and provided several photos of Forrest and his plantation homes. Thanks also to John McVey, who introduced me to Molly Shannahan Taylor, a direct descendent of Pvt. John Henry Kelly Shannahan II; she graciously provided his picture.

I am also indebted for the help and expertise of Kathy Shue, Craig Caba, Jeff Davis, and Mark Nesbitt of the Gettysburg Battlefield Preservation Association; Amber Paranick of the Library of Congress; Grant Gates of the Petersburg National Military Park; Dr. Richard J. Sommers of the US Army Heritage and Education Center; Mary Mannix of the Maryland Room at the C. Burr Artz Public Library in Frederick; Debbie Harner and Damon Talbot of the Special Collections Library at the Maryland Historical Society; John McClure and Lee Shepard of the Virginia Historical Society; Peter Himmelheber and Frankie Tippett of the St. Mary's County Historical Society; Catherine Perry of the Musselman Library Special Collections at Gettysburg College; Bob Caulk of Easton, who is related to Shannahan and Pvt. Francis M. Fairbanks; Shlomi Amiga of Shlomi Amiga Photography for his excellent work in producing the illustrations; and Jeff Penfound of Toronto.

I owe many repeated thanks to the willing, thoughtful, and dedicated help of all those anonymous librarians, archivists, and docents of the Adams County Historical Society; the Archives and Special Collections of the Waidner-Spahr Library at Dickinson College; the David M. Rubenstein Rare Book and Manuscript Library, Duke University; the Enoch Pratt Free Library; the Essex County Museum and Historical Society; Greenmount Cemetery; the Historical Society of Harford County; Loudon Park Cemetery; the Maryland State Archives; the National Archives; the New York State Library; the Northumberland County Historical Society; the Queen Anne's County Historical Society; the Special Collections Library at Virginia Commonwealth University; the Archives of the Virginia Military Institute; and the Albert and Shirley Small Special Collections Library at the University of Virginia.

Finally, I owe a huge thanks to my wife, Pat, for her encouragement and support, who over the years patiently endured countless days and weekends occupying her time while I explored libraries, archives, and battlefields with the guns of the Chesapeake. "They also serve who only stand and wait."

"I LEFT MARYLAND TO LEND MY AID TO THE CONFEDERATE CAUSE"

It was unseasonably warm the first day of January 1862, at the village of Machodoc in Virginia's Northern Neck region. Under a "lurid sky," fifty men gathered to enlist in the Confederate Army, an occurrence that likely all of Machodoc's few residents turned out to see. Virtually every town and village in the United States had already seen companies of local militia and newly recruited soldiers gather and march off to war, but this gathering of prospective soldiers was unique. These enlistees comprised a group of mostly Marylanders, many of whom, rather than enlisting in the local town square, had travelled over a hundred miles from home to do so. As they came from a border state that was not part of the Confederacy, they were forced to enlist in Virginia rather than in their home state. This reflected a commitment that went beyond the typical motivations of men who became soldiers from other states in the Confederacy.[1]

The "Chesapeake Artillery," as they called their group, was organized as a Virginia artillery battery with the official designation "Forrest's Company of Virginia Artillery" of the 4th Virginia Artillery Regiment. Their officers represented some of the wealthiest and most influential families in Maryland. The commander and mustering officer was Capt. Joseph Forrest. The heavily bearded Forrest was a thirty-eight-year-old owner of two plantations and the wealthiest man in St. Mary's County; he was descended from one of the oldest families in the state, the son of an officer of the War of 1812 and the grandson of an officer of the Revolution. He owned forty-five slaves—the only slave owner of the group. Shortly after the war broke out Forrest had formed and commanded a company of infantry known as "Saint

Modern view of the site of the village of Machodoc, Virginia. *Author*

Mary's Rangers." They had made their way to Fredericksburg and became a company commanded by Forrest designated as "Company A" of the prospective 2nd Maryland Infantry Regiment. Not enough recruits could be enlisted to make up the required number of soldiers for a regiment, so the effort was abandoned. Forrest's wealth, slave ownership, and influence in St. Mary's County had caught the attention of occupying Federal authorities: two months prior his wife and their six children, ages two to eleven, had been banished from Maryland for being "Southern sympathizers."[2]

Forrest's second in command was 1st Lt. William D. "Billy" Brown of Baltimore. The light-haired and charismatic Brown was about thirty, single, and came from a prominent and wealthy family. He owned the shipbuilding business started by his father. Brown already had extensive military experience, having served as the captain of the "Lafayette Guards," a prewar militia unit in Baltimore. Described as a "fine company" of thirty-five men, "the bearing of this company on parade was most soldierlike, and their marching bespoke severe drilling." At the start of the war Brown made his way to Richmond and enlisted in the Confederate Army as a 3rd lieutenant of Company E of the Hanover Court House Infantry, an unassigned infantry company; no doubt a number of the Lafayette Guards enlisted with him. This organization later moved to Fredericksburg in late summer 1861, to

Sandgates, Capt. Joseph Forrest's home near Oakville, Maryland, St. Mary's County. Forrest's family was ordered to leave here by Federal authorities in 1861 for being Southern sympathizers. *Library of Congress*

Capt. Joseph Forrest. *Courtesy of Debi Burt*

Lt. William Dawson Brown. This daguerreotype was taken in Richmond in spring 1861, shortly before Brown enlisted in the Confederate Army. *Author's collection*

become the "1st Company" of the prospective 2nd Maryland Infantry Regiment, with Brown as its captain.[3]

The third officer of the organization was 2nd Lt. John E. Plater. Plater had descended from what was once one of the wealthiest and most prominent families in St. Mary's County. His grandfather was a former governor of Maryland, and Plater was a distant cousin of Joseph Forrest. Plater was a graduate of Georgetown University, and was working as a bookkeeper for his uncle in Baltimore at the start of the war. He had been a member of the Maryland Guard Battalion as a sergeant, and then became captain of the Lafayette Guards under Billy Brown. He had also travelled to Richmond in 1861, and had served as a lieutenant in Brown's 1st Company.[4]

No doubt the organization of the Chesapeake Artillery gave a feeling of great pride to Forrest, Brown, and Plater, who had attempted to form a Maryland infantry regiment for service to the Confederacy, but were unable to do so because of a lack of recruits. Forrest and Brown had spent their time recruiting in Richmond while their companies were in Fredericksburg. Forrest received authorization to form a Virginia artillery company in September 1861, and after requisitioning blankets and tents, moved by rail to Norfolk with the men of his company who wished to form an artillery battery. The unit was assigned to the Department of Norfolk's field artillery battalion under Maj. John S. Saunders to train and recruit to company strength.[5]

In October, Forrest's nascent battery had its first experience under fire while engaging a Federal gunboat offshore near Cape Henry. War news in the eastern theater was scarce at the time, and though it was a minor affair, many Southern newspapers reprinted the *Norfolk Day Book's* breathless account of the engagement:

> Information was brought to the city yesterday morning that a large United States transport ship had run ashore [off] Cape Henry beach.
>
> The commanding officer at this post immediately proceeded to the beach. Rifle guns were mounted in a little while, and operations begun [...] the forces engaged on our side were the Huger Artillery, Louisiana Guard Artillery, and Chesapeake Light Artillery, the whole under the command of Major Saunders. Firing was commenced on our side about 4 o'clock, and continued until night set in. It was not returned by the vessel; but, in a short while after we began operations, the steamer *Monticello* hove in sight and opened her fire on us. At first, her shot did not reach us; but changing her position, she threw her shot immediately among us...
>
> None of our guns took effect upon the vessel, nor did any shot from the *Monticello* do us injury...
>
> The *Monticello* remained until nightfall, when she left for Old Point to procure assistance, as is supposed, for the purpose of towing the vessel out [...] Nobody hurt on our side.[6]

By December, the Department of Norfolk had reduced its field artillery strength in favor of siege guns, and Forrest's company became part of the Confederate military Aquia District, commanded by Maj. Gen. Theophilus H. Holmes, and moved to the Northern Neck. Other organizations in the area included the 40th Virginia Infantry Regiment and Meriweather Lewis's and John Tayloe's companies of cavalry—also in the Northern Neck—and the 55th Virginia Infantry Regiment and the Essex Cavalry company across the Rappahannock River in nearby Tapahannock.[7]

Though still without guns, Forrest continued to recruit. Meanwhile, on December 2, 1861, Lieutenant Brown requisitioned uniforms for his company and led those of his men who desired to join the artillery to Machodoc to join the Chesapeake Artillery.[8]

Motivations of these men to fight for the Confederacy were varied. The preservation of slavery was far less a factor for the company compared to the rest of the Army of Northern Virginia, of which they would eventually become a part. Not only was Forrest the sole slave owner, but also, compared to the rest of the Army, only half as many of the men in the battery had lived in slaveholding households. During the Pennsylvania Campaign, Sgt. Peter Williams would write to his father—who owned three slaves—that, "I had a discussion with an old Dutchman on the right of secession & War matters generally...I also had a warm debate with a regular abolition woman. I wouldn't say everything I wished to the woman but if I didn't abuse that old Dutchman, then I am one myself."[9]

Conversely, nearly 80% of the men did not come from slaveholding households, and this large majority had multiple reasons for enlisting. Certainly adventure and excitement was an important motivator, as the group was young, with nearly a quarter of them teenaged.[10]

Southern sentiment was strong in Baltimore and the Maryland counties with shoreline on Chesapeake Bay. Citizens of Baltimore had attacked the 6th Massachusetts Infantry Regiment as it passed through the city in April 1861. Several counties on the Eastern Shore had openly supported secession. In St. Mary's County, Joseph Forrest had been a member of a citizen's committee formed to present a set of resolutions that were unanimously approved by its citizens, stating in part:

> ...we, the citizens of Saint Mary's County, Maryland...do earnestly and devotedly express our sympathies with the cause and people of the States which have seceded from the Union, and, do pledge ourselves by every sacred obligation we can assume, to aid, by every means in our power in securing the Independence of all those States, and that of such others as may join them.

The group subsequently approved funds for arming citizens of the county. Actions such as these led to Lincoln's ordering the Federal occupation of Baltimore and other parts of Maryland, as well as the suspension of the writ of habeas corpus.[11]

This Southern sympathy was an important element to the men's reasons for joining the Confederate Army, as was avoiding persecution from Federal authorities for their support. Lt. Brown's sentiments reflected this, as he wrote of the war, "May it soon end with the independence of our beloved South." Pvt. Philip L. Harrison enlisted "for the purpose of avoiding imprisonment and persecution from the Federal powers."[12]

As Pvt. Thomas Mummey expressed it, "I left Maryland to lend my aid to the Confederate Cause. Why I did not leave sooner was because I then held the Com[mission] of Major...of the 6th Brigade of Md. Militia, and acted by and with the advice of...my friends, by waiting to see what actions, if any, our Old State would take."[13]

Pvt. John Hooff, writing later in the year, expressed Southern nationalism:

> I expect that Old Abraham the first and the last is very sorry about this time that he ever heard of a Southern Soldier. With what pride I write that [...]
>
> Oh! My country, 'tis of thee,
> Sweet land of liberty,
> Of thee I sing:
> Land where my fathers died,
> Land of the pilgrim's pride,
> From every Mountain side
> Let freedom ring.[14]

Whatever the cause, this level of motivation reached to the very nature of their military service; there was an inherent permanence to their enlistment, as Maryland, and home, was behind Federal lines. As Pvt. Andy Egan saw it, "My home is in Baltimore City and I cannot get there 'honorably.'"[15]

Pvt. Edward C. Cottrell, a shoemaker from Somerset County, was an outspoken secessionist. He was arrested in November 1861 for "correspondence with rebels" and imprisoned in Baltimore's Fort McHenry, then sent to Fort Lafayette in New York City. He was offered his freedom in exchange for taking the Oath of Allegiance, but he refused. Not knowing what to do with him, Federal authorities finally released Cottrell unconditionally, and he made his way to Virginia to enlist in the battery.[16]

The newly enlisted soldiers of the Chesapeake had to take extreme measures even to arrive at the enlistment rendezvous. Some men made their way overland and crossed the Potomac River at Harper's Ferry, Virginia. Others crossed the Potomac into the Northern Neck from Leonardtown, in St. Mary's County, or at Mathias' Point in King George County, Virginia. There, as Pvt. Jacob Cook recalled, they "were under the charge of Rodney Watson, whose residence was on the bank of the Potomac, directly opposite Mathias Point. Mr. Watson rendered invaluable services in running Marylanders to the Virginia side, taking fearful risks, and making many narrow escapes from the Federal vessels guarding the river."[17]

Pvt. George Maccubbin of Queen Anne's County travelled with several others from the Maryland Eastern Shore who would enlist with him in the company: John Grason, John Embert, Benjamin Young, Phil Harrison, Watson Webb, and Isaac Blunt. These men boarded the sloop *Sally* in the Wye River and commandeered it from Capt. Burke, forcing him to take them across the Potomac; they landed in Northumberland County, Virginia.[18]

Heathsville

Shortly after their formation, Forrest moved the company twenty miles south to Heathsville. They were still without any armament, and were included in an organization record of the Aquia District on January 14 as one of "two companies of local volunteers." On January 23, the company was presented with a flag of the Confederate national pattern, with eight stars denoting the state of Virginia.[19]

Heathsville had no strategic advantage, but was about a mile from Mill Creek, a large stream that let out into the Coan River and thence to the Potomac River near its mouth at Chesapeake Bay. It was an ideal location to facilitate the enlistment of Marylanders arriving by boat from counties on both sides of Chesapeake Bay, and there was active competition for Maryland recruits in the Northern Neck. As reported by Maj. R. L. T. Beale, provost marshall for the region: "Three gentlemen, with the full endorsement of the Government, captain's commissions, are here recruiting and claiming the right to run boats to Maryland. Any man who crosses is taken in…" The company actively picketed the Potomac River shoreline, and by early March an additional twelve soldiers had entered the Chesapeake's ranks.[20]

The weather had turned more seasonal, with temperatures below freezing at night, rising to about 45°F during the day. Rain was frequent; the region received nearly seven inches of rain that February, with several

Modern view of the historic section of Heathsville, Virginia. *Author*

Flag presented to the Chesapeake Artillery on January 23, 1862. This flag was carried by the battery until June 1864. *Author's collection*

occurrences of snow or sleet. Presumably, the men were sheltered in the tents originally requisitioned by Forrest and Brown for the infantry companies while in Fredericksburg, and the officers billeted in town.[21]

Once established in Heathsville, Forrest wasted no time bringing the company to field readiness as an artillery battery. On February 5, he requisitioned from the Ordnance Department in Richmond two 6-pound cannon, a 12-pound howitzer, and a three-inch Ordnance rifle, as well as carriages, caissons, a forge, a battery wagon, all of the attendant equipment for the guns, and thirty-three horses. This equipment and the horses were delivered on February 12.[22]

No doubt it was a day of great excitement within the unit, but an inauspicious beginning

6-pound field gun. *Author*

as far as their ordnance was concerned. While the three-inch rifle represented the most advanced weapons technology of the day, by 1862, the 6-pound cannon and 12-pound howitzer were already obsolete. These guns had less range compared to the rifled cannon and 12-pound Napoleons prevalent in the Federal artillery branch. Further, the lighter weight of the 6-pound projectiles provided more limited firepower. These limitations would come to affect the battery's deployment and effectiveness on the battlefield.[23]

The officers began training the men right away in artillery methods, tactics, and maneuvering. Their practice was imperfect, resulting in an accident in which eighteen-year-old Cpl. Robert Chew Jones lost his right arm; incredibly, he continued to serve with the company following his recovery. Maintaining equipment and the required complement of horses would be a constant struggle for the battery throughout the war, as evidenced early on. Pvt. John Grason was detailed to seek additional horses as soon as February.[24]

By this time other events were to have an effect on the Chesapeake's movements. Confederate authorities had two concerns regarding the Northern Neck region: the area's citizens and the military. As early as November 30, 1861, Major Beale reported on the mood of the local citizenry in Northern Neck:

> I think I discover many slight indications of disaffection to our cause in this section, and full credence to what I hear would render me really very uneasy. The deprivation of salt, sugar, and coffee is severely felt by the poor [...] The opinion is expressed that the landing of the enemy would witness the raising of the Union flag now, and an officer in the militia, I hear, thinks over half of his company, if they did not openly take sides with, would at least refuse to fight the Yankees.[25]

Col. George E. Pickett, commander of the Northern Neck and lower Rappahannock regions, was so concerned that he travelled to Richmond in person the following month to report to the War Department "the necessity of some immediate steps being taken in the District of the Lower Rappahannock in order to prevent the possibility of the disaffected element from gaining the ascendency."[26]

The Northern Neck was also vulnerable from a military perspective because of the difficulty of defending its extensive coastline, along with the possibility of the region being isolated if Federal gunboats advanced up the Rappahannock River. As Major Beale expressed, "The obvious importance to the North of securing possession of the south bank of the Potomac…would justify strenuous efforts…"[27]

But there was no consensus within the Confederate command on action to be taken. Pickett felt, "Should the Rappahannock close during the winter, which is very likely to occur, then the enemy have it at their option to land from Chesapeake Bay, which will be open, and we cannot re-enforce." But in mid-December, Holmes reported to the War Department his opinion that "If the enemy do not attack our batteries in a few days I think we may conclude that they do not intend doing so…"[28]

Tappahannock

Ultimately Holmes made the decision to abandon Northern Neck; as part of this movement, in late February, the Chesapeake Artillery was ordered to Tappahannock, twenty-five miles west of Heathsville across the Rappahannock River. It was a controversial decision; Gen. Robert E. Lee later wrote to him, "It is not the plan of the Government to abandon any country that can be held, and it is only the necessity of the case, I presume, that has caused the withdrawal of the troops to the Rappahannock. I trust there will be no necessity of retrograding further." The Chesapeake mustered at Tappahannock on March 1. At that point the battery numbered sixty, three officers and fifty-seven enlisted men. Although enlistments continued to steadily increase the size of the company, it was still significantly under strength compared to the normal complement of about 100 officers and enlisted men.[29]

There was a much stronger Confederate military presence in the Tappahannock area than in Northern Neck. The center was Fort Lowry, an earthen walled eight-gun battery on Lowry's Point on the Rappahannock River, approximately four miles south of Tappahannock. Fort Lowry was to protect Fredericksburg thirty miles upriver, as well as the Rappahannock valley's important food production. The fort was manned by the 55th Virginia Infantry, who lived at nearby Camp Byron; the guns were under the immediate command of Lt. Henry Howell Lewis of the Confederate Navy. Four other camps were from one to thirty-eight miles from Fort Lowry.[30]

The Chesapeake was assigned to stay in Tappahannock, probably as field support for the other installations in the area. The extreme hardships of the war were still in the future, and the Marylanders enjoyed the social scene and made friends and acquaintances with people of the town. One prominent family who came to know the men of the company well was that of Maj. William Norvell Ward of the 55th Virginia. Although the family was temporarily living in Tappahannock, its plantation home, Bladensfield, was about ten miles away across the Tappahannock River.[31]

The Wards' daughter Evelyn later recalled the socializing between the soldiers and her older sisters during this time:

> Soldiers came up every evening; the morning's mail brought notes for the grown-up sisters that caused quite a good deal of fluttering. As I remember, they were about engagements for walks and for séances of various kinds […] Sister

Historic Tappahannock, Virginia, looking east toward the Rappahannock River, with the old ferry landing in the background. The Chesapeake Artillery landed here in late February 1862. *Author*

> Matty had her specials. As for Mamie, she was gay, always talking and laughing, always full of pranks. I wouldn't like to have to name the young soldiers who were her followers. She played off one against another and had the time of her life.[32]

These times were remembered with fondness by members of the unit. Lt. Brown later wrote to Ward's wife Mary:

> I know of nothing that would give me more pleasure than to be present around the hearthstone of your pleasant home. My meeting with you all at Tappahannock & at home in my memory is among the pleasing recollections of the war—we often talk of our visit there [...] Lieut. Plater & Grason desire to be remembered to yourself & family. May I ask the same from when you wish to recall them.[33]

Fredericksburg

The battery's stay at Tappahannock would be short. Gen. Holmes wrote to Gen. Robert E. Lee from Fredericksburg that his analysis of Federal movements in Virginia:

> indicate a concentration of the enemy for an attack on Fredericksburg; and I am clearly of the opinion that they should be met and given battle before they reach this city.
>
> I have directed Colonel [Mallory] to concentrate his forces for the defense of Fort Lowry, and I have also caused a battery of four guns to be placed on the Rappahannock 4 miles below here.

The battery Holmes referred to was the Chesapeake Artillery, and it moved to the Fredericksburg area before March 13.[34]

The site occupied by the company on the right bank of the Rappahannock was protected by entrenchments and was "an excellent position." While the battery bivouacked at their position near Fredericksburg, Capt. Forrest returned to Tappahannock and established himself at Fort Lowry to sign recruits and requisition needed supplies, such as mule harnesses and saddle blankets. Fort Lowry was determined by the Confederate Engineer Bureau to be untenable, and the installations in the Tappahannock area were abandoned on April 3. Forrest subsequently returned to the unit.[35]

The abandonment of Fort Lowry opened the Rappahannock River to Federal gunboats entering from Chesapeake Bay. Fredericksburg was considered vulnerable to attack by the Federals because of its attraction as a large depot for Confederate supplies. It was an exciting time, and no doubt the Chesapeakes anticipated their first opportunity to open fire on the enemy, but the sector remained quiet, and no evidence of Federal troop or naval activity was evident.[36]

Richmond

By this time the Federal Army of the Potomac under Maj. Gen. George B. McClellan had landed on the Virginia peninsula and was advancing toward Richmond. Consequently, the battery was ordered to Camp Lee, a camp of instruction and organization at Richmond. They moved fifty miles south and were in Richmond before April 12. Here their training was completed in earnest. Two soldiers from the Richmond Howitzers, Pvts. James Peter Williams and Martin Luther Harvey, had been detailed to instruct the company. They would train the unit to a high level of efficiency.[37]

May 15, 1862, was a momentous day for the Chesapeake Artillery. In February, the Confederate Congress authorized the organizing of Maryland units for service in the Confederate Army. With their training completed, the company was accepted into Confederate service and reorganized as the 4th Maryland Light Artillery Battery. Importantly, on this day they would elect their officers to provide leadership from that date onward.[38]

Lt. Billy Brown's previous military leadership experience had served the company well; despite his organizational abilities, Capt. Joseph Forrest was dropped at the reorganization. The results of the election elevated Brown to captain, 2nd Lt. John Plater and 1st Sgt. Walter S. Chew to 1st lieutenant, and Pvt. John Grason to 2nd lieutenant.[39]

In electing these men as their leaders the Chesapeakes had chosen well. Newly promoted Sgt. Peter Williams referred to them as "three very nice good men." Brown in particular would prove to be an exceptional leader and battery commander who was much admired. Variously described by his superiors and men as "a most gallant and valuable officer," "gallant Captain Brown," "the handsome, dashing, gallant Brown," and a soldier who "has obtained a very high reputation as an Officer, and is very popular with the Generals," he would apply his prewar militia experience to lead the battery with high efficiency.[40]

Brown also had compassion and an interest in the well being of his men, as illustrated in a letter he wrote to Mary Ward regarding her nephew, Pvt. John Hooff, who had enlisted in the battery:

> I regret exceedingly that my Co[mpany] was ordered from the neighbourhood of R[ichmon]d before the arrival of Mrs. H[ooff]. Had she remained there I could have procured a furlough for her son, which would have enabled him to see her. I can appreciate the anxiety felt for her in his behalf, for I too have a mother of whom my thoughts cannot long dwell without giving me much pain for I know how her anxious heart awaits tidings from her son. Rest assured Mrs. Ward that I shall leave nothing undone for the comfort & care of your nephew. I have a brother in the Co[mpany] of his age & shall treat one as the other. Should an engagement occur shortly & my Co[mpany] take part in it, I will write you immediately thereafter.[41]

Speculation abounded as to where the company would be assigned. Sgt. Peter

Williams summed up the camp gossip in a letter home:

> there is a prospect of getting up in the mountains under old Jackson. General Pendleton has promised the Captain to send his battery off, the first time any reinforcements are sent to Jackson. Which atime he says will be next week. He sent the whole battery into Richmond yesterday to have everything about the guns & caissons fixed up & painted over again ready for the march.[42]

With the prospect of active campaigning and the battery's proximity to many displaced Marylanders in Richmond, enlistments surged in May and June. Nineteen men enlisted in the company, increasing its strength to about eighty-five present for duty, its highest level up to that time.[43]

The Chesapeakes were hoping to get into a battle before the war ended. As Williams opined to his aunt:

> I don't think there can be many more days before the big fight will take place when, I sincerely believe the Yankee army will just be annihilated [...] I believe that the whole Yankee army and Government, to use a camp phrase, are about 'played out' & if they are not now, will be in a few months.[44]

On May 23—eight days after their reorganization—the battery was ordered "to report without delay to General J.E. Johnston for service in the field." No doubt this news was received with cheers by the men of the Chesapeake, anticipating going into action at last. The *Richmond Daily Dispatch* announced their assignment with enthusiasm:

> We are glad to record as the first response to the call of reinforcements for Johnston the company of Chesapeake Artillery, Capt. W.D. Brown, who, after full reorganization leaves in a few days to join the victorious army of the Potomac. The command numbers nearly an hundred men [...] and being composed of Marylanders exclusively, the object in attaching themselves to the command is obvious. 'Maryland, my Maryland' is to be changed to 'Home Again.'[45]

The company was not assigned to Johnston's Army of the Potomac in the field but to Battery No. 2, part of the Richmond defense line on a bluff overlooking the James River just southeast of the city. They spent the next several weeks in this static position and could hear the gunfire from the initial Seven Days battles in late June, but did not participate. Finally, they were ordered forward as part of the artillery reserve of Maj. Gen. James Longstreet's command at the Battle of Gaines's Mill on June 27, but were not engaged.[46]

They remained in reserve during the Battle of Malvern Hill on July 1, and Peter Williams expressed the company's disappointment in a letter home:

> I am very sorry to tell you that our company took no active part whatsoever in the fight & consequently I am not able to give any account. We were down within three or four miles of the battlefield [...] and heard all the fighting without being ordered in.[47]

Afterward they returned to Battery No. 2. Disappointment, inactivity, and homesickness became more telling during the weeks the company occupied Battery No. 2. Letters from home were particularly important to the men and hard to obtain, as letters to Maryland had to be sent to friends in Virginia who could then arrange to have them transported across the Potomac. Pvt. John Hooff referred to this arrangement in a letter to his cousin Mamie Ward:

> I told Captain Brown, Lieut. Plater and Mr. [Phil] Harrison about sending letters to you as requested, they requested me in turn to tell you that they were greatly indebted to you for our kindness in offering them an opportunity of sending letters to Md, and I believe that Mr. H. accepted it, and I think wrote to you also.

Captain Billy Brown also wrote to her:

> Will you not let me hear from you again? Nothing would afford me greater pleasure & as I am debarred the privilege of hearing from home, letters from friends are doubly prized.

Pvt. Lewis Warrington wrote a letter to his parents that was included in the same envelope as one Lt. John Grason wrote to his sister, to be delivered by hand: "Today I hear that an opportunity may apper to forward a letter and I add these lines to give you the latest news…"[48]

However, mail was still sporadic and unpredictable—when it arrived at all—and the men expressed their frustration in the most forthright terms. As Pvt. Isaac Blunt wrote to his cousin, "I have longed to hear from you all, but in vain." Cpl. Robert Chew Jones, writing to his mother, referred to the last letter he had received from her a full eight months prior and lamented, "You cannot imagine what a great consolation it would be for me to receive an answer to one of the many letters that I have written to you and my dear friends in Talbot." Grason theorized that letters from home were scarce because "it is forbidden by the Federal government." Hooff sarcastically scolded his cousin Mattie Ward:

> I think that you might have written to me. I have received letters from both Cousin Mary and Eddie but not a word from you. I know that housekeeping occupies most of your time while Aunt Mary is in Richmond, but I think that you could possibly write me a few lines when the others are writing.

Even when he did receive letters Hooff wasn't satisfied, writing to his cousin Mary, "the last note you wrote to me {I can hardly call it a note, it was so short, I should say, one or two lines you wrote me} it was not 1/5 the size of any I have written to you… ."[49]

Peter Williams was even more pointed in a letter to his sister Nannie, writing on June 17:

> I have given up all hopes of ever getting another letter from any of you & had determined not to write again myself until some of you wrote, but I thought this morning that I would write once more to let you know where I am & if you didn't write pretty soon, just to let the correspondence drop. I know you are perfectly horrified at my talking this way, but you need not be surprised at it, when I tell you that the only letter I have received from anybody, with the exception of one from Pa, since the middle of May was one written by Aunt Mary on the 5th April […] I think you might have at lest time enough to write me word where you all are & how you are.[50]

At times the trouble with mail even prevented the soldiers from making the attempt at writing home. Sgt. Thomas LeCompte felt compelled to write his mother:

> It being such a difficult matter to get a letter to you has prevented my writing for 6 months or more, but Frank Stewart, who has recently joined our company, informs me that I am reckoned among the number of the dead, I felt it my duty to try and let you know that I am still in the land of the living […][51]

Finally, on July 14, Gen. Pendleton ordered, "Captain Brown, of the Maryland

Artillery, is assigned, with his battery, to the command of General T.J. Jackson. He will report to-day to Colonel Crutchfield, General Jackson's chief of artillery." No doubt this created the highest level of excitement and relief within the company as preparations were made to break camp and take the field.[52]

McClellan's Army of the Potomac had remained inactive near the James River following the Seven Days battles, and the newly formed Federal Army of Virginia, under Maj. Gen. John Pope, had taken position in northern Virginia. Lee ordered Jackson to take the initiative against Pope before the two Federal armies could join forces. Jackson's command was to be transported by rail to Gordonsville. The Chesapeake Artillery was attached to Brig. Gen. Jubal A. Early's brigade of Maj. Gen. Richard S. Ewell's division. Ewell's division had performed with distinction during Jackson's brilliant Valley Campaign, and no doubt the Chesapeakes were eager to prove themselves to their illustrious comrades in Jackson's command. They would not have long to wait.[53]

"MOST OF THE MEN ARE NICE GOOD FELLOWS"

Sgt. Peter Williams initially enlisted as a private in the 2nd Company of the Richmond Howitzers in April 1861, but was not able to get along with his superior officers. In a letter to his aunt Williams wrote of his situation, "I was treated with a good deal of unjustice by the officers and that the only way to get rid of it was to leave the company." He had developed strong relationships with the members of the Chesapeake Artillery when he was their artillery instructor at Camp Lee during spring 1862. Accordingly, Williams decided to follow his close friend, Sgt. Martin Harvey, who was also originally a member of the Howitzers and an instructor at Camp Lee, and obtained a transfer to the Chesapeake Artillery in late June. In a letter to his mother Williams described his new comrades: "The officers in the company are all nice gentlemen & most of the men are nice good fellows, though some of them are 'right hard cases.'" No doubt this could be said of every unit in the Army of Northern Virginia, but an analysis of census records, Compiled Service Records (CSRs), interment data, and other records shows that as they boarded the trains in Richmond for the trip to Gordonsville, the company had a number of distinct characteristics that made it unique.[1]

Residence

The Chesapeake Artillery was aptly named, for 82% of the unit's members whose antebellum residence is known lived in the port city of Baltimore or counties that had shoreline on the Chesapeake Bay. The unit had a pronounced urban element, with nearly a third of its members living in Baltimore City before the war. This is more than five times higher than the overall rate of soldiers in the Army of Northern Virginia who lived in urban centers with a population over 9,500.[2]

Two distinct profiles emerge of the soldiers from Baltimore City and those from rural counties. Those from rural counties with agriculture-based economies were younger, likely to be farmers or farm laborers, and most lived with or came from middle- or upper-class families; one-third of them came from households that owned slaves. In contrast, the men from Baltimore City were older, more established in their careers, and far more likely to be professionals, or skilled or white-collar workers. They were more likely to come from lower-class backgrounds and none came from slaveholding households, since land and slave ownership was more centered in the middle and upper classes.[3]

Age

One of the most salient characteristics of the battery was its youth; it may well have been one of the youngest units in the Army of Northern Virginia. The company was decidedly young compared to the army as a whole; even versus the Artillery arm, which had the youngest average age of any branch of the service. The average known year of birth of members of the unit was more than two years younger than the average for the Army of Northern Virginia. Despite the Artillery being the army's youngest branch of service, the Chesapeakes were fully a year and a half younger than the average

age of other artillery units.[4] The younger half of the men in the company were born after January 1839—a year younger than in the army as a whole—and it numbered among its members a higher proportion of young men born after 1840, and a lower proportion of older men born before 1830. The company's young men were younger and its older men were younger.[5]

The oldest soldier to enlist with the Chesapeakes was Pvt. William Smith, who was born in 1813 and was forty-eight years old when he enlisted at Machodoc on January 1, 1862. He resided in Baltimore City, was single, and worked as a hatter. Smith served continuously with the unit until he deserted on December 23, 1863. The youngest was Pvt. Edward O. N. Stansbury of Baltimore, a student who lived with his mother, older brother, and two older sisters; his brother supported the family as a railroad conductor. Edward was only fifteen years old when he enlisted at Machodoc the same date as Smith.[6]

Adventure seems to have been an important motivation to join the battery, as teenaged soldiers were likely to enlist as soon as they reached the minimum age requirement for military service (set at eighteen years in 1862, but lowered to seventeen in early 1864). Edwin Kendall "E. K." Culver enlisted in the company when it was at Fredericks Hall, Virginia. Originally from Kentucky, he was eager to enter Confederate service: when he enlisted in April 1864, he was still five months shy of his eighteenth birthday.[7]

The battery's youth was a key factor in determining its other characteristics of occupation and wealth, as well as slaveholding and family status.

Occupation and Literacy

The battery's occupational profile was different from that of the Army as a whole to a significant degree, because the unit had a far lower proportion of farmers and a far higher proportion of professionals, skilled workers, and white-collar workers among its members. Only 23% of the Chesapeakes were employed as farmers before the war, compared to 54% for the army as a whole. Conversely, 52% worked as professionals, skilled workers, or in white-collar jobs, while only 19% of the army as a whole was similarly employed before the war.[8]

The percentage of students in the Chesapeake battery (12%) was similar to that of the army (14%) and equal to the Artillery—an unexpected result considering the company's youth. It suggests many of the men who worked in skilled jobs left school early to learn their trade. Yet the men of the Chesapeake Artillery were highly literate. The literacy rate in the battery was fully 95%; much higher than the 80% literacy rate of the Confederate Army as a whole.[9]

Economic Class and Marital Status

As might be expected because of the unit's lower average age, the members of the battery were earlier in their careers and reflected lower overall levels in economic status. When personal wealth indicated in the 1860 Census is examined, fully 94% of the men of the unit were individually at levels in the lower economic class (wealth of $0 to $799); moreover, only 13% of the men could claim any personal wealth at all. Typical is Pvt. Allen J. Covington, a twenty-two-year-old farmer living with his parents and two siblings in Queen Anne's County. Neither he nor his family's household had any personal wealth. The wealthiest man in the unit was Capt. Joseph Forrest, who was also the wealthiest man in St. Mary's County, a planter whose combined personal property and real estate was valued at nearly $115,000—an enormous figure for the day.[10]

Because of the youth of the soldiers in the battery, nearly 85% lived with their parents or siblings, or boarded with other families—significantly higher than 64% for the army as a whole. Thus, a much more accurate depiction of their economic status is reflected in household wealth rather than personal wealth. When total household wealth is considered a different picture emerges. While nearly half of the company members' household wealth was in the lower economic class, about a quarter of the men lived in middle-class households (household wealth of $800 to $3,999), and a quarter in households of the highest economic class ($4,000 and above).[11]

For example, the battery's bugler, Pvt. Daniel Wilkinson, was a seventeen-year-old farmer residing in St. Mary's County with his father and six siblings. Although he had no personal wealth, his father's real estate and personal wealth totalled $2,400, putting the family in the middle class. Pvt. Frank Fairbanks was a nineteen-year-old clerk boarding with the Talbot family in Easton. Although Fairbanks had no personal wealth, the Talbots' household had a net worth of $7,000. Pvt. Doug McClure lived in Baltimore City with his parents and five siblings and worked as a clerk in his father's store. Although Doug had no personal wealth, his family's household had a net worth of $15,000 and was also in the upper class.[12]

Related to economic class is marital and parental status, and youth influences the number of married men in the unit as well. The 18% of men who were married is less than half of the 37% of married men in the Army of Northern Virginia. Similarly, only 14% of the men (78% of the married men) had children, compared to 31% in the army.[13]

Slaveholding

Another more pronounced characteristic of the Chesapeake Artillery was that, compared to the Army of Northern Virginia and its Artillery, the rates of slave ownership, individually and by household, were far lower.[14]

Only one individual member of the battery was a slave owner—Capt. Joseph Forrest owned three plantations worked by forty-five slaves—while about 37% of those in the Army of Northern Virginia individually owned slaves. A number of the unit's soldiers came from households that had slave ownership or had occupations influenced by slavery, but only 22% of the men did so, including Forrest, in marked contrast to the Army of Northern Virginia at 44%. The number of soldiers in the Artillery who came from slaveholding households was even higher than that of the Army as a whole at 54%.[15]

Pvt. William Pinder was thirty-five and resided in Queen Anne's County when the 1860 Census was taken; he owned no slaves, nor did the household he lived in, but he worked as an overseer. Pvt. Gustavus Porter was a twenty-three-year-old laborer on his older brother's farm in Queen Anne's County; his brother owned three slaves. Pvt. William S. Tarbutton also lived in Queen Anne's County, an eighteen-year-old student who lived with his parents and five siblings; his father owned ten slaves. Pvt. Robert Goldsborough was nineteen years old and boarding with the Fedmann family in Easton; the Fedmanns owned three slaves.[16]

Several factors contributed to the lower incidence of soldiers of the company living in slaveholding households before the war. First, as a border state, Maryland could be expected to have a lower level of slave ownership in general. Second, the soldiers' youth contributed; both they and their families were younger than average, and slave ownership tended to occur among soldiers of higher ages. Their generally lower economic level was also a key dynamic, as slave ownership was more difficult for those in the lower and middle economic levels. Finally, the lower incidence of farming as an occupation in the unit also influenced the level of slaveholding households; notably, all of the soldiers in the battery who lived in slaveholding households before the war came from counties with agriculture-based economies that had shoreline on the Chesapeake Bay.

Officers and Enlisted Men

Two additional distinct groups that existed within the battery were the officers and enlisted men, and they also differed greatly. During the first year of the battery's existence officers were elected, and the profile of these men reflects their accomplishments in civilian life, as well as their influence in the communities they lived in. The characteristics of the men appointed commissioned officers for skill and valor in 1864 reflect a pronounced departure from the elected officers of 1862.

Three officers raised the battery in its initial organization on January 1, 1862: Capt. Joseph Forrest, 1st Lt. Billy Brown, and 2nd Lt. John Plater. Forrest was dropped at the unit's re-organization on May 15, 1862; Brown was elected captain, Plater and Pvt. John Grason 1st lieutenants, and Sgt. Walter Chew 2nd lieutenant. Upon the death of Grason at 1st Fredericksburg on December 13, 1862, Chew was promoted to 1st lieutenant and Benjamin G. Roberts was elected to replace him as 2nd lieutenant. These six men reflected a remarkable contrast to the rest of the company they commanded.[17]

On average, the officers were nearly seven years older than the enlisted men, with half the officers born before May 1831, versus half the enlisted men born before January 1838. Consequently, the officers reflected their greater age and experience in other measures. Fully 80% of the officers came from households with wealth in the upper economic class level, with the remaining 20% in the lower class. The average household wealth of the officers ($38,200) was more than eight times that of the enlisted men at $4,537. Half of the officers came from wealthy planter class backgrounds and 40% came from slaveholding households, a proportion more than double the 18% of enlisted men who came from slaveholding households.[18]

The next officer appointments for the unit occurred in 1864, when the battery had only two officers, both appointed to their positions that year for skill rather than being elected. Chew was promoted to captain and Sgt. Maj. Thomas P. LeCompte was promoted to 1st lieutenant. These two men contrasted oppositely from the elected officers of 1862. They were younger than the enlisted men by more than three years, with an average birth date of June 1841—not quite twenty-three years of age in 1864. Neither had any personal wealth, and their average household wealth was only $1,500. By occupation prewar Chew was a clerk and LeCompte a student. If anything, these officers resembled the enlisted men more closely rather than contrasting; they were young, single, adventurous, had little invested in career or family, and by 1864 were skilled veterans who had proven themselves on multiple battlefields.[19]

Late Enlisters and Early Enlisters

The unit was nearly evenly divided between early enlisters—men who enlisted up until January 1, 1862—and late enlisters (those who enlisted after that date). Of the men whose enlistment date is known and could also be identified in the 1860 Census, 50.5% enlisted on or before January 1, 1862, and 49.5% after.[20]

While the army's late enlisters exhibited a number of differences compared to its early enlisters, there was only one notable difference among the Chesapeake Artillery's late enlisters: their level of household property ownership. The battery's late enlisters were twice more likely than the early enlisters to come from a household that held no property. Further, the value of the property of the late enlisters' households was markedly lower. The average value of household property of the late enlisters was only $4,361, compared to $7,123 for the company's early enlisters. Even if the officers of the company are excluded from both groups, since their greater wealth skews the results, the average household property value of the late enlisters was still only $2,971, compared to the early enlisters at $4,582. This implies the early enlisters of the company rushed to enlist because they were motivated by a desire to protect the value of their personal property and real estate.[21]

Summary

As they joined the Army of Northern Virginia for their first experience in active campaigning, the Chesapeake Artillery was almost certainly a unit like no other. Compared to the Army as a whole, its members were much younger, much more likely to be single, and far more likely to be literate. A much greater proportion was from lower- and middle-class backgrounds, and only half the proportion of Chesapeakes came from slaveholding households compared to the proportion in the army as a whole. The Chesapeakes had a larger urban element and a much higher number whose jobs were as professional, skilled, or white-collar workers, with only a quarter of the men coming from a farming background. At this point in the war the officers were older, wealthier, and much more likely to come from slaveholding households; they were elected not only for their standing in their communities, but also their deportment during the initial six months of the battery's existence.

The motivations of the soldiers of the company for joining the Confederate Army were varied. Many young men were seeking adventure, and those from wealthy households may have come to protect the value of their property and real estate. Some felt strong sympathy to the Southern cause, while others no doubt wanted to protect a way of life that included slavery. Several had been drafted into the US Army and sought to serve in the Confederate Army instead. The Chesapeake's most pronounced characteristic—its youth, with its resultant enthusiasm, optimism, and fearlessness—would resonate in its conduct on the battlefield.[22]

"OH! WE HAVE HAD A MOST GLORIOUS VICTORY HERE..."

Stonewall Jackson's long columns of over 20,000 infantry and artillery soldiers trudged over several roads into Culpeper County. It was August 8, and the men suffered under extreme heat and humidity, with temperatures that day reaching 96°F. Partway along the column following the Culpeper Road the Chesapeake Artillery moved with the rest of Ewell's division. The battery had left their camp near Gordonsville the day before and crossed the Rapidan River at Liberty Mills that evening. Although it was not the Chesapeake's first march, they had never marched under such extreme conditions. They suffered. Water was scarce. Some in the division fell out of rank because of heat prostration.

However, as Pvt. Jacob Cook recalled, they were able to apply what they had learned about marching without unnecessary encumbrances:

> Ever ready for a fight, strict disciplinarians, always well up in their tactics, fully posted in their duties as soldiers [...] they were nevertheless, always in light marching order, detesting anything in the shape of a knapsack, and ever ready to ridicule in friend or foe anything cumbersome, or heavy. They were, however, great admirers of the frying pan and oven, provided they were carried by someone else [...] there was not an oven or skillet in the entire battalion.[1]

The company marched as part of Maj. Alfred R. Courtney's artillery battalion. Shortly after arriving at Gordonsville in July, the artillery of Jackson's command had been reorganized to improve its efficiency. The practice of attaching single batteries to infantry brigades was discontinued. Instead, artillery battalions consisting of several batteries each were assigned to an infantry division, and reported directly to the division commander. This had the advantage of facilitating the concentration of artillery fire, as well as placing deployment of guns in the hands of more senior artillery officers who had a much better understanding of artillery tactics than infantry brigade commanders. The other batteries in Courtney's battalion were the fellow Marylanders of Capt. William F. Dement's 1st Maryland Artillery (Maryland Flying Artillery), along with Capt. Louis E. D'Aquin's Louisiana Guard Artillery, Capt. Joseph W. Latimer's Virginia Henrico Artillery, and Capt. John R. Johnson's Virginia Bedford Artillery.[2]

Jackson had received word that Pope's Federal Army of Virginia was advancing south in the vicinity of Culpeper. Maj. Gen. Nathaniel P. Banks's corps of some 9,000 men was isolated from the rest of Pope's army several miles south of the town. Stonewall intended to advance on Banks and strike him to defeat the Army of Virginia—which outnumbered him—in detail. Ewell's division had been allowed no fires in their camps around the Rapidan on the evening of the seventh because of the proximity of the enemy; they started their march on the eighth at sunrise in the lead of Jackson's command. Because of the heat the column went into camp in the early afternoon. Cavalry of both sides clashed periodically to the north.[3]

Battle of Cedar Mountain

Ewell's men and the Chesapeake did not resume their march the next morning until 0800; the temperature at the time was already 84°F. At midday the column reached the vicinity of Cedar Mountain (also called Slaughter's Mountain), eight miles south of Culpeper, and stopped as Federal cavalry resistance stiffened against Confederate cavalry in the advance. At midday Maj. Courtney was ordered to deploy his artillery and drive the enemy cavalry off. Along with the rest of the battalion, the Chesapeakes turned off Culpeper Road to the right on the lane leading to the Major farmhouse, then dropped trail facing left, or generally east. They were on "a small knoll on which there were growing pines" near the Major house. Before them stretched open, rolling farmland, with Cedar Mountain rising from the plain to their right.[4]

It was the first time the company would go into battery in the presence of the enemy. Courtney described the action in his report:

> Captain Dement's (First Maryland) battery, Captain Brown's Chesapeake Artillery, also from Maryland; Captain D'Aquin's (Louisiana) battery, and the rifle gun of Captain Latimer's battery were posted in a line from the main road, on the left of the mountain, on the right, and as far forward as Majors house [...] From these positions the several batteries named opened upon a large body of cavalry in front as soon as the infantry opened upon their advance guard from the woods on the left. The cavalry having at once fled, and the enemy opening with several batteries in our front and beyond effective range of our guns, I ordered the batteries on the plain to cease firing [...].

Cedar Mountain battlefield looking southeast from the old Culpeper Road near the location of the Major farm lane. The battery fired its first shots from the knoll in the middle distance. Cedar Mountain is in the left background. *Author*

No doubt the cheers and rebel yells of the gunners rang in the fleeing cavalrymen's ears.[5]

There was a lull as the infantry of Ewell's and Brig. Gen. Charles S. Winder's divisions moved from marching column into battle line. Maj. Courtney realized the infantry would need artillery support and critically viewed the armament in the battalion. A number of guns were insufficient for the purpose because of limited range or firepower, including the Chesapeake Artillery's howitzer and two six-pound smoothbores. These guns Courtney ordered to remain behind, and when Brig. Gen. Early ordered the artillery up, Courtney sent Capt. Brown with the three-inch Ordnance rifle forward, as well as two Napoleons from the First Maryland battery.[6]

It was about 1600; Early recalled the scene in his official report:

> Captain Brown, of the Chesapeake Artillery, with one piece, and Captain Dement, with three [sic] pieces, came up through the fields in rear on a gallop, and were posted, by my direction, a little in advance of my right near a clump of cedars, where they had a good cover for their horses and caissons and occupied a commanding position. They very soon opened fire upon the enemy.[7]

The gunners at the clump of cedars had dropped trail and opened fire on Federal artillery nine hundred yards away. As Maj. Courtney recalled:

> From these positions the batteries opened upon the batteries immediately on their front as soon as they took their positions [...]. Though the effect of our artillery fire upon their batteries was evidently terrible, the enemy obstinately held their positions, except to move their pieces a little to the right or left

3-inch Ordnance rifle. *Author*

Cedar Mountain battlefield looking east from the Crittenden farm lane in the foreground toward the location of the clump of cedars in the center background. Capt. Brown's advance, "dashing up" with the rifled gun detachment, was from behind the camera position. *Author*

> occasionally to escape the deadly shower, and moving the battery on their right back to a knoll 300 yards in rear soon after, they were fired on by the three guns of Captains Dement and Brown behind the clump of cedars.

The firing went on for nearly two hours in the intense heat, which reached 98°F that day. Jacob Cook remembered it as "one of the most terrible artillery duels of the war." The barrels of the Napoleons in the adjacent 1st Maryland battery became so hot the sponge rammers sizzled when inserted; these guns had to stop firing temporarily so the barrels could cool. The heat affected the men as well, and a number of gunners had to fall out from exhaustion. Capts. Brown and Dement stepped in to help load and fire the pieces when manpower became short.[8]

By this time the infantry and artillery of Winder's division became engaged with Federals about a thousand yards to the Chesapeake's left, and the remainder of the infantry, under Early's direction, formed a line in the Crittenden farm lane, in the rear of the artillerists' position at the clump of cedars. This relieved the pressure of counter-battery fire on the guns to some degree, but slightly before 1800 the Federal infantry brigades of Brig. Gens. John W. Geary and Henry Prince advanced toward Early's line, with Prince attacking directly against the clump of cedars.[9]

Brown and Dement redoubled their efforts, firing as rapidly as possible as the Federal infantry levelled their rifles at them. A soldier in Dement's battery recalled the Federals attacked "nine times." Pvt. John Shannahan of the Chesapeake, a nineteen-year-old student from Talbot County, was seriously wounded in the thigh by a musket round—the battery's first casualty; this added to the confusion and desperation as he was tended to by his already

Pvt. John Henry Kelly Shannahan II. *Courtesy of Molly Shannahan Taylor*

short-handed group of comrades. Quartermaster Sgt. John Shafer, a twenty-eight-year-old merchant from Harford County, was shot in the face—losing his left eye and much of the sight of his right eye—and had to be helped to the rear. Finally, the Georgians of Brig. Gen. Edward L. Thomas's brigade managed to work their way around the left flank of the attacking Federals, and their fire, in addition to that from the front, drove the attackers back, with Gen. Prince becoming a prisoner in the process.[10]

It was now near sundown, and the guns at the clump of cedars had exhausted their ammunition. They were withdrawn, and the Chesapeake's remaining three guns were sent forward to take their place. The fighting in this sector was over and they did not open. The battle continued to rage on Jackson's left until after dark.[11]

The next day, the two armies held their positions and there was little fighting, except for occasional picket firing and cavalry clashes. A truce was arranged on the eleventh so the dead could be buried, and as Federal reinforcements had eliminated his numerical advantage, Stonewall began moving his troops back to Gordonsville that night.[12]

In their first battle at Cedar Mountain the Chesapeakes had acquitted themselves well, and their excellent performance was duly recognized by their superior officers. Maj. Courtney wrote in his official report:

> As to the conduct of the officers and men of those batteries on the plain—to which I confined my attention —I can but speak in the highest terms...all, without a single exception, so far as my own knowledge goes or has been reported by company officers, were fired with the ardour of men determined to be free."

In his report Gen. Early noted that "Captain Brown, of the Chesapeake Artillery, and Captain Dement displayed great courage, energy, and efficiency." G. Campbell Brown, of General Ewell's staff, remembered "Captain Brown was especially commended."

The company's "rapid and well-directed fire" was also mentioned in Stonewall Jackson's report. While at Gordonsville, as further recognition of their effectiveness as a unit, the battery's obsolete howitzer and two six-pound smoothbores were replaced with two 10-pound Parrott rifled cannon. Added to their 3-inch Ordnance rifle, this brought their armament to three modern, accurate, and long-range rifled guns. It was an auspicious beginning.[13]

Action at Warrenton Springs

Jackson's command had reached Gordonsville on August 12, but took up the march again on the sixteenth. Gen. Robert E. Lee was determined to strike at Pope with his whole army, and Stonewall Jackson was about to embark on one of the most brilliant marches of his career. By late afternoon of the twenty-second the Chesapeake Artillery, marching with Ewell's division, was at the banks of the Rappahannock River near Warrenton Springs. In a pouring rain, the 13th Georgia Infantry Regiment of Brig. Gen. Alexander R. Lawton's brigade crossed the river to secure the opposite bank, followed by the Chesapeake Artillery and the 1st Maryland batteries. Early's Virginia brigade crossed about a mile away over "an old dilapidated dam." At that point, due to darkness, increasing rain, and the difficulty of the crossing, operations for the day were suspended. That night increasing rain caused the Rappahannock to rise six feet, preventing the crossing of further troops the next day and stranding Early's brigade, the 13th Georgia, and Brown's and Dement's batteries on the north side of the river.[14]

It was a highly precarious situation, as these troops were now isolated on the same side of the river as most of Pope's Army of Virginia, and Pope began moving against them. Luckily for the Confederates, Pope believed Jackson's whole force had crossed the Rappahannock, so his approach was cautious. Jackson was able to get an order across the river directing Early to take command of all the stranded troops and plan to resist an attack if necessary. By afternoon the river had fallen, but Federal troops and artillery had arrived and advanced against Early's force.[15]

Brig. Gen. Beverly Robertson arrived from Warrenton about that time with two regiments of cavalry and two cannon, and was directed by Early to take a position north of the springs and open fire. As Early wrote in his report of the action:

> This was responded to by a battery of the enemy in a few moments, and I sent two Parrott guns from Brown's battery to the assistance of Robertson's pieces, which were of short range, and a brisk cannonading was kept up until near sundown, with no damage, however, to my infantry or artillery..."

The infantry and artillery moved from place to place to make it seem as if the number of troops on hand was larger than it really was until night fell.[16]

Early had been ordered to recross the river the next morning—a tricky operation. A soldier of Dement's battery recalled:

> General Jackson planted guns on the other side for our protection, and set the infantry at work tearing down an old barn and several outbuildings to build a bridge, which he done on the remaining rubbish of the old one. We pulled our guns across by hand, and then walked the horses over. Before we got all over the enemy commenced to shell us but all got over safely and we burnt the bridge after us."

Early was pleased with his troops' deportment in avoiding a disaster: "I lost no men killed or wounded." It was another reliable performance by the Chesapeake.[17]

Engagement at Bristoe Station

The reunited division moved to nearby Jeffersonton and was issued rations for the first time in several days. Early on August 25, Ewell's men began marching west to Henson's Mill, where they finally crossed the Rappahannock, then through Orleans, stopping just south of Salem. It was one of Stonewall Jackson's famous marches of twenty-five miles, conducted in humid weather hovering near 80°F and partly in pouring rain. Fires were prohibited to prevent detection by the Federals. The next day, starting early to avoid the midday heat, the column marched nearly another twenty-five miles and reached Gainesville. Ewell sent two brigades ahead to tear up the tracks at Bristoe Station; these brigades then moved five miles east to Manassas Junction, Pope's supply base. The rest of the division, including the Chesapeake Artillery, advanced to Bristoe Station and were deployed to the west of town in anticipation of elements of Pope's army advancing to protect Manassas Junction. They would not be long in coming.[18]

To establish a delaying action, Ewell deployed part of one brigade near Kettle Run, west of Bristoe Station, as well as two batteries. The Chesapeake Artillery was positioned in support of Early's brigade farther east, on the east side of Broad Run, on a rise above the run near the Leachman house, near the Orange and Alexandra railroad tracks. During the afternoon of the twenty-seventh, Maj. Gen. Joseph Hooker's Federal division approached in lines of battle with a battery of artillery. In heavy fighting, and with high casualties considering the number of troops involved, Hooker's division drove the Confederates back across Kettle Run and approached the line at Broad Run. An officer in Early's brigade described the action:

> ...late in the afternoon when [the advance] came we were ready. Gen. Hooker (fighting Joe) was in command and he struck us a hard blow. Our orders were to skirmish with the enemy, hold them in check, but not to stand for a battle.[19]

The Chesapeake opened fire as the Confederates withdrew across Broad Run, destroying two bridges behind them. "Under a heavy artillery fire," they helped keep Hooker's troops back in the bloody fight. During the action Pvt. William Wilson of the

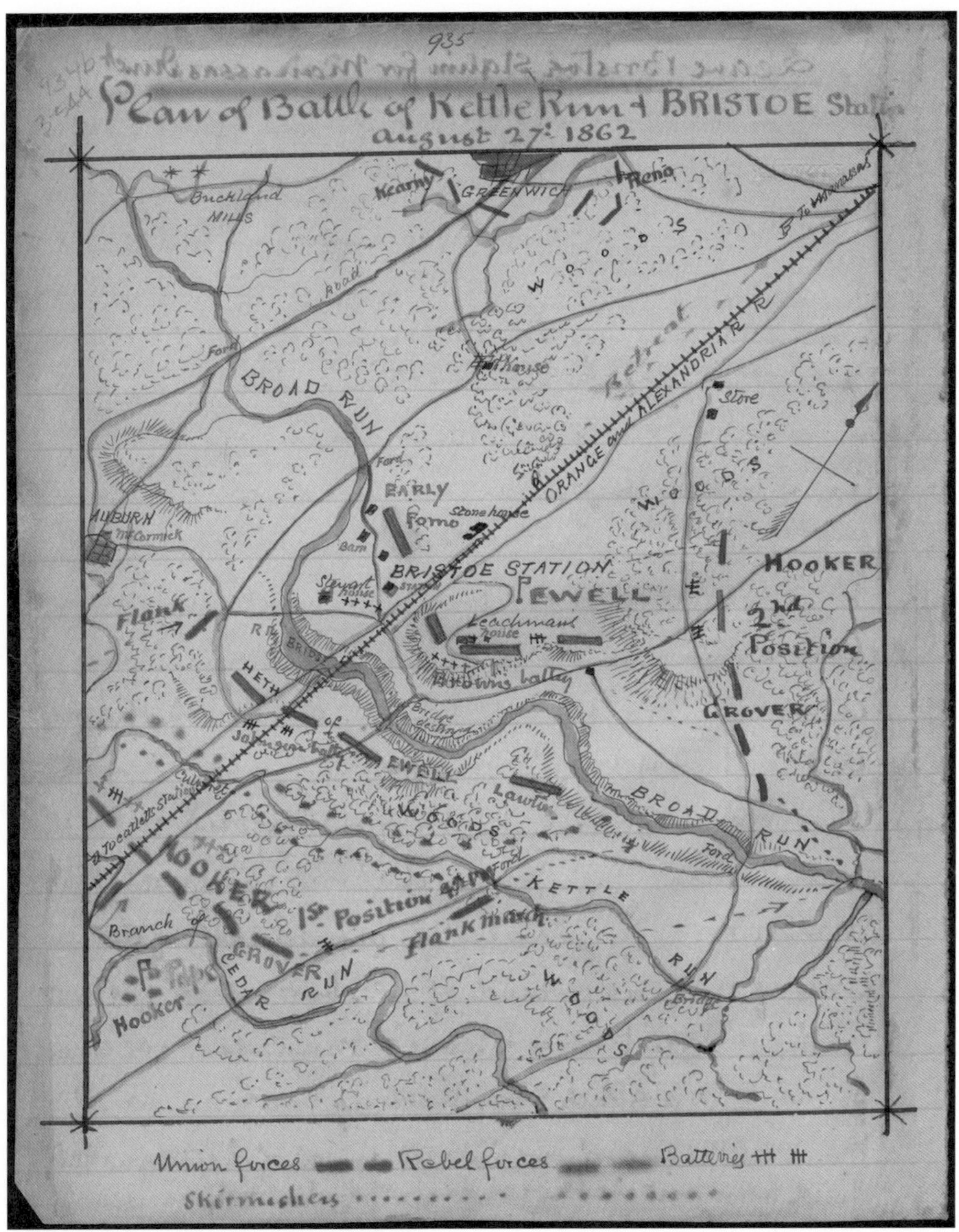

Period map of the battles of Kettle Run and Bristoe Station. The position of the Chesapeake Artillery is marked as "Brown's Battery" at center.
Library of Congress

company was slightly wounded. The battery finally retreated unmolested along with the rest of Ewell's division to Manassas Junction.[20]

Meanwhile, at Manassas Junction, the remaining two divisions of Jackson's troops had set to destroying the immense stores there. The soldiers gorged themselves on sutlers' stores of delicacies and foodstuffs the Confederates rarely encountered. The Chesapeake, along with the rest of Ewell's command, arrived on the scene after dark. As one of Early's soldiers remembered it:

> We hurried on and obtained plenty of heavy rations but all the "knick-knacks" had been carried away or eaten by the cavalry and troops who got in before us. We got plenty of "hard tack," bacon, coffee, sugar, and so on, all we could eat and carry even to the hunks of bacon on our bayonets."

No doubt the limbers of the Chesapeake were filled with more than ammunition that evening.[21]

Battle of Second Manassas

It had already been a gruelling campaign and was about to become more so. As Pvt. John Hooff described it in a letter to his cousin: "After leaving Gordonsville we have never rested in any Camp longer than two days, and hardly even that long, and even when we do stop the Knapsacks are seldom allowed to be taken out of the wagons and have not for any length of time."[22]

Now that Pope had word of Stonewall Jackson's whereabouts and was attempting to concentrate his forces to meet him, Jackson needed to position his command in such a way that he could unite with Robert E. Lee, Maj. Gen. James Longstreet, and the other half of the Army of Northern Virginia—still a day's march away. Accordingly, starting around midnight, after firing the stores at Manassas Junction, Jackson's reunited command marched an additional ten miles or so by a roundabout route to the vicinity of Groveton and concealed themselves in the woods along an unfinished railroad bed that ran southwest-northeast just north of the Warrenton Turnpike. The battery was concealed on a rise known as Stony Ridge behind the unfinished railroad bed. There the soldiers rested in the shade and waited.[23]

At dusk, a column of Federal infantry and artillery trudged along the Warrenton Turnpike from right to left along the front of Jackson's command, unaware they were in close proximity to over 20,000 Confederate soldiers. This was Brig. Gen. Rufus King's division of four brigades and four artillery batteries. Jackson, the former artillery instructor at VMI, was with Ewell's division in the vicinity of his beloved artillery. As King's column passed the intersection of the Groveton-Sudley Road—a little over a mile directly in front of the Chesapeakes' position—Jackson personally ordered Lt. Asher W. Garber's Staunton Artillery to move out of the woods on Stony Ridge and open fire. The guns of the Chesapeake Artillery adjacent to Garber's battery also soon thundered into action with its two Parrott rifles.[24]

Two brigades of Ewell's division and one of Talliaferro's to the right advanced against the surprised Federal column and opened fire in what would become one of the most intense musket battles of the war. Soon the fire of Brown's and Garber's batteries was responded to by Capt. John A. Reynolds's Battery L, 1st New York Artillery, in position at the intersection of the Warrenton Turnpike and Groveton-Sudley Road. The Federal battery was in a hot place, as one of its officers remembered:

> The rebel guns were on an elevated place, somewhat concealed by trees or bushes, and their range on us was perfect. The shot and shell fell and bursted in our midst every minute, striking the fence, exploding in the middle of the

The Second Manassas battlefield looking south along the Groveton-Sudley road from the position of the Chesapeake Artillery on Stony Ridge. *Author*

> road between men and horses, and caissons, throwing dirt and gravel all over us, and making it almost impossible for the cannoniers to man their pieces.[25]

Jackson had stayed to observe the effects of Confederate artillery fire and watched the Chesapeake in action:

> In the midst of the hottest part of the fire, the boys were startled by the sight of Stonewall Jackson, quietly looking on, and evidently much gratified at the execution the battery was doing [...]. The impulse could not be resisted and the fire of the battery was stopped and three hearty cheers were given to the grim old soldier. But this was evidently not to his liking, for he instantly ordered the battery to renew its firing, and the way those guns were made to jump was a lesson to the enemy.[26]

Casualties mounted. Pvt. Richard Hardesty, a twenty-seven-year-old clerk from Baltimore, was slightly wounded, and Pvt. Phil Harrison, a twenty-two-year-old student from Queen Anne's County, incurred a wound that would keep him out of the unit for seven months. Sgt. Thomas P. LeCompte later described the action against Reynolds's battery in a letter home:

> Two of our pieces on that occasion were engaged with 6 of theirs; but when on account of darkness, we were compelled to cease firing only one of their pieces was able to reply, we having disabled the other five with a loss to our battery of 3 horses, a number of our men being

> struck but not being hurt bad enough to leave their post.

Darkness eventually led to the end of the battle, as only muzzle flashes could be used to see the opposing lines of battle; the Federals withdrew and the fighting at Groveton died out. Casualties were heavy, including Gen. Ewell, who received a knee wound that would cost him a leg. Leadership of the division went to Brig. Gen. Alexander R. Lawton.[27]

The soldiers of The Chesapeake returned to their position in the woods and enjoyed the spoils of their foray to Manassas Junction:

> ...the boys sought something refreshing to compensate them in a measure for the danger they had escaped and the severe work they had been compelled to perform; and even a soldier has his moments of enjoyment, and of these is a cup of good Coffee, something to which the Southern soldier was a stranger for a long period of the war, unless it was captured from the enemy....the boys were in luck, and soon a quantity of steaming coffee was being handed around, and that night the campfire was enlivened with song and jest at the expense of the enemy.[28]

During the night and next day heavy Federal reinforcements arrived in the Manassas area. The battery maintained its position on Stony Ridge the next morning, August 29. At about 1000, Federal artillery opened on Confederate positions on Jackson's right and center and pounded the Confederates for two hours. The Chesapeake responded, and also helped repel the attack of Federal Brig. Gen. Robert Milroy's brigade. That afternoon Federal efforts shifted to the Confederate left. With little happening in the center, the company was placed in reserve behind Stony Ridge in a U-shaped depression formed by Catharpin Creek, about a mile behind the Confederate line.[29]

Ironically, this is where the battery suffered its only casualty that day. Pvt. Jacob Cook recalled:

> We were in reserve, snugly ensconced in a beautiful little hollow, the exact shape of a horseshoe, the horses, guns, limbers and caissons standing immediately in our front, at the distance of ten yards. Here a stray shot came bouncing over the top of the hill, and [...] after bursting, it struck Andy Egan in the thigh, tearing out a piece large enough to lame him for life, and Dad Baker had his jacket and shirt torn clean out in front. We could never determine whether it was the concussion, a piece of the shell, or what it was. At any rate, Dad was not even scratched, strange as it may appear. Two of our horses were killed by this truant bomb, than which not many line shots could have done more damage.

Egan, a clerk from Baltimore, was permanently lost to the unit, although he remained in the service. Following his recovery in hospital seventeen months later, he was detailed as a clerk for Ewell's department in Richmond until the end of the war.[30]

The company returned to their position on Stony Ridge, which they held for most of August 30. Little happened in their vicinity until 1500, when they helped repel the massive attack of Maj. Gen. Fitz John Porter's Federal 5th Corps. Cpl. George Smith, a twenty-two-year-old tailor from Dorchester County, was slightly wounded by counter-battery fire. Unknown to Pope and his army, Longstreet had arrived the day before, and by this time had placed a battalion of artillery on Jackson's right, next to a number of combined batteries in the same area. These guns blasted the left flank of the Federal attacking column, breaking the assault and uncovering the area near Groveton-Sudley Road. Longstreet launched the attack of his

25,000-man command; sensing an opportunity, Stapleton Crutchfield "ordered forward... Garber's battery of four guns at a gallop to move down into the plain below, so as to get an enfilading position on their other lines..." Brown's battery was also ordered forward at this time. Just as they deployed in the vicinity of the intersection of Groveton-Sudley Road and Warrenton Turnpike facing east, Confederate infantry approaching from the west rolled over their position, pushing the Federals back and blocking these batteries' field of fire. Now in the Confederate rear, the company held their position.[31]

This was the area Reynolds's New York battery had held during their encounter with the Chesapeake the evening of August 28, and it was the Marylanders' first opportunity to observe the effects of their fire. They saw that "...the ground, where had stood the hostile battery and its supporting infantry was found thickly strewn with dead and wounded men and horses."[32]

The men of the company sought to aid some of the Federal wounded:

> In passing over this ghastly field Lieutenant John Grason, of the Chesapeake, discovered an officer of a New York regiment mortally wounded and dying. This Christian gentleman knelt and prayed with his wounded enemy—not enemy now—whilst the men of the battery stood reverently by until the poor soldier closed his eyes in death.[33]

Federal prisoners were also being marshalled in the area before being taken farther to the rear, and the men of the battery had an opportunity to interact with them. Pvt. John Hoof remembered:

> I had a present of a silver watch from a Yankey Officer, he was a prisoner at Mannassa [sic] and was sick. I gave him a blanket that I did not want, and shortly afterwards he made me...a present of the watch. I refused to take it at first but did so after he had insisted upon my taken it for sometime, I sold it...and got a good price for it, it was of no use to me.[34]

Lee's Army of Northern Virginia had gained a brilliant victory and forced Pope's Army of Virginia from the field. The Federals retreated east toward Washington. Jackson's command was roused early the next morning, September 1, and in a pouring rain moved east on the Little River Turnpike in an attempt to get on Pope's right flank and destroy his army. The tactic did not work, and the infantry fought during a violent thunderstorm near Chantilly in which the artillery was not engaged because of the heavily wooded terrain.[35]

Capture of Harper's Ferry

With no Federal threat in the field in northern Virginia, the way was open for Lee to move his army north, and in so doing not only supply his army, but possibly gain foreign recognition for the Confederacy. Accordingly, the Army of Northern Virginia moved north on September 3. Lee's plan was to split his army into several parts as it moved into Maryland. Jackson's objective was to capture the Federal garrisons of 2,500 men under Brig. Gen. Julius White at Martinsburg and the 10,400 men under Col. Dixon Miles at Harper's Ferry, thus removing them as a threat to Lee's rear as the army moved into Maryland.[36]

Harper's Ferry sits in a low elevation at the confluence of the Potomac and Shenandoah Rivers. The division of Brig. Gen. John G. Walker was ordered to move from Frederick, recross the Potomac River, advance west along the Virginia side of the river, and occupy Loudoun Heights, an eminence overlooking Harper's Ferry to the east, on the east side of the Shenandoah River. A division under Maj. Gen. Lafayette McLaws was to move west along the Maryland side of the Potomac and occupy Maryland Heights, which dominated Harper's Ferry across the Potomac to the north. Jackson was also to move his command west on the Maryland side, recross the Potomac at Williamsport, and approach Martinsburg and Harper's Ferry from the west. By surrounding the town Jackson hoped to force its capitulation.[37]

Accordingly, the Army of Northern Virginia started its move north on September 3. Lawton's division—with the Chesapeake Artillery—crossed the Potomac into Maryland on the fifth with bands playing "Maryland, My Maryland." They were in Frederick by the sixth. Lee and the Confederates had hoped to spur enlistments of Marylanders by their presence in the state, but the reaction of the Northern sympathizing citizens of the western counties was decidedly cool. The Chesapeake had no new enlistments while in Maryland.[38]

The column left Frederick on the tenth and marched ten miles west to beyond Middletown; the following day they crossed the Potomac at Williamsport and reached the vicinity of North Mountain Depot on the Baltimore & Ohio Railroad. The march was hard—twenty-three miles that day—straggling was common, and Federal cavalry was ever present to capture those who fell out of rank. Pvt. William Oldson, a thirty-six-year-old clerk from Baltimore, was captured on the twelfth near Frederick; and Pvt. "Doctor Jack" Bryan, a thirty-three-year-old physician from Culpeper County, Virginia, was captured on the fourteenth. Capt. Brown, riding in the back of the column to collect stragglers, was almost captured as well. Pvt. John Hooff remembered Brown's close call:

> Capt Brown was with us…he had a very hard time coming to us, he was cut off by the Yanks twice and was very near being captured both times, the only thing that saved him was a fleet horse, never did men rejoice so as ours did when they perceived him in the distance ride up to us, the remark was, "Thank god he is safe and with us."[39]

Capt. Billy Brown, likely taken in spring 1862, after his election to captain. *Courtesy of Dave Mark*

Jackson's men reached Martinsburg on September 12; the town had been evacuated and the garrison under White moved to Harper's Ferry. By the thirteenth, the Confederates had reached the vicinity of Harper's Ferry, and on the afternoon of the fourteenth they were approaching from the west in three columns. They took position on Schoolhouse Ridge outside of town, opposite the Federal position on Bolivar Heights, and advanced, but night fell before an engagement commenced. With McLaws's and Walker's divisions in place the Federal bastion was surrounded.[40]

That night ten rifled guns of Courtney's battalion, including the three guns of the Chesapeake, were moved to the east side of the town. Crossing the Shenandoah River at Kelly's Ford, they were pushed by hand to a shelf on Loudoun Heights on a road that had been cut up the mountain to enable this. The guns were in position a couple of hours after dawn. From this position these ten guns commanded the Federal rear on Bolivar Heights. The guns opened fire in concert with Jackson's infantry, which advanced directly against the Federal position. As Stapleton Crutchfield reported:

> In a short time the guns of Captains Brown, [Lieutenant] Garber, Latimer, and Dement, being in position, their fire was directed against this work from the rear. Its battery was quickly silenced, and the men running from their guns, but returning to them in a short time after the guns directed on the work were brought to bear on the enemy's infantry in his intrenchments. These pieces were, therefore, again directed on the work, and in something less than an hour its fire was completely silenced, and our guns being again turned on the enemy's infantry, they soon began to fall back from their intrenchments in great confusion, and the white flag was raised over their works.[41]

Col. Dixon Miles was mortally wounded near the end of the bombardment. The surrender of the Harper's Ferry garrison and its nearly 13,000 men, complete with munitions, horses, and equipment, was the largest single capture of prisoners during the entire war. One of the prisoners was Pvt. Willie Mason's brother Joseph, who was serving with the Federal 3rd Potomac Home Brigade of Maryland Infantry. The men of The Chesapeake were ecstatic with the victory, voiced with enthusiasm by Pvt. John Hooff a couple of days later in a letter to his aunt, Mary Ward:

> Oh! we have had a most glorious Victory here, Captured 18 thousand [sic] Prisoners...48 pieces of artillery & over 30 thousand stands of small arms of ever description and patent, also any amount of clothing and wagons. The enemy were fortified on Boliver [sic] Hights...we got possession of Maryland and Virginia [Loudoun] Hights during Sunday [the 14th] without them knowing anything about it. Gen Jackson sent them an order to surrender on Sunday evening, but they refused, so on Sunday night Jackson posted his Artillery on the highest points of both the Maryland and Va Hights while the infantry lined the rivers both above and below the fortifications so they could not retreat by that route, [McLaws] commanded on the Maryland side and Jackson on the Va. The Yankees were aroused on Monday morning [the 15th] before daybreak by the roar of over 50 pieces of Artillery throwing their iron hail right down amongst them and Oh! such a sight, if you ever saw a man Jump about on red hot, iron, they did it then, you never saw such jumping and dancing about in your life, they tried to man their guns but it was of no use, they broke their ranks Just as if they had walked into a hornets nest, and in about a half or 3 quarters of an hour they hoisted the white flag and surrendered unconditionally. Gen Miles who commanded the Yankees was [killed] just as the white flag...was being hoisted, when our Gen sent us an order to cease fireing our Captain could hardly restrain our boys of sending them another shot, but out of humanity for the retches they refrained from doing so.[42]

It was the capstone to a gruelling six weeks of campaigning. Since leaving Gordonsville on August 7, the unit had marched over 220 miles and participated in six battles. Its horses and equipment were broken down to the point where, rather than joining the rest of the army at Sharpsburg, Crutchfield ordered the "batteries of Captains Brown, Dement, and Latimer…left at Harper's Ferry, as disabled, on account of the condition of their horses." Capt. Brown submitted a requisition for thirty-two horses on the seventeenth, and as Pvt. Hooff summarized it in a letter to Mary Ward the same day, "We are now equipping our battery with new horses, harness, and wagons captured in the fight, our old horses were completely worn out as also were the men, we have now rested 2 days and will start a tomorrow morning to give the Yankees another thrashing."[43]

On September 19, following the battle at Sharpsburg, the Army of Northern Virginia crossed the Potomac River into Virginia. Lawton was seriously wounded at Sharpsburg, and command of the division now fell to Gen. Jubal Early. The 4th Maryland Artillery rejoined Jackson's command, marched with it to Martinsburg, and on the twenty-seventh marched to Bunker Hill. There the tracks of the B&O Railroad were destroyed; the column then moved to a camp near Charles Town for several weeks of much needed rest. Peter Williams described the location:

> We are now in Clarke County on the turnpike leading from Charlestown to Berryville about 15 miles from Harper's Ferry […]. Our Camp here is about 3 miles from the Shenandoah river, and apparently is one of the finest portions of Virginia. The farms around here are magnificent & there are a good many very fine looking country residences.[44]

Morale in the unit soared following the successes of their initial campaign. As Pvt. John Hooff expressed it in a letter to Mary Ward that was gleefully headed, "This is yankee paper captured at Mannassa[s]":

> I am quite an old veteran now, have passed through eight battles safe. The battle of Ceder Creek, of Bristo Station, 4 days fighting at Mannasa[s], battle of the [Warrenton] Springs and the last and the most glorious of all, the battle of Harpers Ferry."

He went on to describe the reputation of the unit:

> …the Generals have a very high opinion of our Company, which is evident from the number of engagements they throgh us into, while a dozen or more other Companies have never been in one. If any battery of the enemy is to be silenced or a position is to be taken, the cry is, where are those two Md batteries at, meaning ours and Capt Dements…send them up and we will have them is the order.[45]

Sgt. Thomas LeCompte expressed relief at passing through battle safely and his good state of health in a letter to his mother:

> …notwithstanding the iron hail that has fallen around me for the last three or four months…I have escaped almost entirely unhurt, with the exception of a slight scratch on the head by a piece of spent shell, which however did not prevent my helping to make the yankees position to hot for them to hold…You have no idea how camp life agrees with me, with the exception of a slight attack of the bilious I have enjoyed perfect health. My weight at present is 169 lbs, but before the winter ends I expect to come up to 180. You have no idea how one feels after rising in the morning from beneath his blankets while white with hoarfrost the atmosphere feels so pure and healthy it gives an energy for drill and rids him entirely of that sluggishness attendant on camp life.[46]

Pvt. Isaac Blunt echoed similar sentiments:

> Willy Stenet joined us the other day and gave us a great deal of news from home he told us that you all heard I was dead but it is a [lie.] I have made three or four very narrow [escapes.] I have been in seven very hard battles [and a] number of skirmishes and have not [had a] single scratch yet [...] I have had better health than I ever did before and you would hardly know me I am so fat.[47]

Capt. Billy Brown was appointed acting chief of artillery for Early's division in the absence of Maj. A.R. Courtney. He was highly regarded by his superiors, as Hooff wrote to Mary Ward: "Capt B has obtained a very high reputation as an Officer, and is very popular with the Generals."

Brown's reputation extended to that of the company as a whole, and the Chesapeake experienced a surge in enlistments. Twenty-two men enlisted in the battery during the months of October and November, bringing its strength by the beginning of December to about 100 men, the highest level it would reach at any time during the war. The Chesapeakes had gained the respect of their comrades in Jackson's command, and had every reason to be proud.[48]

"THEY DON'T KNOW ANYTHING ELSE BUT FIGHT"

Pvt. John Hooff was homesick. Although he was a Virginian, he shared something in common with his Maryland compatriots in the Chesapeake Artillery: his Fairfax home was behind Federal lines and not accessible. Hooff's aunt, Mary Ward, had left Tappahannock with her children and returned to Bladensfield, the Wards' plantation home a few miles from Machodoc, in the Northern Neck. Hooff wrote to her from camp:

> Oh! I would give anything in the world to be with you once more, and I shall try my best to get a forlough, it would be like going into a new world to get down to Bladen[s]field, you may look out for me before long. I should like so much some cold morning, when they are all sitting down to a nice breakfast, before a warm fire, just present my self at the door; wouldn't they be astonished, I want to see Ma so bad that I am nearly distracted. I am so afraid she is sick, night and day, hour, minute and second, and in fact all the time I am thinking about her, sometimes when I am busy attending to working or doing some other work I will become deaf to everything and I have often heard the boys remark "why what is the matter with Hooff, he certainly is asleep or dreaming." Oh! I would give any thing in the world just to see her for a few minutes.[1]

Furloughs were difficult to obtain, as Hooff wrote to his cousin, Mary:

> I have been trying to get a forlough for some time and Captain Brown promised me yesterday that he would try his best

Bladensfield, the Ward family home. *Library of Congress*

to get me one. I hope he will succede I would give any thing in the world to come down and see you all…"

Sgt. Peter Williams was also hoping to go home to Richmond, writing to his mother at this time:

> I am very anxious to hear from you all […]. When I write again, I will probably be nearer home & if we do get down about Gordonsville this winter I mean to go home anyhow.[2]

Those lucky men who received furloughs had difficulty making their way to Maryland. Evelyn Ward remembered:

> When one of the Maryland [soldiers] had a furlough, he was very apt to come to our part of the country and go across to Leonardtown with the blockade runners. While he waited the blockade runner's time, Bladensfield was a good safe place to stay. In that way it happened that we very often had a Maryland [soldier] as guest for a night, a couple of nights, or even a week at a time. My poor dear Mother! It was a pleasure to her to do what she could for those soldier boys who were trying to get a glimpse of home.

It was just as difficult getting back. Pvt. Fred Allston, a ninteen-year-old clerk from Baltimore, was captured on October 20 by Federal authorities while trying to land on the Virginia shore with "a canoe load of goods."[3]

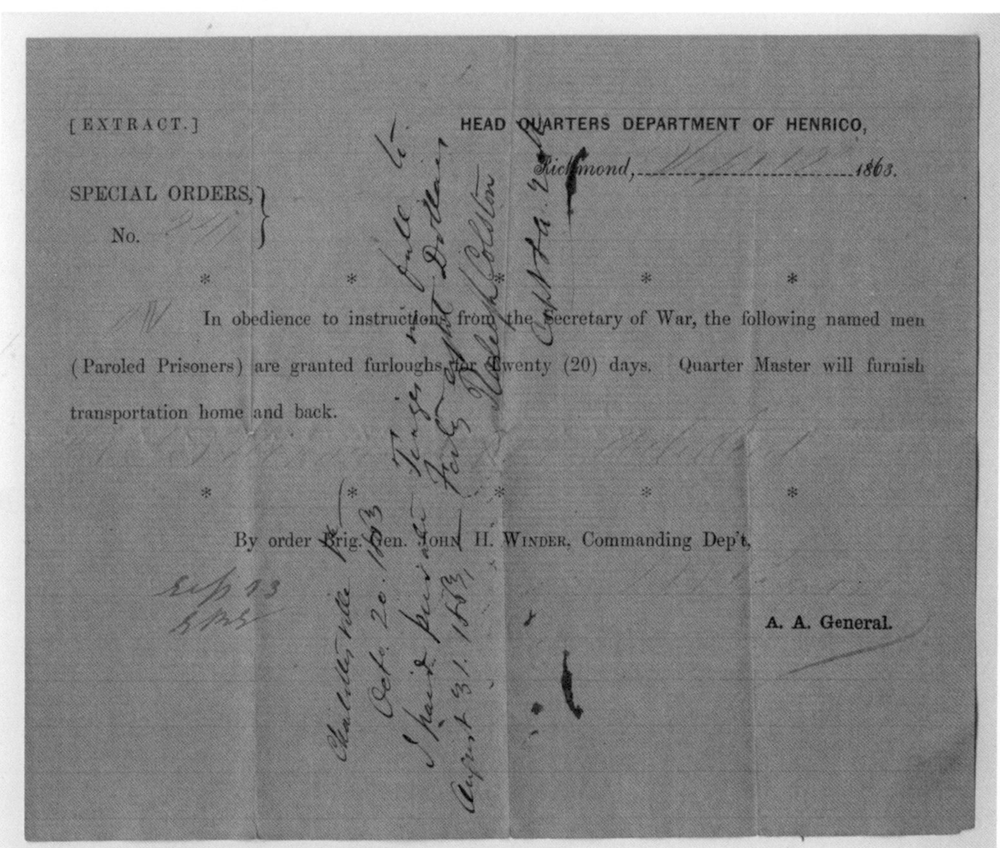

[EXTRACT.] HEAD QUARTERS DEPARTMENT OF HENRICO,

Richmond, ______ 1863.

SPECIAL ORDERS, No. ______

* * * * * *

In obedience to instructions from the Secretary of War, the following named men (Paroled Prisoners) are granted furloughs for Twenty (20) days. Quarter Master will furnish transportation home and back.

* * * * * *

By order Brig. Gen. JOHN H. WINDER, Commanding Dep't,

A. A. General.

Furlough issued to Pvt. Charles Tinges. *Author's collection*

Postwar view of the wharf at Leonardtown, Maryland. Many Confederate Maryland soldiers passed through here on their way to and from the Army of Northern Virginia. *Courtesy of St. Mary's County Historical Society*

The soldiers strove to pass the time in camp. Foraging was a favorite activity to improve rations; squirrels were relished supplements. Peter Williams recounted one particularly successful expedition:

> I went out about 5 miles from Camp yesterday "foraging," down the river. I stopped about 2 O'Clock at a beautiful place right on the banks of the river owned by a man named Lewis. I went in & bought a peck of magnificent apples & got one of the best dinners I ever saw. I met with two ladies, one rather an elder lady—the other very young & very pretty but both married.[4]

As the boredom of camp life set in rumors became common. Williams shared one in a letter to his mother shortly after Jackson's command had finished destroying part of the B&O Railroad:

> When the Yankee Government took the [rail]road at commencement for the war it promised the company to replace the road at the end of the War, in the same condition it was when they took it & to do this now will cost them an immense sum of money.[5]

John Hooff also repeated a number of these rumors in letters home; they reflect the optimism about the Confederate war effort the soldiers of the company felt at this time:

> I suppose that you have heard of the capture of Cincinatta by our troops, and will be held as a ransom for Baltimore.[6]
>
> There is some talk about here about an armistice being agreed upon between the two commanding parties for 60 days, have you heard any thing about it, I hope that it is so I think that if it is it will be the end of the war.
>
> I have heard…that three of Lincoln's cabinet are in Richmond, is it so? if it is the war is over, and also that the Yankey Army has fallen back on Washington but cannot vouch for the truth of it, I only hope it is so…
>
> Have you heard anything about the intervention of any Foreign Power lately.

> I think that if they ever intend doing any thing of that kind, it is high time they were commencing, but I am afraid that [they] never intend doing any thing untill we gain our independence by the work of our own hands, which I hope is not far distant.[7]

Pvt. Isaac Blunt also had a positive outlook on the outcome of the war, writing to his cousin, "I will soon be home the war will not last long it will soon close and I will be with you all once more."[8]

Camp gossip was a favorite topic of conversation, as Hooff wrote to Mary Ward:

> Capt Brown stands a good chance of being promoted to a majorship before long, he has been acting as such [...] and it is the opinion of all that Capt B, will be commissioned [...] and Lieut Plater will be Captain of this Company [...] I should be very sorry to lose him, but still I like Plater very well. Tell Cousin Mattie she had better set her cap for Capt B—major elect.[9]

The soldiers also engaged in gossip from home, as Hooff teased his cousin, Mary:

> So Mr Austin has treated you badly, indeed I am very sorry to hear it. I had no idea that he would treat you in that manner, to stay in a mile or two of his lady love and never let her know of it. oh! it was too bad I declare...How is Charley getting on with Mis Janett?[10]

Talk of the military situation was common around the campfires, and the men of the unit speculated on the multiple possibilities of moves their generals might make. Lewis Warrington wrote home that, "we are expecting to be on the move every day but can not say whether it will be in the direction of Richmond or whether in that of Maryland." Peter Williams opined, "The general impression is that our army is falling back towards Gordonsville upon the same old lines it held last winter. There is very little forage up in this country & I suppose it is too far from Richmond to transport it." But John Hooff ruminated, "would not be surprised if we were to be marching towards Richmond before long. I heard this morning that Gen Earley our Commandant would not grant a forlough as he expected orders to move towards Winchester which is on the route to Richmond and I have also heard that the rest of our army is moving in that direction...."[11]

March to Fredericksburg

Certainly the military situation was developing quickly. Gen. McClellan had been replaced as the commander of the Army of the Potomac with Maj. Gen. Ambrose Burnside. Burnside immediately started his columns south in a feint towards Culpeper, but then began moving toward Fredericksburg, shadowed by Longstreet's newly established 1st Corps. Burnside's plan was to cross the Rappahannock River at Fredericksburg on pontoons and move against Richmond before Lee could reunite his two widely separated corps and respond.

The weather was mild in late October and early November, but by November 5 it was chilly, with cold rain and snow. Two days later it snowed all day, leaving two inches on the ground. On the twenty-first, Jackson's 2nd Corps, with the Chesapeake Artillery, left their camps near Charlestown and marched south on the Valley Pike; they made twenty miles that day. By the twenty-fourth they had crossed Massanutten Mountain at New Market on icy roads that hampered their progress. Pvt. Jacob Cook remembered the difficulty marching through the mountains:

> The day was bitter cold, the wind blowing a perfect gale. The poor horses, broken down through short rations [...] could barely make the ascent. The road wound

> along, around and up the mountain like a huge serpent. A half day was consumed in laboriously reaching the summit, the wind fairly threatened to blow the entire Battalion from off the mountain top. The cold was intensely bitter, cutting like a keen-edge blade, almost stopping the circulation.[12]

After two days spent at Madison Court House, the column was within five miles of Fredericksburg by December 1, and filed into positions on Longstreet's right flank that afternoon; they had marched 175 miles in twelve days, including two days of rest at Madison Court House. Meanwhile, frustration had dogged the Army of the Potomac. Bad weather and bad planning had delayed the pontoon train that was such an integral part of Burnside's plan. It did not reach Fredericksburg until November 25. By that time Longstreet's corps had taken a strong position on the hills west of Fredericksburg and a Confederate brigade occupied the town to contest any river crossing there.[13]

The weather turned cold, with snow during the night of December 5. Jacob Cook recalled life in camp at this time and his own thoughts of home:

> Our park of artillery was near the Rappahannock, whose bank was covered with tall and bare trees, throwing their naked trunks in bold relief against the winter sky. Lying on the cold, wet ground that night, I thought of old, loved Baltimore. The trees looming up before me, seemed in the dim, uncertain light of a winter night, to float above the river, like the masts and spars of shipping. The impression crept over my mind, half dreaming, half waking, that we were at Pratt-street wharf, where I had so often, in the dull, inactive times of peace, seen our merchant marine resting lazily on the dark, quiet water of the fragrant Basin. Reveille brought us to a stern sense of reality. The snow had covered us in the night. The boys were thus enabled to sleep, through the generous warmth afforded by nature's gentle hand. Comfortable as it seemed during the night, when the bugle's shrill notes called us to our feet at early dawn, we awoke cold and shivering.[14]

Burnside decided to initiate several feints, including a crossing fifteen miles downstream at a sharp bend in the river known as Skinker's Neck, and he called on the US Navy to assist. The Rappahannock squadron moved upriver. On December 10, the Chesapeake was ordered south to the area near Skinker's Neck with the rest of Early's division and engaged the navy gunboats. Cook recalled the action:

> We were going in to fight gunboats, the terror of artillerymen. Before reaching our position a shell, as big as a nail keg, came rushing through the air, falling directly in front of our detachment, and killing one of our lead horses. Fortunately, John Montgomery had a good knife, with which we quickly cut the traces, and with the rest of the team made our way into position. The gunboats thundered away, but overshot us, not having exact range.

The action was more noisy than deadly, with the squadron eventually steaming back downriver. Pvt. John Montgomery, a twenty-year-old Baltimorean, was unhurt.[15]

The next day, the Federals bridged the Rappahannock with the pontoons, and forced their way across the river and into the town. Fredericksburg was subsequently sacked by the soldiers of the Army of the Potomac. As the sound of rifle fire carried to their camp at Brooke Farm, the men of Early's division cooked rations and waited. Burnside and his generals spent the next day deploying their forces for the attack on the positions of the Army of Northern Virginia.[16]

Battle of 1st Fredericksburg

Fog covered the ground the morning of December 13, as Early's division marched to join Jackson's corps, positioned on Longstreet's right and stretching for nearly two miles along a range of hills a mile west of the Rappahannock. On Jackson's right and left flanks open ground descended for over a mile down to the river. Lt. Col. R. Lindsay Walker's battalion of fourteen guns was placed on the right flank of the corps, at Hamilton's Crossing. Maj. Greenlee Davidson's battalion of twenty-one guns went into position on the left, on a knoll near the slave cabins of the Bernard plantation overlooking the Richmond, Fredericksburg, and Potomac Railroad tracks.[17]

In the center, extensive woods precluded the placement of the remainder of the corps' artillery, so twelve guns under the command of Capt. John B. Brockenbrough were placed a couple of hundred yards to the front and right of Davidson's guns across the railroad tracks. The center was weak, not only because the artillery on the flanks could not fire directly on this area, but also because few troops had been placed in the low, swampy ground in the woods.[18]

Early's division, including the Chesapeake Artillery, was placed in reserve behind Prospect Hill half a mile to the right rear of the Confederate line. About this time Capt. Brown received an injury that incapacitated him from duty; the duties of the division's artillery chief passed to Capt. Joseph Latimer of the Courtney Artillery, and command of the Chesapeake fell to Lt. John Plater as senior officer present.[19]

As the fog lifted the morning of December 13, Federal batteries on both sides of the river pounded Confederate positions. Confederate guns were ordered to hold their fire until the anticipated infantry attack, so the Federals had difficulty identifying targets, and many of their shots were long, landing beyond the hills where the reserves were waiting. Jacob Cook recalled a close call:

> While seated around the fire at the artillery park, which we had formed after falling back, busily engaged in providing for the inner man, a stray bomb came shrieking through the air and fell square in the fire. There is an old and strong belief among artillerists that a shot never strikes twice in the same place; so, after a very lively scattering, no one being hurt, we rebuilt the fire and resumed operations.[20]

Shortly after noon the Federal divisions of Brig. Gen. John Gibbon and Maj. Gen. George G. Meade—8,000 men in all—began their advance against Jackson's position. Confederate artillery opened fire, and with their targets now visible, Federal artillery blanketed the guns in counter-battery fire. Casualties were heavy in the Confederate batteries, both in men and guns. 2nd Corps Chief of Artillery Col. Stapleton Crutchfield withdrew several of the batteries in Greenlee Davidson's battalion and all of Brockenbrough's guns beyond the railroad, then ordered Latimer into action to replace them near the Bernard cabins. Latimer described the scene they encountered in his report:

> I relieved five of the guns at that point by the two rifles belonging to my battery, and the three rifles composing Captain Brown's. The position on which these guns were posted was not a very advantageous one, but the best that could be selected. It was a small rising in an open field, with a wood to the right, in which a portion of General A.P. Hill's division was posted, and on the left was a ditch and bank running parallel with the railroad, behind which a portion of General Hood's division was posted. In front, at the distance of about a mile, were four of the enemy's batteries, with lines of skirmishers considerably advanced in front of said batteries. We were exposed to quite a heavy fire from these batteries, but gained the position without loss.[21]

The artillery on the knoll just north of the Bernard cabins was supported by Brig. Gen. George "Tige" Anderson's Georgia brigade on their left, Brig. Gen. James Lane's North Carolina brigade to their right front at the railroad, and in the rear by Brig. Gen. William Dorsey Pender's North Carolina brigade and Brig. Gen. Evander Law's Alabama and North Carolina brigade.[22]

Although Latimer located the guns on the reverse slope of the knoll, the position was much exposed to Federal artillery fire, and as the company went into action things began to go wrong almost immediately. Peter Williams recalled:

> Our battery was in a very exposed position and having about fifteen guns playing on us, with infantry at the same time, we suffered a good deal. At about the 6th shot from the enemy, our 2nd Lieutenant (Grayson) fell right at my side, his leg shot almost entirely off above the knee. He was carried off the field but died very soon afterwards.[23]

Grason was taken to the rear, saying to the men near him, "Tell them at home that I died at my post." Shortly after a direct hit on one of the Chesapeake's limbers caused it to explode and Pvt. Edward Graham, a twenty-seven-year-old carpenter from Baltimore, was "blown to pieces" and killed instantly. The explosion also wounded five additional men: Pvt. Isaac Blunt, a twenty-three-year-old farmer from Talbot County; Pvt. James Kemper Harper, a seventeen-year-old student from Talbot County; nineteen-year-old Pvt. Paul Huber; Pvt. Willie Mason, a nineteen-year-old from Harford County; and the company's bugler, nineteen-year-old Daniel Wilkinson, a farmer from St. Mary's County. They had to be helped to safety. One of the company's guns was then disabled by counter-battery fire.[24]

To the company's right front, Lane's brigade caused heavy casualties among Gibbon's advancing columns but ran out of ammunition and had to withdraw; Pender's brigade now supported Latimer's guns from the right rear. The battery switched to double loads of canister as the retreating North Carolinians uncovered the Federal advance. "The head of the column," wrote Greenlee Davidson, "went down like wheat before the reaper."[25]

Col. William B. Hatch's 4th New Jersey regiment advanced directly against the knoll,

The Fredericksburg battlefield, looking northwest from the site of the Bernard cabins. Andrews' Battalion, including the Chesapeake Artillery, was in position on the knoll in front of the tree line in the center background. Federal infantry approached along the RF&P railroad in the right distance. *Author*

crossing the railroad as the 16th North Carolina posted there also ran out of ammunition and withdrew. Sharpshooters took aim at the artillerists from 200 yards away, causing numerous casualties: Pvt. John "Little" Green, a twenty-year-old farm laborer from Dorchester County, went down with a gunshot wound above his left knee, as did his friend, Pvt. Vincent "Big" Green—also a farm laborer from Baltimore County—with a wound to his left thigh. Pvt. Thomas Toy, a twenty-five-year-old bookkeeper from Baltimore City, received severe gunshot wounds to both legs, and Pvt. Phil Oldner, who had just turned twenty the week before, went down with a gunshot wound as well. The Federals also began shooting down the battery's horses. The gun crews of Latimer's battalion could not hold their position and ran for safety to the woods along Deep Run on their left.[25] As Pvt. Jacob Cook recalled:

> With colors flying, with bright bayonets flashing in the sun, to the drum's loud roll [...] the enemy advanced. On they come! We [...] poured shot and shell fast and furious into their ranks. As gaps after gaps are broken in their line, they fill them up; and still they advance. They are within a quarter of a mile, and many brave men have fallen on both sides [...]. And still they come. Our guns are yet pouring death and destruction into their lines, but we can never hold our own against such heavy force. "Will our support never be ordered up?" is the question on every lip.[26]

Law saw the artillery was in trouble and he advanced two regiments to drive the New Jersey soldiers away; he was joined on the left by Anderson's Georgians. The Chesapeakes returned to their guns and began firing shell at the retreating Federals, then switching to canister. As Crutchfield reported, the "pieces were excellently managed, and though losing heavily from the enemy's sharpshooters, drove back their lines with canister, and caused them great loss by an uncommonly accurate and rapid shell-fire, as they were driven back by general Law's brigade in their attempted advance."[27]

Capt. Latimer reported, "I was kept constantly engaged at this point from 11 a.m. (when I gained it) until night, repelling repeated advances of the enemy by the use of canister." A couple of days later Sgt. Peter Williams wrote a letter to his uncle to let his family know he was safe:

> Day before yesterday we were in the fight all day and the fight exceeded anything I have ever seen yet [...] we had one private killed by the explosion of a limber chest and five wounded; at the other guns we had four more wounded and lost a good many horses. We remained on the field until ten o'clock at night, when we were relieved. [...] We are so disabled that we can only go in again with two guns. We are trying our best this morning to get up enough men and horses to go in again.[28]

The company had again performed well under trying circumstances. Gen. "Tige" Anderson, commander of the Georgia brigade to the Chesapeake's left, lauded the battery's efforts, as Jacob Cook remembered:

> During the engagement he sent over to enquire what battery "he had the honor of seeing upon his right, making the most stubborn resistance he had ever seen, and against overwhelming odds." On the next day he proved his appreciation by sending over to camp two wagon loads of clothing; of which we stood greatly in need, our boys being nearly naked.[29]

Cook also recalled that a Maryland soldier in Anderson's brigade, "has since related to me that, when we beat the enemy back into the river, one of his comrades in arms said to him: 'Look here, Baltimore, what kind of men have you got in Maryland, anyhow? They don't know anything else but fight.'"[30]

The Chesapeake had been battered in the conflict: in addition to the disabling of one of the guns and the destroyed limber the unit had lost sixteen horses. The battery's casualties (two killed and nine wounded) were greater than the total casualties of all their engagements combined to that time and included its first battle deaths.[31]

The loss of Lt. John Grason was particularly felt by his men and superiors. Capt. Billy Brown referred to him as "the noble Grason," and Latimer in his report echoed similar thoughts, saying he "fell nobly at his post." Cook described his loss: "Lieut. Grayson has been killed at his post, brave to the last," and Sgt. Peter Williams remembered him as, "one of the bravest and best men I ever knew." Ben Roberts, a twenty-two-year-old farmer from Queen Anne's County, was elected to replace Grason as 2nd Lieutenant.[32]

Following the day's exertions, hunger became the most important factor to deal with. Cook recalled a humorous foraging expedition he undertook later that night in the camp of Anderson's Georgia brigade with Pvt. Smith Warrington, a sixteen-year-old student from Baltimore:

> That night, after having been engaged all day without anything to eat, Smith Warrington and I concluded to forage; every old Confed knows what that means. We started out, guided by the camp fires of Lee's line. All that mighty host, after a hard day's fight, were trying to snatch a little sleep...But [ovens] were lying around loose in the brigade, among the Goobers, and Warrington was the boy to find them. After scouting around for over an hour, we struck the trail, and a big fat oven presented itself to our delighted gaze. Now the question was how to get possession of the aforesaid oven; for be it known that the aforesaid Goobers were very sensitive where ovens were concerned, and woe to the unlucky compatriot caught in the act of "confiscating" one of the aforesaid ovens. In response to this question, I suggested that Warrington should do the borrowing. He, although never known to shirk, begged to be excused. We compromised by deliberately walking up to the oven under consideration, he taking one side and I the other, and very quietly walking off with it. After trotting...a considerable distance, we stopped to hold an inspection, and a glorious treat repaid our long and weary search for grub; for reposing within the depths of that oven were biscuits, bacon and potatoes. Now, how in the name of everything sacred, these Goobers could manage to get such grub together, no Marylander ever could find out. However, we knew how to enjoy it.[33]

The Army of the Potomac withdrew from the Fredericksburg area the night of December 15–16. Not knowing if Burnside would make another attempt to cross the Rappahannock, Lee spread his army among the various crossings up and down the river, but Burnside made no further attempt, other than his aborted "Mud March" of early January.[34]

Christmas, 1862

Lee allowed more soldiers to go home on furlough, and the lucky ones who could made their way to friends' homes to celebrate Christmas. Several were present at the Wards' home, Bladensfield, for the holiday season; the Wards were still grieving over the loss of their oldest son Will, who died that August from a wound received at the Battle of Gaines's Mill. As Evelyn Ward remembered it:

> We had a crowd of [Maryland soldiers] at Christmas. Mamma said, "We must

> do all we can to make them have a good time." The silver came out of the cabbage patch, the glass out of its hiding. Mamma made a fine fruitcake, having the sugar Charley had run the blockade to get. She used her dried cherries for raisins, and homemade citron...So, trying to make things merry for us children and for the Maryland soldiers, Mamma stilled her heartache this first Christmas without our Brother Will. She had a Christmas tree in the studio trimmed with long strings of hollyberries and lighted by nub ends of candles. We had no presents for the soldiers, so we made them little round pincushions, but put no pins in them. Pins were scarce and precious in those days.[35]

Capt. Billy Brown recovered from his injury at Bladensfield and was a participant in the Christmas celebrations there. In a letter thanking her, Brown assured Mary Ward, "Mr. Harrison is absent sick. I have a pin cushion for him which I will deliver on his return."[36]

Sgt. Peter Williams spent a cheerless Christmas in camp and missed being home:

> This Xmas was the dullest I ever spent in my life; I remained in Camp all day & dined on the meanest rations that the Government has furnished us for six months. Within the last few days however one of my tent mates has received two large Boxes; one filled with potatoes, Peas & dried Peaches; the other containing a pot of Butter, a box of eggs & a box of Sausage meat, a bag of cakes and some magnificent apples. We have been having our Xmas ever since. We have eggs and sausage every morning for breakfast & just eat apples all day long.[37]

Winter Camp near Bowling Green

In late December, the battery moved with the rest of the artillery of the 2nd Corps, and soon were in winter camp at DeJarnette's Woods in Caroline County, five miles south of Bowling Green, Virginia.[38]

The men immediately began building winter quarters, as described by Peter Williams in a letter home on January 12:

> The infantry of General Lee's army are still stretched along the line of the Rappahannock, but all the artillery except one Battery to each division has been ordered to the rear and are building winter quarters. Three other fellows besides myself went to work about ten days ago, as soon as we got here, and put up a really first rate comfortable log cabin. We built it out and out ourselves, I being the 'Boss' carpenter. It is ten foot square inside, with a nice brick hearth and fireplace, and has a little hole about a foot square in one end with a plank to open and shut for a window. We scoured the whole country for a window sash, but couldn't find one. The three young men in the house with me are very nice fellows and we have a very pleasant time. [Sergeant] Martin Harvey is one of these and one is a young man from a large business house in Baltimore and is named [Cpl. Henry] Buckmaster, the third is a young law student from Baltimore named [Sergeant Robert] Crowley.[39]

Jacob Cook recalled his own experiences building winter quarters at that time:

> We were camped in a thick grove of pines. Going vigorously to work, we soon had quite a little village in the heart of the forest. Many a tall pine came to grief in providing logs for the cabins and fuel to keep them warm after their erection. Our mess was composed of [Quartermaster Sgt. John] Hickey,

[Pvt.] Smith Warrington, [Pvt. Philip] Oldner, [Pvt.] Jack Brian and myself. The non-commissioned officers were our next door neighbors —Serg'ts Harvey, Crowley,[Williams], and Corp. Buckmaster, occupying a very neat and orderly little cabin. Sergt. [Thomas] LeCompt[e] was quartered with [Pvt. Phil] Harris[on], [Pvt. John] Shannahan, [Private Henry] Wil[l]son, and a number of others, they having the largest and most commodious house in the entire company. Corp. [Tom] Carberry and [Pvt.] Doug McClure had quite a cosy little arrangement. In fact, all the boys were snugly fixed in comparison with their mode of life on the march.

These cabins were comfortable, having but one large room, with a huge fire-place extending across the entire building, and in it, with plenty of wood, a good back log was continually burning. Our bunks were at the other end, one above the other. No furniture, save a plain table of rough pine boards, and a couple of benches of the same material. It must be evident to the dullest comprehension that we were luxuriously provided for [...].

Occasionally a chimney would take fire. Then the Baltimore boys would turn out to such inspiring cries as "New Market—Big 8!" "Independent—Big 6!" and other rallying cries of the old volunteer department, familiar to Baltimoreans in the ante-bellum days.[40]

The company had a busy daily schedule, as outlined by Cook:

OUR PROGRAMME

Bugler's Call, 4.55 A.M.; Reveille and Roll Call, 5 A.M.; Surgeon's Call, 5.20 A.M.; First Call for Guard Mounting, 8.45 A.M.; Second Call for Guard Mounting, 8.55 A.M.; Adjutant's Call, 9 A.M.; Bugler's Call, 1.15 P.M.; Dinner Call, 1.30 P.M.; Bugler's Call, 5.45 P.M.; Supper Call, 6 P.M.; Assembly of Companies and Roll Call, 6.45 P.M.; Adjutant's Call, 7 P.M.; Dress Parade, Retreat 7.10 P.M.; Tattoo, 10 P.M.; Taps, 10.30 P.M.

On Sundays the battalion drill was omitted, and inspection of the battalion substituted for the same hour. Bugler's call was on that day at 9.45 A.M., and church call at 9.55 A.M. This was the daily routine.[41]

In spite of this, Cook remembered "we managed to extract leisure enough." Peter Williams outlined some of the pursuits the soldiers could engage in:

I think it is a very pleasant neighborhood and we are very conveniently located, being only two miles [sic] from Bowling Green where there is a Post office, two churches and one or two little stores and only two miles from Milford Station. Yesterday I went up to church and heard a most excellent sermon from Mr. Friend the Episcopal minister. Although the weather was very threatening, there were 35 or 40 ladies out, a few male citizens and the rest of the church was crowded with soldiers. Mrs. Friend played the Melodeon very sweetly and the singing was as good as it generally is in little country churches. On next Sunday there will be preaching at the Carmmellite Church and on Sunday week again at the Episcopal church.[42]

There was also time for other activities, as Cook recalled a "little game of draw run by a certain gentleman, now standing high in theological circles. On reflection, if I am not mistaken, this ecclesiastical gentleman was indebted to Jack Brian, on breaking camp, to the lively tune of $50,000, Confederate currency."[43]

The constant desire for letters from home remained unabated, as expressed by Peter Williams in a letter to his aunt: "I hardly know what to think of them at home; I have not gotten a line from there in a month...I think I will have to go up there before long & have a regular quarrel with them all."[44]

At this point in the war Williams seems to have resigned himself to the irregular postal service, as he despaired in another letter to his aunt a couple of weeks later:

> I have not received but one letter from you since I left the Valley [...] at least two of my letters to you were lost about that time. I wrote again however and as I have not heard from you since I take it for granted that one was miscarried too. It seems that all of my letters are destined to be lost.[45]

Although a greater number of furloughs were being granted at this time, Williams's unsuccessful attempts to obtain one demonstrate the difficulty of doing so. In a January 1 letter to his aunt he wrote, "By the by, I sent in a application today for a short leave of absence & I feel very certain that I will be able to get down to Richmond sometime next week...to remain a day or two." Twelve days later he told her in another letter:

> I am well as usual, but nearly dead to get home. I intend to make every effort to get home this winter, for if I don't and the War continues next spring I don't know when I will have another opportunity. There have been some few furloughs granted lately and I am going to make application for one myself in a few days. Martin Harvey got one a few days ago and went down to Richmond.[46]

Illness also caused losses along with battlefield casualties, and during this time the battery lost several of its members. Pvt. Richard Hardesty, a twenty-seven-year-old clerk from Baltimore, died of smallpox in a Richmond hospital on December 21. He left behind his wife and a son not quite three years old. W. Cooper, one of the company's African American servants, also took ill at this time and was too sick to move with the unit to their winter camp. He died at Guinea's Station on January 10.[47]

Pvt. Edward Stansbury was the youngest member of the company; when he enlisted at Machodoc he was only fifteen years old. He suffered from poor health while in the service and had been in a hospital in Richmond with tuberculosis since the previous September. A volunteer nurse wrote in her diary on April 15 about two patients she was particularly concerned about:

> One is a youth of seventeen years, who has been seventeen months in service. Poor boy! He is now sinking with consumption, and has lately been brought to our hospital from another. His case elicits great sympathy and kindness. His name is Stansberry, and he is from Baltimore. We have reason to hope that he is prepared to meet his God.
>
> The next day she wrote:
>
> On going to the hospital yesterday I found that young Stansberry had died, surrounded by sympathizing friends, and having a bright hope of a blessed immortality."

He was also the youngest member of his Baltimore family, composed of his mother, two adult sisters, and an adult brother.[48]

As spring approached, in anticipation of a return to active campaigning, changes were made in the structure of the artillery organization of Jackson's 2nd Corps. On April 16, 1863, the Chesapeake was assigned to fellow Marylander Lt. Col. R. Snowden Andrews's battalion, and Capt. Joseph Latimer was promoted to major as its executive

Lt. Col. Richard Snowden Andrews. Smith, ed., *Richard Snowden Andrews: Lieutenant-Colonel Commanding the First Maryland Artillery (Andrews's Battalion) Confederate States Army: a Memoir*

officer. Latimer was one of the most brilliant young artillerists of the Army of Northern Virginia; known as the "Boy Major," he was only nineteen years old. The other batteries in the battalion included Capt. Joseph Carpenter's Alleghany Artillery, Capt. William F. Dement's 1st Maryland Artillery, and Capt. Charles I. Raine's Lee Artillery. With its commander and two of its batteries from the Old Line State, the battalion was known as the "Maryland Battalion."[49]

The Army of the Potomac had undergone changes, too. Gen. Ambrose Burnside was relieved after the Fredericksburg campaign, replaced with Maj. Gen. Joseph Hooker. Hooker streamlined the structure of his army and improved morale by introducing corps and division badges, improving rations, and re-equipping his men. Lee was still holding his lines at Fredericksburg with Jackson's 2nd Corps and two divisions of Longstreet's 1st Corps, Longstreet having taken his other two divisions on a raid toward Suffolk. Hooker's plan was to demonstrate against Fredericksburg with Maj. Gen. John Sedgwick's VI Corps and Maj. Gen. John Reynolds's I Corps to keep Lee pinned there, then cross the Rappahannock to the north and get into Lee's rear from the west. Hooker expected Lee to then retreat in the direction of Richmond. Hooker was confident: his 130,000-man army outnumbered Lee's force along the Rappahannock by more than two to one.[50]

Battle of 2nd Fredericksburg

Hooker marched with three of his corps on April 27; two additional corps from the Fredericksburg area would follow, a total of 70,000 men. They crossed the Rappahannock at Ely's Ford three days later, opposed by only one regiment of Confederate cavalry. Sedgwick and Reynolds crossed at Fredericksburg the morning of April 29, pushing back three regiments of Confederate infantry.[51]

The same day Andrews's battalion, with the Chesapeake, was ordered to move; they would take position with the rest of Jackson's Corps on the same range of hills west of Fredericksburg they had occupied during the battle of December. It was a difficult march. The battalion left its winter camp at 1500 without pausing to eat and with no rations issued. The roads were still muddy from winter snow and spring rains, and a heavy rainstorm added to the mud and the soldiers' discomfort. The men had to literally put their shoulders to the wheels to push the guns and caissons along. They marched continuously through the night, finally reaching the vicinity of Hamilton's Crossing on what would be Jackson's right flank at about 1000 on the thirtieth. Here they were issued rations and the weather cleared.[52]

The company was put in position behind gun emplacements on Prospect Hill along

The Fredericksburg battlefield looking north toward the Federal line of attack on Jackson's position. The Chesapeake Artillery initially occupied the embrasures in the foreground. *Author*

with Capt. Archibald Graham's 1st Rockbridge Artillery, all under Andrews. Jacob Cook described it as "one of the best positions I have ever seen for artillery. Our guns were run into embrasures cut into the brow of the hill giving us a clean sweep of the field," and Peter Williams exclaimed, "a splendid position it is." The other guns of the battalion were placed on Jackson's left flank near the Bernard cabins site under Maj. Latimer. Remembering how exposed the position was in the battle of December, Latimer immediately had gun emplacements dug to protect the gunners, horses, and caissons. Federal infantry was a mile to the east, as were heavy concentrations of artillery on both sides of the river.[53]

Sedgwick was relatively inactive in the Fredericksburg area on May 1, or as Peter Williams remembered it:

> Early Friday morning [May 1st] we took position on the centre of the lines, from which position another battery had fired some the day before. We had nothing however to do that day, having no orders to fire, and the Yankee batteries in front of us not seeming inclined to fire either.[54]

Hooker had advanced with his columns from the west that day. When Lee learned of their approach he did not withdraw as Hooker expected, but attacked with the divisions of Maj. Gens. Richard H. Anderson and Lafayette McLaws. He also ordered most of Jackson's corps west to assist. Jackson left Early's division and Brig. Gen. William Barksdale's Mississippi brigade to keep watch over Sedgwick's force at Fredericksburg, then hastened to join Lee. The determined Confederate resistance surprised and unnerved Hooker, who then assumed a defensive position around Chancellorsville to await developments. Early and Barksdale occupied the same defensive line as the Army of Northern Virginia in December, but there was one important difference: their force only numbered about 10,000 men to oppose Sedgwick's 40,000.[55]

On May 2, Andrews reported:

> At an early hour I was ordered to feel the enemy with my guns [...] I opened fire with the Rifle guns of Captain Graham and Brown on the enemy's Infantry on this side of the river, compelling them to recross the River. Two of the enemy's Batteries on the other side and one on this side opened fire upon Captains Graham and Brown's guns wounding severely a brave Corporal ("Carberry") of Brown's Battery.[56]

The firing in this action was severe, as Peter Williams remembered it in a letter he wrote to his sister that afternoon "On the field":

> Yesterday we did not fire any at all but opened on the Yankee batteries (number in all about 20 pieces) this morning at half past seven with our two Parrott guns (one of them under my command) & with 4 Parrott guns of the Rockbridge Art'y which is along side of us. We fired about ¾ of an hour as rapidly as possible & the Yankees did the same thing. Their shots were the poorest I ever saw but were so frequent that we had a pretty hot place.

At one point the battery lost its 3-inch Ordnance rifle:

> One of our guns [...] became useless after firing about 25 rounds, from the vent piece becoming sprung, so as to render any more firing dangerous.[57]

The wounding of highly regarded Cpl. Tom Carberry of Baltimore was a noteworthy event in the minds of his batterymates. As Peter Williams remembered it, "In this engagement, which was terrific, one of our gunners, a man named Carberry, had his leg shot off below the knee." Jacob Cook also described it:

> The boys had strict orders not to show themselves above the parapet, but they were not to be restrained. We were doing so well that Corporal C[arberr]y, after having made what he considered an exceptionally good shot, jumped upon the parapet and while cheering was knocked back into the embrasure, losing his right leg below the knee.

Carberry survived his wound but never returned to the unit.[58] Cook also remembered a close call at this time:

> As going on to show on what a slight thread the life of a soldier depends [...] Immediately in the rear of our position we had stretched a small fly tent, such as were carried for the use of two or three men; having fixed it in such manner that it kept the sun (it being a very hot day) from some half a dozen or so in our detachment, while not engaged in firing. We had made room for Capt. Brown, and were enjoying a glorious rest when he suddenly ordered us to resume firing. Hardly had we reached our guns when a shell, having ricocheted from the face of our position passed square through our fly tent, being but a minute too late to catch us.[59]

The Chesapeake's firing was highly effective; as Andrews reported, the "guns were then turned upon the battery of the enemy on this side of the River—near the Pratt House—and in a short time drove it from its position and compelled it to recross the river." In a letter to his sister written that afternoon Williams recalled the battery's fire "disabled two pieces of one battery which held a position from which they have since retired & our men have been there on the spot...Since we ceased firing about an hour ago the Yankee ambulances have been rolling down to their batteries taking off wounded & they have nearly all fallen back now."[60]

An independent observer also sought out the Chesapeakes to report on their effectiveness. Williams recalled in his letter to his sister:

> A gentleman named Corbin who lives a mile or two down the river from here & who had a fine view of the fight from his house, has just come over & says that we fairly slayed them & said that the ladies (God bless 'm) at his house, when one of our pieces above mentioned stopped firing so suddenly, became so excited that they insisted on his coming over to see what was the cause of it. We returned our thanks to the ladies with the names of the two batteries on cards & a large rifled shell fired by the Yankees.[61]

As Cook remembered it:

> The battery did such good service that a messenger was dispatched from the residence of a gentleman living in the vicinity, asking what battery it was effecting such havoc with the enemy, and conveying the complements of the ladies of his family. You may rest assured that the message and compliments—particularly the latter —were received with three rousing cheers and a Maryland tiger.[62]

The men of the company were exhilarated at their success that morning. In the letter he wrote "on the field" that afternoon Peter Williams gushed, "I am still live and kicking & just now in as good a humor & as fine spirits as I ever was in my life." But there was more fighting to be done; in his report to Early, Andrews noted that "about two o'clock I received orders from you to march with your Division...I replenished my supply of ammunition and obtained three days' supply of corn for my horses, and awaited the arrival of the division." As Williams continued, noting the time as about 1430, "While I write this an order is received to limber up & be ready to move at a moment's notice, so I must close though I intended on writing more. The real big fight will be above Fredericksburg & it is reported now that we have routed them up there."[63]

It was a false alarm; through a misunderstanding of orders, Early withdrew most of his division and artillery from its position south of Fredericksburg and advanced west on Telegraph Road. Meanwhile, Stonewall Jackson had marched around Hooker's right flank and attacked in the Chancellorsville area, routing the Federal XI Corps. When the mistake was understood and he was recalled Early returned to his original lines and the Chesapeake to their redoubts on Prospect Hill at about 2300.[64]

That night, the Federals threw a new pontoon bridge across the river at Fredericksburg and troops soon began to stream across. Sunday, May 3, dawned foggy along the Rappahannock, with the guns of Early's division "in the precise position of the day before." Early, seeking to understand Sedgwick's intentions, ordered the Virginia brigade of Brig. Gen. William "Extra Billy" Smith to push back the Federal brigade of Brig. Gen. Joseph Bartlett, where Bartlett had achieved a lodgement along the railroad near the Bernard Cabins south of Deep Run. Latimer had located Dement's and Raine's batteries on the same knoll the Chesapeake had occupied in the December battle. These guns had to contend with Bartlett's troops advancing on their left up the wooded ravine of Deep Run and two Federal batteries near the river; they were taking casualties in their exposed position.[65]

While these guns were able to keep Bartlett's infantry at bay with canister, Andrews "observed the enemy were bringing up two additional Batteries and placing them beyond the range of Dement's Napoleon guns. I immediately ordered Dement's guns to be withdrawn and sent to the rear and their places to be supplied by Captain Brown's 10 pds. Parrotts and Captain Graham's 2 twenty pds. Parrotts." The Chesapeakes had to advance across open ground under artillery fire from these Federal batteries. Sgt. Peter Williams described the scene:

> We knew from experience that we were going into the hottest place on the field & another proof too was the wounded of the 1st Md Battery whom we met being born off the field. The last 4 or 5 hundred yards of the road leading to the position was through an open flat & for this distance we were exposed to a raking fire from 3 Yankee batteries about 600 yards off. I rode at the head of my piece in a gallop; Capt. Brown was about 10 yds ahead of me & the shell & shrapnel were flying under & over us as thick as hail. I saw three or four solid shot pass right between his horse & mine & I was just expecting every minute for my horse to roll from under me. When we got to the position we had to unhitch our horses from our pieces & hitch them to the pieces of the other battery to take them off as their Horses had been sent to the rear. Our horses were nervous, had never been under fire before & you may know it took us some time to do this. I have never been under such a fire before; it was what might really be called "iron hail."[66]

It was a difficult maneuver to complete at the best of times, and seeing their friends and acquaintances of the 1st Maryland Artillery wounded and killed must have been unnerving. By this time the members of the company were experienced veterans and they unlimbered quickly. As Andrews observed, "Captains Graham's and Brown's Batteries, while relieving Captain Dement, therefore, went into position under very disadvantageous circumstances, tending to create confusion, but the officers and men with a few exceptions behaved very handsomely under them, displaying bravery and coolness."[67]

The Federal artillery fire, unabated by counter-battery fire while this movement was being executed, was heavy and deadly. A twenty-year-old student from Talbot County, Cpl. Alexander "Bey" Hopkins, was killed. Three additional men were slightly wounded but did not leave their posts: Pvt. Charles F. Dallam, a twenty-eight-year-old clerk from Baltimore; Pvt. James Harper, an eighteen-year-old student from Talbot County; and Pvt. John Shannahan. For Harper and Shannahan it was their second wounding of the war.[68]

Once they had taken position behind the artillery lunettes built that morning and went into battery with their two remaining Parrott rifles, the company was subjected to the fire of sharpshooters from the 5th Maine Infantry hidden in the wooded ravine of Deep Run on their left. Col. Clark S. Edwards, commander of the 5th Maine, reported:

> the ground at this point in the ravine is much broken, and covered with a thick undergrowth, and during the movement it was impossible to keep the files well closed. The regiment remained in this position about three-fourths of an hour, during which time a portion of the men were employed as sharpshooters and skirmishers.[69]

Jacob Cook recalled this fire:

> Doug McClure was standing right in front of me, I being seated on a sponge bucket. Remarking that the minnies

> were skipping around very lively, McClure suggested that we had better lie down in the embrasure, until we were ordered to resume firing. We did so, and not a minute too soon; for on that instant a Minnie ball passed clean through our bucket, leaving us in a bad fix for water for some time after.[70]

Not all the men were so lucky; several were wounded by the 5th Maine's sharpshooters. Pvt. Richard Langley, a nineteen-year-old farmer from St. Mary's County, received a severe gunshot wound in the shoulder; he would not return to the company until November. Sgt. Robert Crowley, the twenty-one-year-old law student from Baltimore, was wounded in the face. And Pvt. James Sparks, a twenty-seven-year-old farm laborer from Queen Anne's County, was severely wounded in the hip, resulting in several months of absence.[71]

Eventually Smith's brigade, in concert with Brig. Gen. Robert F. Hoke's North Carolina brigade, drove Bartlett's men back from the railroad, and Brown's and Graham's batteries were able to shift their fire from the Federal infantry and concentrate on the batteries near the river. Andrews reported, "Major Latimer, who was in command of the eight rifle guns, then, with great judgment, concentrated their whole fire on each of the enemy's Batteries successively and soon succeeded in driving them from their positions." As Peter Williams described it: "As soon as we got our guns in position, though, & opened on them, they commenced firing wildly & after about 3 hours fight...we silenced them."[72]

Although Federal attacks had been repulsed from Deep Run south to Hamilton's Crossing by midday, north of Deep Run an assault by three Yankee brigades on Marye's Heights routed parts of Barksdale's brigade and captured six guns. Sedgwick now had a position on Early's left flank, and Early responded by withdrawing his artillery and infantry southwesterly to a new line east–west along Telegraph Road. This allowed Early to face the Federal threat and protect the approach to Richmond. Sedgwick had been ordered to Chancellorsville and marched west on the Orange Plank Road, leaving a small force behind to maintain his position on Marye's Hill.[73]

On May 4, to connect with the right flank of Brig. Gen. Cadmus M. Wilcox's division, Early ordered an attack to retake Marye's Heights. Brig. Gen. John Gordon's Georgia brigade, along with Graham's battery, attacked and re-occupied the Heights. The Chesapeake was ordered to take a position there, from which they had a clear view of Lee's general attack on Hooker's lines now concentrated near the Rappahannock. Recalling the advance of Brig. Gen. Harry Hays's Louisiana brigade, Cook described what he saw:

> What sound is this in our rear: There are no troops who charge to such inspiring music as that, save the valiant sons of Louisiana. They are approaching. It is the "rebel yell!" The brave Louisianians, our old support, come pouring past our line to hurl themselves upon the trembling foe. With bayonets fixed, they charge, and woe to the enemy before them. They give, they break, they fly![74]

It was a memorable sight, as Peter Williams also recalled in a letter home:

> At half past 5 o'clock we heard the signal gun & we could see our lines advancing steadily up the hill from every direction & as soon as the top of the hill was reached our men charged with a yell. The Yankee batteries opened at the same time a murderous fire upon our infantry but our brave fellows charged onward, onward, until we could see them no longer for the dust & smoke. The Yankees fled in every direction.

> The Louisiana brigade of Early's Division charged entirely through one Yankee line & was going on at a double quick when [Gordon's] brigade came up & swept the Yankees off from their rear. We took several batteries & routed them at every point.[75]

Hooker began withdrawing his army on May 5. The soldiers of the Army of Northern Virginia were ecstatic with their victory. As Peter Williams expressed it, "Old Hooker certainly made a very good fight & got an awful slashing. The loss on both sides was very heavy; we have taken a large number of prisoners, a good many pieces of artillery, etc." Their mood was tempered somewhat by the news that Stonewall Jackson had been wounded; he would die a week later.[76]

That afternoon the "rain fell in torrents and soon our trenches were filled with water." Jacob Cook described the state of the men following the battle:

> Worn out with hunger and fatigue, having had very little to eat during the two or three day's hard fighting, drenched to the skin with the rain that had been pouring incessantly, our boys threw themselves down—some in the mud, others, more fortunate, on the limbers and caissons, with no covering but the dark, drizzling, threatening clouds. For there were no blankets on hand; everything of that character had been left with the wagons, of which we had seen or heard nothing for three days. No one but a soldier can easily believe that those brave boys slept, and slept well [...]. By degrees a quiet stole over the entire field.[77]

The rain continued through the night, but the battery had been ordered to resume its position at Hamilton's Crossing:

> Then the sergeants were heard busy with their detachments, getting them off to the rear, and the boys had hard work that night. The poor horses we had left were so completely broken down, they could do very little pulling, so that we had to put our shoulders to the wheel, in the full sense of that term, to jerk the guns out of the mud. The mud had become very thick, sticking to the wheels to such an extent that we were compelled to take every horse in the battery to haul each separate piece off the field. Never can I forget that night.[78]

Having not been issued rations for several days, the men were finally able to eat, an occasion joyously remembered by Cook:

> Half starved as we were, you can well imagine that Hickey, our Commissary, was the most popular man in our command, when he met us with grub enough to satisfy all hands. On the next morning Capt. Brown, in order to test the esprit de corps of his company, called for volunteers to relieve a company at the front. Broken down as those heroes were, ragged, naked, many of them without shoes to protect their bleeding feet, how many do you suppose responded to the summons? At roll call, they were "all present and accounted for!"[79]

A few days later, in a letter thanking Mary Ward for a tobacco pouch she had sent to him as a gift, Capt. Billy Brown referred to how difficult the battle had been, but also the pride he felt in the unit:

> I had just brought my battery off the bloody field of Fredericksburg when the kind letter of my dear friends & its beautiful accompaniments was placed in my hands —worn out & fatigued with the smoke & dust of battle still about me, my heart was more than cheered to know, that tho' so long separated, I was not forgotten by the kind friends who had rendered my short

> stay near Tappahannock so pleasant... It may please you to know that our battery has made its mark in all the battles from the "Cedar Mountain" to Fredericksburg.[80]

Andrews' battalion was finally withdrawn to Guinea's Station to rest and re-equip. Lee's great victory was celebrated throughout the Confederacy, and the citizens of Richmond waited for details as news trickled in. Rumors were also rampant at this time, as reported by the *Richmond Daily Dispatch* on May 6: "A rumor prevailed extensively that Capt Brown, of the Chesapeake Artillery, and a large number of his men, had also fallen in the engagement on Monday."[81]

The *Richmond Examiner* trumpeted their more accurate report the next day:

> THE CHESAPEAKE ARTILLERY—From the wounded received in the city yesterday on the several ambulance trains, we have definite intelligence from the Chesapeake Artillery, Captain W.D. Brown, and are glad to have it in our power to contradict the report that the battery had been completely cut up and lost. But one member, Charles [sic] Hopkins, of St. Michaels [sic], Maryland, was killed, and six or eight wounded, one or two severely. The horses of the battery were nearly all killed or disabled, but the guns are, with one or two exceptions, safe and in good condition.[82]

Luckily for the soldiers of the Chesapeake the rumor was not true, but it was an eerily accurate foreshadowing of what was to come.

"OUR POSITION WAS WELL CALCULATED TO DRIVE CONFIDENCE FROM THE STOUTEST HEART"

Sgt. Peter Williams could barely contain his excitement in a letter he wrote to his Aunt Mary a little over two weeks after the battle of 2nd Fredericksburg. He apologized for not writing sooner, as, "we have had so many things to attend to since the battle that it is hard to find time to write. I have had to be running about getting ammunition and getting horses, etc., as we have just gotten two more Parrott Guns for the battery. We have now 4 ten pounder Parrott Guns."[1]

Maj. Gen. Edward "Old Alleghany" Johnson. *Library of Congress*

These two additional Parrott guns, which replaced the 3-inch Ordnance rifle rendered unserviceable at the battle of 2nd Fredericksburg, brought the Chesapeake's armament to four rifled guns in readiness for the next campaign. Following the death of Stonewall Jackson, Lee reorganized his army, creating a third corps for efficiency and greater ease of command: Longstreet still commanded the 1st Corps; Lt. Gen. Richard Ewell, having returned from the loss of his leg at 2nd Manassas, was given command of the 2nd Corps; and Lt. Gen. A.P. Hill commanded the newly created 3rd Corps. Lt. Col. R. Snowden Andrews's "Maryland Battalion," with the Chesapeake Artillery led by Capt. Billy Brown, now became part of Maj. Gen. Edward "Old Alleghany" Johnson's division of Ewell's corps.[2]

Williams speculated as to what the Army of Northern Virginia would do next:

> The army here is pretty much in the same position it was before the battle, though I can't believe we will remain inactive very long. We are now encamped on the Telegraph road near Guinea's Station.

What he didn't know was that the battery's preparations were leading up to Lee's initiative to take the war into Pennsylvania, to obtain supplies and possibly defeat the Army of the Potomac on its own ground.[3]

March to Pennsylvania

The campaign got off to an ominously poor start for Andrews's battalion. Leaving Hill's corps at Fredericksburg to pin down the Army of the Potomac, Rodes's division of Ewell's corps pulled out of its position to move west and then north, followed by Johnson's and Early's divisions on June 6. Hooker, noticing the activity, sent elements of Sedgwick's Federal VI corps across the Rappahannock on a reconnaissance. This movement met firm resistance by Hill's corps, but prompted the return of the remainder of the army. As Pvt. John Ford Hatton of Dement's 1st Maryland Artillery of the Maryland Battalion recalled:

> We were called from our slumbers by the shrill notes of the Bugle about 2 O'Clock A.M., and left camp about light, marched no more than five hundred yards, turned about, returned to the starting point and parked our guns in the same place. This sham of a march was made because the enemy were discovered on a move as though they would cross the river to do us some harm. We remained in this camp till evening, then resumed our march; proceeded westward six or seven miles through heat and dust; and encamped about 11 O'Clock P.M., and was visited by a heavy storm of rain which gave us a good soaking.[4]

Notwithstanding, the morale of the Army of Northern Virginia was high following their smashing victory over Hooker and the Army of the Potomac. As Johnson described it, "Nothing occurred worthy of particular note during the march, which was steady and regular, the command being in good condition and excellent spirits." The column marched through the Blue Ridge Mountains at Chester Gap, passed through Front Royal, crossed both branches of the Shenandoah River, and reached Cedarville—ninety miles from Guinea's Station—by June 12.[5]

On the thirteenth, Johnson's and Early's divisions advanced on the 8,000 men of Federal Maj. Gen. Robert Milroy at Winchester. Milroy's forces were driven out of Winchester and soundly defeated on the fifteenth at Stephenson's Depot with a loss of twenty-three pieces of artillery, 4,000 prisoners, horses, wagons, and stores. Although the Chesapeake Artillery was not engaged in this action, much of the rest of the battalion was. Dement's 1st Maryland Artillery incurred heavy casualties, and Lt. Col. Andrews suffered a serious flesh wound to his right arm. Although Andrews would report for duty when the division reached Hagerstown a few days later, he was only able to serve in an advisory capacity, so command of the battalion passed to Maj. Joseph Latimer.[6]

The bands played "Maryland, My Maryland" as the troops crossed the Potomac River into Maryland on the eighteenth. They rested for three days at Sharpsburg before moving on to Hagerstown, described by Peter Williams as "a pretty little town in Maryland & contains some good Southern men." On the twenty-third, Johnson's division crossed into Pennsylvania and marched to Greencastle. To the men of the Chesapeake—more familiar with the bleak and war-worn landscape of Virginia—the farms of

Pennsylvania made a remarkable contrast. As Peter Williams wrote to his father:

> we have been marching constantly & through the finest country I ever laid my eyes on…Pa, I never saw such wheat & corn in my life. Every man has a little bit of a dwelling house & a magnificent barn, probably about 80 or 90 feet long.[7]

Williams went on to explain how well the army had been living off the land:

> Genl Lee has issued positive orders against individual plundering & burning, but tells the Q[uarte]r Masters to pitch right into everything they see that is needful for the army. At Chambersburg the Qr Masters emptied every store in the place and our men are living luxuriously. We bought everything we wanted at our own price in the town, & the country is full of everything good to eat. We get as much Butter, Lard & Molasses as we want, & vegetables too…Our army is in fine spirits & a straggler is something that you never see now […]. We have splendid horses for our Artillery, and abundance of forage for them & the men draw rations of everything.[8]

Williams found the sentiments of the inhabitants also represented a distinct difference compared to those in Virginia, remarking the region was populated with:

> the hardest looking set of people—abolition Dutch. We have passed through such a number of little towns that I cant recollect the names of half of them but the principle ones were Chambersburg & Shippensburg. The former is a place of about 10,000 inhabitants, all Dutch & the meanest looking white people I ever saw. They were scared nearly to death at the bare idea of having the rebel army among them & evidently expected to be burnt alive.[9]

The Army of the Potomac had shadowed the Army of Northern Virginia at a distance, with Hooker trying to determine its location while at the same time developing a plan to respond. Speculation as to the campaign's objectives ran high within the Confederate ranks, along with a certain amount of relish to engage the local militia. Writing from near Carlisle on June 28, Williams expressed this:

> The greatest consternation prevails all through Yankee-dom & they are busy sending on the "Milish" to meet us at Harrisburg. We will leave here, I think, tomorrow, & Harrisburg is only 18 miles distant. It will be rare fun fighting the "Milish." Old Hooker is perfectly at a loss what to do. He cant bring his army up here & he doesn't know what to do with it where he is. I don't know what Genl Lee's plans are, of course, but it is generally hoped & believed that after taking Harrisburg, he will sweep down the Susquehanna on Baltimore & Washington, having destroyed their great line of communication North […]. This corps, I believe, can whip all the Militia in the United States.[10]

Soon developments would change that outlook. In a disagreement over strategy with General in Chief Maj. Gen. Henry Halleck, Joseph Hooker resigned, and the same day Williams wrote to his father, Maj. Gen. George Meade was made commander of the Army of the Potomac. Both armies were scattered: Lee's from Chambersburg to the west, Carlisle to the north, and Wrightsville to the east; and Meade's in the area around Frederick, Maryland. Meade immediately began concentrating his army and moving it north toward Gettysburg; when Lee learned of this, he ordered his army to concentrate in the area of Cashtown and Gettysburg.[11]

Accordingly, Johnson's division and the Chesapeake, accompanied by the 2nd Corps's reserve artillery and wagons, were ordered to counter-march back toward Chambersburg from near Carlisle. They went into camp between Green Village and Scotland, near Chambersburg, where they rested on the thirtieth. That day the 4th Maryland Artillery mustered for pay under Capt. Brown, with eighty men—four officers and seventy-six enlisted men—present for duty with four Parrott guns. The men knew events were developing rapidly: Williams had closed his letter home to his father with some foreboding: "Don't be uneasy because you don't hear from me. I will write as often as possible. Goodbye."[12]

Advance to Gettysburg, July 1

The next day by 0700, Johnson's division was on the march east toward Gettysburg, and "the men were in great spirits, notwithstanding almost one-third of them were barefoot." Several miles beyond Fayetteville the column encountered Longstreet's troops and there was a traffic jam with the 1st Corps's wagon trains. Johnson's columns had to wait until the wagons cleared the road, and even then made slow and tedious progress. At this point the battery lost one of its gun crew chiefs. Sgt. Peter Williams had requested a transfer to the Richmond Howitzers of the 1st Corps, whose ranks included many of his friends from home in Richmond. The transfer had been approved in mid-June, but could not be executed during the march to Pennsylvania. As Williams described it in a letter home:

> Ewell's corps started down in the direction of Gettysburg & had to pass Longstreet. In the meantime I had gotten my transfer to the Howitzers & happening to pass right by them, I joined them the day before the fight, so I am now in that Company.

Cpl. James A. Wall was promoted to 1st sergeant and command of the 4th gun detachment in Williams's place.[13]

After marching about seventeen miles, the column reached Cashtown, and they could hear "the roar of cannons ahead of us, reverberating over the hills, sounding rapidly, and louder than the rattle of our own gun wheels." Johnson's division moved with as much speed as possible, but the sound of battle died before they reached Gettysburg. Just before dark they reached the scene of the battle of that morning. "The field bore evidence of a sharp fight. Dead horses and men were scattered over the ground, intermingled with spent balls, fragments of shell, discarded muskets and accoutrements... the surface of the ground in many places was torn up."[14]

It was difficult moving the entire division, in addition to Latimer's battalion and the reserve artillery, over the obstacles and debris presented by this scene. Ewell had ordered Johnson to a position east of the town; to prevent observation from the Federals on Cemetery and McKnight's (now Stevens') Hills the guns took a "zigzag" route through the town on side streets, while the infantry marched along the Gettysburg and York Railroad bed. After pausing north of the town and then near the railroad station for several hours, Capt. Brown led the battery across Rock Creek on the York Pike after dark along with the rest of the division. Johnson then deployed the division in line of battle south of the York Pike on the eastern slope of Benner's Hill, across the fields of the Wolf, Shriver, and Lady farms, parallel with the Hanover Road. It was late at night by the time this deployment was completed, and having marched over twenty-five miles that day, the men fell in place and slept on their arms.[15]

Engagement on Benner's Hill, July 2

The next morning dawned damp and cloudy, and at first light (0403), the men of Latimer's battalion "were aroused from our slumbers by the booming of cannon." This was the Federal response to the advancement of Confederate skirmishers from Brig. Gen. John M. Jones's Virginia brigade to the southwest along Rock Creek, who "before an hour of daylight elapsed had stirred up a hornets' nest in their front." The sporadic firing of skirmishers and the occasional reply of cannon would continue throughout the day, as each side sought to determine the other's strength and position.[16]

Johnson had been ordered to attack the Federal right flank on Culp's Hill and Cemetery Hill as a diversion to Longstreet's attack on the Federal left. "Old Alleghany" wanted his artillery to support the infantry by battering Federal lines prior to the attack. By dawn, Maj. Latimer had already scouted the area east of Gettysburg for the most advantageous position. There was only one possibility: Benner's Hill, the open rise to the immediate right and front of Johnson's division, running 1,400 yards nominally from northeast to southwest and bisected by Hanover Road. It rose 460 feet above sea level at a knob on its northern crest and sloped gradually to 450 feet at its southern end. The flat crest was about 1,000 yards northeast of Culp's Hill and 1,500 yards east and northeast of Cemetery Hill—well within cannon range. Rock Creek flowed at its western base.[17]

Later that morning, on the northern crest of Benner's Hill, a couple of hundred yards north of Hanover Road, Latimer posted the four long-range twenty-pound Parrott guns of Capt. Archibald Graham's 1st Rockbridge Artillery, of the 2nd Corps's artillery reserve. In addition, also placed there under the command of Lt. William W. Hardwicke were a section of two twenty-pound Parrotts of Capt. Charles I. Raine's Lee Artillery of his own battalion. Because of their range these guns were out of reach of the Federal cannon, but could still strike Cemetery Hill with their fire. They fired several times during the day to determine the elevation and range to the Federal positions. The remainder of the battalion's guns stayed in the fields behind Benner's Hill; to put them in position on the crest south of Hanover Road beforehand, in the open and within range of Federal guns, was too dangerous.[18]

The southern crest of Benner's Hill below Hanover Road was not an ideal position for the rest of the battalion. As Andrews summarized it:

> The ground offered very few advantages, and the major found great difficulty in sheltering his horses and caissons. The hill which he selected brought him directly in front of the wooded mountain [Culp's Hill] and a little to the left of the Cemetery Hill. All the guns excepting [Raine's] two long-range guns had to be crowded on this small hill, which was not in our favour.

Although there was ample room for the battalion's guns to operate, there was no room to maneuver, meaning the men of

Maj. Joseph White Latimer. *Courtesy of the Virginia Military Institute Archives*

Latimer's command would be stationary targets well within range of the Federal guns on Culp's Hill and Cemetery Hill. Further, both hills occupied by the Federals were of slightly higher elevation than Benner's Hill, giving Federal guns the added advantage of delivering a plunging fire on the top of the Confederate position, as well as converging fire from two positions.[19]

Latimer must have expressed his misgivings to Johnson at the Lady farm. He and Andrews later conducted a second examination of the ground with no different result. Almost certainly, Latimer led Capt. Brown and the other battery commanders to the top of Benner's Hill at some point to observe the position and discuss the battalion's deployment, and they conveyed their concern about the work ahead of them to their officers. The apprehensive perceptions of the men influenced their descriptions of the terrain, magnifying the differences in elevation between Cemetery Hill and Culp's Hill compared to Benner's Hill. As Pvt. Jacob Cook described it, "the towering, almost perpendicular cliffs against which we stormed in vain; our own miserable position flat as a pancake." Pvt. Chris Lynch, a twenty-one-year-old farmer from Queen Anne's County, recalled:

> our position was well calculated to drive confidence from the stoutest heart. We were directly opposed by some of the finest batteries in the regular service of the enemy, which batteries, moreover, held a position to which ours was but a molehill.[20]

Alleghany Johnson was also concerned. He asked Maj. William W. Goldsborough, of the 1st Maryland Battalion in Brig. Gen. George H. "Maryland" Steuart's brigade, to advise him as well. Goldsborough, from Baltimore and well acquainted with Capt. Brown, remembered:

> About noon on the 2d of July, 1863, General Edward Johnson having been advised that I was somewhat familiar with the country around Gettysburg, suggested, for it was not a command, that I reconnoitre a hill that loomed up about a mile to his front and right, the division at that time being in line of battle along the road leading to Hanover. On this hill known as Benner's Hill, General Johnson wished to station some artillery if the elevations would admit of it, as it was certainly the only point along his front in the least adapted for artillery…By a little twisting and turning I reached the top of Benner's Hill without being observed, and once there I had a good view of the open country that lay between me and the enemy's position, running from Culp's Hill to Cemetery Hill, along the ridge of which I could see numerous batteries in position, as well as their infantry supports. At a glance I was satisfied that Benner's Hill was commanded by the more elevated positions held by the enemy, and I hardly thought it possible that General Johnson would send artillery there after I had made my report to him. However, I was spared this duty […] the General […] with his staff rode up. After carefully surveying the opposite heights for a few minutes, to my surprise he sent an aide to order Major Lattimer's [sic] batteries to come up. My heart leaped to my mouth at this order, for in that command was the Chesapeake Artillery, of Baltimore, and certain death and destruction stared them in the face. Nearly every man in that battery was known to me from Captain Brown down, many being from Baltimore, and the remainder from the several counties of Maryland.[21]

Latimer readied his command. He positioned the battalion's remaining fourteen

Maj. William W. Goldsborough. *Courtesy of "Company D," 2nd Maryland Infantry*

guns in column in the fields of the Wolf farm at the northern base of Benner's Hill. First were the remaining two ordnance rifles of Raine's Lee Artillery, followed by the four Napoleons of Dement's 1st Maryland Artillery, the two ordnance rifles and two Napoleons of Carpenter's Alleghany Artillery, and then the Chesapeake Artillery's four 10-pound Parrotts. At the command, the battery commanders were to advance their guns at the gallop up the northern slope of the hill through Daniel Lady's knee-high corn field, move south along its crest, and deploy in Daniel Benner's wheat field south of Hanover Road. Raine's two guns would take position at the extreme southern end of the hill on the left flank, and Brown's guns just at the Hanover Road on the right flank. This would place the lower range capabilities of Dement's four Napoleons and the two Napoleons of Carpenter's battery at the southern tip of Benner's Hill closest to Cemetery Hill; the longer-range guns were thus placed to advantage, with Raine's two ordnance rifles anchoring the left flank and the rifles of Carpenter's battery, as well as Brown's Parrotts farther back as Benner's Hill angled away from Cemetery Hill to the northeast. While this was going on, Johnson advanced Jones's Brigade to the southern base of Benner's Hill as support for the artillery.[22]

Federal artillery commanders also made adjustments that afternoon. Maj. Thomas W. Osborn, commanding the artillery brigade of the Federal XI Corps, established a line of ten guns facing Benner's Hill from the vicinity of Evergreen Cemetery. In front of Osborn, on the eastern brow of Cemetery Hill, was another line of twenty-five guns arrayed by Col. Charles S. Wainwright, artillery brigade commander of I Corps. Included were four 20-pound Parrott rifles of Capt. Elijah Taft's 5th New York Independent battery brought up to neutralize the 20-pounders of Graham and Raine on the northern crest of Benner's Hill. In addition, one 10-pound Parrott of Knap's Independent Pennsylvania Battery E was placed on Culp's Hill.[23]

The men were anxious to begin, and Pvt. Lynch remembered "our impatience at what we deemed unnecessary inaction, our eagerness at the word of command from our handsome Captain Brown." At about 1600, Latimer received the order to advance. Goldsborough recalled, "I see them now, those gallant boys, few above the age of nineteen, as they obey the command: 'Cannoneers to your posts!'" Pvt. Cook described the military pageantry of the charge with flags flying: "Our Battalion rushed into position at the full gallop, with Latimer at the head of the command…And never shall I forget the handsome, dashing, gallant Brown, as with drawn sabre high above his head, he led the van, guiding the Chesapeake on to death or victory."[24]

A member of the 1st Maryland Battalion remembered admiringly that the charge was "a splendid sight. Sixteen [sic] guns, sixteen caissons, with their attending cavalcade of company and field officers, streaming over the field in bustle and busy speed and enveloped in clouds of dust."[25]

Pvt. Edward Moore of the 1st Rockbridge Artillery, already in position on the northern crest of Benner's Hill, also saw them as they advanced:

> the day passed quietly until nearly four o'clock. At this time Andrews's battalion of artillery, led by Major Latimer, passed in front of us and went into position two hundred yards to our left, and nearer the enemy. The ground sloped so as to give us a perfect view of his four batteries. Promptly other batteries joined those confronting us on Cemetery Hill, and by the time Latimer's guns were unlimbered the guns on both sides were thundering.[26]

The Chesapeakes went into position and unlimbered quickly, but there was a pause, likely because other guns had difficulty deploying. As Pvt. Chris Lynch wrote, "Well do we remember our position upon a piece of rugged, rocky ground and in full view of

Postwar view of Benner's Hill looking southwest toward Cemetery Hill in the left background, with Hanover Road in the foreground. The Chesapeake Artillery was in position here on the immediate opposite side of the fence. *Author's collection*

the almost impregnable position of the enemy." Pvt. Jacob Cook recalled:

> The enemy expect our coming from their impregnable heights, their inaccessible position. They shower down their welcome, and a right royal welcome it is! Shot and shell fall thick and fast, rending the air, tearing the ground in their angry career. We gain our position unharmed, untouched... As we look up to the frowning heights above us, which continue to thunder forth their iron storm; as we glance around upon our flat, rocky position, with no swelling hill-top behind whose brow we could oppose the cliff above us, we have a premonition that defeat is in the very air...The Rockbridge remains silent. The Chesapeake has not spoken. Why this inaction, the most trying ordeal through which a soldier has to pass (while the enemy are thundering away) and, on account of orders, compelled to remain quiet?[27]

Capt. Brown ordered the men to lie down for safety. Sensing their apprehension, he rode to the front of the battery and "addressing us as sons of Maryland" spoke to the company: "Strike for your homes, boys," he shouted above the roar, "stand by your guns, and give it to them hot and heavy." Shortly after Latimer dashed up, and "with sword aloft, he cries: 'Battalion attention! Fire by detail! Sponge, load, fire!' This is all done just as coolly as if we had been on dress parade, the sergeants even giving the numbers according to the manual."[28]

Lynch recalled, "our feelings of almost exultant satisfaction as the enemy's shot fell in our rear, out of range." Cook echoed:

> At the command "Fire!" the very earth seemed to tremble, for every gun in the Rockbridge and Chesapeake spoke at once. Relieved from their being now engaged, the boys went earnestly to work, having acquired the requisite steadiness. It was now "Fire at will!" Cheer after cheer went up from the boys in each battery, the enemy continuing to overshoot us. We fondly imagined that we were getting the best of them.[29]

The fire of Latimer's battalion, according to Col. Wainwright, was "the most accurate fire I have ever yet seen from their artillery." Pvt. Moore of the 1st Rockbridge Artillery recalled: "In less than five minutes one of Latimer's caissons was exploded, which called forth a lusty cheer from the enemy. In five minutes more a Federal caisson was blown up, which brought forth a louder cheer from us."[30]

But "the enemy soon got our range" with solid shot and spherical case. Goldsborough remembered of the Chesapeake that:

> At first, through their splendid practice and the excellent calibre of their Parrott guns...they did good execution, but it took only a short time to convince them that they were overmatched.

Cook thought the battery:

> might as well have been firing so much blank cartridge. Nature had set her seal on their position to render it impregnable! How about their range? They must, in connection with their advantage of position, have had a most excellent battery opposed to us, for they steadily corrected their range.[31]

A case shell exploded just to Capt. Brown's left, killing his horse and shattering his left knee. His horse fell to the right, breaking Brown's right leg and ribs and pinning him to the ground. Shocked, the men nearby rushed to extricate him—an excruciatingly difficult process. They made him as comfortable as possible while stretcher bearers were called. Brown was carried four hundred yards down the east side of Benner's Hill along the Hanover Road to the stone Lady farmhouse, now being used as an aid station. The scene at the Lady farm was chaotic: couriers rushing about with orders, wounded streaming into the yard, and overshots from Federal batteries landing in the yard and even crashing into the barn, which was also being used as an aid station. The soldiers of Johnson's division were marshalled along Hanover Road, anxiously waiting to go into action against Culp's Hill.[32]

The 1st Maryland Infantry Battalion of Brig. Gen. George H. "Maryland" Steuart's brigade was near the Lady house, including in its ranks many men from Baltimore who knew Brown. Cpl. Washington Hands of Baltimore, who served in the 1st Battalion, described the scene as the stretcher bearers approached:

> Latimer is working his guns savagely, but is being terribly handled, for three times his number of guns are concentrated upon his little batteries, rending and tearing him to pieces. Caisson after caisson shoot high up in the air as they are exploded by the enemy's shell [...]. Here comes a litter from that direction with a wounded man [...] we were shocked to behold the familiar face of the Chivalrous Capt. Wm Brown, of the Chesapeake Artillery. His face was pale as death, and although both legs had been horribly shattered by a cannon ball, he smiled as he recognized us. Turning to Capt. Torsch, he said in a weak voice; "Captain, if you should get home, tell my poor old father I died endeavouring to do my duty."
> "We are making out badly up there," said one of the litter bearers.

Lt. John Plater maintained command over the unit's caissons, and Lt. Walter Chew took command of the guns.[33]

Other men also received wounds and had to step away from the guns. Pvt. William Williams of Queen Anne's County was wounded in the face by a shell fragment. Pvt. Henry Parker, a nineteen-year-old farmer from St. Mary's County, was also wounded. Pvt. Willie Mason, a twenty-year-old from Harford County, received a wound that would cause his absence from the battery for six weeks.[34]

Major Goldsborough described the scene:

> The command devolving upon Lieut. Chew, he fought the battery for all it was worth, and the guns became so hot through incessant firing that premature discharges were threatened.

Goldsborough's fears regarding the position on Benner's Hill had become reality; as he continued:

> Position is everything to artillery. Bad position means certain defeat and death. This was so at Gettysburg, for the Chesapeakes fought under great disadvantage.

Jacob Cook recalled, "Having secured our range, they poured plunging shot after shot into us." From Chris Lynch's standpoint: "Benner's Hill was simply a hell infernal... Every shot we fired ricochetted clean over and above them —here, there, and everywhere, except where they could do execution."[35]

Indeed, although Federal casualties mounted, many of the shots of Latimer's battalion passed over Cemetery Hill, and many of those that landed failed to detonate: Confederate shell and fuses were notoriously ineffective. The superior Federal ammunition and firepower were highly damaging. Another soldier of the 1st Maryland Battalion near the Lady Farm described the action:

> The roar was deafening and incessant, with no distinguishable pauses, even of seconds. The very earth trembled,

> and the Heavens seemed "hung with black" with the smoke of the conflict.[36]

Jacob Cook remembered the destruction of the Chesapeake's 2nd gun detachment, of which he was a member:

> Holding No. 1 position at the piece, and no ammunition coming up, I went to the limber to see what had become of No. 5, the only man to be seen belonging to our detachment. Was Sergt. Crowley preparing ammunition to bring it to the piece himself? On asking him what had become of our boys, the brave veteran, with tears in his eyes, pointed to Cusick, with his head torn off; to Corp. Dan Dougherty, literally cut in half; to Dr. Jack Brian, with his head off, and to a number of the boys lying around severely wounded.[37]

Pvt. Fred Cusick was a twenty-one-year-old clerk from Charles County. Pvt. "Doctor Jack" Bryan, a thirty-four-year-old physician from Culpeper, Virginia, left behind his wife and ten-year-old daughter. Irish-born Cpl. Dan Dougherty, a twenty-six-year-old moulder from Baltimore, was wounded by several case shot that entered his back and hip and left frightful exit wounds in his abdomen. He was also carried to the Lady farmhouse, where he died shortly thereafter. With so many casualties in his detachment, Sgt. Robert Crowley ordered his remaining men to join the 3rd gun detachment, whose chief of piece was Sgt. Phil Brown, Capt. Brown's brother.[38]

Sgt. Brown's detachment fared no better. As Cook continued:

> ...a shell came bouncing past to our right, striking directly in front of Thad Parker, who was holding the lead horses in that detachment, and exploded, disembowelling him and killing the two horses. After extricating and carrying him, with Crowley's assistance, out of range, (the poor fellow begging all the while to be put out of his misery), I reported to Sergt. Phil Brown's detachment. His No. 2 had been wounded. On taking that position, after receiving a charge for the piece and having inserted it, a shell struck the right-hand wheel, and, exploding, tore it to pieces, wounding Sergt. Brown, Privates [Phil] Oldner, mortally; Smith Warrington, severely, and Henry Wilson, severely. Poor Oldner had just barely recovered from a wound received at Fredericksburg.[39]

Pvt. Thad Parker, a 25-year-old farmhand from St. Mary's County and the brother of Henry Parker, who had also been wounded, died before he could be taken to the Lady farmhouse. Pvt. Phil Oldner had suffered a severe knee wound, as had Pvt. Henry Willson of Queen Anne's County; both were carried off. Pvt. Smith Warrington received a face wound.[40]

At this point the gun of the Chesapeake's 4th detachment was disabled and could not be serviced; newly promoted Sgt. James Wall was slightly wounded; Pvts. Frank Smith and James Stephens, friends who lived in Baltimore's 12th Ward and had enlisted together a year prior in Richmond, were both severely wounded. So, too, was Pvt. Charles Tinges, a 21-year-old clerk from Baltimore. The battery now had only one gun in action.[41]

A lull settled over the field, as Goldsborough recounted: "During a lull in the firing Chew took stock. There was but little left...The gallant Latimer came charging up and eagerly inquired why the battery had ceased firing. But he required no answer, for the ghastly evidences around him were too palpable." During this lull both sides cleared debris and wounded and consolidated their positions. Oldner, Willson, Smith, and Stephens were taken to the Lady farm. Pvt. Lynch remembered that Sgt. Phil Brown, wounded earlier, "stepped down to Rock Creek, close to our position, bound up his

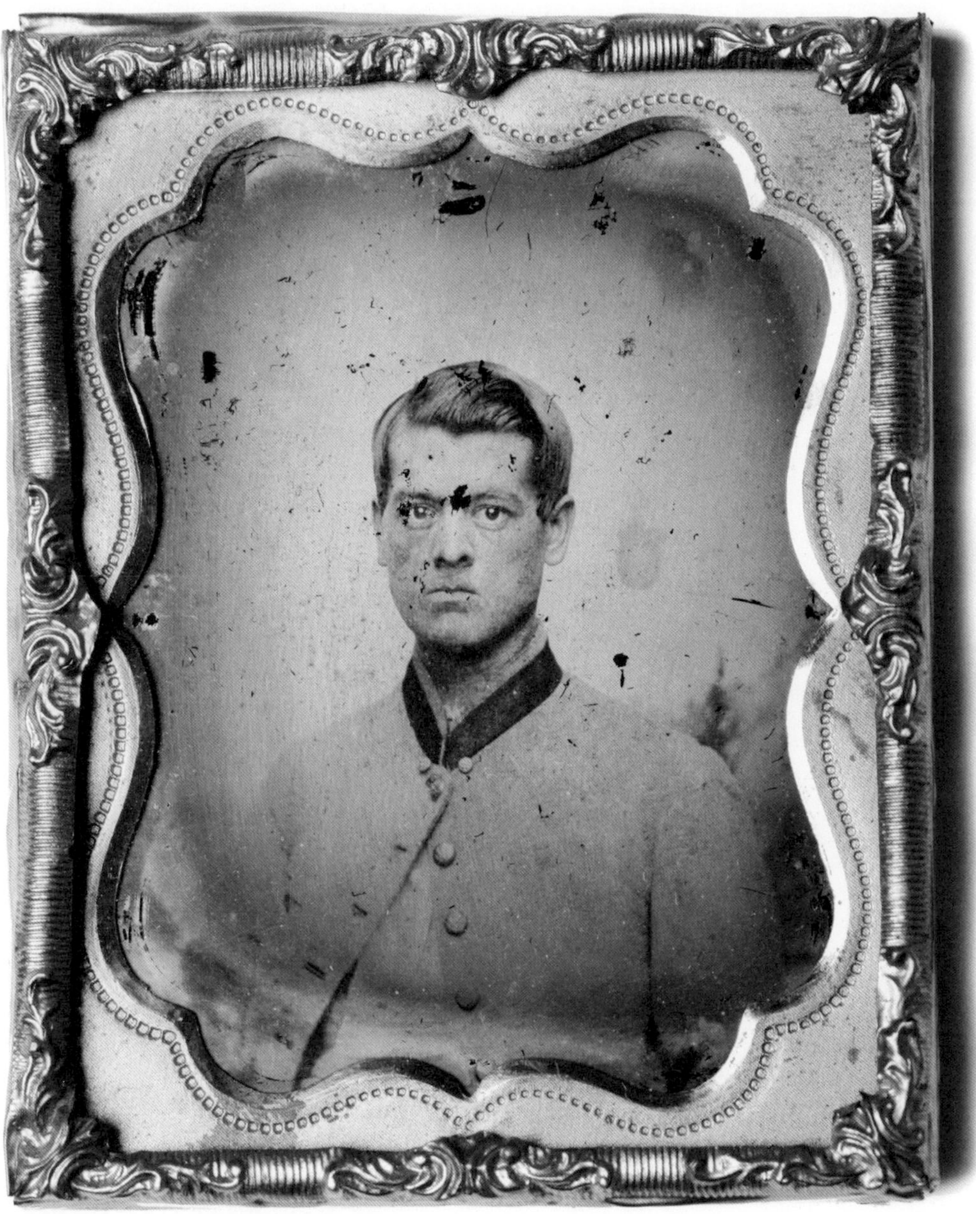

Cpl. Daniel Dougherty. *Author's collection*

wound, and returned to jack up his gun, put on a spare wheel, and resumed firing."[42]

At the same time Federal artillerists worked to improve their position. Concerned about the effect of Latimer's fire on the infantry of the XII Corps, as well as the fire of Graham's and Hardwicke's 20-pound Parrotts north of the Hanover Road, Lt. Edward D. Muhlenberg, commanding the artillery brigade of that corps, placed two additional 10-pound Parrotts and two Napoleons on Culp's Hill, and had fields of fire cut through the trees and brush. This brought five guns to bear on Latimer's position in a left-front enfilade; from their position atop Culp's Hill these guns could

Sgt. Philip Auld Harrison Brown. *Courtesy of the Photograph Collection, Archives and Special Collections, Dickinson College*

fire down nearly the length of the line of Confederate artillerists. The number of Federal guns on Cemetery Hill and Culp's Hill opposing them now more than doubled those in Latimer's battalion.[43]

Presently, at Latimer's word, "Chew's voice rang out clear and strong: 'Resume firing!'" To John Hatton of the 1st Maryland Artillery, it seemed as if "all the guns of the Battalion was discharged at the same time, and the ground upon which we stood trembled from the jar. So promptly did the enemy reply that it seemed as though they caused our own shell rebounding against us, after the manner of a boomerang." The Federal guns on Culp's Hill from the left flank, now joining those on Cemetery Hill from the left front, caught Carpenter's Alleghany and the Chesapeake batteries in a deadly crossfire. These units suffered the highest casualties of the day.[44]

Raine's two guns on the southern end of Benner's Hill, as well as Dement's four Napoleons and two guns of Carpenter's battery, were turned to the left to face the new threat from Culp's Hill and their fire was effective. Two pieces of the 1st Maryland Artillery expended all their ammunition and the 20-pounders north of Hanover Road were silenced.[45]

The Chesapeakes continued firing with their two remaining guns but casualties mounted. Shortly after firing started again a shell exploded behind Lt. Ben Roberts; he was seriously wounded by fragments in his back and both arms and would not return to the unit for two months. Sgt. Maj. Thomas LeCompte, a twenty-two-year-old farmer from Dorchester County and chief of piece of the 1st detachment, was also wounded, bringing to three the number of casualties among the four gun chiefs. Pvt. John Lane, a twenty-seven-year-old laborer from Cecil County, received a head wound from a shell fragment and would be absent for a month. Cpl. Henry Buckmaster, a twenty-eight-year-old clerk from Baltimore, was wounded as well and taken to the Lady farmhouse. Also taken to the Lady farm was Pvt. James Harper, the eighteen-year-old student from Talbot County, with his third wound of the war. Pvt. John "Little" Green, who had been wounded at 1st Fredericksburg, was wounded again, as was Pvt. Charles Dallam, a twenty-nine-year-old clerk from Baltimore, who proudly stated that in spite of his wound, he "did not leave my command." Pvt. John Richardson, a twenty-two-year-old laborer from Worcester County, was also wounded.[46]

The men of the battery had bravely stood to their guns under the most trying circumstances. The scene on Benner's Hill could only be described as horrific, with comrades and horses literally blown to pieces, the bloody wounded being taken to the Lady farm, explosions from Federal shell showering the Chesapeake's position, and a horrendous casualty rate among its officers. Pvt. John Ford Hatton of the 1st Maryland Artillery, serving with his battery less than one hundred yards away from the Chesapeake's position, recalled the scene in his memoirs:

> Solid shots were whistling by us, striking among the few scattered bunches of trees along the hill side and tearing up the ground in several places; and the shells were bursting over us, around us, and among us, keeping the air in a continuous vibration like a severe storm raging.

The Daniel Lady farm on Hanover Road. Several members of the Chesapeake Artillery were buried across the road from the farmhouse in the immediate foreground. *Author*

> Horses were killed in harness while others were plunging from fright and wounds. Men were struck, wounded and killed, while their comrades continued at their duties regardless of the cry's of agony and moans of the dieing.

After about two hours, Latimer could see the battalion's efforts were futile and deadly. Having sought permission from Alleghany Johnson to withdraw because he was no longer able to hold his position, Johnson ordered him to do so, but to keep four guns on the hill as ongoing support for the infantry attack.[47]

As Cook recalled, "Lieut. Chew braced the dismounted pieces up with the spare wheels, and got the Battery off the field. It was now growing dark." The unit had lost so many horses that two of the guns had to be drawn off by hand. They did not withdraw on their line of approach along the crest of Benner's Hill, but quickly brought the guns over the hill's brow onto its reverse slope, out of sight of the Federal guns.[48]

The scene they left was one of devastation. One of the company's limber chests was so damaged it was replaced with the large wooden box Capt. Brown used for his personal belongings. Chris Lynch gave a grimly succinct summation of the engagement: "in a short while, on the spot which a few minutes ago was filled with strong, buoyant and brave men, there remained but broken cannon, bloody corpses, and a few sad-hearted." Even from their position on Cemetery Hill Federal officers could observe that Brown's was one of the batteries that had "suffered greatly," and later counted twenty-eight dead horses on the crest of Benner's Hill.[49]

Robert Stiles, acting lieutenant and adjutant of Col. Henry C. Cabell's artillery battalion of the 1st Corps, was bearing a message to Gen. Johnson and came upon the scene on Benner's Hill just after the battalion had withdrawn:

> Never, before or after, did I see fifteen or twenty guns in such a condition of wreck and destruction as this battalion was. It had been hurled backward, as it were, by the very weight and impact of metal from the position it had occupied on the crest of a little ridge, into a saucer-shaped depression behind it; and such a scene as it presented—guns dismounted and disabled, carriages splintered and crushed, ammunition chests exploded, limbers upset, wounded horses plunging and kicking, dashing out the brains of men tangled in the harness; while cannoneers with pistols were crawling around through the wreck shooting the struggling horses to save the lives of the wounded men.[50]

The bloody action on Benner's Hill was not finished, as the infantry of Johnson's division started their attack on Culp's Hill. Andrews reported:

> Soon after this, Major Latimer again opened on the enemy with the four guns left in position to cover the advance of our Infantry, which drew a terrible fire on him, and it was here that the accomplished and gallant Latimer was severely wounded in the arm...The command then devolved on Captain Raine, the senior captain of the Battalion. Night coming on, Captain Raine, at Major Latimer's suggestion, withdrew the command a short distance and encamped for the night.

The battalion camped several miles northeast of Gettysburg on the York Pike. The Chesapeake had incurred eight killed or mortally wounded and sixteen wounded while in action for less than two hours.[51]

The men of the Chesapeake had still more exertions to complete that day. Cook recalled that, along with several others, "I volunteered to bury our boys left on the battle ground. With picks and shovels, we made our way back. The spot where they fell was so stony that we had to carry them a long distance before we found a suitable place. We buried them all in one grave." This place, where "Doctor Jack" Bryan, Fred Cusick, and Thad Parker were buried, was approximately four hundred yards west of the crest of the hill on Daniel Benner's farm, "back of Rock Creek under a large walnut tree." Cpl. Dan Dougherty was buried across the road from the Lady farmhouse. Capt. Billy Brown was later taken to the widow Elizabeth Weible's farm two miles to the northeast, where his left leg was amputated. He would die there nine days later, eulogized by Cook as "the lamented Capt. Brown, than whom no more gallant, brave and devoted patriot laid down his life on that bloody field."[52]

Withdrawal from Gettysburg, July 3

The next day the Chesapeake, along with the rest of the battalion, was ordered to have their ammunition chests replenished, repairs made, and rations issued, and then await further orders. Johnson's infantry was engaged on Culp's Hill early that morning, but there was no repeat of the advance of the artillery on Benner's Hill in support. That evening, at about 2200, Johnson's division was ordered to pull back to the vicinity of Seminary Ridge, the scene of the first day's battle that the Chesapeake had entered on July 1. They were put into position on the Chambersburg Road.[53]

Most of the wounded were to be brought back with the column, but those more seriously injured had to be left behind. Cpl. Henry Buckmaster and Pvt. James Harper had been taken to the Weible farm; Pvts. Frank Smith and James Stephens were left at the Lady Farm. Smith and Stephens died during the night of July 3/4. Smith was a thirty-three-year-old tailor from Baltimore. Stephens, a thirty-two-year-old merchant from Baltimore, left behind his wife and two daughters, ages eight and ten. Federal soldiers moved into the area vacated by Johnson's division Saturday, July 4, and took Buckmaster and Harper as prisoners of war; they were both transferred to Federal hospitals. Daniel Lady and his family also returned to their farm that day; a family friend later related that they found the "buildings were used for hospital purposes, upon the return of the family on Saturday, wounded soldiers were in the house and dead bodies lying around which they were obliged to bury." With no one to identify their remains, Smith and Stephens were buried by the Lady family as unknowns across the Hanover Road from their farmhouse, near Cpl. Dan Dougherty.[54]

Even the short distance travelled by the company that day was too painful for Pvts. Phil Oldner and Charles Tinges; they were taken to a field hospital at the David Stewart farm a few miles west of Gettysburg on the Fairfield Road. When Federal soldiers moved into the area on the fifth, Tinges was taken as a prisoner of war and transferred to a Federal hospital. With his knee so badly injured he could not be moved, Oldner lingered at the Stewart farm until he died on July 20, and was buried there, "east of the barn and near [a] row of trees."[55]

Some of the men were unnerved by their experience on Benner's Hill. Pvt. Jacob Cook had never had an absence of any kind during his service; but after seeing close friends in his detachment blown apart and then burying them that evening, he slipped away the next day and gave himself up to the Federals. Pvt. Henry Russell also left about this time; these were the company's first desertions. The popular Lt. John Plater, who had performed creditably and also commanded the battery at the battle of 1st Fredericksburg, also lost his composure on Benner's Hill. In command of the caissons during the engagement, in his haste to leave the field he abandoned a caisson and then misrepresented the circumstances behind it. He was placed under arrest by acting battalion commander Capt. Charles Raine, pending charges of misbehavior before the enemy, as well as conduct unbecoming an officer and a gentleman.[56]

March to Virginia

Andrews's battalion was in the line of battle in a steady rain all day on the fourth, expecting an attack from the Army of the Potomac that never came. On July 5, the Chesapeake, along with the rest of Johnson's division, started the march back to Virginia along the Fairfield Road while the rain continued. It was difficult marching, especially for the ambulatory wounded. Federal cavalry made frequent attacks on the column and were a constant presence to "gobble up" any stragglers. In the confusion many soldiers became separated from their units.[57]

Johnson's division reached Hagerstown, Maryland, at 1200 on July 7. Sgt. Phil Brown and Pvt. Smith Warrington, both struggling with their wounds, were captured near there, along with twenty-year-old German-born Pvt. Paul Huber. Pvt. John Myers and Pvt. William Schaefer—a twenty-five-year-old music teacher from Baltimore—had become separated from the company and were marching ahead of Johnson's column with the division of Maj. Gen. George Pickett; they were both captured near Williamsport the same day that Pickett's division crossed the Potomac at that point.[58]

Johnson's division crossed the Potomac on July 13, and reached Darkesville, Virginia, by the fifteenth. Another member of the company who had become separated—Pvt. "Johnny Trigger" Tregoe, a twenty-two-year-old farm laborer from Dorchester County—was captured by the Federals near Front Royal on the eighteenth. Johnson was ordered to retrace his steps to Martinsburg to destroy the B&O Railroad and repel elements of the Army of the Potomac in the area. The next day Pvt. John Gore, a forty-two-year-old clerk from Baltimore, was captured near Martinsburg. Although the battalion was deployed in line of battle, they were not engaged. The division next marched to Winchester, and on the twentieth Pvt. John Canfield, also of Dorchester County, was captured near there. The column continued, reaching the vicinity of Winchester on the twenty-second; Pvt. John Vansant, a twenty-two-year-old farmhand from Queen Anne's County, was captured the next day. This brought the total number of men of the battery captured on the retreat to Virginia to eight. In addition, two more discouraged men deserted from the company.[59]

Johnson's division finally went into camp near Montpelier on August 1. The same day Joseph Latimer died in Harrisonburg of the wound he received on Benner's Hill. When the Chesapeake Artillery arrived at Orange Court House, only fifty-one members of the company remained of the 80 that had mustered near Chambersburg on June 30. Eight had been killed, eleven were prisoners of war (five of them had also been wounded), four were absent wounded, four had left the company, Lt. John Plater was under arrest, and Peter Williams had transferred out. The missing twenty-nine men accounted for over 36% of the unit's strength. Of these, twenty-six would never return to the battery. The Pennsylvania campaign had been devastating for the Chesapeake. The *Richmond Examiner*'s report now mirrored the incorrect one of the *Daily Dispatch* that appeared after 2nd Fredericksburg:

> Capt. W.D. Brown, of the Chesapeake Artillery, has died of his wounds in the hands of the enemy. A cannon shot carried one leg away and shattered the other. His brother, Sergeant Philip Brown, is wounded and a prisoner. All the Maryland organizations in the field stand in immediate need of recruits to fill their shattered ranks.[60]

Peter Williams, now a corporal in the 1st Company of the Richmond Howitzers, had heard of the company's disastrous engagement on Benner's Hill and anxiously inquired after the fate of his former comrades. On July 7, during the march to Virginia, Williams wrote to his father to provide assurances of his safety, and although his information was inaccurate, he was able to articulate the scope of the Chesapeake's ordeal on Benner's Hill:

> Our army was very badly crippled but the Yankee army is said to be cut to pieces terribly. There own men admit that they were really whipped & that they commenced falling back as soon as we did. The artillery firing was the most terrible, it is said, that was ever known...I have heard from the Chesapeake; they lost terribly too; Capt. Brown was wounded, it is thought mortally; the 2nd Lt. & seven privates wounded & four men killed dead [sic]. None of my particular friends were hurt.[61]

Williams's sister Nannie wrote to him in reply and made a tribute to the sacrifice the Chesapeake Artillery had made at Gettysburg: "But doesn't it seem almost providential that you joined the Howitzers the very evening before the battle, when the poor Chesapeake suffered so terribly...Three cheers for the Chesapeake! They are gallant fellows. Heaven bless them!"[62]

"ALL THE OFFICERS AND MEN ACTED WITH THEIR USUAL COOLNESS AND GALLANTRY"

In spite of his wound, Snowden Andrews immediately began to restore the Chesapeake to campaign readiness. He started by addressing its needs in leadership. With Capt. Billy Brown dead, Lt. Ben Roberts absent wounded, and Lt. John Plater under arrest pending his court-martial, of the commissioned officers only Lt. Walter Chew was left to oversee all the operations of the Chesapeake. The battery's non-commissioned officer ranks had also suffered: Sgt. Phil Brown was wounded and in Federal hands, and Sgt. Maj. Thomas LeCompte and Sgt. James Wall had also been wounded, although they remained with the unit.

In a report he wrote on August 6, Snowden Andrews outlined the battalion's needs in officers and how they related to the Chesapeake:

> Whilst there is no official information of the fact, I have no reason to doubt that Capt. Brown has died of his wounds recd in "Battle of Gettysburg"—I respectfully and earnestly recommend 1st Lt. Chas. S. Contee Senior Lt. of Capt. Dements 1st Maryland Battery, for promotion as Capt of the Chesapeake Battery—for the following reasons—Lieut. Contee is the senior Lieut. of these two Maryland companies, having been commissioned 1st Lieut July 13th, 1861. By his uniform Soldierly conduct generally…Another important reason is that no officer with the Chesapeake Battery is competent or suitable to be made Captain. The senior officer, Lieut. Plater, will have charges preferred against him by myself for improperly leaving a caisson at Gettysburg without the knowledge of the officer then commanding The Battalion, and also for conduct unbecoming an Officer and a gentleman in misrepresenting to […] the Officer in Command, that this caisson had been left by order of Maj. Braxton, and afterwards reporting the Caison was left by order of Capt. Raine; and when contradicted by Capt. Raine he assumed the responsibility of having left it of his own accord. Charges were about being preferred against him by Maj. Latimer for unsoldierly conduct during the Battle of Gettysburg. Since the death of Maj Latimer, of which I just have been informed, it becomes my duty to prepare them which will be done promptly.[1]

Plater appeared before a court-martial on September 5 and was dismissed from the service. Although Contee's appointment to captain was supported up the chain of command as far as Lt. Gen. Ewell, he had been seriously wounded at Stephenson's Depot on June 15, and had not yet returned to duty in the field. For the time being 1st Lt. Walter Chew remained in command of the company. Second Lt. Ben Roberts recovered from his Gettysburg wounds and returned to the battery by the beginning of September.[2]

The company's enlisted ranks had also been materially reduced at Gettysburg. Only two of the men who were wounded at Gettysburg returned to duty after a brief recovery period: Pvts. John Lane and Willie Mason came back to the company in August. Two recruits had joined the battery during the Pennsylvania campaign: two residents of Baltimore's 12th Ward—students Walter L. Burke, seventeen, and George Goodhand, eighteen—had made their way to Dover, Pennsylvania, an area known for its Southern sympathy, as the Army of Northern Virginia marched into the state. They enlisted there when Confederate cavalry entered the town on June 28.[3]

On July 30, the *Richmond Examiner* reported Maryland units required recruits, and that, "officers, detailed to recruit for them, are now in the city." However, because of the difficulty of reaching Virginia from Maryland the response was weak, and the Chesapeake only gained one additional member. Thomas Ennis, a twenty-two-year-old apprentice shoemaker from Talbot County, enlisted on August 1.[4]

These additions still only brought the number of officers and men present for duty

Battle flag of the 4th Maryland Artillery issued in fall 1863 and carried by the battery until the end of the war. *Author's collection*

with the company to fewer than sixty—barely more than half that of the full complement of soldiers needed to service four guns. Consequently, the Chesapeake's armament was reduced to two 10-pound Parrott guns. About this time the units of Johnson's division were issued new battle flags of the Army of Northern Virginia's pattern with battle honors painted on them in white lettering. The Chesapeakes' flag bore the honors "Cedar Run," "Manassas," "Fredericksburg," and "Gettysburg"; honors all hard-won and at high cost.[5]

The Bristoe Campaign

Gen. Meade and the Army of the Potomac had advanced into Virginia and crossed the Rappahannock River in mid-September. Robert E. Lee, anxious to take the initiative, and learning the Federal XI and XII Corps had been transferred to the western theater, determined to march north to turn the Army of the Potomac's right flank. Accordingly, Hill's 3rd Corps and Ewell's 2nd Corps were ordered to move in an arc around the Federal army. Ewell's corps moved on October 9, with Andrews's battalion moving behind Alleghany Johnson's division. They crossed the Rapidan River at Barnett's Ford and camped at Jack's Shop; they had marched twenty-one miles. The Confederates marched along hollows and ravines to avoid being observed. No fires were allowed.[6]

The Army of Northern Virginia anticipated forcing Meade into a battle near Culpeper Court House the next day, but, realizing the movement was taking place, Meade withdrew his force from the area. On October 12, the Confederate column moved to Warrenton Springs, forced back a small force of Federal Cavalry, and began crossing the Rappahannock River. Andrews's battalion and the Chesapeake were posted in line of battle on the south side of the river to protect the bridge and ford at that location. The march was continued the next day and Andrews's battalion went into camp just south of Warrenton.[7]

The Maryland Battalion was on the march by daylight on October 14 and passed through Warrenton. They heard cannon fire to their front as artillery of Maj. Gen. Jeb Stuart's cavalry division engaged that of Brig. Gen. John Caldwell's Federal infantry division. Ewell advanced his corps to the hills surrounding the town of Auburn, which lay in a hollow formed by Cedar Run. Federal artillery was well positioned on a hill just northeast of the town, so at about 1000 Andrews called up his long range rifled guns, including the two Parrott guns of the Chesapeake Artillery, to a position in the Confederate center.[8] As it was reported by Andrews:

> The long-range guns were at once ordered up, consisting of two 3-inch rifles, commanded by captain Carpenter; two 10-pounder Parrotts, commanded by Lieutenant Chew; one 3-inch and one 10-pounder Parrott, commanded by Lieutenants Hardwicke and Early, which were placed in position on the left of the road leading to Auburn…and were ordered to open upon the enemy, directing their fire upon the batteries occupying a commanding hill to the left of Auburn. This order was given about 10 a.m., and the fire was continued about an hour […]. All the officers and men acted with their usual coolness and gallantry.[9]

The battalion of Lt. Col. Thomas H. Carter of Rodes's division had gained a position on the Federal left flank to the right of Andrews's battalion, and the combined crossfire of the two battalions caused the Federals to withdraw. There were no casualties in the company in this engagement. The battalion was then ordered to Bristoe Station, where elements of A. P. Hill's 3rd Corps were engaged in a disastrous attack on the Federal II Corps but did not see action.[10]

The following day, Lt. Col. Andrews was assigned to the Bureau of Ordnance. Command of the battalion was given to Maj.

Carter M. Braxton. The artillery of Ewell's division stayed in the vicinity of Bristoe Station during the morning, and at noon advanced half a mile and went into battery near Broad Run, but was not engaged. They then "prepared to cook rations, but suffered disappointment because the provision train failed to put in an appearance." On October 16, the battalion was placed in position on a hill overlooking Bristoe Station while the infantry destroyed the railroad. That evening, "it was raining, blustering, and chilly, causing the men much exposure and suffering, not having tents to protect themselves from the inclemency of the weather."[11]

The weather improved considerably the next day, allowing the men to dry their clothes and also get warm. Meade, having moved his army to a safer position near Centreville, on October 18 the Army of Northern Virginia withdrew and began crossing the Rappahannock River. Andrews's battalion remained in position near the river at the Orange and Alexandria Railroad bridge until all the artillery of the 2nd Corps had crossed. The battery mustered for pay on November 1 while in camp there; sixty officers and men were present for duty. On November 4, the company continued its march south and crossed the Rapidan River at Rapidan Station, "returning to and camping on the 9th of November at the camp abandoned by it on the 9th of October."[12]

The Mine Run Campaign

By the time the Chesapeake had settled into their camp below the Rapidan Meade, the Army of the Potomac had already started moving forward again. The Federals forced a crossing of the Rappahannock River at Rappahannock Station and Kelly's Ford on November 7, and Lee brought his entire army south of the Rapidan River north of Culpeper; Meade remained unsure of Lee's intentions. Andrews's battalion was later moved to a position near Morton's Ford in support of Alleghany Johnson's division.[13]

The weather turned cold in November, and the first snow of the season occurred on the ninth. There were several days of rain mid-month. Supplies for the Army of Northern Virginia became a concern, especially rations and clothing. Pvt. James Harper returned to the unit, having recovered from the wounds he received at Gettysburg. About this time Lt. Ben Roberts left the company and was admitted to the Confederate General Hospital in Charlottesville with typhoid fever on November 18. Once again, Lt. Walter Chew became the company's only commissioned officer, and Roberts's duties were taken up by Sgt. Maj. Thomas LeCompte.[14]

Meade planned to cross the Rapidan with five of the Army of the Potomac's corps beyond Lee's right flank and advance to a position in the Army of Northern Virginia's rear near Robertson's Tavern. Heavy rain delayed the movement from November 24–26, but on the latter date the Federal II, III, and VI Corps crossed the river just below the position of Johnson's division at Morton's Ford, led by Brig. Henry Prince's division of the III Corps. Mud, narrow roads, and higher water levels had delayed the advance of the Federals considerably, and the crossing was not completed until after dark.[15]

The Confederate response was swift. At 0400 on the twenty-seventh, Braxton's battalion and the Chesapeake were ordered to follow Johnson's division and move south on the Raccoon Ford Road, preparatory to taking a blocking position on the Army of Northern Virginia's left flank. Carpenter's battery advanced behind Jones's Virginia brigade, the Chesapeake moving with the 1st Maryland Artillery and the Lee Artillery behind the third brigade in the column. The division moved along the narrow road that passed through heavy forest on both sides with skirmishers out to the left, wary of the presence of the Federals. At about 1500, elements of Prince's division unexpectedly crashed into the left of Johnson's column in the vicinity of the Payne farm near Jacob's

Ford Road. The artillery battalion concentrated in a small clearing to the right of the road between Jacob's Ford Road and a lane leading to the Payne farm. Johnson deployed his brigades along the left of the road and attacked Prince's troops. As Braxton outlined it in his report:

> The country being an almost unbroken forest, the battalion was retired at once to a small field to the right of the road, where it came into battery [...]. At 4 p.m. a section of Napoleons from Carpenter's battery was placed on position at the junction of the road [...] in the woods. It opened fire and kept it up until 7:30 o'clock, when it was retired. A section of Napoleons from the First Maryland Battery...was placed in position on the left [...] This section was engaged but a short time when the enemy pressed our left wing back, necessitating the withdrawal of these guns under a heavy flank fire from infantry [...] opening at the same time with canister, soon compelled the enemy to retire.[16]

Although deployed, the other guns of the battalion could not engage because of the dense woods. The Chesapeake had no casualties during this action, but Pvt. Doug McClure, a twenty-three-year-old clerk from Baltimore, had straggled during the march and was captured.[17]

Lee established a strong line facing south across Mine Run; Braxton's battalion was placed in position on Lee's left near Zoar Church. As Braxton continued:

> The enemy was quiet on our front during the 28th and 29th, but a little after sunrise on the morning of the 30th he opened on our left, at a distance of 800 or 1,000 yards, with Napoleons, and soon thereafter from the front and right with guns of various caliber, ranging from 10-pounder to 30-pounder Parrotts. The enemy's fire was returned first by Captain Raine, then by Lieutenant Chew and Captain Carpenter.[18]

Although an attack was planned all along the line, the Army of Northern Virginia's position was deemed too strong, the attack was called off, and the Army of the Potomac withdrew to a position north of the Rapidan around Culpeper Court House. Andrews's battalion picketed the area around nearby Verdiersville for several weeks.[19]

Winter Camp, 1863–64

In late December the Chesapeake, along with the rest of the artillery of Ewell's 2nd Corps under Brig. Gen. Armistead L. Long, went into winter camp near Frederick's Hall Station on the Virginia Central Railroad. Shortly after arriving, the men of Chew's battery learned that Lt. Ben Roberts had died of typhoid fever on December 1. He was not immediately replaced. The hard campaigning and poor weather had affected the soldiers' health; as a staff officer of Maryland Steuart's brigade described it: "The physical condition of the men...I did not consider good. Their rations had been systematically reduced to the smallest quantity and there was almost no variety." Desertions within the Army of Northern Virginia were widespread at this time because of supply problems and disappointment in the recent results of the Confederate war effort. Two additional men deserted from the Chesapeake a few days before Christmas.[20]

In the new year 1864, the company benefitted from the return of three of the men wounded at Gettysburg. After recovering from their wounds Pvt. Charles Tinges was exchanged in January and Cpl. Henry Buckmaster in March; both returned to duty. In addition, Pvt. Henry Willson returned to duty in February, having also recovered from his Gettysburg wound. Lt. John Plater was returned to duty on February 20; his dismissal from the service had been commuted to suspension and forfeiture of pay by Jefferson Davis. It appears he did not rejoin the unit in the field. Maj. Carter Braxton was promoted to lieutenant colonel in January and given formal command of the battalion.[21]

In late February, there was considerable excitement in the 2nd Corps Artillery camp when Federal cavalry, led by Col. Ulric Dahlgren as part of a joint raid on Richmond with Brig. Gen. Judson Kilpatrick, approached Frederick's Hall. Armistead Long described his efforts to resist the raid:

> [February 29th] about 12 m. the enemy were reported advancing in considerable force upon my position. I immediately placed my artillery in position to resist cavalry. With the assistance of 120 sharpshooters I was in hopes of being able to repel any attack that might be made. The enemy, about 1,000 or 1,500 strong, advanced to within half a mile of my advanced camp, but finding a force in front of them, changed their direction to the left, taking farm roads towards Bumpass Station. They struck the railroad about 3 miles below me, above Bumpass. They hastily tore up a few rails and passed on in the direction of Cartersville.[22]

Capt. John F. B. Mitchell, commanding the 2nd New York Cavalry, continued the narrative in his report written after Dahlgren's death:

> The command amounted to 500 men [...]. The colonel pressed on to Spotsylvania Court-House, which he reached at early dawn on the 29th February, marched on in the direction of Frederick's Hall till 8 a.m., when he halted for fifteen minutes to feed the horses; then pressed on again to within three-fourths of a mile of Frederick's Hall Station, which we reached about 11 a.m. On the road we captured 16 artillery soldiers belonging to the Maryland Battalion. They told us that at the station there were three different camps, eight batteries in each, in all about ninety-six guns; that there was a regiment of infantry near at hand and a battalion of sharpshooters in each camp. Here we captured also 12 artillery officers on court martial.[23]

One of the men captured was Pvt. George Rice of the Chesapeake, a twenty-one-year-old farm laborer from Talbot County. Although many of the captured officers later escaped, Rice was not so lucky, and was sent to Point Lookout prisoner-of-war camp in St. Mary's County, where he would remain for the next twelve months.[24]

The Maryland Line

Col. Bradley T. Johnson was one of the Army of Northern Virginia's most talented officers from Maryland. Born in Frederick in 1829, he was a state's attorney before the war. He helped raise the 1st Maryland Infantry Regiment, rising to colonel and commanding the regiment during Jackson's Valley Campaign and the Seven Days' battles. Along with Maryland Steuart, Johnson wanted to consolidate all the Maryland units and Maryland soldiers serving in other units into one unified command.[25]

Johnson had been granted a commission by the Confederate secretary of war on June 22, 1863, to consolidate the Maryland units in the Army of Northern Virginia into one organization to be known as the Maryland Line. Johnson did not reach the army until the same day Ewell's Corps was preparing to attack Culp's Hill. As Johnson described it, "I joined the army on July 2d, but,—as, in the graphic language of General Ewell, 'This is no time for swapping horses'—I did not get my command to which I had been ordered."[25]

On November 1, Lee ordered Johnson to move to Hanover Junction, and also

Col. Bradley Tyler Johnson. *Library of Congress*

ordered the 1st Maryland Infantry Battalion (soon to be re-designated the 2nd Maryland Battalion), the 1st Maryland Cavalry, and the Baltimore Light Artillery to join him there. The other Maryland units were to join Johnson later. During winter 1863–64 this force guarded the bridges over the South Anna River. On March 23, 1864, General Orders No. 38 from the adjutant and inspector general's office authorized Marylanders serving in other Confederate units to transfer to Maryland organizations in the Maryland Line.[26]

Completing the organization of the Maryland Line took time and effort, as commanders were reluctant to give up experienced units. In a letter to his wife from Hanover Junction on April 1, 1864, Johnson outlined his progress and frustration: "I have got the Chesapeake Battery the commanding officer of which reported last night + will bring all of it here day after tomorrow. Genl Lee refuses to give up the 1" Md." The rest of the Chesapeake would finally arrive the evening of April 14. Johnson was also recruiting Maryland soldiers who had originally enlisted in Virginia and South Carolina units. On April 18, he was able to report to his wife: "Our prospects for the Line are brightening greatly, dear wife. The Chesapeake Battery arrived last week and 1" Maryland will come this evening. I have sent in 50 applications for transfers + hope to get them today or tomorrow [...]. Every thing is in motion."[27]

The Maryland Line under Bradley Johnson's command consisted of the 2nd Maryland Infantry Battalion, the 1st Maryland Cavalry, and the 1st (Maryland Flying Artillery), 2nd (Baltimore Light Artillery), and 4th (Chesapeake Artillery) Maryland Artillery batteries. The Chesapeake benefitted greatly from this initiative. Through April, May, and early June four men enlisted in the battery and an additional six transferred in from other units. With this increased size to sixty men present for duty, Bradley Johnson reorganized the company from section to battery strength. Its armament was increased with the addition of a 3-inch Ordnance rifle to the two 10-pound Parrott rifles, bringing their armament to three rifled guns. On April 13, Lt. Walter Chew requisitioned a travelling forge and enough harnesses, halters, and saddle blankets for horses to draw the additional gun. Lt. Charles Contee of the 1st Maryland Artillery, the recommended next commander of the unit, was declared unfit for field duty as a result of the wounds he received at Winchester during the Pennsylvania Campaign. Johnson recommended Chew be promoted to captain and Sgt. Maj. Thomas LeCompte to 1st lieutenant; both promotions became effective June 6. At the same time John Plater was dropped from the rolls. The blue-eyed, light-haired Chew stood only five feet, six inches tall, but made up in battle-tested leadership what he lacked in stature.

Although seasoned veterans, the newly appointed officers of the battery reflected its youth: at the time of their appointments each was just twenty-three years old.[28]

These actions completed nearly a year of rebuilding the company, now officially referred to as the 4th Maryland Artillery, following the devastation of Gettysburg. As the Chesapeake was now led by men from their own ranks, no doubt morale was high, and the feelings of the men reflected that of one of Bradley Johnson's staff officers who wrote, "the Maryland Line in this position enjoyed the association of comradeship and constituted the recognized representation of Maryland in the Army of Northern Virginia." A soldier in the 2nd Maryland Battalion similarly remembered that his unit:

> was in better condition than it ever was afterward. Those wounded at Gettysburg had returned to the ranks, and some few accessions had been made from other organizations, and in esprit, if not in size, the command was fully equal to what it was a year past it had entered the Pennsylvania campaign.[29]

The Maryland Line was assigned to Maj. Gen. Matt Ransom's command in the Richmond Defenses. On April 21, the artillery and cavalry of the Maryland Line was ordered to cook three day's rations, and on the twenty-third left for Hanover Court House. In early May, the Army of the Potomac, still under the command of Maj. Gen. George Meade, but the immediate supervision of Lt. Gen. Ulysses Grant, crossed the Rappahannock River and over the next weeks engaged the Army of Northern Virginia in the battles of the Wilderness and Spotsylvania. Following the stalemate at Spotsylvania, Grant moved south, attempting to get around Lee's right flank. The Maryland Line was ordered to the North Anna River, in the vicinity of the Virginia Central railroad bridge, and the 4th Maryland Artillery, with the other two batteries of the Line, was posted in forts overlooking the bridge.[30]

Needing to make good the losses incurred at the Wilderness and Spotsylvania, Lee assigned the Maryland Line to Maj. Gen. John C. Breckinridge's division, which was ordered to join the Army of Northern Virginia. Beginning a period of several days of marching and countermarching, Breckinridge first advanced to Hanover Junction. The command then moved to near Taylorsville, on Telegraph Road, in anticipation of an attack there by elements of the Army of the Potomac. As a soldier in the 2nd Maryland Battalion wrote in his diary on May 20, "Remained in line of battle all night. Chew's Battery took position in the entrenchments about 50 yds. from, & immediately to the rear of our line of battle. [The enemy], however, failed to make his appearance." The next day, the Maryland Line's artillery horses were unhitched and allowed to graze, but a false alarm caused the horses to quickly be harnessed and made ready to repel another attack that never materialized.[31]

Lee concentrated his army on the south bank of the North Anna River to contest Grant's advance over the river across the bridges near Hanover Junction. He had established a clever position in the shape of an inverted "V" with its apex on the river and fortified lines extending to the southeast and southwest. This would force Grant to make unsupportable attacks by columns isolated from each other by the river. Breckinridge's division marched to a position west of Hanover Junction near the Virginia Central Railroad in the lines south of the North Anna River, where several days had been spent constructing log breastworks. Later, the division was moved east to a position overlooking the railroad behind Ewell's 2nd Corps. The night of the twenty-fourth, lightning flashes lent an air of drama to heavy cannonading.[32]

On May 25, the 4th Maryland Artillery was engaged in repulsing several attacks against the Confederate right flank by the Federal II Corps, and incurred no losses. Lee was hoping to draw Grant into making an ill-advised broadscale attack against an almost impregnable position, but Grant, recognizing the danger, entrenched. The night of May 26, he withdrew his troops north of the river. Grant again sidled around the Army of Northern Virginia's right flank, and by May 28, the Army of the Potomac was crossing the Pamunkey River east of Richmond.[33]

On May 27, Breckinridge's division had marched to Ashland, rested for several hours, then continued the march as far as Atlee's Station. On the twenty-eighth, they marched several more miles to a position near Totopotomoy Creek, and the Maryland Line went into camp as part of the division's reserve. The next day the division advanced in line of battle, and a sporadic artillery exchange occurred with Federal batteries on the east side of the creek. On May 30, the batteries of the Maryland Line opened on Federal work parties building fortifications, and Northern artillery replied. Recalled a soldier of the 2nd Maryland Battalion:

> Artillery duel commenced about ten o'clock this morning, and lasted, with but little intermission, through the whole day [...]. We could see distinctly the balls passing through the air...Just at nightfall, the enemy commence a most terrific shelling upon our lines [...]. Fortunately, however, no one was injured.[34]

By this time it became clear that the Maryland Line's organization of units from different branches of the service was impractical, as the cavalry was required to operate in different areas than the infantry and artillery. Moreover, Bradley Johnson had proven himself to be a highly capable cavalry officer and his services were needed with that arm. Consequently, Johnson and the 1st Maryland Cavalry were assigned to the Cavalry corps; Johnson would be promoted to brigadier general in late June. The 2nd Maryland Infantry Battalion stayed as a separate unit in Breckinridge's division. The 2nd Maryland Artillery was also assigned to the cavalry corps as horse artillery, while the 1st and 4th Maryland Artillery batteries were assigned to Lt. Col. David G. McIntosh's artillery battalion in Lt. Gen. A. P. Hill's 3rd Corps. The brief history of the Maryland Line had come to a close.[35]

Lt. Col. David Gregg McIntosh. Wise, *The Long Arm of Lee*, vol. 2

There were four units in McIntosh's battalion in addition to the 1st and 4th Maryland Artillery batteries. The other batteries were Capt. William K. Donald's 2nd Rockbridge Artillery, Capt. William B. Hurt's Alabama Light Artillery, Capt. Berryman Z. Price's Danville Artillery, and Capt. Valentine J. Clutter's Jackson Flying Artillery. The evening of June 1, the battalion marched south with Hill's corps in a pouring rain to a position near the Chickahominy River, and stayed in this wet location all day on the second.[36]

Battle of Cold Harbor

Following the Battle of Totopotomoy Creek (also known as the Battle of Bethesda Church) Lee concentrated the Army of Northern Virginia on a line nominally north-south reaching to the Chickahominy River near Cold Harbor, and it was soon well entrenched. By June 2, Lee's right flank was anchored near the river by Maj. Gen. Cadmus M. Wilcox's division, with Breckinridge's troops to the left of Wilcox. On a rise known as

Turkey Hill, McIntosh's battalion was positioned behind Wilcox and to the immediate right of Breckinridge. The 1st Maryland Artillery was positioned on a rise east of the Watt house, overlooking Boatswain's Creek behind a low swampy area, and the 4th Maryland Artillery with the rest of the battalion to its right. The rain had widened the creek, so the Confederate defenders had been pulled back from their entrenchments in this area. Maj. Gen. "Billy" Mahone's division was in the rear as a reserve. Federal artillery directed heavy fire against the position of McIntosh's guns that night, but the Confederates did not reply.[37]

Fog covered the ground early on the morning of June 3, partly obscuring the advance of the Army of the Potomac across Lee's front at dawn. The lines of Wilcox and Breckinridge were attacked by all three divisions of the Federal II Corps. The 4th Maryland opened fire with the other guns of McIntosh's battalion, but the brigade of Brig. Gen. Francis C. Barlow broke through the Confederate lines in the swampy ground south of Boatswain's Creek, capturing prisoners and the guns of Capt. William H. Caskie's Hampden Artillery. The 2nd Maryland Battalion counterattacked, and assisted by members of the 1st Maryland Artillery recaptured the guns and turned them on the Federals.[38]

The 4th Maryland shifted their aim to the left front and fired canister at the Federal infantry during the breakthrough at a distance of a few hundred yards. Federal fire was heavy. The battery's bugler, Pvt. Daniel Wilkinson, received a gunshot wound in the foot, his second wound of the war. Pvt. Charles Garrett, who had enlisted less than three months previously, suffered a gunshot wound to his left arm. The counterattack by the 2nd Maryland was effective in driving out the attackers, and with the additional weight of Brig. Gen. Joseph Finegan's Florida brigade the entrenchments were retaken. The Army of the Potomac was repulsed all along Lee's lines with heavy casualties. As reported by Lee's artillery chief William Pendleton, "all the guns of this line were engaged in the battle of the 3d and materially assisted in checking the enemy's advance." That evening a second attack was made against Breckinridge's line and easily repulsed.[39]

On June 4, the battalion marched a short distance south and bivouacked behind entrenchments in the bottom lands of the Chickahominy. Here rations were issued, consisting of cornmeal, coffee, sugar, and half a pound of salt pork per man. The next day the men spent sleeping, exhausted by the rigors of the past few days. Although the battle at Cold Harbor was over, the shooting was not; firing across the lines was frequent. A truce to tend to the wounded caught between the lines and to bury the dead was called on June 7, the only break in the tension.[40]

Advance to Petersburg

Grant determined to attack the lightly held defenses at Petersburg; by taking the city he would sever the supply lines of the Army of Northern Virginia. On June 13, Grant began moving the Army of the Potomac south to cross the James River and get around the Army of Northern Virginia's right flank. Lee, expecting the move but not appreciating how quickly and secretively it had been executed, did not follow. That same morning, McIntosh's battalion was advanced and went into battery at the intersection of the Charles City and Long Bridge roads near Glendale, following the cavalry action at Riddle's Shop but was not engaged. The 4th Maryland Artillery would remain here with McIntosh's battalion for the next two days with Federals in position on nearby Malvern Hill. Except for a few artillery exchanges the battery was not engaged, but sharpshooters were active: Pvt. Edward Cottrell received a flesh wound in his left arm near the elbow on June 15. He refused to leave the company, but was compelled to enter a hospital eight days later and would be absent for five months. That same day a weak attack on the Petersburg lines by the Federal XVIII Corps was repulsed by a patchwork force of reserve troops and militia.[41]

The Army of Northern Virginia began to move toward Petersburg the morning of June 16. McIntosh's battalion left their camp in the morning and marched seven or eight miles to near Drewry's Bluff, and "found the roads very dusty and disagreeable." The 1st and 4th Maryland batteries were left in one camp, while the rest of the battalion moved to a nearby camp. The next day, a much-needed clothing issue was made within the battery, as Capt. Chew had requisitioned jackets, pants, drawers, and shoes. That evening, cannonading and musketry was heard from the direction of Petersburg as Ambrose Burnside's IX Corps attack was turned back in front of the trenches there.[42]

On Saturday June 18, camp was broken at 0400 and the battalion marched with Mahone's division toward the James River on the Richmond Road. They crossed the river on a pontoon bridge near Drewry's Bluff at about 0900, and after marching seven miles or so on the Richmond-Petersburg Road stopped to unhitch and water the horses at noon. Firing could again be heard from the direction of Petersburg, caused by attacks of the Federal II, V, VI, IX, and XVIII Corps. Resuming the march, the column crossed Duck Creek—a small stream four miles north of Petersburg—crossed the Appomattox River, entered Petersburg, and went into park on the south side of the town in the early evening, having marched about fifteen miles that day. As a soldier of the battalion remembered it:

> The citizens of Petersburg, who had just been in a measure at last relieved from the menacing attitudes of the Federals, rejoiced to see their deliverers and defenders marching the streets. The Ladies waved handkerchiefs and flags, and collected on the sidewalks with buckets of water for the soldiers. Nothing could have been more acceptable for the tired soldiers.[43]

The battalion took a position in the trenches south of the city. With the arrival of the Army of Northern Virginia, Grant's opportunity to quickly take Petersburg had ended. The next day, the three rifles of the 4th Maryland Artillery, as well as those of Clutter's battery, were detached and recrossed the Appomattox to take a position on a shelf about half a mile upstream from Archer's Hill, an eminence that rises approximately 100 feet above the left bank of the river. Both batteries were under the command of Maj. Marmaduke Johnson; there were rifled guns from three other battalions on the crest of the hill as well. From this position these longer range guns had the ability to fire on Federal entrenchments across the river in enfilade.[44]

Lee had thwarted Grant once again, and following their rejuvenation as a unit, the repulse of the Federals at North Anna and Cold Harbor, and their triumphant welcome by the citizens of Petersburg, no doubt the Chesapeakes felt cheered by their prospects. They could not have known that for the Army of Northern Virginia and the 4th Maryland Artillery it was the beginning of the end.

"CHEW'S BATTERY BEHAVED SPLENDIDLY"

With a sudden blast, the three rifled guns of the 4th Maryland Artillery jerked in recoil. As the sound reverberated from the sides of Archer's Hill, the three shells arced over the Appomattox River and exploded among Federal troops on the other side at the right flank of the Army of the Potomac. It was June 20, 1864, the day after the company had taken its position at Archer's Hill on the left bank of the river, and more than fifty guns in position there all opened fire. As Brig. Gen. William Pendleton reported, "these guns opened upon the enemy with such power—from their number and from the direction in which they struck flank and reverse—as to produce much confusion in his ranks, and compel him to effect a sudden change of position."[1]

The members of Chew's and Clutter's batteries had worked through the night of the nineteenth, digging embrasures for their protection. In time the low earthwork they built up would come to be known as Fort Memminger. The protection was needed: they faced heavy opposition from Federal batteries Numbers 1 and 5 across the river. These works contained 10-, 20-, and 30-pound Parrott rifles, as well as a 13-inch mortar known as "The Dictator." With the building of earthworks by both armies Grant's Overland campaign was transformed into trench warfare.[2]

The Petersburg Campaign

A soldier of a Georgia battery also on Archer's Hill described life at this position: "We have to fight a little every day and work nearly evry night so you see we are engaged nearly all the time." A Louisiana artilleryman serving with his battery near the Archer house recalled the action June 21:

> Our guns provoked a duel this morning, the enemy using 10 and 20-pounders from the river bank on our right [...]. The affair lasted for two hours, the Yankees indicating in an unpleasant manner that they had the exact range of our works [...]. Along the line of earthworks stood the gunners, half naked, working like fiends, shouting words of encouragement or chanting the refrain of some patriotic song [...]. Strong men [...] frequently fell, fainting from fatigue, at their posts, and were dragged away by detailed stretcher-bearers, to be placed under the shade of the trees. With lungs full of smoke, almost to the point of strangulation, the brave fellows swabbed the hot guns, stood like statues with thumb on vent, and as the command "Fire!" rang out, fell back of the axle, and there, with brawny arms, hurled the heavy gun back from its recoil, and shouted with the strange joy of action.[3]

The artillery firing was intense at times. A few days later the adjutant of one of the battalions on Archer's Hill remembered "the Yankees yesterday threw 10,000 lbs of iron at the lowest calculation. We threw a great deal of their ammunition back at them."[4]

On June 24, Gen. Pendleton euphemistically reported:

> our guns opened by order along the entire line, those on the north of the Appomattox especially exerting their whole power with a view to a vigorous attack on the enemy's right. Circumstances prevented the full execution of the design, but the development of our artillery strength apparently exerted a wholesome influence upon the enemy.[5]

June stretched into July. Chew made further clothing requisitions for the men. The weather was typically "Clear, hot, and dry," and in spite of a couple of showers the prevailing condition was drought. As Pendleton described the artillery's actions:

> Throughout the month of July sharp skirmishing day and night and desultory cannonading were continued, but nothing material was developed till near the close of the month [...]. About dawn of July 30 a mine was sprung by the enemy under the salient [...] near the right of General Beauregard's line [...]. Our guns on the north of the Appomattox meanwhile put forth their strength [...] to occupy the enemy elsewhere and prevent his too great concentration at his point of attack.

During the Battle of the Crater on July 31, Federal artillery also responded heavily. Pvt. John "Little" Green sustained a serious flesh wound and contusion of his forehead from a shell fragment and was admitted to a hospital a couple of days later. The twenty-two-year-old farmer from Dorchester County would be absent from the company for over a month; it was his third wound of the war.[6]

August was much the same, the weather "very hot; very dry; very dusty," with afternoon temperature readings at ninety degrees or higher more than half the time, but September brought some relief, with noticeably cooler temperatures and rain. On September 1, an inspection of McIntosh's battalion, including the 4th Maryland Artillery, gave insight into its condition at the time. The inspection report described an organization that was well officered, disciplined, and efficient, but struggling to maintain its needs and those of its men. Its military bearing was rated as "soldierly," and its military appearance and discipline both "good." The officers and men were well instructed in drill and the officers rated as "efficient." The battalion's arms were "clean," and its ammunition and equipment "good." However, both the number of accoutrements and horse equipment's were "deficient." The battalion's clothing was described as "poor." Although the policing of quarters and trenches was "good," and the soldiers' personal cleanliness was considered "neat," sanitary conditions were rated as only "fair." Public animals were well treated and properly fed and groomed.[7]

From their position on the Appomattox River, the Chesapeakes were not exposed to the deadly sharpshooting that occurred in the front lines, but the danger from periodic artillery duels at Petersburg continued. Pvt. James Dean, a twenty-eight-year-old laborer from Dorchester County, suffered a serious shell fragment wound in his right thigh on September 21, and would be absent from the company for over three months. Lee decided to increase troop strength in the lines around Richmond by transferring several divisions and batteries to that sector from Petersburg; on September 29, Clutter's battery left Fort Memminger. The 4th Maryland Artillery stayed in place.[8]

Meanwhile, significant developments within the ranks of Capt. William F. Dement's 1st Maryland Artillery, that in time would affect the 4th Maryland, came to resolution in October. The 1st Maryland Artillery had been organized as the Maryland Flying Artillery and was accepted into Confederate service in Richmond in July 1861; the men enlisted for three years. In July 1864, their terms of service having expired, the men of the battery asked for discharges, which Dement asked President Jefferson Davis for. The war department denied the request, citing the Conscription Act of 1864 that held all soldiers in the ranks indefinitely until the end of the war. The soldiers of the 1st Maryland sued Dement for a writ of habeas corpus on the basis that, since their residence in Maryland was not part of the Confederate States, they could not be held in the service. A judge in Richmond agreed, ordering Dement to release all soldiers in that unit who had served three years and sought a discharge. The subsequent loss in manpower in the battery from discharges and desertions caused it to be disbanded; the 1st Maryland Artillery relinquished its guns, and its remaining members were ordered to be consolidated with another unit at Drewry's Bluff in the Richmond defenses.[9]

The 1st Maryland Artillery's horses were turned over to the 4th Maryland Artillery on October 23. They were much needed: in a June 30 requisition for supplies Capt. Chew had indicated the company only had thirty horses, while more than forty horses would have been required to efficiently transport the unit's three guns with caissons, its forge, battery, and company wagons, and to bear its commissioned and non-commissioned officers.[10]

About this time the 4th Maryland Artillery was ordered to occupy Fort Gregg, a newly constructed open earthen fort on the west side of Petersburg, just north of the Boydton Plank Road near its intersection with Church Road, and about 400 yards behind the main works. The fort's irregularly shaped walls faced generally east, south, and west, were ten feet wide at the top, and rose fifteen feet high. The fort was about seventy-five yards in length and fifty yards wide and surrounded with a moat. There was a gun embrasure in each of its west and south orientations and two that faced southeast. A traverse separated the two south- and west-facing embrasures from the two facing southeast. The rear of the fort consisted of a log palisade with a sally port and shooting embrasures. An enclosed earthen fort (Fort Whitworth) was 700 yards to the north; entrenchments were being built to connect the two forts. These forts were designed to provide defense in the event of a breach in the outer lines. The outer works in front of Fort Gregg were manned by Brig. Gen. Edward L. Thomas's Georgia brigade, with Brig. Gen. James Lane's North Carolina brigade to Thomas's right. To Fort Gregg's right rear, and in front of Fort Whitworth, was positioned Brig. Gen. Nathaniel Harris's Mississippi brigade.[11]

The battery's two 3-inch Ordnance rifles along with their caissons were placed in the two south-facing embrasures of the work—one on each side of the traverse—and the Parrott rifle in the west-facing embrasure.[12] The company also established a camp near the abandoned Gregg farmhouse about 400 yards north of Fort Gregg, out of the confines of the earthwork and a safe distance to the rear.[13] The men took turns in detailed groups cooking rations at the camp and bringing the prepared food back to the men in Fort Gregg. In addition to the Chesapeakes, about one hundred 3rd Corps artillery drivers trained as infantry and carrying muskets were also at Fort Gregg.[14]

Chew's battery mustered for pay on October 31. Although eighty-six men were carried on the rolls, only sixty were present for duty. The weather had turned colder, with much rain and some snow. With their position behind the main lines, the company suffered no casualties during October, November, or December. In spite of the hardships endured by the Army of Northern Virginia, unit cohesion and morale among the Chesapeakes remained high. The Army of Northern Virginia experienced its highest desertion rate of the entire war during the last three months of 1864, but no soldiers from the 4th Maryland Artillery deserted in the same period. During 1864, only two men had deserted from the company—far below the Army's average.[15]

Winter of 1864–65

A Georgia soldier, one of the artillerymen trained as infantry, recalled the shelters the men in Fort Gregg built for themselves as winter quarters:

> As the winter on that bleak hill was quite cold and wood scarce, we divided up into mess squads of from four to eight men and dug square pits in the ground that our tents would stretch over, about four feet deep, digging a small chimney fireplace in one end of our pits and finishing our chimneys by building a funnel above the ground with mud and sticks. And we thought we were pretty well fixed for the winter.

One of the Mississippi soldiers described life in the camp, "We used water from the ditch that was dug around the fort. I broke the ice many a cold morning to make coffee when we could get the sorghum seed to make it out of."[16]

On December 31, the 4th Maryland Artillery mustered again. The company still carried eighty-six men on the rolls with sixty-one present for duty, two 3-inch Ordnance rifles, and the 10-pound Parrott gun. January 1, 1865, was momentous for two reasons. First, it marked the third anniversary of the formation of the battery; of the fifty men who had originally enlisted at the company's organization at Machodoc, twenty-four were still present with the unit. Second and more significantly, it meant the three-year enlistment terms of these men were completed and they were eligible for discharges. In addition, another eight men who had enlisted in other units more than three years prior before transferring into the company were also eligible for discharges. Four more men would be eligible for discharge by the end of March. Considering discharges, these thirty-six men represented well over half of the unit's strength present for duty.[17]

No doubt there was considerable discussion about the merits of continuing to serve in the army versus going home. While unit cohesion was strong, the cold, rainy weather, constant mud, inadequate rations, and the bleak prospects of the Confederate war effort were certainly factors affecting the men's considerations. Over the next three months, nineteen men would receive discharges. Included were Pvt. Henry Parker, who had been wounded at Gettysburg, where his brother Thad was killed; Pvt. John Shannahan, who was wounded at Cedar Run and 2nd Fredericksburg; and Pvts. "Big" and "Little" Green. Discharges went to men in the company's leadership as well, with Lt. Thomas LeCompte and Quartermaster Sgt. George Maccubbin leaving the company. In their requests for discharges, the men wrote of Federal persecution at home, and that they had been absent from their families for longer than originally anticipated. Pvt. Phil Harrison's request was typical:

> I left my home in Queen Anne Co. Md. for the purpose of avoiding imprisonment & persecution from Federal powers and to join the Confederate Army, expecting to be absent from home not exceeding 12 months, and it is still my intention to return to my home in Maryland when with safety I can do so.[18]

Three of the men who had already served three years left the company of their own accord without the formality of obtaining a discharge; two more who were within a couple of months of three years' service also left. Pvt. John Hooff obtained a position as captain and aide de camp to the army's Chief of Artillery, William Pendleton, and left the company in March. Two others deserted. On March 7, Pvt. Charles Tinges was admitted to a hospital in Richmond with measles. Pvt. James Stewart was one of those who obtained a discharge but changed his mind about leaving the army, staying with the company. Bugler Daniel Wilkinson also elected to stay with the company; he reenlisted and received a furlough.[19]

In anticipation of the opening of active campaigning in the spring, Gen. Pendleton developed a plan to reorganize the artillery of the Army of Northern Virginia. One of Pendleton's objectives was to improve the condition of the artillery of the 2nd Corps, and on March 17, he proposed to Lee:

> Certain inefficient batteries now with Third Corps to be transferred, as agreed upon between General Walker and myself, viz: Chew's remnant of a Maryland battery and Dement's remnant of another to be consolidated, and the resulting company left in charge of the guns on the line between Battery Dantzler and Battery Semmes. Chew has 36 men present, Dement 44. The former 19 absent, the latter 14.

Lee rejected this plan, agreeing that improving the efficiency of the 2nd Corps Artillery was necessary, but not "at the expense of other commands."[20]

The next day Pendleton submitted a revised plan that was accepted. In it he recommended:

> The remnant of a Maryland battery under Captain Chew, McIntosh's battalion, I respectfully recommend to be consolidated with another Maryland battery (Griffin's) [2nd Maryland Artillery], Breathed's battalion horse artillery. Captain Chew has already formally applied for this union and assures me it will be agreeable to the other company. The two together will only make one good strong company.

Subsequently, Special Orders No. 13 was issued on March 20, ordering this consolidation. In addition, it ordered that:

> [Captain John H.] Chamberlayne's battery, [Lt. Col. William M.] Owen's battalion, now with the Third Corps, will be detached from its present connection and assigned in place of Chew's to McIntosh's battalion. Lieutenant-Colonel Owen will be assigned as second field officer to McIntosh's battalion...The armament, horses, and equipment and transportation of Chew's battery, McIntosh's battalion, will also be turned over to Lieut. Col. C.M. Braxton, and Captain Chew will proceed with his men to Richmond and report to Lieutenant-Colonel [R. Preston] Chew, commanding horse artillery, for orders in connection with his consolidation with Griffin's battery, Breathed's battalion.[21]

On March 25, Owen established his headquarters at the Gregg House, but the order to consolidate the 4th Maryland Artillery was never carried out, probably because at the time the 2nd Maryland Artillery was

Lt. Col. William Miller Owen. *Courtesy of Glen Cangelosi*

serving with the cavalry in the Shenandoah Valley. By the time Griffin's battery was in the vicinity of the Richmond-Petersburg lines and the order could be executed events had overtaken Chew's battery and the Army of Northern Virginia. The 4th Maryland Artillery turned in its guns, horses, and equipment, but for the time being retained its separate status and remained in Fort Gregg, with Chew still in command of the earthwork.[22]

Although at the company's muster on March 1 there were forty men present for duty, discharges, the aforementioned desertions, illness, and detail assignments caused this number to quickly dwindle to twenty-nine present by the end of March, consisting of only Capt. Chew, Commissary Sgt. John Hickey, and twenty-seven privates. This prompted Chew to reorganize the company's command structure. Pvt. John D. Richardson, a twenty-three-year-old laborer from Worcester County, was promoted to sergeant and Pvt. William Pinder of Queen Anne's County, a thirty-nine-year-old overseer who was married and had four children, was promoted to corporal.[23]

Col. David McIntosh was assigned to temporary duty as the chief of artillery for the 2nd Corps, and Owen took over nominal command of the battalion, in addition to the works in the vicinity of Fort Gregg. He ordered the defenses in the area to be strengthened. An additional small earthwork was built in the outer works about 500 yards south-southwest of Fort Gregg to replace a broken dam just east of the Fort that had caused Rohoic Creek to flood as it ran north into the Appomattox River along the front of the inner works. On March 29, Lt. Henry A. Battles of the Washington Artillery's 4th Company occupied this position with two 3-inch Ordnance rifles from the battalion's 1st Company, and the work was named Fort Owen. The day before, Lt. Frank McElroy of the 3rd Company, Washington Artillery, had entered Fort Gregg with sixty-four men—"supernumerary" artillerists and drivers who carried muskets and had been trained as infantry.[24]

In spite of these improvements, Owen was apprehensive. In a diary entry written at 2200 on March 29 he recorded:

> The firing in front of Petersburg is very heavy, the enemy evidently making a desperate attempt to force through our lines and prevent any more troops being sent to [Brigadier General George] Pickett. Our lines are very weak; the men in the trenches stand two yards apart…Rumor says Grant has 200,000 men. Lee has 35,000 only. The odds are certainly fearful.

Three days later, on the night of April 1, Federal batteries bombarded the Confederate positions for four hours. Owen wrote, "Bad news from Pickett. He has been overwhelmed at Five Forks by the Fifth corps of the Federal army and Gen. Sheridan's cavalry. We are in a tight box now, and only wondering where and when our lines will be broken."[25]

They would not wonder for long.

Attack on Fort Gregg

Capt. Walter Chew narrowed his eyes, straining to see through the dim predawn light of Sunday, April 2. He had not slept much the night before: the Federal artillery barrage had started at 2200 and pounded the Confederate trench lines for hours, and the bastion at Fort Gregg had been on the alert. The first order of the day was to organize a detail to cook rations for the men of the company. But just before 0500 the cannonading was followed by heavy small arms fire a mile to the southwest. This immediately caught Chew's attention. He was used to the occasional artillery barrage and the isolated shots of sharpshooters, but this volume of rifle fire was different. Most of the fighting around Petersburg had been away from the trenches in conflicts over possession of the railroads of Lee's supply lines. From the time the battery had taken position near the outer lines the previous October, not a single Federal attack had been made directly against the Confederate trenches. Soon staff officers and couriers could be seen racing from the direction of the firing. The lines had been broken, and Federal infantry columns were moving into the Confederate rear. The rations would have to wait.[26]

What Chew could not discern was the attack of Maj. Gen. Horatio G. Wright's entire Federal VI Corps, which had broken the thinly held Confederate defense lines near the Banks house a mile west of Fort Gregg, splitting Lane's North Carolina brigade in two, capturing men and artillery, and forcing Thomas's Georgia brigade from its trenches. Lt. Gen. A.P. Hill—the 3rd Corps commander—riding to assess the situation, had been shot and killed by Federal infantrymen. What remained of Lane's and Thomas's brigades retreated to the east toward Fort Gregg, followed by part of the Federal brigade of Col. Joseph E. Hamblin, who advanced along the Confederate trench line capturing artillery and soldiers. Chew alerted the men inside Fort Gregg and ordered them to prepare to receive an attack.[27]

Hamblin's men eventually approached and attacked Fort Owen, capturing Lt. Henry Battles and his section of artillery. The Federals turned the guns toward Fort Gregg and began firing ineffectively at the earthwork. Lt. Frank McElroy and the supernumerary artillerists of Fort Gregg fired back with their rifles, but at 500 yards the range was too great to be effective. The men of the 4th Maryland Artillery, without rifles or cannon, were helpless to respond. McElroy led part of his contingent of the Washington Artillery converted to infantry in an attack on Fort Owen. The Federal infantrymen, outnumbered and unsupported, fell back and left the guns to McElroy. Lt. Col. Owen ordered him to move west along the Boydton Plank Road

Fort Gregg looking north from the Boydton Plank Road in the foreground. *Author*

with the two guns to support Confederate infantry forming to contest the advance of Hamblin's brigade. Chew ordered the remaining supernumerary artillerists to also advance as infantry.[28]

The men of the 4th Maryland Artillery were unable to stand by as mere observers, as one of the men recalled: "The Chesapeake not only held Fort Gregg, but volunteers under Corporal Pindar went out from the fort to work a piece of artillery under heavy fire and did much good until recalled." The guns and artillerists fought alongside the remaining elements of Lane's and Thomas's brigades in a line perpendicular to their trench lines near the Banks house. In addition, Harris's Mississippi brigade had arrived from north of the Appomattox River to take a position on the right. Under this opposition, Hamblin's attack lost momentum, ground to a halt, and was forced back by the mixed force of Confederates.[29]

Soon advance elements of Maj. Gen. John Gibbon's Federal XXIV Corps advanced forward from the site of the breakthrough, and led by the brigade of Col. Thomas Osborn, pushed the Confederates back. A pause came over the field as Lane's, Thomas's, and Harris's brigades, as well as the supernumerary artillerists and McElroy's section, retreated to the vicinity of Fort Gregg. As they came into the work, the soldiers picked up rifles dropped by the other retreating troops so that each man had two or three to fire. It was about 1100. Pvt. Edward Cottrell of the 4th Maryland Artillery recalled:

> I was in the early morning fight (about daylight), and after the enemy had been driven back through the aid of the infantry there was quiet, neither side making any movement for about two hours. In the meantime a detail of men, myself of the number, was sent back to the yard of an unoccupied dwelling house about four hundred yards in the rear of the fort, to cook rations for the men.

Chew had ordered the detail to the Gregg house under Sgt. John Richardson; this left him with only eleven other men of the company in Fort Gregg.[30]

The leadership vacuum created by A. P. Hill's death caused confusion in the 3rd Corps's senior ranks. Maj. Gen. Cadmus Wilcox, the division commander for the infantry troops in the area of the breakthrough, had arrived in time to order Harris to attack Hamblin's brigade. Wilcox now ordered Harris to split his brigade, taking his 19th and 48th Mississippi regiments to Fort Whitworth and placing the 12th and 16th Mississippi regiments—under Lt. Col. James H. Duncan of the 19th Mississippi—in Fort Gregg. Meanwhile, some of Lane's men had taken refuge in Fort Gregg while the rest continued east and took position near the broken dam on Rohoic Creek. Lane argued with Wilcox that Fort Gregg and Fort Whitworth were untenable and that both bastions should be evacuated. Wilcox allowed Lane to take a position near the Rohoic Creek line, and, after exhorting the officers in Fort Gregg to defend it to the last, made his way to the Gregg house to make it his headquarters; Lane ordered those of his North Carolinians who were in Fort Gregg to fall back to the Rohoic Creek line, but not all heard his order. The 3rd Corps chief of artillery, Brig. Gen. R. Lindsay Walker, sharing Lane's sentiments, ordered Owen to withdraw the artillery from Forts Gregg and Whitworth. Owen knew this would be counter to Wilcox's plan and rode to the Gregg house to confer with him. Wilcox countermanded Walker's order, and Owen delivered this message to Fort Gregg. However, the courier with the original message had already continued on to Fort Whitworth and the new message was never delivered. This would come to have major implications for the men in Fort Gregg.[31]

As one of the supernumerary artillerists from Virginia put it, "Capt. Chew and his men who were quartered just in rear of Gregg all winter, and who were horseless and gunless, taken refuge in the Fort, but could not take any part in the fight." Capt. Chew immediately recognized this, and, as the senior artillery officer present, ordered the artillerymen of one of McElroy's guns to pick up their rifles and resume their role as infantrymen, while the eleven men of the 4th Maryland stepped forward to serve the piece. No doubt the Chesapeakes did so with a cheer. As one of the supernumerary artillerists recalled, "we were... under the command of Captain Chew, of Maryland, with Frank McElroy, of the 3rd Company, Washington Artillery, as our lieutenant." Gen. Lane later remembered the positions taken by the troops: "My [North Carolina] men were on the right and centre, the supernumerary artillerists on the left, and Chew's battery was in the centre, so as to give the pieces the widest possible range of fire." Chew had his men roll their gun into the southwest-facing embrasure on the west side of the traverse, while McElroy's gun crew took the southeast-facing embrasure on the east side of the traverse. Duncan's Mississippians were spread out along the back of the fort at the log palisade. In all, counting the two Mississippi regiments, Chew's and McElroy's guns, the supernumerary artillerists, the group of soldiers from Lane's brigade, and about forty Georgians from Thomas's brigade, Fort Gregg held between 300 and 350 men; Fort Whitworth, with four guns, had about 200.[32]

While this was happening, Gibbon's XXIV Corps began deploying to the south and west of Fort Gregg with orders to assault the inner works and attack Petersburg. A Federal battery in the vicinity of Fort Owen, as well as another in the vicinity of the Banks house, began shelling Fort Gregg, and the two guns under Chew replied. Apprehension in the fort ran high, and some men started to leave for the rear. As Capt. A. K. Jones, commander of the 12th Mississippi, remembered it:

> Men were continually leaving, remarking that they were separated from their commands and would be considered deserters, and if hurt away from their friends would not receive proper attention, &c. As soon as General Wilcox rode away, at my suggestion no more men were permitted to leave, no matter what the excuse.[33]

Surgeon George W. Richards also recalled this scene:

> They had never made their escape from any place...and begged to go to the rear, and after hesitating to comply with their request [Jones] at last concluded to let them go, provided they would leave their guns with him; and to that they readily assented [...]. I suggested to Captain Chew, of Maryland, to surrender, as there was no chance of ultimate success by holding out any longer."

Chew demurred, saying that Duncan was the senior officer present, so the decision was not Chew's to make. Speaking loudly enough for his men to hear he shouted over the din, "Let the fight go on as it will; I will not surrender."[34]

Gen. Lane asked Wilcox for permission to leave the fort to be with the larger part of his brigade at the dam, and permission was granted. Lane observed the 4th Maryland serving its gun and later recalled: "even before I left the work, two or three men were shot down in rapid succession while attempting to discharge a single gun." At that moment Pvt. Thomas Everngam of Queen Anne's County was killed; he was within days of his thirty-fourth birthday and left behind a wife and young son. Pvt. Chris Lynch was slightly wounded. At the same time Lane saw the four guns withdrawn from Fort Whitworth, which from that point onward could not provide artillery support to the defenders in Fort Gregg. Rushing from his location farther east McIntosh described what he saw:

> The scene which met my eyes as I mounted the ramparts staggered me.

> No troops of ours could be seen beyond the dam. The open plains beyond were thickly dotted with long lines of the enemy rapidly forming for an assault on Fort Gregg.[35]

At about 1300 the Federal brigades of Osborn from the south and Col. George B. Dandy from the west rolled forward in the attack on Fort Gregg. The six brigades arrayed in front of forts Gregg and Whitworth would bring between 7,000 and 7,500 Federal infantry to bear against the Confederate defenders' 500. Pvt. Cottrell and the other men on the cooking detail at the Gregg house were stunned:

> We had not finished our work when the enemy again attacked [...]. Believing the fort would eventually be captured, and realizing the fact that the rations could not be gotten to our comrades at that juncture, we sheltered ourselves as best we could [...][36]

Dandy described the attack in his after action report:

> The assault was commenced at a distance of from 200 to 300 yards from the works, and was made at the double-quick, without a halt, under the most terrific fire of musketry and artillery I have ever witnessed. Many of our brave men went down, but the work was reached without faltering [...]. The First Brigade came up with us on the right and inclosed the work, but the moat was so deep and wide that it was impossible to cross at that point. The garrison, although surrounded, refused to surrender and continued to fire upon our men.[37]

Pvt. Chris Lynch later recalled what he saw from inside Fort Gregg:

> This large body of Federals advance upon this devoted little band, expecting no resistance, anticipating an easy, triumphant entry into the fort. They indeed approached so close that the Confederate line in the distance feared the fort was about to surrender without a struggle. But not so, for when in close range the guns of artillery and infantry belched forth, amidst clouds of white smoke, death and terror to the too-confiding foe. Amazed and terror-stricken they retracted, staggering, broken.[38]

Federal casualties were particularly heavy as Chew's guns fired rounds of double canister. Soldiers in the attacking columns later described how destructive the artillery fire was: "[Canister] was being planted, not as farmers plant corn, two to four in a hill, but by the bucket full, perhaps barrel, for two of the men of my company who were killed each had three [canister] through them," remembered one. "When we moved forward the enemy opened on the solid column, first with one piece of artillery, then with another, cutting a wide swath the full length of the column, and eight or ten feet wide," recalled another. McIntosh observed, "Line after line of the enemy was broken as they moved up to the work, and the dead could be seen at the distance of a mile lying in piles around it."[39]

The attack had stalled, and many of the Federal soldiers huddled near the moat at the base of Fort Gregg's walls, unable to go forward and unwilling to go back and be subjected to the same fire again. As one soldier in the fort described it, "when the first charge was driven back, there were left under the guns of the fort in a deep ditch more than two thousand men, who had chosen to stay there rather than be shot in the back on the first retreat." Dandy sent for reinforcements, and two additional regiments came to the attack. This attack also lost momentum, breaking against the fort's walls with heavy casualties. During an ensuing lull the men in Fort Gregg could hear those in Fort Whitworth and the inner trench lines cheering their encouragement.[40]

Those observing were amazed at the resistance put up by the fort's defenders and struggled to put what they saw into words. As Gen. Harris put it, "Gregg raged like the crater of a volcano emitting its flashes of deadly battle fires, enveloped in flame and cloud, wreathing its flag in honor as well as in the smoke of death." Gen. Wilcox later wrote that the work "was now nearly surrounded. The heroism displayed by the defenders of Battery Gregg has not been exaggerated by those attempting to describe it. A mere handful of men, they beat back repeatedly the overwhelming number assailing them on all sides." Lt. Col. Owen—at the Gregg house—wrote, "It was a glorious struggle."[41]

Gibbon, impatient to capture the two works and attack Petersburg's inner defenses while there was still daylight, ordered three additional brigades of the division of Brig. Gen. John W. Turner to move to the attack: one against Fort Whitworth and the other two against Gregg, bringing its total number of attackers to about 4,000. The garrison again exploded with fire from rifles and artillery. Ammunition was running low and Lynch remembered, "After exhausting our ammunition Lieutenant [sic] Chew's gray coat was pressed into service, and we loaded our pieces with such projectiles as could be picked up."[42]

Federal soldiers eventually forced their way into Fort Gregg by sheer numbers, as remembered by one of the supernumerary artillerists:

> they rallied and came, but in double-quick time and never stopped until they jumped into the big ditch around the fort and into water two feet deep. They then dug steps from the bottom of the ditch to the top of the fort and attempted to scale the fort by charging up the steps [...]. We had the advantage of being able to shoot them in the top of the head as they climbed up the fort before they could see to shoot us, and the dead falling down the steps knocked others down and confused them.

From his position to the east McIntosh could see Federal soldiers enter the ditch:

> Into it they poured until it seemed to be over-flowing, and then clambering up the scarp they mounted the parapet and the last struggle joined. Three times more the guns fired after the parapet was lined with men and at each discharge a generous and sympathising cheer went up from the crowd who were distant spectators.

Brig. Gen. Robert S. Foster, commander of the Federal division, reported, "The fighting on both sides at this point was the most desperate I ever witnessed, being a hand to hand struggle for twenty-five minutes after my troops had reached the parapet." A Confederate soldier remembered:

> At the third charge these men came out of the ditches and advanced in such great numbers that the men in the fort could not kill them all. The enemy appeared exasperated and gave no quarter, and the men in the fort, having no time to reload, broke the stocks from their guns and fought with the barrels.

A Federal soldier recalled "the cannoneers being clubed to the death with muskets." The defenders even threw rocks and bricks taken from the chimneys of the winter quarters still standing in the fort.[43]

The 4th Maryland Artillery was overrun at its embrasure. Cpl. William Pinder was struck in the head and seriously wounded during the melee. Pvt. William Culver, a twenty-seven-year-old farm laborer from Worcester County, was killed; he left behind a wife and six-year-old daughter. Though wounded, Chris Lynch vividly remembered the final scene:

> Billy Holtzman, as the columns [...] swarmed over the ramparts, still showed fight. A big fellow seized the boy and seemed intent on distinguishing himself by some sanguinary deed, but a young Lieutenant who divined the brute's intentions, put a stop to it by ordering Holtzman to the rear under a prisoners' guard. Billy couldn't understand why the fellow wanted to wreak summary vengeance upon him until he reached the trench surrounding the ramparts and found it choked with the man's comrades, which he had attributed to the fire of the Chesapeake battery. Although Pinder was severely wounded in the head, he and Culver fought like tigers at the ramparts. Poor Culver; his young life was sacrificed while fighting with a clubbed rifle, with which he had been doing deadly work, for he was a dead shot, and during intervals of firing by the battery he was busy at the ramparts with his rifle.

McIntosh thought the entire garrison was killed or wounded, "as the enemy could be seen firing their pieces for some time from the ramparts, with the muzzles pointed downwards. Eight flags could be seen floating from the works and may be taken as an evidence of the number brought against it."[44]

The defenders of Fort Gregg were forced to capitulate, and those that survived became prisoners of war. Casualties among the defenders totalled 57 killed, 243 wounded and captured, and the remaining 33 unwounded also taken prisoner. Federal casualties in the attacks on forts Gregg and Whitworth exceeded 800. The defense of Fort Gregg and Fort Whitworth on April 2 had so delayed and disrupted Gibbon's advance that the XXIV Corps would not be able to attack the inner defenses until the next day, allowing the Army of Northern Virginia to evacuate Petersburg and withdraw across the Appomattox River that night.[45]

Capt. Walter Chew and the other nine soldiers of the 4th Maryland Artillery who survived were marched off to spend the rest of the war in prison camps. As Fort Gregg fell, Brig. Gen. Nathaniel Harris led his two regiments out of Fort Whitworth, accompanied by Lt. Col. Owen and the remaining seventeen members of the 4th Maryland Artillery at the Gregg house.[46]

The artillerymen in Fort Gregg earned the respect of their fellow soldiers in the Army of Northern Virginia and the Federal attackers. McIntosh declared:

> The defense of Fort Gregg by its two guns under Captain Chew and manned by a detachment of his company and the other by Lt. McElroy of the Washington Artillery with a detachment made up of drivers, together with its garrison of muskets will always be remembered by those who witnessed it as one of the bloodiest, most obstinate, and most gallant contests of the war.

Lt. Col. Andrew Potter, commander of one of the Federal brigades in the assault, also reported, "The attack was gallantly made and most stubbornly resisted. The enemy refused to yield till we were fairly within their works." Brig. Gen. James Lane praised the 4th Maryland's performance in particular: "Chew's battery behaved splendidly," and an officer of Lane's brigade remembered, "The artillerists fought bravely, resorting to small arms after being unable to use their cannon, and appeared to me as if commanding themselves: they were of Captain Chew's battery."[47]

The Appomattox Campaign

With his army cut in two, by 2000 on April 2, Lee had started quietly evacuating his lines from Petersburg and Richmond to reunite his forces on the other side of the Appomattox River. At Petersburg, after blowing up their munitions and burning tobacco warehouses, the army crossed the river on four bridges, burning these behind them as well, and by midnight the whole army had passed over. The remaining men of the 4th Maryland Artillery were placed in charge of one gun as the army's rear guard, as McIntosh recalled:

> Getting my Battalion together upon the north side of the Appomattox, and stopping for a few minutes to feed the horses, the line of march was immediately taken upon the "Rim Road" and continued all night [...] the roads were in places very bad and by daylight only seven or eight miles had been accomplished. One of my own Baltimore pieces being placed as the rear guard under Lt. Col. Owen left me with little assistance.[48]

Federal infantry of the XXIV Corps marched into Petersburg the next morning to find the Confederates had gone. In the confusion commensurate with the withdrawal, many soldiers became separated from their units, were cut off when the bridges were burned, and were captured the next day. Two soldiers of the 4th Maryland Artillery met this fate: Pvts. Francis McCummins, a nineteen-year-old student from Cecil County; and John Torrington, a twenty-three-year-old wood turner from Baltimore, were both captured at Petersburg on April 3 and sent to Hart Island prison in New York Harbor.[49]

Lee's initial objective was to reach Amelia Court House, thirty miles to the west on the Richmond and Danville Railroad. The columns from Petersburg and Richmond would concentrate there and continue to march west and south, eventually linking with Gen. Joseph E. Johnston's Army of the Tennessee in North Carolina. The fifteen remaining members of the 4th Maryland Artillery led by Quartermaster Sgt. John Hickey marched with the other four batteries of McIntosh's battalion, still commanded by Lt. Col. William Owen. The other batteries in the battalion included Hurt's Alabama battery, Price's Danville Light Artillery battery, Chamberlayne's Virginia battery, and Donald's 2nd Rockbridge Artillery. Following his death, A. P. Hill's 3rd Corps was combined with James Longstreet's 1st Corps, which took the lead.[50]

Owen remarked in his diary that he experienced "a feeling of relief at getting out of the trenches and on the road once more," although he also noted "Sheridan's cavalry are after us sharply." McIntosh noted in his diary that shortly after dawn he called a halt of a couple of hours to feed the horses, after which the march was resumed. Gen. Pendleton characterized the march on the third as "fatiguing, and very slow, on account of the immense number of carriages with the army." The army had about two hundred pieces of artillery and over one thousand wagons. Many Confederate soldiers, unused to the hard marching, fell behind and were captured by Federal cavalry. Pvt. George Goodhand of the 4th Maryland Artillery became separated from the rest of the column and made his way toward Richmond without realizing it had been evacuated. Although he managed to elude Federal patrols for over a week, he was eventually captured at Manchester, Virginia, ten days later. The column continued marching through the night.[51]

After recrossing the Appomattox River at Goode's Bridge, Owen noted that the column reached Amelia Court House during the afternoon of April 4, "having marched with scarcely a halt for forty-four hours. Have not eaten a regular meal since last Sunday—three days." McIntosh remembered the men "had lived chiefly on parched corn, with a few bags of flour and a little meat which the Sergeants picked up in the country." The army had to wait to be joined by Ewell's column, delayed because a pontoon bridge had not been constructed over the Appomattox River at the Genito Road. When the Richmond troops arrived, Pvts. Charles Tinges, Phil Harrison, and George Rice rejoined the company. Tinges had been released from Robertson Hospital in Richmond on April 2 when the city was ordered to be evacuated, the same day as the attack on Fort Gregg. Rice, who had been captured a year before during the Dahlgren raid, was exchanged, and arrived at Camp Lee in Richmond in late March. Harrison had been detailed as a clerk in the Confederate Paymaster department in Richmond; he followed the army even though he had been discharged for three years' service. All three had marched with Ewell's column of Local Defense Troops until it rendezvoused with the rest of the Army of Northern Virginia at Amelia Court House. This brought the company's strength to seventeen men.[52]

With the column encumbered with extra wagons and guns, at this time Lee ordered that the number be consolidated, with the surplus sent ahead of the army. Pendleton had each battalion reorganized to reduce the number of guns to that commensurate with the number of men in each battery. McIntosh's battalion was "fitted up with the best guns and horses from the Corps, the compliment of guns being 8 Napoleons and 4 other [three] in. Rifles." Price's and Hurt's batteries were at nearly full strength, and Owen created a third battery by consolidating Chew's, Donald's, and Chamberlayne's units into one battery that had about the same strength and four guns. The next day Gen. R. Lindsay Walker left with a column of the surplus guns, and ninety-five caissons and their ammunition were destroyed.[53]

Ewell's column having finally arrived, the army was again put in motion at about 0100 on April 5. The one-day lead Lee's army had on the Army of the Potomac was lost, which Lee later characterized as "fatal, and could not be retrieved." Owen described the continuance of the march:

> Marched all day and nearly all night. When the batteries halt to rest, the men throw themselves upon the ground and immediately go to sleep. When the order is given to move forward, the horses often move on without their drivers, so hard is it to arouse the men. Tired and hungry we push on. It is now a race for life or death. We seldom receive orders now. The enemy has the shortest line to Danville and Burkesville, and is heading us off.[54]

The battalion continued on the march the next day, with frequent clashes from attacks by Federal cavalry. At Riceville, the battalion was formed into line of battle and fired several rounds to drive cavalry off their line of march. To the column's rear, nearly 8,000 Confederates of Ewell's column were casualties at the Battle of Sailor's Creek, the great majority captured. That night the march was taken up again, with progress impeded by ankle-deep mud.[55]

Battle of Cumberland Church

The battalion's column reached Farmville the morning of the seventh and went into park to rest. Rations were issued for the first time during the campaign: "casks of bacon being knocked open on the road-side, the tired and hungry troops helping themselves as they passed by," and receiving "as much as we could carry." The column recrossed the Appomattox at Farmville and dragged the guns uphill through axle-deep mud north on the Cumberland Court House Road, passing wagons that had been set afire to reduce the size of the army's train. They went into camp in the vicinity of Cumberland Church to cook rations; to the east, Confederate infantry of Maj. Gen. Billy Mahone's division formed a line of battle and dug breastworks. An attack by Humphrey's Federal II Corps was repulsed that afternoon, but it was determined that Longstreet's corps, its wagon trains, and its artillery would resume the march in the interest of safety. The column moved west down a narrow country road surrounded by woods described by McIntosh as "wretched beyond description, and the woods filled with new tracks. I was much alarmed for fear I would be unable to get my guns over the bad road before dark and I should have to abandon them in the mud."[56]

While the column struggled in the mud of the narrow road, it was attacked on its flank from the south by Federal cavalry of Brig. Gen. J. Irwin Gregg's brigade charging up the intersecting Buckingham Plank Road. McIntosh remembered, "the cavalry guarding our left flank was stampeded, and fled right through my guns." Teamsters desperately tried to get their wagons out of danger. Hardaway's artillery battalion fled. Confederate cavalry regrouped and beat off the attack, capturing Gen. Gregg in the process, but the Federal cavalry re-formed in line of battle across the fields on either side of the Buckingham Plank Road and charged again. As Owen described it:

> bullets began to whistle around our ears [...] and feeling assured that the enemy was upon us [I] gave the order at the top of my voice, "Tention! Fire to the left, in battery!" With great promptitude the guns were wheeled into position ready for action just as the Federal cavalry came charging to the crest of the high ground. With shell cut for close range, and canister, our twelve guns were let loose, and such a scattering I never saw before.[57]

These would prove to be the last shots fired by the 4th Maryland Artillery.

Surrender

The march was resumed, and continued through the night. Owen later wrote:

The Cumberland Church battlefield looking south from the 4th Maryland Artillery's position. The Buckingham Plank Road is at right. Federal cavalry formed at the tree line in the background and advanced against this position. *Author*

> And so the retreat rolls on. We are passing abandoned cannon, and wrecked and overturned wagons, and their now useless contents belonged to the quartermasters. Horses and mules dead or dying in the mud. At night our march is lighted by the fires of burning wagons, and the hoarse roar of cannon and rattle of small arms before, behind, and on our flanks, are ever in our ears. The constant marching and fighting without sleep or food are rapidly thinning the ranks of this grand old army. Men who have stood by their flags since the beginning of the war now fall out of ranks and are captured, simply because it is beyond the power of physical endurance to go any farther.

The seventeen men of the 4th Maryland Artillery managed to stay with the column.[58]

At about 0900 on April 8, the battalion went into camp on Rocky Run a mile from Appomattox Court House. The march was to be resumed the next day; McIntosh's and Hardaway's battalions were to accompany the army, while the rest of the artillery was to move ahead in hopes of reaching North Carolina. On the morning of the ninth, Owen put the battalion on the road and it began moving up the hill above the Appomattox River. McIntosh was told to park the guns in the hollow, but as "the enemy was in such force in our front the march could not be resumed and it was not improbable a surrender would be the result." By 1500 that day the surrender agreement was complete, and word spread through both armies that the war for them was over.[59]

Hundreds of soldiers of the Army of Northern Virginia, including battalion commander Col. David McIntosh and most of the cavalry, determined to strike out on their own to reach other Confederate armies and continue the fight. Sgt. John Hickey and Pvts. George Rice, Phil Harrison, and Charles Tinges left the company. Likely riding on battery horses, they rode north through the wooded ravine of the headwaters of the Appomattox River, making their way to the James River and west toward Lynchburg.

Incredibly, all four would elude capture by Federal cavalry and surrender in other locations. Tinges and Harrison surrendered in Lynchburg a few days later. Rice and Hickey made their way to Greensboro, North Carolina, arriving about April 15, only to find out the next day that Joe Johnston's Army of Tennessee had been halted pending surrender negotiations. Rice surrendered there on May 9. The resourceful Hickey determined to reach Lt. Gen. Richard Taylor's army of the Department of Alabama, Mississippi, and East Louisiana, and was able to get as far as Meridien, Mississippi, a journey of over 650 miles. Here he found that Taylor's force had also surrendered and was finally paroled there on May 13.

This left the Chesapeake with only thirteen in number, and Sgt. John Richardson was now in command of the company.[60]

April 10 dawned cool and rainy, and a steady downpour continued throughout the day. Rations were issued to the Confederate soldiers by the Army of the Potomac. Lt. Col. Owen recalled on this day, "I had the Battalion assembled and informed the men of the terms of the surrender, which were as follows: that each officer and man were to go to their homes after receiving a parole… the rolls were then called and but few men were found to be missing." Parole slips were printed and signed by Owen; the formal surrender for the artillery arm of the Army of Northern Virginia was scheduled to occur on Tuesday, April 11.[61]

The rain continued that night; during the morning of the eleventh Owen led McIntosh's battalion of twelve guns and marched with the rest of the Army of Northern Virginia's

Location of the surrender of the Army of Northern Virginia's artillery at Appomattox. In the foreground are traces of the Lynchburg Stage Road. *Author*

artillery units along the Richmond-Lynchburg Stage Road, halting just east of Appomattox Court House. Sgt. John Richardson of the Chesapeakes proudly recalled that in addition to himself, "I surrendered 12 men and one gun." The other men of the company present at the surrender were Pvts. Allen Covington, Edward Cottrell, Robert Grimes, John Hill, John Lane, John Lond, John Mowbray, James Pratt, Bedingfield Spencer, William Tarbutton, William Williams, and William Yates. Of the initial fifty men who had enlisted with the Chesapeake Artillery on January 1, 1862, only John Lane remained. The battle flag the battery had been issued after Gettysburg "was not surrendered at Appomattox C.H." It had been retained by Richardson, and only a flagstaff was turned in with the company's gun and equipment. The 4th Maryland Light Artillery Battery was no more.[62]

As Lt. Col. Owen recalled, the next morning (April 12) the battalion was "assembled for the last time in front of our camp-fire," and Owen read to them Robert E. Lee's farewell address to the army:

> GENERAL ORDERS,} HDQRS. ARMY OF NORTHERN VIRGINIA,
> No. 9 } April 10, 1865.
>
> After four years of arduous service, marked by unsurpassed courage and fortitude, the Army of Northern Virginia has been compelled to yield to overwhelming numbers and resources. I need not tell the brave survivors of so many hard-fought battles, who have remained steadfast to the last, that I have consented to the result from no distrust of them. But, feeling that valor

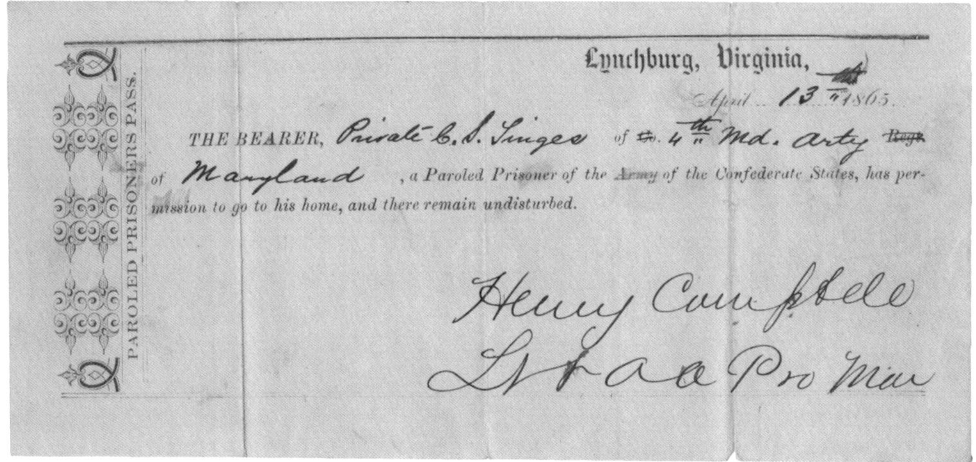

PAROLED PRISONERS PASS.

Lynchburg, Virginia, April 13th 1865.

THE BEARER, Private C. S. Tinges of ~~Co.~~ 4th Md. Arty ~~Regt~~ of Maryland, a Paroled Prisoner of the ~~Army~~ of the Confederate States, has permission to go to his home, and there remain undisturbed.

Henry Campbell
Lt & a a Pro Mar

Parole of Pvt. Charles S. Tinges of the 4th Maryland Artillery issued at Lynchburg, Virginia. *Author's collection*

and devotion could accomplish nothing that could compensate for the loss that must have attended the continuance of the contest, I determined to avoid the useless sacrifice of those whose past services have endeared them to their countrymen. By the terms of the agreement officers and men can return to their homes and remain until exchanged. You will take with you the satisfaction that proceeds from the consciousness of duty faithfully performed; and I earnestly pray that a merciful God will extend to you his blessing and protection. With an increasing admiration of your constancy and devotion to your country, and a grateful remembrance of your kind and generous considerations for myself, I bid you all an affectionate farewell.

R. E. Lee,
General[63]

Owen continued his narrative:

The men listened with marked attention and with moistened eyes as this grand farewell from our old chief was read, and then receiving each his parole they every one shook my hand warmly and bade me good-by; and breaking up into parties of three and four, turned their faces homeward […]. I watched them until the last man disappeared with a wave of his hand around a curve of the road […].[64]

"MARYLAND MAY WELL BE PROUD OF SUCH SONS"

Former Sgt. John Richardson, the last commander of the 4th Maryland Artillery, trudged along the muddy road between Appomattox Court House and Fredericksburg on his way home to Cuttsville, in Queen Anne's County. It rained almost every day that April, and progress was slow. He was with a group of five other former soldiers of the Chesapeake, all from Maryland's eastern shore: Allen Covington and James Pratt were also from Queen Anne's County; John Hill, John Lond, and John Mowbray were going home to Dorchester County. After several days they reached Fredericksburg; no doubt they spoke among themselves of the two great battles they had fought there, and remembered Lt. John Grason, as well as Pvts. Edward Graham and "Bey" Hopkins of the Chesapeake, who all lay in graves near Hamilton's Crossing.[1]

The Journey Home

On April 22, the group reached Washington, DC, and, as required, reported to the provost marshall general there. The men then made their way home. Richardson married his wife Kate in 1868; they would have a son and a daughter. He supported his family as a storekeeper in Delaware. By 1920, Richardson was living in the Maryland Line Confederate Soldiers' Home in Pikesville. Of his service with the battery, he later said he "enlisted October 1862 in the Fourth Maryland 'Chesapeake' Artillery for the war at Richmond as a private. Then promoted to sergeant. Engaged in the battles of… Fredericksburg, Gettysburg, and others. I surrendered 12 men and one gun at Appomattox Court House April 1865." He died at the home on October 24, 1925, at age eighty-four, and was buried at Druid Ridge Cemetery in Pikesville.[2]

Former Pvts. Edward Cottrell and Frank Yates also travelled together from Appomattox and arrived in Washington on April 18 to report to the provost marshall general. Yates returned to his home in Leonardtown, in St. Mary's County, but Edward Cottrell eventually settled in Fairfax County, Virginia. Cottrell was the firebreathing secessionist who was imprisoned in Fort McHenry in 1861 for "Corresponding with Rebels." After refusing to take the Oath of Allegiance to secure his release, Federal authorities, not knowing how to respond, eventually released him unconditionally, and he enlisted in the Chesapeake Artillery at Richmond in June 1862. He served with the unit until wounded two years later and refused to leave the company until, after eight days, the nature of his wound forced him to seek hospitalization; he did not return to duty for five months. Cottrell became a schoolteacher after the war, and no doubt his history lessons were enhanced with the exploits of the Chesapeake. He married Mary Eliza Money in 1882 when he was forty-seven years old and was widowed nine years later. In 1894, at age fifty-eight, he married again to Emma Buckley. He was active in the John Q. Marr Camp of the United Confederate Veterans in Fairfax and wrote two articles in *Confederate Veteran* magazine on the battery's participation at Fort Gregg. Cottrell died on October 30,

1910, at age seventy-five; he had never taken the Oath of Allegiance, remaining "unreconstructed" to the end.[3]

William M. Williams of Queen Anne's County had enlisted in the company at Richmond in November 1862 for the war. He served in all of the subsequent campaigns, skirmishes, and battles of the Chesapeake without an absence of any kind, in spite of a face wound received at Gettysburg. Williams surrendered at Appomattox and registered at the office of the provost marshall general in Washington. He then walked out the door and disappeared into history among the nearly 5,000 other William Williams living in the United States at the time.[4]

George Maccubbin met with considerably more difficulty during his journey home. A thirty-year-old land agent from Queen Anne's County, married and with four children, he had made his way to Heathsville in late January 1862, in company with a group including John Grason, John Embert, Phil Harrison, Benjamin Young, Watson Webb, and Isaac Blunt; all enlisted in the Chesapeake. To cross the Potomac River, the men confiscated the sloop *Sally* in St. Mary's County and forced its captain to take them across the river. Maccubbin had served in the company without absence until he was granted a discharge in March 1865. The sloop captain reported the incident to Federal authorities, however, and when Maccubbin reported to the provost marshall general in Baltimore on March 31, he was arrested and charged with piracy. He was acquitted in June and released when it was determined "he did not Desert but was honorably discharged [from] the Rebel Service—his term of service having expired." He was allowed to return to Queen Anne's County. Maccubbin later moved to Mathews County, Virginia, where he died as the result of a homicide in 1870.[5]

The Prisoners of War

It took former Pvt. John Gardner longer to get home. The carpenter from Queen Anne's County had enlisted at Richmond in November 1862, along with Thomas Everngam and William Tarbutton, after the three had been drafted into the US army. He participated in all the company's campaigns until he was captured at Fort Gregg, where his friend Everngam was killed. Gardner was confined at Point Lookout and released on June 12, 1865, when he returned to Queen Anne's County. He became a farmer, was married, and had two children. Gardner died in 1900 and was eulogized by Chris Lynch: "Among all these brave hearts there was none that beat with higher courage or in stricter time with duty...His was a life quiet, unassuming, and obscure (except for those troublous times), yet such a life it was that all who knew him well could stand up and say, 'this were a man.'"[6]

Pvt. John Torrington had also been taken as a prisoner of war. A nineteen-year-old wood turner from Baltimore, he had originally enlisted in a South Carolina artillery unit at Castle Pinckney, Charleston, South Carolina, even before the war started in March 1861. He served in the Charleston Harbor defenses until transferring to the 4th Maryland Artillery in June 1864, at the formation of the Maryland Line. Torrington served in the battery throughout the Petersburg campaign and was a member of the cooking detail sent to the Gregg house on April 2, 1865, so was not part of the defense of Fort Gregg. He was captured as a prisoner of war by Federal troops the next day in Petersburg, along with Pvt. Francis McCummins, and both were sent to Hart Island prison in New York City. Conditions there were harsh and Torrington developed a severe case of chronic diarrhea from which he died on June 10, just ten days before McCummins took the Oath of Allegiance and was released. He was buried in Grave #2971 at Cypress Hills National Cemetery in Brooklyn, the last casualty incurred by the company and the only member to die as a prisoner of war.[7]

The Captains

Walter Chew, the company's last captain, was also a prisoner of war when the company surrendered its last gun at Appomattox. Following his capture at Fort Gregg he had been sent to Johnson's Island, a prisoner of war camp for officers in Sandusky Bay in Lake Erie. He took the Oath of Allegiance on June 2 and returned home to Georgetown, DC. Ironically, the former Confederate commander earned his living as a clerk in the capitol building in Washington. He married but had no children.[8]

Chew remained in touch with his former comrades, endorsing Bedney Spencer's application to the Maryland Line Confederate Soldiers' Home and probably others. John Richardson gave Chew the battery's battle flag retained at Appomattox; it was a treasured possession. While touring the Petersburg battlefield decades after the war, Chew came upon another relic of the battery's service: Capt. Brown's wooden trunk pressed into service as a limber chest following the Battle of Gettysburg: "It was carried into every battle for the rest of the conflict. Lost at the fall of Petersburg, it showed up in a shop there a quarter of a century later! It was secured by the Chews."[9]

Chew led a peaceful life after the war. He refused to become embroiled in a postwar controversy over which units had fought at Fort Gregg, even though in an article published in the Southern Historical Society Papers he was challenged by former Lt. Col. William Owen, who claimed the only artillerymen in Fort Gregg comprised McElroy's section of the Washington Artillery: "I have never seen any statement from…Chew claiming the credit of the action of the artillery at Fort Gregg, or that it was his battery that was entitled to the credit of the gallantry shown; but as by his silence he has accepted the verdict due a brother officer, will he not give us his account of the defence of Fort Gregg?" Chew preferred to let his record and that of the company speak for him. He died in 1900 at age fifty-eight, and was buried at Oak Hill Cemetery in Washington.[10]

The Chesapeake's first captain, Joseph Forrest, left the company after he was defeated for re-election at the company's reorganization in May 1862. He had moved his family and slaves to Virginia, but with the conflict coming in such close proximity decided to move farther south. After the war he applied for a pardon to President Andrew Johnson and his application outlined his wartime experiences:

> in February 1861 he found himself largely indebted to various creditors, and to an amount nearly equal to the value of his real estate, and being the owner of fifty six slaves, he removed them to the Southern States with the hope of relieving himself of his large indebtedness—that soon after their removal, the rebellion broke out and the undersigned removed his family to the State of Louisiana and that whilst there […] on the 24th of April 1863 he left his home with his family, and travelled as far as New Iberia in the Parish of St. Martin, La. with the intention of returning to Maryland, but that owing to the unsafe condition of the route and troubled state of the country, he was unable to procure a passport at this time, and being promised protection and advised by the United States Provost Marshall […] to return to his plantation, which he did […] after the evacuation of the country by the Federal troops, he removed his family to the State of Texas and there resisted the right of the rebel government to force him into its military service, and did so successfully […] he was unable at any time to leave the State of Texas and so soon as your Excellency's Proclamation of Amnesty was issued, he took the oath prescribed and has returned to Maryland and as the undersigned comes within the exception of your Excellency's Proclamation, he most respectfully asks your Excellency

> for a special, unconditional pardon, so that he may enjoy all the rights and privileges of a loyal citizen of the United States residing in Maryland.

Forrest returned to St. Mary's County to find that, although his wife and children had been banished from Maryland by Federal authorities for being Southern sympathizers, his two plantations had been declared "abandoned" in May 1864, and appropriated to be run as government farms for the Freedman's Bureau. He probably applied for a pardon as a way to re-acquire his land. Forrest received his pardon in fall 1865, but did not recover his property until March 1866. He and his wife Henrietta eventually had twelve children, only seven of whom lived to adulthood. Debts continued to plague him, and one of his plantations and the family home "Sandgates" was ordered into receivership in 1878. Forrest and his family moved to his other plantation, Cole's Farm. He continued to provide leadership to the community. As president of the trustees of the Confederate Cemetery at Point Lookout, Forrest led the fundraising for the Maryland Monument dedicated there in 1876. Described as "a gentleman of the old school," he died at Cole's Farm in 1889 at age sixty-seven and was buried in the cemetery at St. Francis Xavier Roman Catholic Church in Newtown.[11]

Capt. Billy Brown's brother, Sgt. Phil Brown, never returned to the company after he was wounded at Gettysburg and subsequently captured near Hagerstown. Following his recovery he was exchanged in late December 1863, joined the Confederate Signal Corps in February 1864, and served as a signal officer on a blockade runner. Brown returned to Baltimore at the end of the war and took the Oath of Allegiance there in May 1865.[12]

If he hadn't heard of it already, surely Brown's family told him of a controversial incident that occurred during his brother Billy's funeral that underscored the enmity that existed between occupying Federals and Southern sympathizers in the city. Brown's father had arranged to have the captain's body removed from its initial burying place at the Weible farm near Gettysburg and sent to Baltimore for re-interment at Greenmount Cemetery. As it

Postwar view of Cole's Farm, one of Joseph Forrest's plantation homes. Forrest died here in 1889. *Courtesy of Debi Burt*

was reported in the *Baltimore Gazette* on August 3, 1863:

> The friends of the deceased were invited, through the press, to attend the funeral... at the cemetery. The father, with a number of acquaintances, repaired to the spot at the appointed hour, when the body was removed to the cemetery chapel. Here [...] when the funeral service [...] was gone through [...] the coffin was then carried to the burial lot, and deposited in the ground. After this last rite had been performed and whilst those present were about leaving the cemetery, a military guard apperred at the gate, the officer in command stating that his orders were to arrest all parties attending the funeral. The attendants, to the number of nineteen, were then taken under escort to the Gilmor House [Hotel], and placed in a room in the second story [...]. The gentlemen arrested were kept under guard until about nine o'clock [...]. The gentlemen were dismissed to appear before the authorities at ten o'clock today.

Brown's body had allegedly been buried in a Confederate uniform, and it was only after the undertaker reported it was a gray cloth that covered the body that the participants were released. The men were invited to take the Oath of Allegiance but all declined.[13]

Phil Brown entered the ministry, and served as the rector of Christ Church in Cooperstown, New York. He later was vicar of Trinity Parish in New York City for nearly thirty-five years. He married and had eight children. It was the fun-loving Brown whom Jacob Cook later recalled in winter camp participating in a "little game of draw run by a certain gentleman, now standing high in theological circles [...] indebted to Jack Brian [...] to the lively tune of $50,000, Confederate currency." Brown died on

Bottony Cross worn by Capt. Billy Brown. *Author's collection*

September 15, 1909, at age sixty-seven. His obituary read in part:

> ...a life of intense interest has been, for this world, concluded, and not only close ties of friendship here, but relationships that reached far and wide have been severed [...] his personal character and record was among the most highly esteemed of clergy in the American church [...] Mr. Brown was a southerner [...]. In spite of the protests of his family, being then but nineteen years of age, he enlisted in the Confederate Army, and served under his brother, Capt. William D. Brown, who was in command of a Maryland battery. He was afterward signal officer on a blockade runner flying between Nassau and Chesapeake Bay. During the war he was engaged in thirteen battles.[14]

The Chroniclers

Former Pvt. Jacob Cook had also returned home to Baltimore. The apprentice plumber had enlisted at Machodoc at the battery's formation at age nineteen. Cook had deserted the day after the Chesapeake's horrific action on Benner's Hill and was released from Point Lookout in September 1863. He married and worked as a reading clerk for the

Baltimore City Council. Cook became a highly respected member of the community, serving in the Mt. Vernon chapter of the Grand Lodge of Maryland as well as the Society of the Army and Navy of the Confederate States of Maryland veterans' organization, and endorsing applications of his former comrades to the Maryland Line Confederate Soldiers' Home. He was also the most prolific chronicler of the Chesapeake, writing several articles in the *Baltimore Telegram* about the battery's fellow members and the company's service. He died in 1898 at age fifty-seven and was buried at Loudon Park Cemetery.[15]

Another of the company's historians, former Pvt. Chris Lynch, enlisted in the battery in November 1862, at age twenty. He was wounded and captured at Fort Gregg, sent to Point Lookout, and not released until he took the Oath of Allegiance in June 1865. Lynch returned to Queen Anne's County, became a successful farmer, married, and had three sons. He wrote about the Chesapeake's actions at Gettysburg and Fort Gregg in W. W. Goldsborough's *The Maryland Line in the Confederate Army*, as well as compiling the unit roster and casualty list. Lynch also recounted in local newspaper articles his experiences visiting the Gettysburg battlefield after the war, and a brief account of the battery's part in the attack on Fort Gregg. He died in 1905 at age 63 and was buried at Spring Hill Cemetery in Easton.[16]

John Hooff, who corresponded with his aunt Mary Ward and his cousins at Bladensfield, enlisted in the Chesapeake Artillery at Richmond in April 1862, when he was only seventeen years old. He was absent on several occasions because of illness, but served with the company consistently up until March 1865, when he received an appointment as captain and aide-de-camp to Gen. William Pendleton. During the Appomattox Campaign he was one of those that struck out on his own, but was not able to make his way south to join another Confederate army; he was eventually paroled at Harper's Ferry in May 1865. After the war Hooff lived in Baltimore and worked as a wholesale hardware dealer; he married, had two sons, and was a captain in the Maryland National Guard. Later he moved to Pittsburgh, Pennsylvania, and worked as a railroad agent, then settled in Alexandria, Virginia, where he was an active member of the R. E. Lee Camp of the United Confederate Veterans. Hooff became a resident of the Maryland Line Confederate Soldiers' Home and died there on May 7, 1921, at age seventy-six; he was buried at Saint Paul's Cemetery in Alexandria, Virginia.[17]

A diligent correspondent with his family in Richmond, former Sgt. Peter Williams had originally enlisted in the 2nd Company, Richmond Howitzers, in 1861, and was one of the Chesapeake's instructors at Camp Lee in spring 1862. He subsequently transferred to the battery and served with it for a year before transferring back to the Howitzers on July 1, 1863, the day before the Chesapeake's disastrous engagement at Gettysburg. Williams served with the 1st Company of the Howitzers through the remainder of the war and surrendered with them at Appomattox. After the surrender he returned home to Richmond; he later married, had four children, and became a freight agent and superintendent of the Lynchburg division of the James River and Kanawha Canal. Williams died in Lynchburg in 1893 at age forty-nine.[18]

The Youth

Some of the returning veterans of the Chesapeake had given their youth to the Confederate war effort, having enlisted as teenagers, and they returned as men to start their lives anew.

Smith Warrington of Baltimore enlisted with his brother Lewis at Machodoc on January 1, 1862, when not quite sixteen years old. Smith had accompanied Jacob Cook on his successful foraging expedition in the camp of the "Goobers" of Anderson's Georgia brigade after the battle of 1st Fredericksburg.

He served without absence until he was wounded in the face at Gettysburg and captured near Hagerstown, Maryland. Exchanged in February 1865, after the war he moved to Georgetown, Washington, DC, and was employed as a clerk at a lumber yard.[19]

Francis McCummins, a student from Cecil County, was only sixteen years old when he enlisted in the 9th Virginia Cavalry at Fort Lowry in October 1861. After serving in that unit he enlisted in the 4th Maryland Artillery in July 1864 at Petersburg, the company's last enlistee. McCummins was captured at Petersburg the day after the assault on Fort Gregg, and was sent to Hart Island, New York, along with John Torrington. After the war he married and worked as a driver in Washington, DC. He died in 1924 at age sixty-eight; McCummins and his wife Amanda are buried together in the Confederate section of Arlington National Cemetery.[20]

Originally from Kentucky, former Pvt. "E.K." Culver enlisted at Fredericks Hall in April 1864 when he was seventeen years old. He served without absence until the company was ordered to be disbanded and consolidated in March 1865, at which time he deserted. "E.K." was detained at Point Lookout and released that same month when he took the Oath of Allegiance. In June he appeared before the provost marshall general in Washington, DC, claiming to be a member of the 16th Georgia Infantry Regiment, and thereby obtained transportation to Lincolntown, North Carolina; he settled first in Cecil County, then Little Rock, Arkansas. He was married and had three children; when his first wife died he remarried and had seven more children with his second wife. Culver appears to have had an active imagination and a well developed sense of humor: in censuses and city directories through the late 1800s and early 1900s he alternately claimed to be living "at home" in a boarding house and worth what at the time was an astronomical $17,000, a gardener, a laborer, a clerk, a solicitor, a janitor, an attendant at the state insane asylum, and a sheep herder! He died on January 5, 1915, at age sixty-eight, and was buried at Thomas Cemetery in North Little Rock.[21]

Henry Parker was a seventeen-year-old farmhand from St. Mary's County when he enlisted with his brother Thad at Machodoc. The Parker brothers served with the company through all of its operations until the Battle of Gettysburg, where Henry was wounded and Thad was killed. Henry returned to duty in August 1863, and served continuously with the company until March 1865, when he obtained a discharge after three years' service. Parker became a farmer in Amelia County, Virginia, was married in 1868, and with his wife Martha had thirteen children, eight of whom lived beyond infancy. When Martha died he remarried and had another child. He died in 1917 at age seventy-five.[22]

Walter Burke was also seventeen years old when he left his home in Baltimore along with his friends Billy Holtzman and George Goodhand in June 1863. They made their way to Dover, Pennsylvania, and enlisted in the Confederate Army during the Pennsylvania campaign. Burke and Goodhand enlisted in the Chesapeake Artillery. Walter served without absence until February 1865, when he deserted and returned home. But he and Holtzman remained friends; after the war they owned a retail store together on Lexington Street in Baltimore for a short time. Walter eventually moved to Towsontown and became a lawyer, married, and had six children. He died before 1900.[23]

The Displaced

The disruptive influence of the war prevented more than one member of the Chesapeake from returning to Maryland.

George Ewell enlisted in the battery as a sergeant in spring 1862, and was detailed as a nurse to Hospital No. 18 in Richmond that September. He had a talent for medicine and was appointed a hospital steward at a Confederate hospital in Fort Gaines, Georgia, the following January. There he met Ann Wardlaw, and they were married in December 1864. He stayed in Georgia at the close of the war, eventually becoming a druggist in Early County, Georgia, and later moving to Henrico County, Virginia, where he owned a drug store. He was widowed and remarried twice and had several children. Ewell died in December 1914 at age eighty-three and was buried at Blakely City Cemetery in Early County, Georgia.[24]

Thomas Toy was a twenty-three-year-old bookkeeper from Baltimore when he enlisted in the battery in October 1862; he left a wife and two young daughters behind at home in Baltimore. Weeks later, at the battle of 1st Fredericksburg, he received serious gunshot wounds to both legs. He entered a hospital in Richmond and was later transferred to a hospital in Lynchburg, but his recovery was slow, and he did not return to the unit until after Gettysburg. Toy continued to have difficulty with his wounds and was declared unfit for field duty in January 1864; he had to be hospitalized again because of complications in February. He applied to be detailed as a clerk in the Confederate Treasury Department, writing in his application, "I have been in the Army for fifteen months as a private in the Chesapeake Battery, Andrews's Battalion, Johnson's Division, Ewell's Corps, but am unfit for service in consequence of wounds received in both legs at the battle of Fredericksburg. I am twenty four years of age, and an accountant by profession."[25]

Toy had strong recommendations to accompany his application. A friend of the Toy family wrote to Secretary of the Confederate Treasury Christopher G. Memminger:

> It gives me pleasure to call attention to the claims of my young friend Mr. Thomas B. Toy to the office he now seeks. He left a comfortable home and loved ones in Baltimore and entered our army as a private soldier, was in the battle of Fredericksburg, where he was wounded in both legs. After his recovery would allow it he reported to his company for duty where he remained until his health failed him...I have known Mr. Toy's father and family for thirty years—their character & standing in society will justify any commendation the son may now need.[26]

Another wrote of him:

> ...it gives me more than ordinary pleasure to commend his claims to your favourable consideration. Mr. Toy to my own knowledge served the South faithfully in the field until wounded in both legs at the battle of Fredericksburg, from the effects of which he has not yet recovered. He is an accomplished and energetic clerk, and a gentleman of the strictest morals, so that the Government can find no man of better character and higher qualifications for the place to which he aspires....[27]

Toy was detailed to the Confederate Treasury Department in Richmond in February 1864, and served in that capacity until March 1865. At that time he deserted, likely due to pressure from his family because of his father's poor health, and returned to Baltimore. There Federal authorities, as was customary with Confederate deserters from Maryland, paroled him on the condition that he go "north of Philadelphia." Following the death of his father Toy received special permission to remain in Baltimore for the funeral. He then settled in Castleton, New York, with his family and was able to re-establish his career as a bookkeeper. He died during the 1870s at about age forty.[28]

Originally from Baltimore, Pvt. Phil Harrison was a married twenty-nine-year-old clerk who lived in Queen Anne's County when he enlisted for the war at Heathsville in February 1862. He served with the battery until the battle of 2nd Manassas, where he was seriously wounded. Harrison did not return to duty for nearly eight months, but by that time his health was seriously compromised and he had to return to the hospital because of chronic dysentery just five weeks later. He was never able to return to active field duty and was detailed as a clerk to Maj. J. B. Cary, Confederate paymaster in Richmond. Harrison excelled in this role, as Cary requested Phil's permanent assignment in October 1864, writing that he "is an 'Expert' and a very skillful clerk & is absolutely indispensable, at this time, to the prompt official discharge of my duties." Harrison had enlisted in the 3rd Virginia, Local Defense Troops in Richmond, but his dysentery gave him continued difficulty, Cary saying that, "Mr. Harrison was detailed by Gen. Lee, on account of physical disability, under which he has continued to labor, to a greater or less extent, & is, at present, under treatment for his disease."[29]

Phil had received a discharge in late March 1865, but when the city was evacuated following the Federal breakthrough at Petersburg he accompanied the Local Defense Troops on the march to Appomattox, eventually rejoining the company and making his way with Pvts. Charles Tinges and George Rice to Lynchburg, where he was paroled on April 13, 1865. Harrison never settled again in Maryland. After the war he and his wife moved to Louisville, Kentucky, where he worked as a clerk, and still later moved again to Fauquier County, Virginia. He died by 1900 at about sixty years of age.[30]

Disgraced Lt. John Plater never returned to Maryland, either. No doubt wishing to avoid the criticism of Baltimore society, he moved to the remote silver ore mining town of Hamilton, Nevada, and resumed his career in the financial industry as a clerk in a bank. He later managed a bank in Eureka County, and in an industry that required honesty and integrity prospered well. By 1883, he had moved to Los Angeles and became a partner in the Los Angeles County Bank; he later founded Los Angeles Savings Bank and served as its president. He married, and with his wife Sallie moved into an apartment in Los Angeles's posh Baker Block, which was described as "the grandest thing in Southern California, three stories of magnificence." As "the most desirable in the city, with many families of wealth and fashion living there, the Baker Block was the social center of the city. Mrs. Plater, a woman of great charm, was the social leader and dictator of that period."[31]

When Plater recounted his war experiences, he understandably dwelt on his creditable record before Gettysburg. Referred to as "Captain" Plater, he was known to have "served with high honors. He particularly distinguished himself at Fredericksburg." Sallie died in 1906 and Plater retired a few years later. After several years of declining health he died in 1926 at age eighty-six—one of the last surviving members of the company—and was buried in Sacramento City cemetery. He certainly achieved a measure of redemption, eulogized in his obituary as "a pioneer banker, the founder of the city's first savings bank, and a gentleman of the old school of the South."[32]

The Wounded

Some of the soldiers of the Chesapeake had additional difficulties to deal with after they returned home from the war. These were the men who had suffered serious and in some cases crippling wounds, and they demonstrated a remarkable ability to overcome this adversity.

The company's first casualty was Cpl. Robert Jones, an eighteen-year-old farmhand from Talbot County who lost his arm in a training accident in February 1862 just weeks after enlisting while the unit was still in Heathsville, Virginia. Incredibly, he returned to duty following his recovery and was present for the company's muster on March 1. By October 1862 he found the rigors of service more than he could manage, writing to his mother, "I think under my circumstances that I am perfectly right in leaving the field. I have lost my right arm and have been in battle since but I now find a soldier's life to be too hard for me. I have done more than I expected to do, and am now about to leave the field with the proud consolation of having been a Southern Soldier in southern perils." In a recommendation for other duties written a few days after the battle of 1st Fredericksburg, Lt. John Plater wrote of Jones:

> I regard it as due him to state that whilst he continued in the Army the duties imposed upon him were performed with a willingness to which too much praise cannot be given. Having lost his arm soon after enlisting he was at that time entitled to a discharge, but at his request was allowed to continue as a member of the company until the present time....[33]

Jones sought an appointment to the provost marshall's office and was assigned to duty as a clerk there in Richmond. In September 1863, he was commissioned as a 2nd lieutenant and enrolling officer in the 12th Congressional District, CSA. After the war Jones became a lawyer in Easton, Maryland, married, and had two children. In 1868, he moved to Cumberland to establish his own law practice. He died there in November 1879 at age thirty-six and was buried at Rose Hill Cemetery in Cumberland.[34]

At the Battle of Cedar Mountain, August 9, 1862, Pvt. John Shannahan, a student from Easton, was nineteen years old when he received a serious gunshot wound in the thigh during the attack of Prince's Federal brigade, the company's first battle casualty. His recovery took two months, at which point he received a furlough and returned to duty, only to be wounded again at the battle of 2nd Fredericksburg. Shannahan received a discharge in January 1865 after serving three years and returned home, built a house on the Miles River in Royal Oak, married, and raised two sons.[35]

Shannahan had a remarkable career as a businessman after the war. As reported in *Confederate Veteran*, he "constructed and put into operation the first ice plant on the eastern shore of Maryland; later he organized a corporation, of which he was president, for the sinking of artesian wells, which organization...has conducted a most successful business throughout Maryland... His ability along this line made him a prominent engineer for consultation." Shannahan also started a company called the Shannahan & Wrightson Hardware Co., sole agents for Oldsmobile in the area. On September 7, 1901, the *Easton Gazette* reported Shannahan bought the first automobile in the county, a curved dash Oldsmobile runabout, "elegant in appearance, weighing only 550 pounds." It can truly be said that he ushered Talbot County into the twentieth century.[36]

Shannahan died of heart trouble May 20, 1916, at age seventy-four. His obituary read in part: "During his service in the Army John Shannahan was untiring, courageous, and attentive to his duties and won the admiration of all his associates. In his business affairs he showed the same energy, skill and good judgement."[37]

Cpl. Tom Carberry of Baltimore lost his leg when he jumped up on his gun's embrasure to cheer a shot at the battle of 2nd Fredericksburg. He was struck by an artillery projectile that took his left leg off below the knee. A surgeon completed the amputation and Carberry faced a long recovery period. Nearly a year later he requested and received an artificial limb. Although eligible for a disability discharge, he instead retired to the Invalid Corps, where he was assigned as a clerk in the quartermaster's department in Macon, Georgia. He eventually rose to the rank of quartermaster sergeant and was paroled upon taking the Oath of Allegiance at Albany, Georgia, in May 1865.[38]

Pvt. Richard E. Langley was eighteen years old when he enlisted in the battery at

Machodoc on January 1, 1862. Orphaned at an early age, he lived and worked as a farmhand in St. Mary's County at the home of his uncle, a carpenter who owned eleven slaves. At the battle of 2nd Fredericksburg Langley suffered a serious wound in his shoulder from rifle fire. He returned to duty five months later, but his wound continued to give him difficulties. In June 1864, he was hospitalized for over a month because of debility, then again in November because of complications with his wound. He finally retired to the Invalid Corps the next month. He was captured by Federal cavalry near Frederick's Hall in March 1865 and held as a prisoner of war at Point Lookout until he took the Oath of Allegiance in June and was released.[39]

Langley returned to St. Mary's County and worked as a carpenter following the war. He never married, but led an active life, with travels to India, and serving as a county judge of elections. The projectile had never been removed from Langley's wound, and he would suffer for years with suppuration and the discharge of pieces of bone. Remarkably, in 1896—more than thirty-three years after the battle of 2nd Fredericksburg—the bullet worked its way out of his wound. A relieved Langley wrote of the occurrence to his local newspaper, "My long deferred hope is realized, and I have the would-be fatal messenger of death securely preserved. I shall treasure it as an impressive reminder of the days that tried every true Confederate's soul." Richard would live for another sixteen years, dying in 1912 at age sixty-nine.[40]

The Veterans

The former members of the 4th Maryland Artillery endeavored to put the war behind them and quietly build normal lives for themselves and their families.

James T. "Delaware" Moore, a thirty-year-old millwright from Delaware, enlisted in the Chesapeake at Machodoc. He served with the unit through all of its campaigns and battles, as well as taking on extra duty as a blacksmith. Moore obtained a discharge after three years' service and went to Maryland. He worked as a laborer and a carpenter in Montgomery and Baltimore counties; he and his wife Martha raised seven children. Moore died in Gaithersburg in 1920 at age eighty-eight.[41]

Charles Sewall Tinges was born into a Baltimore family of privilege. His father George was a very wealthy commission merchant and banker, with combined property and real estate worth $25,000. Charles was educated at St. James College boarding school in Washington County and worked as a clerk in his father's office. He made his way to Winchester and enlisted there as a private in the Chesapeake Artillery on October 1, 1862, at age twenty-one.[42]

Tinges missed the battle of 1st Fredericksburg because of illness and did not return to the company until early January 1863. He was seriously wounded at Gettysburg and captured at the field hospital at the Stewart farm on July 5. Sent to DeCamp General Hospital on Davids Island, Tinges recovered, was exchanged in early September, and was back with the unit late that year. He served continuously throughout the Overland and Petersburg campaigns until hospitalized in Richmond with measles in March 1865. Tinges was released from the hospital April 2—the same day Richmond was evacuated—and rejoined the company during the Appomattox campaign. When news of the Army of Northern Virginia's surrender was announced he left the unit with several others and made his way as far as Lynchburg, eventually being paroled there on April 13. He took the Oath of Allegiance in Richmond and was given transportation home to Baltimore.[43]

After the war Tinges again lived at his father's home with his other siblings and clerked in his father's office. In 1880, he married and purchased a house on West Lanvale Street in Baltimore; he was an active

Portrait of Pvt. Charles Sewall Tinges, ca. 1885. *Author's collection*

member of the Mount Calvary Episcopal Church in Baltimore, serving as a lay delegate to the diocese's annual convention. By 1900, he had retired and moved to West Lafayette Avenue. Later he opened an office at the Central Savings Bank building and was very successful selling real estate and insurance. Tinges died in Baltimore on November 30, 1918, at age seventy-seven.[44]

As the years passed, veterans' organizations such as the Society of the Army & Navy of the Confederate States in the State of Maryland, and the United Confederate Veterans, among others, became prominent. They attracted many former Confederate soldiers in Maryland, and the former Chesapeakes were no different. An article in the *Baltimore Sun* reported on the massive scope of the ceremonies for the dedication of the monument to the 2nd Maryland Battalion at Gettysburg on November 19, 1883, which demonstrated the number and diversity of veterans' organizations:

> …the first monument marking the position of a Confederate command on the battlefield of Gettysburg, was dedicated yesterday […]. It was erected by the surviving members of the Second Maryland regiment [sic] and their friends, and the dedicatory ceremonies were witnessed by two thousand people, including the members of the Second regiment, the Maryland Line, the Society of the Army and Navy of the Confederate States, the Murray Association, the Ladies' Confederate Memorial Association, Com-

> pany C, First Maryland cavalry, the Fifth Maryland regiment acting as escort, and survivors of the first Maryland infantry, First Maryland artillery, Chesapeake artillery, and a large number of ex-Confederate soldiers from other States, gentlemen and ladies of Baltimore, Frederick and Gettysburg....[45]

Billy Holtzman of Baltimore was an active member of the Society of the Army & Navy of the Confederate States in Maryland. Holtzman and his friends Walter Burke and George Goodhand had enlisted in the Army of Northern Virginia by making their way to Dover, Pennsylvania, during the Pennsylvania Campaign; all three were still in their teens. Billy originally served with the 5th Virginia Cavalry before transferring to the 4th Maryland Artillery at the formation of the Maryland Line. He had narrowly escaped serious injury or death at Fort Gregg when a Federal officer prevented one of his men from striking Holtzman with his musket. Billy was sent to Point Lookout and released in June 1865. After the war Holtzman owned a retail store together with Burke in Baltimore, and then worked as a successful advertising agent. He died on November 4, 1901, at age fifty-eight.[46]

The Ladies' Confederate Memorial Association, formed in 1866, was the first organization dedicated to helping Confederate veterans and preserving Maryland's Confederate history. One of the association's aims was to return to state soil the remains of Maryland Confederate soldiers who had died in service and were buried elsewhere; a committee of Society of the Army & Navy of the Confederate States in Maryland was formed to disburse funds appropriated by the Maryland legislature for this purpose. An area of Loudon Park Cemetery in Baltimore, known as Confederate Hill, was set aside for these burials. In 1873 and 1874, the remains of a number of the Chesapeakes who died during the war were brought to Loudon Park Cemetery. Pvts. Phil Oldner and Thad Parker were re-interred from their graves at Gettysburg, as was Pvt. "Bey" Hopkins from near Hamilton's Crossing at Fredericksburg. Lt. Ben Roberts and Pvts. James Hardesty and young Edward Stansbury were brought back from their resting places at the sites of the hospitals in Virginia where they had died. The *Baltimore Sun* noted the occasion of Roberts's and Hardesty's burials:

> The remains of several Confederate soldiers, which had been brought from the battle fields of Virginia, were reinterred in the Confederate inclosure. These comprised the remains of, [among others...] J.R. Hardesty, Chesapeake artillery [...] B.G. Roberts, Chesapeake artillery, and one unknown. The procession after reaching the place of burial marched around the lots, and after forming around the newly made graves in which the remains had already been deposited, but not filled up, the funeral services took place. Rev. T.U. Dudley, of Christ Episcopal Church, read the impressive burial service of that church, during which he threw a small quantity of dirt into each grave [...]. After the conclusion of the obsequies the flowers not already placed upon the graves were distributed, the band in the meantime playing a dirge.[47]

Former Pvt. Charles F. Dallam was also highly engaged in veterans' activities after the war. The former clerk from Baltimore enlisted in the Chesapeake the day after his twenty-eighth birthday, was wounded at 2nd Fredericksburg and at Gettysburg, had been captured at Fort Gregg, and was sent to Point Lookout prisoner of war camp in St. Mary's County. He was not released until he took the Oath of Allegiance on June 26; as acting sergeant major, he had signed the last morning report at Point Lookout the day before. Charles made his way to Washington, and on reporting

"Confederate Hill" at Loudon Park Cemetery in Baltimore. Several members of the 4th Maryland Artillery are buried there. *Author*

to the provost marshall general was provided with transportation home to Baltimore on the B&O Railroad's Washington branch. Dallam became a partner in an importing business postwar and was later the city clerk. He was also active in the Maryland National Guard, serving in the 5th Regiment of Infantry for twenty-five years and rising to the rank of lieutenant, as well as in the Society of the Army & Navy of the Confederate States in Maryland. He was proud of his service with the Chesapeake Artillery; in an interview after the war he summarized:

> Enlisted as a private in the Chesapeake Artillery, Fourth Maryland Battery, Captain William D. Brown, in the spring of 1862. Was in all the engagements my battery took part in from the First Battle of Fredericksburg to the close of the war. Acted as Provost Guard at Bowling Green, Caroline County, VA, during the winter of 1862 and 1863. Was slightly wounded at the Second Fredericksburg battle and the battle of Gettysburg, but did not leave my command. Was taken prisoner at Fort Gregg April 2, 1865, and sent to Point Lookout where I remained until June 28, 1865 [sic]. Shortly before being released acted as Sergeant Major of the pen.[48]

He became a resident of the Maryland Line Confederate Soldiers' Home in July 1898. Possibly his wounds had disabled him; his application, endorsed by former members of the company Jacob Cook and Billy Holtzman, stated he was unable to provide support for himself because of "physical disability," and that his two daughters had been adopted by his sister. Dallam worked as a clerk at the home. An entry in the home's logbook for February 13, 1913, reads, "Charles F. Dallam our late Comrade died this morning about 5 or 6 o'clock. He was stricken in this office suddenly yesterday morning at breakfast time 7.30 o'clock & never rallied any great deal though he rallied sufficiently to recognize relatives & friends." He was seventy-nine years old.[49]

The Maryland Line Confederate Soldiers' Home

As the veterans aged, it became apparent there was a need to provide assistance to those who were not able to care for or support themselves. The Maryland Line Confederate Soldiers' Home was established in Pikesville in 1888. Governed by the Association of the Maryland Line, its purpose was to provide a care facility for indigent and disabled Confederate veterans of Maryland. Eventually at least ten former members of the 4th Maryland Artillery would come to reside there.[50]

Former Pvt. Benjamin Young was the first of the Chesapeakes to take up residence at the home. He was living in Alexandria, Virginia, at the start of the war and enlisted on February 1, 1862, at Heathsville at age forty-two; he was one of the group that had commandeered the sloop *Sally* in Queen Anne's County to cross the Potomac. Young served without any absences until he obtained a discharge in March 1865. He said of his service: "Born in Prince George's County, Md. Enlisted February 1862 at Heathsville, Va., as a private in the Chesapeake Artillery, Fourth Maryland. Served until January 1865 at the time I was discharged at Petersburg, Va."[51]

Young applied for residence at the home on August 31, 1891, at age seventy-two because of "Physical Disability." He had been a farmer in Kent County, and his nearest relation was his sister in Rock Hall, Maryland. A notation in the logbook on March 31, 1905, read: "…Our late old brother Benjamin Young who had been failing a long time died

The Maryland Line Confederate Soldier's Home.
Author's collection

at 1.30 A.M. Interment next Monday." Young was buried at Loudoun Park Cemetery; he was eighty-six years old.[52]

Bedney Spencer applied to the home on January 29, 1895. He was originally from Queen Anne's County, but lived in Anne Arundel County in the years immediately before the war, working for his uncle, a wealthy lawyer who owned four slaves; his cousin was an officer in the US Army. Spencer had enlisted at Richmond in April 1862, at age twenty-three, and served in all of the battery's campaigns without absence until he surrendered with it at Appomattox. Postwar he married Nannie Tilghman and was a farmer for many years in Church Hill, in Queen Anne's County. His application, endorsed by "W. Scott Chew Capt 4th Md Arty, C.S.A.," stated he was unable to support himself because of sickness; he was only fifty-seven years old and his wife still lived in Church Hill. He recalled of his service: "Born in Kent County, Md. Enlisted spring of 1862 at Richmond as a private in the Chesapeake Battery, Fourth Maryland Artillery for 3 years. Reenlisted in same command for the war. Participated in both battles of Fredericksburg… Harpers Ferry, Gettysburg, and all other actions in which my command was engaged. Paroled at Appomattox when General Lee surrendered." Spencer died at the home on July 31, 1900, at age sixty-two; his funeral service was held there, and he was buried in Queenstown. His plain, unadorned headstone reads simply:

> Bedingfield H. Spencer
> Born June 26, 1838
> Died July 31, 1900
> Chesapeake Battery[53]

George Douglas "Doug" McClure was a twenty-two-year-old clerk from Baltimore when he enlisted in the Chesapeake Artillery at Fort Lowry in April 1862. It was McClure who Jacob Cook recalled as having a close call at the battle of 2nd Fredericksburg, lying down in an artillery embrasure moments before the bucket he had been standing in front of was struck by a bullet. He was captured at the Battle of Payne's Farm, November 27, 1863, and spent the rest of the war at Fort Delaware; he took the Oath of Allegiance on May 5, 1865, and was released. McClure applied for residence to the home on January 24, 1897, at age fifty-seven, because he was "out of imployment." At the time he lived with his wife in Baltimore. McClure proudly remembered of his service:

> Born at Bunker Hill, Berkeley County, Va., February 25, 1840. Enlisted March 1862 at Fort Lowry on the Rappahannock River in the Chesapeake battery, Captain Forest in command, where I remained during the war. Cedar Mountain was the first engagement I was in. Then came Harpers Ferry, the Second battle of Manassas, Fredericksburg, Chancellorsville […] Gettysburg. When we fell back from Pennsylvania was ordered to the Wilderness […].[54]

McClure suffered from declining health during his years at the home, and by June 1905, at age sixty-five, was described as "a poor fellow, not long to live." The home's logbook entry for July 20, 1906, read:

> …In the afternoon six more Members of this Home were detailed to act as pallbearers to our late Brother G.D. McClure who died yesterday at the homeopathic Hospital on Mount St. Balto. He was interred in the Confederate Lot of Loudon Park Cemetery Rev. Wm M. Dame Pastor of Memorial Church Balto officiating clergyman.[55]

Henry Willson of Queen Anne's County was not yet twenty-one years old when he enlisted in the company at Heathsville on March 1, 1862. He suffered a serious shell wound to his right knee at Gettysburg that affected the flexor tendons. Henry was absent from the unit for nearly eight months, returning in February 1864, and serving until the end of December that year, when he transferred to the 1st Maryland Cavalry. By 1920, he was a resident of the home, saying of his service: "Born in Queen Anne's County, Md. Enlisted January 1862 at Heathsville, Va., as a private in the Fourth Maryland Artillery. Transferred December 1864 to Company B, First Maryland Cavalry. Paroled at Richmond June 6, 1865. Wounded at Gettysburg by a shell in the knee." Willson died there on May 18, 1923, at age eighty-two—one of the last surviving members of the company—and was buried at Loudon Park Cemetery.[56]

Vincent Green, eleven months older than his friend John Green, was nicknamed "Big," while John was known as "Little." They were farm laborers, Vincent from Baltimore County and John from Dorchester County. At twenty and nineteen years old, respectively, they had enlisted in the battery for the war at Machodoc on January 1, 1862, and came to be two of the most stalwart soldiers in the company. "Big" Green was seriously wounded at 1st Fredericksburg and "Little" was wounded three times during the course of the war. "Big" Green remembered his service:

> Born in Baltimore County, Md. Enlisted...at Machoda Creek [sic] on the Potomac River in the Chesapeake or Fourth Maryland Artillery. Was engaged in [...] Fredericksburg, Chancellorsville, Second Manassas, Gettysburg, Warrenton Springs, Mine Run, [...] and other actions in which my command took part. Wounded at Fredericksburg in left leg above the knee by a minie ball [...].

Both friends received discharges in January 1865, following three years' service. After the war "Big" Green returned to Baltimore County as a farm laborer; by 1900 he was living at the Maryland Line Home. "Little" Green eventually moved to Baltimore City, became a stationary engineer, was married, and had three children. He had entered the home by 1910. "Big" Green died on February 16, 1919, at age seventy-seven, and was buried at Loudon Park Cemetery. "Little" Green was one of the last two surviving members of the Chesapeake Artillery, passing on June 12, 1928, at age eighty-five, and was also buried at Loudon Park Cemetery.[57]

The Chesapeake in Remembrance

John Shafer's life embodied many of these postwar experiences. He was nearly twenty-eight years old and a merchant from Bel Air, in Harford County, when he enlisted as quartermaster sergeant with the company at Machodoc. At the Battle of Cedar Mountain he advanced to the Cedars position with Capt. Brown's forward gun detachment. During the subsequent Federal infantry attack Shafer received a serious gunshot wound across his face, losing his left eye and impairing the sight of his right eye. It was not until the following April that he was able to take on light duties as a nurse at a hospital in Richmond, and he was discharged for disability in May 1863.[58]

Unwilling to take the Oath of Allegiance as a requirement for returning to Maryland, Shafer instead made his way to South Carolina, where he taught school and married. He then moved with his wife and two stepdaughters to Mecklenburg County, North Carolina, where he was a successful farmer and raised four more children. Postwar he was an active member of United Confederate Veterans Camp 382 of Mecklenburg County. Shafer also worked as a railroad stationmaster. In his later years he lived with his son in Macon, Georgia.[59]

Shafer delighted in relating stories about his life and experiences with the battery, and was prone to embellishment to enhance them. He claimed he was born in Valley

Forge, Pennsylvania, though he was born in Harford County, Maryland. He liked to say he and John Wilkes Booth were childhood playmates and that Booth was a "handsome and lovable boy"; although the Booths did build a summer home in Bel Air, at the time Booth was thirteen years old and Shafer was seventeen and working in the hotel his family owned. Shafer stressed that his brother Daniel C. Shafer fought opposite him in the Union army during the Civil War; no soldier of that name had served in any Maryland unit on either side. He elevated his exploits during the war to heroic status and promotion well into the commissioned officer ranks as captain and major. Although he had never advanced beyond the rank of quartermaster sergeant, he was referred to by his comrades in UCV Camp 382 and the citizens of Macon as "Major Shafer."[60]

Shafer died on August 21, 1929, at age ninety-five, and was buried at Elmwood Cemetery in Charlotte, North Carolina. He was the last surviving member of the company, and as he passed away so, too, did the Chesapeake Artillery, 4th Maryland Light Artillery Battery, pass into history.[61]

During their time in the field as a full strength battery, the men of the Chesapeake Artillery established themselves as one of the most effective and reliable of the Army of Northern Virginia's 2nd Corps. As Jacob Cook wrote of the company, "Maryland may well be proud of such sons…this splendid Maryland Battery, composed, as it was, of such splendid material," and Chris Lynch referred to it as "the famous 'Chesapeake Battery,' which served with signal glory throughout the civil war." But their record was not consequent on fading postwar memories and hyperbole. During the war the company was consistently cited for its bravery and effectiveness, and its esprit de corps reflected this. As Pvt. Thomas Mummey recalled in 1864: "The 'Chesapeake' took part in all the battles fought by Jackson's Corps—never for a day was it with the 'Reserve Art[illery],' and I am proud to say…I was always with it." A few weeks before his death at Gettysburg, Capt. Brown wrote, "our battery has made its mark from the 'Cedar Mountain' to Fredericksburg. I am proud of my command & would not relinquish it for a regiment." Well might Lynch have summarized the unit's deeds: "The history, written and unwritten, of the manly privates and splendid officers of Chesapeake Battery challenges yet the admiration of mankind and lends a lustrous halo to the memory […]."[62]

APPENDIX A

Myths

There are several stories about the Chesapeake Artillery that originally appeared in a number of primary sources and have since been widely repeated in modern histories involving the unit. Although these stories—promulgated by veterans of the company themselves—make for interesting reading, they have no basis in fact.

How the Battery Obtained Its Parrott Guns
Pvt. Jacob Cook wrote a partial history of the Chesapeake Artillery that was published in the *Baltimore Telegram* after the war and sometime before 1879. The document is included in publisher S. Z. Ammen's scrapbook *Maryland Troops in the Confederate Army from Original Sources*. In relating events during the Battle of Cedar Mountain, August 9, 1862, Cook wrote:

> At Cedar Mountain Capt. Brown, with the [rifled] gun detachment, was opposed to a Federal battery. His detachment did such excellent service on that hotly contested field, that Capt. Cushing, of the Federal battery (2d [sic] U.S. Artillery), when captured, requested that his four beautiful ten-pound Parrotts should be handed over to the brave men who, with one gun, had so ably withstood him during the engagement. His letter embodying this request, was read to the boys on the following day, together with a highly complimentary order from Gen. Early, conveying the guns to our company.[1]

William W. Goldsborough repeated this story in his 1900 edition of *The Maryland Line in the Confederate Army*. Goldsborough borrowed material from veterans of the units to compile his history of Maryland troops and used Cook's history as well:

> ...so well did the Chesapeake battery acquit itself in this engagement that General Early complimented the men by presenting them with Cushing's regular battery of four ten-pound Parrotts captured in that battle, thus enabling them to discard the old smooth-bores that had prevented the battery from participating more conspicuously in other engagements.[2]

Brown did move forward with a detachment of the battery to an advanced position at Cedar Mountain along with a section of Dement's Maryland battery, but it was a three-inch Ordnance rifle that was used, not a Parrott rifle. The total complement of guns the battery had at the time of the Cedar Mountain battle consisted of two six-pound smoothbore cannon and a twelve-pound howitzer in addition to the three-inch rifle.[3]

Alonzo Cushing was a lieutenant at the time of Cedar Mountain, having just graduated from West Point the previous year. Although he later commanded the 4th United States Artillery, Battery A, Cushing was in charge of only a two-gun section of that unit temporarily assigned to Joseph M. Knap's Independent Pennsylvania Battery E at Cedar Mountain; he was not captured in the battle. Knap's battery was armed with six ten-pound Parrotts but did not lose any guns, as Knap outlined in his report of the battle: "I was forced to leave two caissons on the field, empty and disabled, one of which has been recovered. One gun was disabled late in the action by a cannon-shot, but was brought off the field."[4]

In his report of the battle at Cedar Mountain, Col. Stapleton Crutchfield, chief of artillery for Jackson's command, makes no mention of the capture of any Parrotts in the battle: "We captured one 12-pounder Napolean (spiked) and carriage and caisson, with two other caissons and a limber, all of which were brought off. The gun and caisson were sent to Richmond, one caisson exchanged into Captain Poague's battery, and the other caisson and limber also sent to Richmond." George W. Booth, formerly an officer in the 1st Maryland Infantry Regiment and an aide to Gen. Richard S. Ewell at Cedar Mountain, echoed Crutchfield's report, summarizing Federal losses as heavy, "including one piece of artillery and some 5000 small arms."[5]

The first mention of the Chesapeake Artillery ever using Parrott rifles is in Brig. Gen. Jubal A. Early's report of the 2nd Manassas campaign, outlining the action at Warrenton Springs on August 23, 1862: "...I sent two Parrott guns from Brown's battery to the assistance of Robertson's pieces, which were of short range, and a brisk cannonading was kept up until near sundown." This suggests the battery received two Parrott rifles to replace their three smoothbores while Jackson's command was at Gordonsville following the battle at Cedar Mountain, prior to the start of the 2nd Manassas campaign. It is probable they received this upgraded ordnance in recognition of their performance at Cedar Mountain, generating an element of truth to the story.[6]

Certainly the battery had only two Parrott guns by the close of the Maryland Campaign, as a summary of armament for the artillery of the Army of Northern Virginia dated September 20 states that the Chesapeake was armed with two Parrotts and one 3-inch

10-pound Parrott field rifle. *Author*

rifle. Moreover, Crutchfield made a very detailed account of guns and equipment replaced or exchanged from the captures at Harper's Ferry with no mention of any new ordnance assigned to the Chesapeake Artillery at that time.[7]

The Chesapeakes did not receive an additional two Parrotts until May 1863, following the Battle of 2nd Fredericksburg. Sgt. Peter Williams wrote to his aunt on May 21, "I have had to be running about getting ammunition and getting horses, etc., as we have just gotten two more Parrott Guns for the battery. We have now 4 ten pounder Parrott Guns." Their armament in the subsequent Pennsylvania Campaign consisted of these four Parrott rifles.[8]

The genesis of this story appears to come from within the ranks of the 1st Maryland Artillery, Dement's Battery, which was also part of Courtney's Battalion. At Cedar Mountain a detachment of this unit advanced with two Napoleons, along with Brown and his three-inch rifle, and kept up an effective fire from this position. According to the memoirs of Pvt. Jonathan Thomas Scharf of Dement's Battery:

> We drove the Yankees from their guns and they left one on the field and we took possession of it. The next day it belonged to a Maryland Co. Captain [Clermont L.] Best from Williamsport, Maryland, the lieutenant of the piece, left a note directed to the officer commanding the two guns, complimenting him upon his accurate firing and distinctive shots. The letter was brought to Captain Dement by General Ewell.[9]

This incident is also included in the chapter on the 1st Maryland Battery in the 1900 edition of Goldsborough's book: "So terrible and accurate was the fire of the First that the battery to which it was opposed was literally cut to pieces, and fell into the hands of the infantry. In a limber chest was found a note signed by a Lieutenant, which read thus: 'Take this gun, and make as good use of it as I have.'"[10]

Scharf's memoirs were not published until 1992, so were not in circulation when Goldsborough's book was published. Scharf was a prolific writer and historian, and since he is the only source for this incident, it is almost certain he authored the 1st Maryland Artillery's history in Goldsborough's book, using his memoirs as the basis for the narrative. However, the occurrence is unconfirmed. John William Ford Hatton, also a private in the 1st Maryland Battery at the time of Cedar Mountain, makes no mention of it in his memoirs, which were based on a diary he kept during the war. It is possible that Scharf confused the events at Cedar Mountain with those of the Seven Days battles around Richmond, where the 1st Maryland Artillery traded their 6-pound smoothbores for four Napoleons captured from the Federals.[11]

The Chesapeake replaced their three smoothbore guns with two Parrotts sometime between August 12, when Jackson's command returned to Gordonsville, and August 16, when the Second Manassas campaign began. It is highly probable the Chesapeakes received the two Parrott rifles in recognition of their excellent performance at Cedar Mountain, and this is consistent with Cook's version of events. Moreover, since the unit had performed so well, it was advantageous from a military standpoint to improve an efficient battery's range and firepower.

It is unknown how this incident involving the 1st Maryland Artillery grew to become the myth that the Chesapeake Artillery was awarded four Parrott rifles captured at Cedar Mountain. It may have been a camp rumor involving Dement's Battery that grew in proportion over the years and somehow became attached to the 4th Maryland Artillery, or was remembered incorrectly by members of the company. Cook himself admitted that "this rambling account is taken wholly from memory." Moreover, it could be that Cook embellished the story to make for more interesting reading of his article.[12]

A Fatal Last Shot

At Harper's Ferry the battery crossed the Shenandoah River, pushed their guns up a newly cut road to a shelf on Loudoun Heights, and took a position on the east side of the town. There, along with Dement's, Latimer's, and Garber's batteries, they fired directly into the rear of the Federal position, contributing to the capitulation of the garrison by its commander, Col. Dixon S. Miles. Shortly after a white flag was raised Miles was mortally wounded by one of the last artillery rounds fired, and died the next day. In Goldsborough's chapter on the Chesapeake briefly describing the action at Harper's Ferry on September 15, 1862, he says: "… fiercely those guns were worked that day, and one of the last shells fired by the battery cost General Miles his life."[13]

Although there is a distinct possibility the battery did fire the fatal shot, this story also appears to be apocryphal. It is highly unlikely the Chesapeakes could have known at the time that any particular shot had killed Miles, or that any of the Federals in Harper's Ferry could have known which battery fired the fatal shot. Members of the unit would not even have known that Miles had been wounded until after the battery had entered Harper's Ferry, since it was retained there to refit and exchange horses. Although it is possible soldiers of the company could have believed one of them fired the shot, it would have been highly speculative.

Visibility in the Harper's Ferry area that morning was quite limited, owing to fog and considerable battle smoke from the artillery exchange. Pvt. John Hooff, in a letter to his aunt Mary Ward, refers to this directly, "The smoke was so thick around us when the flag was hoisted that we did not know anything about it untill our Gen sent us the order to cease firing."[14]

In the same letter Hooff refers to Miles's wounding, but significantly makes no mention that the company's fire was in any way connected to this:

> […] in about a half or 3 quarters of an hour they hoisted the white flag and surrendered unconditionally. Gen Miles who commanded the Yankees was [killed] just as […] the white flag was being hoisted, when our Gen sent us an order to cease fireing our Captain could hardly restrain our boys of sending them another shot, but out of humanity for the retches they refrained from doing so.[15]

It is apparent no discussion of which battery made the fatal shot occurred at the time, as no contemporary accounts by members of other artillery units refer to it, regardless of their position on the field. Cook made no mention of it in his article in the *Baltimore Telegram*, leaving the action at Harper's Ferry out of his narrative entirely. Similarly, Pvt. John William Ford Hatton of the 1st Maryland Artillery, which was also in position on Loudoun Heights near the Chesapeake, leaves Harper's Ferry out of his memoirs as well. Accounts by members of Confederate artillery units on other parts of the field also fail to make mention of any battery being deemed responsible for the shot that killed Miles. In his postwar reminiscences, Pvt. Clarence Fonerden of Carpenter's Virginia battery made no mention of the fatal shot in his discussion of Harper's Ferry; this battery was positioned opposite Bolivar Heights to the south. Similarly, Pvt. Edward E. Moore, serving with the 1st Rockbridge Artillery northwest of the town, mentions Miles's death, but not any battery being credited with it.[16]

As with the myth of the Parrott rifles, this story also appears to have its roots within Dement's Battery. Pvt. Jonathan Scharf of that unit recalled in his memoirs, "we saw a large group of officers passing along the road and we fired, and it happened a shot from Corporal Scott's gun struck in the crowd, and it was the shot from his gun that took the leg from General Miles…" It is possible the men of Dement's Battery saw a group of officers and fired at them, but it could not have been a group that included Miles; he was on foot at the time of his wounding. Considering the poor visibility at the time, it is unlikely the gunners would have been able to distinguish any individual person or riders, especially taking into account Hooff's description from a position adjacent to Dement's unit. If they did see a group of officers, it could only have been early in the battle before smoke obscured the landscape, a further indication that it could not have been Miles.[17]

Scharf is the only source for this myth, and he may have told the tale to Goldsborough, who then confused which unit it pertained to and repeated it as he understood it in his book. Based on a practical consideration of the factors operative at Harper's Ferry at the time the story appears to be mere hyperbole on the part of Scharf.

APPENDIX B

Actions at the Battle of Second Manassas

It is difficult to determine the positions and actions of the Chesapeake Artillery at the battle of Second Manassas during August 28–29 and 30, 1862. The battery was engaged on each of the three days as reflected by casualties, but their mention in the official records for this time period is nearly absent. In his official report of the battle at Second Manassas, Col. Stapleton Crutchfield, chief of artillery for Jackson's wing, makes no mention of six of the twenty-one batteries under his command—over one-quarter of the total—with Brown's battery included among the six. His reporting for each of the three days of the battle varies: he mentions only four of the total batteries under his charge by name for August 28, ten for August 29, and a different ten batteries for August 30. Further, Maj. A.R. Courtney, battalion commander for the Chesapeake, did not file a report for the Second Manassas campaign. Maj. Gen. Richard S. Ewell was severely wounded in the knee on August 28, losing his left leg, and also did not make a report of the campaign; neither did his replacement, Brig. Gen. Alexander R. Lawton, who was seriously wounded at Sharpsburg a little over two weeks later. By applying participant accounts of known locations and actions of the battery in this time frame to other activities of the artillery of Jackson's command, the Chesapeake's part in these battles can be determined with a high degree of certainty.[1]

August 28

Through confusion in marching orders, Jackson's divisions marched too far east of Groveton from Manassas Junction in the morning, eventually concentrating on Matthews Hill, on the old First Manassas battleground. They then marched west along an unfinished railroad bed with Brig. Gen. William B. Talliaferro's division in the lead, followed by Ewell's division and then Maj. Gen. A.P. Hill's last. When the column halted in the woods and faced south toward the Warrenton Turnpike this put Ewell's division in Jackson's center. Although the artillery of Jackson's command was initially concentrated near Sudley Mill on the Confederate left, at the opening of the battle on August 28, Crutchfield ordered the various battalions to rejoin their respective divisions.[2]

During the first day's battle on August 28, historians Alan Gaff and John Hennessy place the Chesapeake Artillery in the vicinity of Lt. Asher W. Garber's Staunton Artillery, also of Courtney's battalion, in Jackson's center near the intersection of the railroad bed with the Groveton-Sudley Road on Stony Ridge. Stony Ridge was a rise immediately behind the railroad bed and an ideal artillery position. Jackson, who after reconnoitering his right had joined Ewell's division, personally ordered Garber's battery into action from this point. The Chesapeake also went into action here shortly after the infantry fight started; Goldsborough recounts Jackson watched the battery approvingly at this time and then peremptorily ordered them back into action when they paused to cheer him. The Chesapeake engaged Capt. J. A. Reynolds's Battery L, 1st New York Light Artillery,

Second Manassas battlefield, looking north at the intersection of the Groveton-Sudley Road and Warrenton Turnpike. On August 28, from Stony Ridge in the center background, the Chesapeake Artillery engaged Reynolds' Federal battery located here, and on the thirtieth advanced toward the camera position to take position just east of here. *Author*

which was positioned 1,800 yards to the south at the intersection of the Groveton-Sudley Road and Warrenton Turnpike. Lt. John Breck of Reynolds's battery described the position of the Confederate batteries as being at "the Groveton and Sudley Road, in the neighbourhood of the independent line of the Manassas Railroad, posted in a piece of woods." This would place Brown's battery in front of Stony Ridge at the Groveton-Sudley Road. Garber described the position as in an "open field on a little knoll," which Goldsborough indicated gave the battery "an advantageous position."[3]

The company incurred two casualties in this action.[4]

August 29

Crutchfield reported that Federal attacks on Jackson's right were renewed in the morning, "while our troops occupied pretty generally the same position." He mentions only three batteries as exceptions that changed positions during the course of the battle, and every one of the thirteen other batteries Crutchfield mentions on multiple days of the battle remained stationary. It is clear from Crutchfield's report that most batteries of Jackson's command maintained their position throughout the battle, with only minor adjustments.[5]

When Federal infantry was repulsed in their attack of the morning, Crutchfield reported that Confederate artillery:

> did not all come into action at once. The enemy endeavoured to cover his repulse by batteries thrown into position to play on the first of ours that opened on his retiring infantry. These were answered by fresh batteries of ours, and thus began a very fierce artillery duel, which lasted till about 10 a.m., our batteries being gradually withdrawn and the enemy moving around more to our left to select another point of attack.[6]

Crutchfield listed the batteries initially engaged in this action on the Confederate right in great detail, and the artillery on the Confederate left was not yet engaged. Thus, the "fresh batteries" he refers to could only be those in the center, including the Chesapeake. As one of the batteries withdrawn, Pvt. Jacob Cook placed the company in reserve following the action of the twenty-ninth in a horseshoe-shaped depression formed by Catharpin Creek behind Stony Ridge, about one mile directly behind their position near the Groveton-Sudley Road. This is where they incurred their only casualty of the day.[7]

August 30

Little occurred until 1500, when heavy attacks against Jackson's center and left were made and the Chesapeake went into action, likely in the same location, incurring one casualty. As the Federal attacking column's left flank was exposed it was smashed by massed artillery of both Jackson's and Longstreet's wings positioned on Jackson's far right. The Federals fell back to their right (Confederate left), uncovering Jackson's center and the Groveton-Sudley Road. At this point, with their front in this sector clear, Crutchfield ordered Garber's battery to advance "at a gallop to move down into the plain below, so as to get an enfilading position on their other lines when they should be repulsed from the woods in which they were engaged with our infantry." However, the advance of Confederate troops eastward toward the retreating Federals blocked Garber's field of fire so the artillery was unable to take advantage of this movement.[8]

Three incidents indicate the Chesapeake Artillery was almost certainly also ordered forward, down Stony Ridge along the Groveton-Sudley Road to where it intersects with the Warrenton Turnpike. Goldsborough describes the scene where Reynolds's New York battery received the Chesapeake's fire on the twenty-eighth, as members of the battery observed that "the ground where stood the hostile battery and its supporting infantry was found thickly strewn with dead and wounded men and horses." He places the timing of the company's observance of the casualties incurred by Reynolds's battery as the morning after the first day's fight on August 29. However, it would have been difficult to discern individual casualties at a distance of over a mile and impossible to know whether they had been caused by artillery or rifle fire. The only way the company could have inspected the damage caused by their firing would be if they were at the scene. Goldsborough also has Lt. John Grason comforting a dying Federal officer at this time, and in a letter Pvt. John Hooff recalled he traded a blanket for a pocket watch with a Federal prisoner. These incidents could only have happened in the Confederate rear, free from active fighting.[9]

The only place and time where these three events could have taken place and also be in the Confederate rear is the vicinity of the Groveton-Sudley Road and Warrenton Turnpike intersection after Longstreet's columns had pushed the Federals to the east and there was no longer any fighting in this sector. This is where Reynolds's battery had stood in the fight the evening of the twenty-eighth, so it is also the only place the Chesapeakes could have observed Federal casualties as a result of their fire during that encounter. Since the Chesapeake had been positioned on Stony Ridge behind Confederate infantry during the entire battle, this is also the only place members of the company could have interacted with Federal wounded and prisoners, so it had to have happened on August 30. This interaction was possible because Garber's and Brown's batteries were not engaged once they reached the road intersection, since their field of fire was blocked by Confederate infantry to the east.

Moreover, these incidents also establish the company was in the vicinity of Garber's battery at the same time Garber advanced. This area had been occupied by Federals continuously during the battle from the evening of August 28 until late afternoon of the thirtieth. The next morning Jackson's command, with the Chesapeake Artillery, moved to Chantilly. Thus, the only time the battery could have been in the area was at the same time as Garber in the late afternoon and early evening of the thirtieth.

Summary

The Chesapeake occupied a position in Jackson's center on Stony Ridge behind the unfinished railroad bed near its intersection with the Groveton-Sudley Road and were engaged the evening of August 28 against Reynolds's New York battery. On the twenty-ninth, the battery participated in the artillery duel of the morning and was then withdrawn and placed in reserve behind Stony Ridge the remainder of the day. Late in the afternoon of the thirtieth they advanced down Stony Ridge along the Groveton-Sudley Road to the vicinity of the Warrenton Turnpike with Garber's and possibly other batteries of Courtney's battalion, but were not engaged at this time. The company incurred casualties on each day, with four men wounded in total during the course of the battle.[10]

APPENDIX C

Losses in the Pennsylvania Campaign

In the confusion attendant on the casualties in leadership of the Maryland Battalion at Gettysburg, errors were made in the reporting of losses the Chesapeake Artillery had suffered there, as well as how they occurred, before the smoke over the blasted debris of Benner's Hill had barely cleared. Primary accounts by members of the battalion, even contemporary with the battle, contained inconsistencies as to how many killed and wounded the battery had incurred and who they were.

Contemporary primary accounts were left by battalion commander Lt. Col. R. Snowden Andrews in his report of the battle, and in letters by Sgt. Peter Williams. In addition, postwar accounts were written by Pvts. Chris Lynch and Jacob Cook of the Chesapeake, as well as Maj. W. W. Goldsborough and Pvt. Washington Hands of the 1st Maryland Infantry Battalion. Most of these contain errors and omissions, some of which have been widely cited in secondary accounts of the battery's participation in the Battle of Gettysburg. The total number of casualties in these reports ranges from sixteen to twenty; some include soldiers who were not even present at the battle and exclude several soldiers whose CSRs clearly indicate they not only received wounds at Gettysburg, but also had subsequent medical treatment as a result.

The two earliest accounts of the Chesapeake's casualties at Gettysburg are a letter recounting the battle written by Sgt. Peter Williams to his father on July 7, 1863, and Andrews's draft of his official report written on August 5. Andrews stated four enlisted men were killed and ten wounded in addition to Capt. W. D. Brown and Lt. B. G. Roberts; Williams counted the Chesapeake's casualties as nine wounded and four dead. Both accounts contain errors.[1]

Williams, in an earlier letter to his sister, had listed his best friends in the battery as Sgts. Phil Brown, Robert Crowley, and James Wall, as well as Cpl. Henry Buckmaster. In his July 7 letter he states "none of my particular friends were hurt," ignoring the fact that Wall, Brown, and Buckmaster had been wounded and the latter two were also captured! In the August 5 draft of his official Gettysburg report that was included in his memoirs, Andrews stated two officers were wounded in addition to four enlisted men killed and ten wounded, and lists some of the killed and wounded by name. However, only twelve names of these sixteen casualties are included in the list. Andrews's final report was not updated, continuing to include both Brown and Oldner among the wounded; although both had died of their wounds by July 20, this was unknown to Andrews at that time. It is possible Andrews under-reported the unit's casualties as part of the Army of Northern Virginia's practice of not reporting slightly wounded men among its casualties.[2]

Two of the most frequently repeated errors were initially made by Pvt. Chris Lynch in a casualty list he compiled soon after the war and Pvt. Jacob Cook in an article he wrote on the Chesapeake Artillery in the *Baltimore Telegram*, which was included in F. Z. Ammen's scrapbook

Benner's Hill from a similar camera position as that on page 75. *Author*

Maryland Troops in the Confederate Army from Original Sources. Cook includes Lt. Benjamin Roberts among the killed at Gettysburg, while Lynch lists Roberts and Pvt. Richard Hardesty. Neither is correct. Roberts was severely wounded in the back and both arms at Gettysburg, but returned to duty by September 2; he died in a hospital in Charlottesville of typhoid fever on December 1. Hardesty was not even with the unit at Gettysburg; he died of smallpox on December 8 the previous year. With Lynch as the author of the account of the unit's participation at Gettysburg in Goldsborough's *The Maryland Line in the Confederate Army*, these errors were repeated. Lynch made the same mistakes again in an article he wrote in the *Centreville Record* in May 1900. These errors have been cited in numerous modern publications of the unit's participation at Gettysburg.[3]

Several diverse primary sources were used to clarify the company's losses and burials at Gettysburg to develop the list here. These include the Compiled Service Records (CSRs) of members of the unit in the National Archives in Washington, DC, burial and re-interment records, contemporary letters and accounts by unit members, newspaper accounts, and even the uniforms and equipment used by members of the battery at Gettysburg.

Within the muster records of the 4th Maryland Artillery, a consistent recording pattern when a battle death occurred was the practice of abruptly dropping the name of a soldier killed in action from the rolls; the only notation regarding his death occurred if he was included in a separate casualty report, with no reference to his death in the muster records. Andrews's final report did not include the names of the killed and wounded in the battalion, only the numbers of killed and wounded for each battery, so no official casualty list for the company exists as such. However, two contemporary burial records confirm several of the Chesapeake Artillery's Gettysburg battle deaths.

The first record of Confederate burials at Gettysburg was made during the three years following the battle by Dr. John W. C. O'Neal of Gettysburg. Born in Virginia, O'Neal had moved to Gettysburg from Baltimore in February 1863, and noticed the hundreds of Confederate graves in the countryside and town following the battle. Rightly thinking these soldiers' families would want to claim their remains when the war was over, he endeavored to record the markings and locations of Confederate graves as he made the rounds of his practice. O'Neal recorded many of the names and units on the marked graves, although his list is not complete. Further, over time many of the markings were obliterated or became indistinct.[4]

The second Gettysburg burial list was developed by Dr. Rufus B. Weaver. Weaver's father Samuel had been contracted by several Southern ladies' memorial societies to recover, pack, and ship the remains of Confederate soldiers at Gettysburg to their home states in the South. Samuel Weaver died before he could complete the task, and the bulk of the work was done by Rufus Weaver in 1873 and 1874. Using O'Neal's lists as a guide, he kept careful records of the names, locations, and shipments of remains he made. Weaver recorded some additional names that O'Neal had missed. Together O'Neal and Weaver recorded the gravesites of approximately 1,100 Confederate soldiers in the Gettysburg area.[5]

Capt. William D. Brown's death was one of prominence and has been recounted often, although many primary accounts as to the nature of his wounds are incorrect. Cook recalled that, while mounted, a shell passed through Brown's left leg and then through his horse, who fell to the right, breaking Brown's right leg. In Lynch's recounting of this incident in Goldsborough's book the projectile is changed to a solid shot. Pvt. Washington Hands of the 1st Maryland Battalion described Brown's wounds as, "both legs had been shattered by a cannon ball." The *Richmond Examiner* further embellished the story in reporting Brown's death: "A cannon shot carried one leg away and shattered the other."[6]

The most accurate account, which would have come from Brown's family, is included in his obituary that appeared in the *Baltimore Sun*:

> He was wounded by a shell that shattered his left leg, and broke the right one. The left leg was subsequently amputated near the thigh, but the injury was of such a severe nature that but little hope was entertained for his recovery.

Indeed, Federal hospital records in Brown's CSR recount that both his legs were fractured and "one amputated."[7]

Further, the uniform Brown was wearing when wounded, as well as his equipment and several of his possessions, exist as a historical record in several private collections today. Their evidence supports both his medical records and the account given in his obituary. An examination of his uniform revealed the bloodied left leg of his uniform trousers was surgically cut off at a level just above the knee. The left skirt of his horse's saddle has a hole the shape and size of a case shot at the approximate location of where Brown's knee would have rested against it. A testament that Brown carried in his vest pocket at the time also has a case shot embedded in it. It is clear Brown was wounded by the explosion of a case shot shell in his close proximity and that a case shot round passed through his left knee, killing his horse and causing it to fall to the right, fracturing Brown's right leg; subsequently his left leg was amputated above the knee. He died on July 11.[8]

Brown was initially treated at an aid station established on the Daniel Lady farm on the Hanover Road, four hundred yards east of the crest of Benner's Hill. Pvt. Washington Hands of the 1st Maryland Battalion wrote that his unit waited in the vicinity of the Lady farm during the artillery bombardment prior to the attack of Johnson's division on Culp's Hill. Brown was recognized and heard to speak to one of the 1st's officers as he was carried down the hill by stretcher bearers.[9]

O'Neal's burial records place the location of Brown's amputation, death, and initial burial at the Elizabeth Weible farm, approximately two miles northeast of Gettysburg between the York Pike and Hunterstown Road. The Weible farm was established as a field hospital for the Confederate 2nd Corps during the battle and used in that capacity until mid-August; access was effected via a farm lane that connected the Lady farm on the Hanover Road with the Wolf farm on the York Pike, slightly over half a mile northwest of the Lady property.[10] Although Brown's family arranged to have his body removed and sent to Baltimore prior to his July 31 funeral at Greenmount Cemetery, his grave marker still stood at the Weible farm.[11] O'Neal recorded it there in May 1866 as "Capt. W.B."[12] Only one other captain with the initials "W. B." was killed at Gettysburg. This is Capt. William R. Bissell of Co. A, 8th Virginia Infantry Regiment, who died on July 16 of wounds received July 3; however, he was buried at the Presbyterian Graveyard on High Street in Gettysburg, duly noted by Dr. O'Neal. Other burials at the Weible farm included members of several 2nd Corps units, and this is also where Maj. Joseph Latimer's arm was amputated following his wounding on July 2.[13]

Pvt. Phil Oldner incurred a severe knee wound as well and would also have been treated initially at the aid station established at the Lady farm, although he was not moved to one of the 2nd Corps's field hospitals at that time. Before 2400 on July 3, Andrews's battalion was included with Johnson's division as it began its withdrawal from the Confederate left flank and established a new line on Oak Ridge northwest of Gettysburg. Subsequently, the 2nd Corps joined the retreat of the Army of Northern Virginia by

The Weible farmhouse on Shaler Road near Gettysburg. Capt. Billy Brown died here and was initially buried near the barn. *Author*

taking the Fairfield Road. The Corps' wounded who had not been taken to field hospitals were removed to a number of newly established field hospitals along the Fairfield Road southwest of Gettysburg, Oldner included. He was recorded as present at the David Stewart farm two miles east of Fairfield when Federal medical authorities moved into the area on July 5. Oldner died there on July 20, and was buried "east of the barn and near row of trees," according to Weaver's records. His remains were shipped by Weaver to Hollywood Cemetery in Richmond, Virginia, on May 17, 1873, in Box 3-286, and subsequently moved to Loudon Park Cemetery in Baltimore in 1874.[14]

Pvts. Fred Cusick, Thad Parker, and "Doctor Jack" Bryan were killed outright during the artillery action on Benner's Hill. Cook stated they were buried together on the evening of July 2 "a long distance" from Benner's Hill. O'Neal recorded their burial location as approximately four hundred yards west of the crest of the hill on Daniel Benner's farm "back of Rock Creek under a large walnut tree." By 1873, only Parker's grave identification was still legible; he was removed to Loudon Park Cemetery in Baltimore on July 4, 1873, while Cusick and Bryan were buried with the unknowns in the Gettysburg Dead section at Hollywood Cemetery in Richmond, VA.[15]

Cpl. Daniel Dougherty's wounds, as described by Cook, caused him to be "entirely cut in half." However, although the wounds were severe and fatal, it appears Dougherty survived them long enough to be taken to the Lady farm for treatment. An examination of the battle shirt that Dougherty wore at the time of his wounding, which is still extant in a private collection, indicates three case shots entered the small of his back, causing frightful exit wounds in his abdomen. Andrews stated in his draft report that Dougherty also received a wound in the hip. O'Neal recorded Dougherty's burial on the south side of the Hanover Road directly across from the Lady house. Dougherty would only have been buried there if he had died at the Lady house; there would be no other reason to bury him nearly half a mile away from the burial location of Cusick, Parker, and Bryan.[16]

According to O'Neal's records from 1863, Dougherty was buried next to "Lt. P.W.H." The only lieutenant of the 2nd Corps with those initials killed at Gettysburg was Lt. Pinckney W. Hatrick of the 53rd North Carolina Infantry Regiment, who was mortally wounded early on the morning of July 3 during the renewal of the fighting on Culp's Hill and died later that day at the Lady farm. There was no unit identification on Hatrick's grave marker, and O'Neal incorrectly indicated he was a member of the Chesapeake

Hat worn by Cpl. Dan Dougherty at Gettysburg. *Author's collection*

Artillery. In 1873, Weaver recorded an additional five unidentified burials at this location on the south side of the Hanover road across from the Lady house. By that time Dougherty's and Hatrick's grave markings had been obliterated, and all seven soldiers were removed to the Gettysburg Dead section at Hollywood Cemetery as unknowns in Box 1-V on May 17, 1873.[17]

The Chesapeake incurred two additional battle deaths at Gettysburg; postwar primary sources consistently state eight men of the battery were killed in the action on Benner's Hill. These sources typically list Roberts and Hardesty, but since they were not killed at Gettysburg, the additional two deaths have to be accounted for by two other men. The recording of Pvts. James Stephens's and Francis Smith's presence in the company's muster rolls abruptly stops after they were marked present for duty on June 30 at Chambersburg, the same pattern that occurs in the rolls for William D. Brown, Oldner, Cusick, Parker, Bryan, and Dougherty. There are no medical or capture records for either Stephens or Smith, neither are reported "Absent, Deserted" in subsequent musters as is consistently the case with other soldiers in the unit who deserted after Gettysburg, and neither appears in the 1870 Census. It is apparent both were mortally wounded in the action on Benner's Hill and taken to the Lady farm like Brown, Oldner, and Dougherty. They likely died around the time Johnson's division left the area so were not transported to the Stewart farm, leaving no opportunity for them to be buried by other members of the battery like Dougherty, and before Federal medical authorities had arrived and could record their names. Similar to Brown and Oldner, this also indicates why they were not listed as killed by Peter Williams or Snowden Andrews in those soldiers' contemporary reporting, and they, like others, were not included in Andrews's incomplete list of the names of wounded for the company.[18]

Daniel Lady's claim for compensation described the scene when he and his family returned to his farm after the Confederate withdrawal on July 4: "buildings were used for hospital purposes, upon the return of the family on Saturday [July 4], wounded soldiers were in the house and dead bodies lying around which they were obliged to bury." Almost certainly Stephens and Smith were among these dead and buried by the family across the road from the Lady house in the same location as Dougherty and Hatrick. Since no other company members were present at that point to identify them they were buried as unknowns, and subsequently removed to the Gettysburg Dead section at Hollywood Cemetery.[19]

By supplementing Andrews's report with contemporary accounts, newspaper records, and CSRs, the number of identified wounded in the battery at Gettysburg total sixteen, including Lt. B. J. Roberts, closely aligning to Cook's tally that "some fifteen of our boys were severely wounded." Five of the wounded were captured during the withdrawal and retreat to Virginia.[20]

Sgt. Phil Brown was wounded slightly in the face and breast. He was captured at Hagerstown, Maryland, on July 7, during the retreat from Gettysburg, sent to Point Lookout, and exchanged December 24.[21]

Cpl. Henry Buckmaster received an unspecified wound, was probably left behind at the Weible farm, and captured there on July 4, when Federal forces moved into that area. He was sent to the US General Hospital at West's buildings in Baltimore on July 28, to Point Lookout on August 20, and exchanged March 17, 1864.[22]

Pvt. Charles Dallam was slightly wounded "but did not leave my command."[23]

Pvt. John "Little" Green received an unspecified wound.[24]

Pvt. James K. Harper received an unspecified wound, was left behind and probably captured at the Weible farm on July 4th. Sent to West's buildings, he was paroled for exchange on September 25.[25]

Small gun marker flag of the 2nd Detachment of the Chesapeake Artillery found on Benner's Hill by a local citizen after the battle. *Author's collection*

Pvt. John Lane received a laceration wound in his head from a shell fragment. He was admitted to General Hospital No. 9 in Richmond on July 21 and returned to duty August 5.[26]

Sgt. Maj. Thomas P. LeCompte received an unspecified wound.[27]

Pvt. Willie Mason received an unspecified wound. He was admitted to General Hospital in Staunton, Virginia, on August 2 and returned to duty on the 17.[28]

Pvt. Henry Parker, Thad's brother, received an unspecified wound.[29]

Pvt. John Richardson received an unspecified wound. He is mistakenly listed among the wounded on several rosters as Pvt. Nick Richardson, but Nick Richardson was in a hospital being treated for rheumatism, and was not present at Gettysburg.[30]

Second Lt. Benjamin Roberts was wounded severely in the back and both arms. There are no medical records extant for him, but he returned to duty by September 2, 1863.[31]

Pvt. Charles Tinges received an unspecified wound, and was most likely left behind at the Stewart farm. He was captured

July 5 and sent to DeCamp General Hospital at Davids Island military prison, New York, New York, on July 17; he was later paroled and returned to duty on January 26, 1864.[32]

Sgt. James A. Wall received an unspecified wound.[33]

Pvt. Smith Warrington received a slight wound to the face. He was captured at an unknown date and not exchanged until February 21, 1865.[34]

Pvt. William M. Williams received a slight wound to the face.[35]

Pvt. Henry Willson received a severe wound from a shell fragment affecting the flexor tendons of his right knee. He was admitted to General Hospital No. 9 in Richmond, Virginia, and treated in various hospitals over the next several months for ulcers in his leg, as well as erysipelas. He was granted a three-day furlough on February 20, 1864, and returned to duty. Willson was no longer able to withstand the rigors of artillery service and transferred to the 1st Maryland Cavalry Regiment in December.[36]

In addition, although not mentioned in any of the contemporary or postwar accounts by veterans of the unit, seven unwounded members of the company were captured during the retreat from Gettysburg: on July 7, Pvt. Paul H. Huber was captured at Hagerstown, Maryland, as were Pvts. John Myers and William Schaefer at Williamsport; Pvt. John Tregoe was captured July 18 at Front Royal, Virginia; Pvt. John W. Gore on July 19 in Berkeley County, Virginia; Pvt. John W. Canfield on July 20 at Winchester, Virginia; and Pvt. John Vansant on July 23 at Front Royal, Virginia.[37]

Finally, there were additional casualties that were never reported, nor understood well at that time. The horrific scene on Benner's Hill unnerved a number of the soldiers of the unit; although post-traumatic stress was not a well-understood concept, these men were clearly affected. Lt. John Plater, who had served credibly up to the time of the battle, even commanding the battery at 1st Fredericksburg, lost his composure, left a caisson behind in his haste to leave the field, and misrepresented the circumstances surrounding the incident; he was later cashiered. Pvt. Jacob Cook, who had served continuously since enlisting at the battery's organization in Machodoc, gave himself up to the Federals the day after the action on Benner's Hill (July 3). Pvts. Thomas McClure and Andrew McElwee, both of whom had served without an absence of any kind since their enlistments in June 1862, deserted sometime after the battery left Pennsylvania. These were the first desertions in the unit and their timing is significant. In the eighteen months the unit had been in existence, these men had had ample opportunity to desert or give themselves up to the enemy, especially during the Maryland Campaign or around the time of either of the Fredericksburg battles. Along with Plater, this resulted in an additional four members permanently lost to the battery's service.[38]

The Chesapeake Artillery was devastated by losses during the Pennsylvania campaign. The battery's total confirmed casualties at Gettysburg were eight killed or mortally wounded, sixteen wounded, five of the wounded captured, and seven unwounded and captured, for a total of thirty-one unduplicated casualties. Their casualty rate of 39% of the men present for duty was astoundingly high for an artillery unit and ranked among the highest in casualty rates of the sixty-two batteries in the Army of Northern Virginia during the Pennsylvania Campaign. The company's total twenty-two killed, disabled by wounds, and captured represents fully 28% of the men present for duty at Gettysburg who would never return to the unit. If Plater and the missing men who deserted in the aftermath of the battle are included, this number increases to twenty-six, or 33%—a third of the battery's membership permanently lost. The company would never again reach the size of the complement of men it mustered near Chambersburg on June 30.[39]

APPENDIX D

Unit Strength

As with other units in the Army of Northern Virginia, the total strength of the Chesapeake Artillery fluctuated during the war, affected by casualties and other absences, as well as enlistments and transfers. The only muster rolls that survive in the National Archives are for the battery's six musters of March 1, 1862; June 30, 1863; November 1, 1863; November 1, 1864; December 31, 1864; and February 28, 1865. Because its recruiting base was behind Federal lines during the entire war, recruiting and maintaining manpower levels were constant challenges, even prompting Capt. Brown to advertise for recruits in a Richmond newspaper.[1]

By adding enlistments on January 1, 1862, from individual CSRs, it can be concluded the company numbered fifty men present at its initial organization, with three officers and forty-seven enlisted men. By the time of the battery's first muster roll in Tappahannock two months later on March 1, this number had increased to a total of sixty men carried on the rolls and fifty-nine present for duty, or 45% of its total enrolment during the war. Although enlistments and transfers into the Chesapeake continued from the time of the unit's organization up until July 1864, they largely occurred during three periods. The first was during June 1862, when the battery was stationed in Richmond and seventeen men enlisted. The second was in October and November following the Maryland Campaign, when twenty-two men enlisted. Finally, when the Maryland Line was established in 1864, ten enlistees or Maryland soldiers serving in other units who transferred into the company were added during May, June, and July. These three enlistment waves accounted for an additional 37% of the battery's total enrolment.

Where muster rolls are missing, by using individual CSRs to account for enlistments and absences it can be determined the company numbered approximately eighty-five present for duty at the time it joined Jackson's command for active campaigning in July 1862, and peaked at its highest level at about 100 men present for duty by December 1, 1862, shortly before the 1st Fredericksburg battle. The number of men present for duty dropped precipitately after Gettysburg and never returned to its former levels, with the company's number present dipping to only fifty enlisted men in addition to Lt. Walter Chew in the early months of 1864. After additional enlistments and transfers in April, May, and June 1864, following the formation of the Maryland Line, the number of soldiers carried on the unit's rolls remained in a remarkably consistent range of between eighty-five to ninety-three men with sixty or sixty-one present for duty up to January 1, 1865. After that discharges and desertions reduced the unit to its lowest strength level of sixty-one men carried on the rolls for the muster of March 1, 1865, with only forty present for duty. By mid-March, there were only fifty-five men on the rolls, with thirty-six present for duty, and only twenty-nine men present by the end of that month. This led to the order on March 22 for the battery to be disbanded and consolidated with Griffin's Battery, although the consolidation was never carried out. Additional discharges and details, losses in the action at Fort Gregg on April 2, 1865, and captures during the Appomattox Campaign reduced the company to the thirteen men present at Appomattox on April 9, 1865.[2]

The final enumeration for April 9, 1865, is not taken from a muster roll, as the company's last muster was on March 1; it is a compilation of the final dispositions of members of the unit on April 9, 1865, as noted on their individual service records. This reflects discharges and desertions after March 1, as well as the captures and battle deaths at Fort Gregg and during the retreat to Appomattox. The same recording practices were used in this compilation that were used by the company throughout the war; that is, men who were killed at Fort Gregg and those marked as absent or deserted on March 1 have been dropped, with only new desertions noted.

Chesapeake Artillery Unit Strength by Muster Date

			Absent						**Roll**
Muster Date	Present for Duty		Wounded	Detailed	Sick	POW	Furlough	AWOL	Total
March 1, 1862	Officers	3	0	0	0	0	0	0	3
	Enlisted	56	0	1	0	0	0	0	57
	Total	59	0	1	0	0	0	0	60
June 30, 1863	Officers	4	0	0	0	0	0	0	4
	Enlisted	76	5	5	3	0	0	0	89
	Total	80	5	5	3	0	0	0	93
November 1, 1863	Officers	2	0	0	0	0	0	0	2
	Enlisted	58	4	5	4	7	0	5	83
	Total	60	4	5	4	7	0	5	85
November 1, 1864	Officers	2	0	0	0	0	0	0	2
	Enlisted	58	4	6	7	4	1	4	84
	Total	60	4	6	7	4	1	4	86
January 1, 1865	Officers	2	0	0	0	0	0	0	2
	Enlisted	59	1	8	7	3	2	3	83
	Total	61	1	8	7	3	2	3	85
March 1, 1865	Officers	2	0	0	0	0	0	0	2
	Enlisted	38	1	9	4	2	2	3	59
	Total	40	1	9	4	2	2	3	61
April 9, 1865	Officers	0	0	0	0	1	0	0	1
	Enlisted	13	1	4	0	15	3	2	38
	Total	13	1	4	0	16	3	2	39

APPENDIX E

Losses

The historical record for casualties and losses for the Chesapeake Artillery is incomplete. Only three casualty reports were compiled for the unit that are known: Capt. Billy Brown's report of casualties for Bristoe Station, 2nd Manassas, and 1st Fredericksburg (Cedar Mountain is not included), and Lt. Col. R. Snowden Andrews's reports for 2nd Fredericksburg and Gettysburg, which include casualties. All three reports have errors, and neither of Andrews's is complete. While Brown did report Pvt. Andy Egan as missing following the battle of 2nd Manassas (Egan had been severely wounded on the battle's second day, then captured while in a field hospital), he did not mention either of the other two men captured and missing during the Maryland Campaign. Andrews's reports for 2nd Fredericksburg and Gettysburg both have names missing.[1]

In addition, several casualty lists were compiled by veterans of the unit postwar. Pvt. Chris Lynch developed a casualty list for the battery that was included in W. W. Goldsborough's unit history in his book *The Maryland Line in the Confederate Army, 1861–1865*, and another that was published in the *Centreville Record* in 1900. Pvt. Jacob Cook also listed casualties in the partial unit history he wrote for the *Baltimore Telegram* that was included in S. Z. Ammen's *Maryland Troops in the Confederate Army from Original Sources*. A number of errors were made by these veterans of the unit postwar, as these casualty lists were compiled using memory as a guide; moreover, none of the men captured or discharged for disability during the course of the war, with the exception of Cpl. Robert Jones, are mentioned in any contemporary reports or postwar reminiscences.[2]

This complete list of the unit's losses during the war is based largely on individual Compiled Service Records in the National Archives, supplemented with official casualty lists, hospital records, burial and interment records, contemporary letters and accounts by unit members, and newspaper accounts and postwar reminiscences.

This compilation indicates the Chesapeake Artillery incurred total losses during the course of the war of 58%, far higher than expected for an artillery unit in the Army of Northern Virginia.[3] Thirteen members of the battery—nearly 10% of total enrolment—were killed or mortally wounded in battle during the course of the war, more than double the rate of killed in action for the artillery arm as a whole.[4] Most of these battle deaths (eight) were incurred at Gettysburg. Twenty-eight members of the unit (nearly 21%) suffered one or more wounds during the war, more than half at Gettysburg.[5] A total of 28 men in the company were captured during the war (about 21% of total enrolment); this rate is much higher than expected compared to the infantry capture rate (14%) and soldiers captured in the Army of Northern Virginia's artillery branch (12%).[6] The greatest number of captures occurred during the course of the Pennsylvania Campaign and in the defense of Fort Gregg. Five members of the company died of disease during the war, including Pvt. John Torrington, the only member of the battery to die as a prisoner of war. Similarly, only four of the unit's soldiers were discharged for disability during the war.[7]

The percent of casualties incurred by the unit in each action represents an adjusted

Robertson HOSPITAL,
Richmond VA. Apl 3d 1865

Private C. S. Tinges Co. 4th Md. Regiment Arty. has this day been returned to duty, and ordered to report directly to his command. No case of Small Pox has occurred in this Hospital during the last sixty days.

State here date of Vaccination or Re-vaccination, or why unnecessary.

Surgeon in Charge.

This Ticket will be delivered by the Soldier to the Surgeon of his Regiment.

Release issued to Pvt. Charles Tinges from Robertson Hospital in Richmond. *Author's collection*

total of all men present for duty at the muster date nearest to the date of that action, with exceptions for 1862. The numbers of men the unit had present for duty during the campaigns of 1862 are estimates based on the muster rolls for March 1, 1862, with adjustments during the intervening periods for enlistees, casualties, and absences. The percent of totals for men who died of disease or were discharged for disability are based on the unit's total enrolment of 135 men.[8]

Losses of the Chesapeake Artillery, January 1, 1862–April 1865: (Losses as a Percent Present for Duty)

Cedar Mountain, August 9, 1862 (2%)
Wounded in Action (2%)
Quartermaster Sgt. John S. Shafer
Pvt. John Shannahan

Bristoe Station, August 27, 1862 (1%)
Wounded in Action (1%)
Pvt. William Wilson

2nd Manassas, August 28–30, 1862 (5%)
Wounded in Action (4%)
Pvt. Richard Hardesty
Pvt. Phil Harrison
Pvt. George Smith

Wounded and Captured (1%)
Pvt. Andy Egan

Maryland Campaign, September 1862 (4%)
Captured (4%)
Pvt. John "Doctor Jack" Bryan
Pvt. Andy Egan
Pvt. William Oldson

1st Fredericksburg, December 13, 1862 (12%)
Killed or Mortally Wounded In Action (2%)
1st Lt. John Grason
Pvt. Edward Graham

Wounded in Action (10%)
Pvt. Isaac Blunt
Pvt. John "Little" Green
Pvt. Vincent "Big" Green
Pvt. James Harper
Pvt. Paul Huber
Pvt. Willie Mason
Pvt. Phil Oldner
Pvt. Thomas Toy
Pvt. Daniel Wilkinson

2nd Fredericksburg, May 1–3, 1863 (9%)
Killed in Action (1%)
Pvt. Alexander "Bey" Hopkins

Wounded in Action (8%)
Sgt. Robert Crowley
Pvt. Tom Carberry
Pvt. Charles Dallam
Pvt. James Harper
Pvt. Richard Langley
Pvt. John Shannahan
Pvt. James Sparks

Pennsylvania Campaign, June–July 1863 (41%)
Killed or Mortally Wounded in Action (11%)
Capt. Billy Brown
Cpl. Dan Dougherty
Pvt. John "Doctor Jack" Bryan
Pvt. Fred Cusick
Pvt. Phil Oldner
Pvt. Thad Parker
Pvt. Francis Smith
Pvt. James Stephens

Wounded in Action (14%)
2nd Lt. Ben Roberts
Sgt. Maj. Thomas LeCompte
Sgt. James Wall
Pvt. Charles Dallam
Pvt. John "Little" Green
Pvt. John Lane
Pvt. Willie Mason
Pvt. Henry Parker
Pvt. John Richardson
Pvt. William Williams
Pvt. Henry Willson

Wounded and Captured (7%)
Sgt. Phil Brown
Cpl. Henry Buckmaster
Pvt. James Harper
Pvt. Charles Tinges
Pvt. Smith Warrington

Captured (9%)
Pvt. Paul Huber
Pvt. John Myers
Pvt. William Schaefer
Pvt. John "Johnny Trigger" Tregoe
Pvt. John Gore

Pvt. John Canfield
Pvt. John Vansant

Payne's Farm, November 27, 1863 (2%)
Captured (2%)
Pvt. Doug McClure

Kilpatrick-Dahlgren Raid, March 1864
Captured (2%)
Pvt. George Rice

Cold Harbor, June 6, 1864 (4%)
Wounded in Action (4%)
Pvt. Charles Garrett
Pvt. Daniel Wilkinson

Near Glendale, June 15, 1864 (2%)
Wounded in Action (2%)
Pvt. Edward Cottrell

Petersburg Campaign, June 18, 1864–April 1, 1865 (6%)
Wounded in Action (4%)
Pvt. James Dean
Pvt. John "Little" Green

Captured (2%)
Pvt. Richard Langley

Fort Gregg, April 2, 1865 (41%)
Killed in Action (7%)
Pvt. William Culver
Pvt. Thomas Everngam

Wounded and Captured (7%)
Cpl. William Pinder
Pvt. Chris Lynch

Captured (28%)
Capt. Walter Chew
Pvt. Charles Dallam
Pvt. John Gardner
Pvt. Billy Holtzman
Pvt. Joseph Peters
Pvt. Gustavus Porter
Pvt. James Sparks
Pvt. James Stewart

Appomattox Campaign, April 3 and after, 1865 (20%)
Captured (20%)
Pvt. George Goodhand
Pvt. Francis McCummins
Pvt. John Torrington

Date Unknown
Wounded in Action
Pvt. Frank Yates

Died of Disease (4%)
2nd Lt. Ben Roberts
Pvt. Richard Hardesty
Pvt. John Poisal
Pvt. Edward Stansbury
Pvt. John Torrington

Discharged for Disability (3%)
Pvt. William Barchus
Pvt. Robert Jones
Pvt. John S. Shafer
Pvt. John Valentine

APPENDIX F

Desertions

Of the battery's total enrolment, fifteen (about 11% of the men in the unit) deserted during the course of the war. This is lower than the Army of Northern Virginia's desertion rate (16%), as well as the artillery branch's nearly 12%. A cursory analysis implies the company's desertion level was lower than, yet similar to other units in the army, but a closer examination of the factors underlying desertion reveals the Chesapeakes were far more steadfast in their duty than it initially appears.[1]

There were four important factors that contributed to desertion in the Army of Northern Virginia: a higher propensity for older soldiers, poorer soldiers, and unskilled workers and farmers to desert, as well as loss of morale in 1863 and 1864. None of these determinants were operative among the soldiers of the Chesapeake Artillery who deserted.[2]

The average age of deserters from the company was almost two years older than the unit's average age, and the difference in age distribution of the deserters in the unit compared to the battery as a whole was similar. Conversely, the difference in age of deserters in the battery compared to deserters from the Army of Northern Virginia was significant because they were younger, reflecting the youth of the company overall.[3]

A comparison of the economic status of the battery's deserters indicates no differences between these men and the unit as a whole, nor of the Army of Northern Virginia. In other words, deserters in the battery were not poorer, but reflected the same distribution of economic classes as they occurred within the company and the army. However, in comparing the occupations of deserters in the company to the Army of Northern Virginia, there is a marked difference due to the lower proportion of unskilled workers and farmers and a greater proportion of skilled and white-collar workers. This reflects the different levels of these occupations in the unit as a whole compared to the Army. When the occupations of deserters are compared to the occupations of the other members of the company there is no difference. Therefore, unskilled workers and farmers were not more likely to desert from the battery.[4]

Finally, a loss of morale in 1863 and 1864 was not evident within the unit as reflected in desertions. For the Army of Northern Virginia, by January 1, 1865, 15% of its soldiers had deserted, compared to only 6% of the Chesapeake Artillery. Clearly the company had a strong sense of unit cohesion and esprit de corps.[5]

The battery's deserters were representative of the rest of the company when age, economic status, and occupation are considered. Further, the unit experienced a much lower rate of desertions up until January 1, 1865. Other factors were operative that influenced desertions within the Chesapeake and warrant further examination. A full 73% of desertions within the company occurred during two brief time periods. The first was during July 1863, in the aftermath of the horrific action at Gettysburg and its high casualties. Four men deserted at this time, and the timing of these desertions is important. These were the first desertions ever from the unit, and no doubt were a direct result of the stress and despair caused by the scene on Benner's Hill (see appendix B for a complete discussion of the battery's losses at Gettysburg). None of these men had absences of any kind until that time.[6]

The second occurrence of desertions of significance was during February and March 1865, when seven men deserted. The timing of these desertions is important also. During the previous October a judge in Petersburg, Virginia, had ruled that Maryland soldiers, because they did not come from a state that was part of the Confederacy, could not be forced to comply with its conscription laws and were eligible for discharge after three years of service. The three months following January 1, 1865, marked three years' service for those who had initially enlisted in the Chesapeake Artillery. Therefore, nineteen soldiers from the unit were discharged. This had a marked impact on unit strength, as these soldiers represented nearly a third of the men present for duty on January 1. This reduction led directly to the March 22 order for the battery to be disbanded and consolidated with Griffin's battery.[7]

Three of the seven men who deserted at this time (Pvts. Frank Fairbanks, Charles Mettee, and Henry Corry) had already served over three years in the Confederate Army, and an additional two (Pvts. Alexander Green and Frank Kirby) were just a few months short of the three-year standard. Clearly these five men understood they were also eligible to leave the army and did not go through the formality of obtaining a discharge. If these men are excluded from the totals the desertion rate for the unit is just over 7%; less than half that of the Army of Northern Virginia and even lower than the artillery arm. It is likely the company's desertion rate was among the lowest of any unit in the Army of Northern Virginia.[8]

These two events explain why those soldiers of the company who deserted did so, and why the factors that influenced desertion in the Army of Northern Virginia were largely not operative within the Chesapeake Artillery. Morale and a sense of duty remained high within the unit compared to the Army as a whole.

APPENDIX G

Chesapeake Artillery Armament

February 1862:
1 3-inch Ordnance Rifle
1 12-pound Howitzer
2 6-pound Field Guns
Initial armament as requisitioned by Capt. Joseph Forrest.[1]

August 1862:
1 3-inch Ordnance Rifle, 2 10-pound Parrott rifles
Armament improved with the addition of two Parrott rifles in place of the 6-pound Field Guns and 12-pound Howitzer.[2]

May 1863:
4 10-pound Parrott rifles
2 Parrotts replace the Ordnance rifle damaged during the battle of 2nd Fredericksburg.[3]

September 1863:
2 10-pound Parrott rifles
Armament reduced due to losses in the Pennsylvania campaign.[4]

April 1864:
2 3-inch Ordnance rifles, 1 10-pound Parrott rifle
Armament increased to three guns with additional transfers and enlistments in the unit at the formation of the Maryland Line.[5]

December 28, 1864:
2 3-inch Ordnance rifles, 1 10-pound Parrott rifle
Armament as it appears on a tabular list of armament of the Army of Northern Virginia.[6]

Late March 1865:
None
The battery turned in its guns and equipment preparatory to consolidation with the 2nd Maryland Artillery; the consolidation was never carried out.[7]

April 5, 1865:
4 Guns, unidentified
The company is consolidated with Donald's and Chamberlayne's batteries, with four guns.[8]

April 9, 1865:
1 Gun, unidentified
The 4th Maryland Artillery surrenders at Appomattox with 13 men and one gun.[9]

12-pound field howitzer. *Author*

APPENDIX H

Misinformation, Veterans' Memories, and the Historical Record

An interesting postwar incident illustrates the difficulty in reconciling divergent sources of information in the historical record with veterans' faulty memories, as well as their motivations to misrepresent their experiences.

Pvt. Doug McClure was a twenty-one-year-old clerk from Baltimore when he enlisted in the Chesapeake Artillery at Fort Lowry on April 1, 1862. He served in the battery without absence, other than for illness, until the company's muster of November 1, 1863, when it was recorded he had deserted. He had not deserted, but was absent without leave, and returned to the unit shortly thereafter. McClure was captured several weeks later at the Battle of Payne's Farm on November 27, 1863. He had likely straggled, and since he carried no weapon, Federal authorities initially listed him as a deserter, but his status was quickly revised to prisoner of war, and he was imprisoned as such at Fort Delaware. McClure was held at Fort Delaware until after the war ended; he took the Oath of Allegiance in May 1865 and was released.[1]

McClure lived at the Maryland Line Confederate Soldiers' Home in Pikesville following his successful application in February 1897. As a routine part of the application process, the home requested a soldier's service records from the War Department in Washington, DC. Through an oversight, McClure's records were not requested until May 1905. At that time the War Department reported McClure as a deserter, since he was absent on the last roll on which his name appeared, thus ignoring his capture in battle and prisoner of war record, even though McClure had reported this in his application. Since deserters were not admitted to the home McClure was ordered to be discharged. At this point he apparently sought the help of the Maryland Division of the United Confederate Veterans; in a June 19, 1905, letter to James P. Wheeler, chairman of the home's board of governors, division commander Maj. Gen. Andrew C. Trippe fairly thundered:

> Sometime since I made application to you for the admission of George Douglas McClure late private in the Chesapeake Artillery, (a Maryland battery in the service of the Confederate States) to the Home at Pikesville...He is a poor fellow, not long to live, and I do not intend to ask the authorities of the Home again to admit him, but simply to say to you, in refutation of the slander on his name, and that the authorities of the Home shall have no excuse of their action that McClure and the late Jacob F. Cook both members of the Chesapeake Artillery (Maryland) P.A.C.S., were captured shortly after the battle of Gettysburg (between Winchester and Front Royal) by the 1st New York Cavalry, and sent to Fort Delaware, and, as exchanges had ceased, remained there to the close of the war and were paroled from there. And if the persons who appear so ready to discredit him are as ready to do him justice, they can find the fact in the records of the War Office at Washington which they have

> searched for other purposes. But I will say further that I do intend to take steps for the protection of the soldiers of our Maryland commands against misjudgement and injustice.[2]

Subsequently, the home requested further details on McClure's capture from the War Department. When the full record was received he was allowed to remain and lived there until his death the following year.[3]

It is difficult to explain how McClure's capture came to be understood by Trippe as occurring during the retreat from Gettysburg. No records to that effect exist in his Compiled Service Records. McClure further confused his service record by inexplicably stating in 1900 that he had surrendered with Lee's army at Appomattox in April 1865! His capture, imprisonment, and release records are very clear that he was captured the same day as the Battle of Payne's Farm and incarcerated at Fort Delaware until he took the OOA in May 1865, a month following the surrender.[4]

It is also odd that Trippe referred to Pvt. Jacob Cook in his letter, as Cook had died by that time and his record was not related to McClure's in any way. Cook, a nineteen-year-old apprentice plumber from Baltimore, had enlisted on January 1, 1862, at Machodoc and served without absence until July 3, 1863. His Compiled Service Records clearly state he gave himself up to the Federals the day after the battery's horrific experience at Gettysburg and was not captured during the army's retreat back to Virginia. Moreover, this is the only way Cook could have fallen into enemy hands that day, as the Federals did not move into the Benner's Hill area occupied by Johnson's division and the Chesapeake Artillery until July 4. The Chesapeake was not in the area between Winchester and Front Royal until July 18. Federal records are clear that Cook was detained on July 3 at Gettysburg and that he was a deserter; the company's muster rolls of November 1, 1863, also record him as having deserted.[5]

After initially being sent to Fort Delaware, Cook was transferred to Point Lookout in September 1863. After that there are no further entries in his Compiled Service Record; he presumably took the Oath of Allegiance and was released. A far less likely possibility is Cook somehow managed to accidentally wander past Confederate pickets to the east of Johnson's division's lines—the opposite direction from Rock Creek, where he had helped bury some of the soldiers killed that day—and into Federal lines on July 3, was captured and held at Point Lookout until the end of the war, and his release or exchange records were lost. (Although prisoner exchange became more limited after Gettysburg, Trippe was mistaken in stating that it had ended; of the seven members of the company captured during the retreat from Gettysburg, four were exchanged or paroled for exchange.) This possibility still does not account for Cook being recorded in Federal capture records as a deserter. All things considered, with Federal and Confederate records in agreement, Cook's CSR appears to be correct in spite of the missing information about his final release from detention.[6]

The most likely origin for the story of Cook's and McClure's capture on the retreat from Gettysburg and subsequent incarceration at Fort Delaware until the end of the war is Cook, which is why he is mentioned in Trippe's letter to Wheeler. Cook occasionally embellished some details of the battery's service in articles he wrote for the *Baltimore Telegram* after the war, and in several instances confused details of the timing and sequence of events. Likely Cook had applied for residency at the Soldiers' Home and was denied because of his desertion record. It is entirely possible he misrepresented his leaving the army to avoid embarrassment.[7]

Cook had reason to be proud of his record with the unit up to and including the action on Benner's Hill. He had served without absence until that time, experienced the horrific scene at Gettysburg on July 2, and assisted burying his dead comrades that evening near Rock Creek. His decision to desert the next day was made at a time of extreme emotional distress and no doubt he came to regret it. Cook wrote several lively articles about the Chesapeake in the *Baltimore Telegram*, and it is obvious he held his comrades and the company's record in high esteem. Later he was an active member of the Society of the Army & Navy of the Confederate States in Maryland veterans' organization, as well as the Grand Lodge of Maryland, and even signed applications to the Soldiers' Home for former members of the company certifying their fitness for residency.[8]

Why McClure would state he had surrendered at Appomattox can only be surmised; it could be the result of a failing memory, or an embellishment that he felt made his service more interesting than being captured. Because of this, the history of his service was misunderstood in contemporary times and the final dissolution of Cook's service can't be confirmed with certainty. Failing veteran memories, mistakes, and deliberate misrepresentations, along with incomplete records, all contributed to errors in the historical record.

THE ROSTER

Introduction to the Roster

A total enrolment of 145 men are listed with the Chesapeake Artillery in the Compiled Service Records (CSRs) of Maryland Confederate Soldiers in the National Archives in Washington, DC. These records consist of an envelope of cards for each individual soldier; each card has a notation of their presence at company musters, details of special duty, capture records, hospital records, death, discharge, transfers, etc.[1]

In addition, several historical rosters of the battery were developed by Confederate veterans in the decades following the war that have been widely referred to and cited. Although much of their information is confirmed when cross referenced with other sources, these rosters contain numerous, and in some cases extensive, errors and omissions.

The earliest known roster of the unit was developed about 1865 by Pvt. Christopher Goodhand Lynch, and also includes a list of casualties. Consisting of 139 names, it appears to have been compiled immediately after the war, and is included in Lynch's papers in the US Army Education and History Center in Carlisle, Pennsylvania. Among numerous errors in spelling and incorrect first names Lynch omitted fifteen members of the unit, included four soldiers twice under different first names, and included ten names of men who never served with the battery.[2]

A partial roster was published in the *Baltimore Telegram* by Pvt. Jacob F. Cook sometime before 1879, and was included in S.Z. Ammen's newspaper scrapbook *Maryland Troops in the Confederate Army from Original Sources*. It includes only seventy-nine names, and although some of the errors in Lynch's roster are duplicated, it appears Cook compiled his roster independently; there are numerous unique errors and nicknames that are not part of Lynch's roster, in addition to the sixty names that appear in Lynch's roster but not Cook's. Based on these unique entries, it appears Jonathan T. Scharf used this roster in his *History of Western Maryland*, published in 1882.[3]

The most accurate historical roster, although incomplete, was published in 1894 in George W. Booth's *Illustrated Souvenir for the Maryland Confederate Soldiers' Home*. This roster includes 103 names, and appears to have been developed from the unit's muster rolls. It is highly accurate, and to a great extent matches the information in the National Archives, with one name duplicated. Curiously, the only soldier included who had died up until that time was Capt. William D. Brown, accounting for the numerous omissions; it is possible this roster was meant to appeal to veterans of the unit still living who were potential residents of the home. The original roster is in the Manuscript Collections of the Maryland Historical Society in Baltimore.[4]

In May 1900, Lynch published another roster "secured from the War Department at Washington," along with a brief history of the Chesapeake Artillery, in the *Centreville Record*. This version, which includes 138 names and was largely adapted from his original roster, has more spelling mistakes than the original, likely because of transcription errors to the newspaper edition. Although four names are included that were omitted from the original roster, an additional two names do not appear, making a total of thirteen soldiers excluded. In addition, seven soldiers appear twice under alternate spellings, and nine names are included of men that did not serve with the unit.[5]

In the same year William W. Goldsborough published a revised and expanded version of his 1869 book *The Maryland Line in the Confederate Army*, including a brief history of the 4th Maryland Artillery and a roster. It appears Goldsborough compiled Lynch's and Cook's published rosters, as he repeats errors that occurred uniquely in each. In format, the inclusion of incorrect names, and the list of casualties, Goldsborough's roster most closely conforms to Lynch's first list. Considering Lynch almost certainly wrote the part of Goldsborough's book on the Chesapeake Artillery's participation at Gettysburg and Fort Gregg, it appears Lynch was asked by Goldsborough to develop this roster for his book's first edition, but it was not included until the second edition. In addition to multiple spelling errors this roster lists 136 names, including nine names of men who did not serve in the unit, three soldiers mentioned twice with different spellings, and eleven omissions.[6]

The roster in the following pages has been developed from the Compiled Service Records of Maryland Confederate Soldiers in the National Archives in Washington, DC, supplemented with census records where found, court-martial records, casualty lists, contemporary accounts, veteran reminiscences, burial records, newspaper articles, family histories, and the records of the Maryland Line Confederate Soldiers' Home. While it is likely a definitive list, there is still information to be added for many of the individual soldiers.[7]

There are several key considerations taken into account for the compilation of this roster. The roster records are a combination of those for the entire history of the Chesapeake Artillery, i.e., Forrest's Virginia Artillery and the 4th Maryland Light Artillery Battery. If he originally enlisted in Forrest's Artillery Company and continued service through the time the unit was designated the 4th Maryland Artillery, a soldier's record is considered seamless between the two units. A soldier who is listed with multiple CSRs in the National Archives due to different spellings of his name has had all records combined into one entry with the correct name.

Muster records for the unit only exist for six periods: January/February 1862, dated March 1, 1862, at Tappahannock, Virginia; May/June 1863, dated June 30, 1863, at Chambersburg, Pennsylvania; September/October 1863, dated November 1, 1863, at Camp near Brandy Station, Virginia; and September/October 1864, dated October 31, 1864, November/December, 1864, dated December 31, 1864, and January/February 1865, dated February 28, 1865, all at Petersburg, Virginia. It appears through cross referencing with other documents that the unit also mustered for at least five additional periods—July/August 1862, November/December 1862, January/February 1863, March/April 1863, and May/June 1864—but these records are lost.

There are two significant gaps in the unit's records: the fourteen months between March 1, 1862, and April 30, 1863, and the ten months between November 1, 1863, and August 31, 1864. The only notations in CSRs during these time periods are for activities that happened outside the unit, such as detail service records, hospital records, casualty reports, and Federal capture records. This means it is possible for a soldier to have no record of service if he enlisted and left the unit between March 1, 1862, and May 1, 1863, or between November 1, 1863, and August 31, 1864. For this reason, five soldiers who appear to have served during the periods of these lost records and do not have service records in the CSRs for the unit are listed here: William H. Culver,[8] Robert Henry Goldsborough,[9] Edward (L. W.) Graham,[10] John Poisal Jr.,[11] and Lewis Warrington.[12]

These men are all mentioned in multiple postwar rosters and reminiscences. Only two are mentioned in National Archives records, both of whom were killed in battle: Edward Graham (listed as L. W. Graham) appears as killed in action at 1st Fredericksburg on a casualty list compiled by Capt. William D. Brown for 1862; and Robert Goldsborough, who was killed at Sailor's Creek in 1865, has service records with Co. B, 39th Virginia Cavalry Regiment and as a staff officer.[13] Notably, two of the other three soldiers also died in the service according to primary accounts: John Poisal Jr. died of illness in hospital and William Culver was killed in action at Fort Gregg on April 2, 1865. Since Culver was present outside the periods of the missing records he may have been serving in an informal capacity, while the service of Goldsborough, Graham, Poisal, and Warrington occurred entirely within the time of the company's lost records. Warrington is the only one who appears in the 1870 Census; specific details of their service with the battery remain to be discovered. Conversely, James Grason, who is mentioned in two contemporary letters but nowhere else in the battery's historical record, is not included.

Three soldiers who do have CSRs in the National Archives records for Forrest's Virginia Artillery are not listed here as members of the Chesapeake Artillery: Andrew Adams, Francis Bogue, and William Jackson. Although all three men enlisted with Capt. Joseph Forrest on January 1, 1862, at Machodoc, they appear to have been bounty jumpers, as all three also deserted together five days later and have no further record with the unit. Significantly, none of their names are recorded in any of the historical rosters. Since they never served with the unit they are included here under the section "Other Names Associated with the Chesapeake Artillery." Nine names are listed in the company's records in error, two are duplicates under different spellings, and one is not a soldier, but an African-American servant. With these adjustments, and the duplicate names and those listed in error eliminated, the total number of men who served in the battery is 135.

There are several distinct reporting patterns in the CSRs. These patterns were consistent throughout the war and verified by other sources and can be used to draw conclusions about the nature of a soldier's service.

When a soldier was marked as absent—whether detailed, furloughed, wounded, or a POW—it is consistently noted throughout the absence period in the muster rolls. When a soldier deserted it was noted once and the soldier's name was dropped from the rolls. When a soldier was killed in action there was no notation in the rolls, and the soldier's service record abruptly ceased beginning with the next muster after his death. For the purposes of this roster, battlefield deaths were determined when there was an abrupt end to the soldier's service record following an engagement with a concomitant absence of medical records, Federal capture records, and appearance in census records after 1860.

The most difficult and complex determinant in the CSRs is whether a soldier had deserted, especially for Maryland soldiers, who may also have been discharged late in the war. In the Chesapeake Artillery's records, as a consistent pattern, a soldier was marked as "Absent, Deserted" once and there was no further record. Some soldiers were marked as having deserted who had been captured; this was corrected later when notification of their capture was received from Federal authorities. For the purposes of this roster two criteria were used to determine whether a soldier was a deserter or not. First, if marked on a muster roll as being "Absent, Deserted," in the absence of further records it is so indicated in the roster. Second, if a soldier is marked as having deserted and this is supported by Federal detention records (e.g., he is identified as a deserter, takes the Oath of Allegiance shortly thereafter, joins a Federal military unit, etc.) he is also considered as having deserted. If a soldier is marked as "Absent, Deserted," but Federal Records indicate he is a prisoner of war and/or incarcerated in a prisoner of war camp, he is indicated as having been captured.

One additional pattern in the CSRs occurred only during January through March 1865. In October 1864, a court ruling in Richmond, Virginia, as the result of a writ of habeas corpus brought by members of the 1st Maryland Artillery against their captain, William F. Dement, determined Maryland soldiers could not be detained in service once they had served three years, and that they could be discharged. Four soldiers in the 4th Maryland Artillery applied for discharges and the records show these were granted in February 1865. Several men who had served for three years or nearly so decided to leave of their own accord at this time without the formality of applying for a discharge; four men were recorded as having deserted in February 1865, while an additional two appear in Federal records as deserters in March.

The records of an additional nineteen soldiers end abruptly at some time during January–March 1865; only one of these was detained or required to report to Federal authorities and their records give no indication they had deserted. Deserters were commonly captured and detained by the Federals, making it highly unlikely this large number of men could have deserted, yet avoided detention or incarceration, and it is also too large a number to represent soldiers killed in action at that time in the war. Moreover, these were some of the battery's most reliable soldiers, men who had served consistently through the whole war, been promoted, returned to duty following recovery from wounds, and included in their number Lt. Thomas P. LeCompte, an officer who was promoted from the ranks for "Valor & Skill." It is almost certain these men did not desert, but were discharged.

Presumably these men had a letter from a superior officer or paperwork of some kind indicating this; it is possible these men were formally discharged and at that late date in the war the records were lost. Pvt. Benjamin Young appears to have been granted a discharge on March 28, 1865. He reported to Federal authorities and took the Oath of Allegiance in Richmond on April 17, but was not detained or recorded as a deserter or prisoner of war. There is no record of his having been discharged other than his attesting to it after the war. Soldiers whose records terminate in 1865 are not listed as "Absent, Deserted," and have no Federal records indicating detention or that they are deserters or prisoners of war, are considered as having been discharged, and are noted here as "appears to have been discharged."[14]

The roster is divided into three sections. The first section lists men who enlisted or were transferred into and served with the unit. Second, the only known African-American servant. Third, Other Names Associated with the Chesapeake Artillery; these are men who are listed in historical rosters in error or mistakenly have CSRs in the Chesapeake Artillery's records but never served with the battery. All locations are in Maryland unless otherwise noted; enlistments are in Forrest's Virginia Artillery/4th Maryland Artillery unless otherwise noted. Wealth as recorded in census data is \$ Value of Real Estate/\$ Value of Personal Estate; personal wealth is \$0 if not noted. Birth and death dates are noted if known. Nicknames are noted in parentheses if known. Rank is private unless otherwise noted.

Abbreviations Used in the Roster

A.C.: army corps
ADC: aide de Camp
adm.: admitted
a.k.a.: also known as
Appmtx: Appomattox
apptd.: appointed
Art.: Artillery
ass.: assigned
AWOL: absent without leave
b.: born
brn.: brown
bur.: buried
Capt.: Captain
Cav.: Cavalry
Cem.: Cemetery
cen.: census
cmplx.: complexion
Co.: Company
corp.: corporal
cptd.: captured
CSA: Confederate States of America
CSR: Compiled Service Records
CV: Confederate Veteran Magazine
d.: died
DC: District of Columbia
DEL: Delaware
disch.: discharged
det.: detailed
el.: elected
enl.: enlisted
exch.: exchanged
Ft.: Fort
G.H.: General Hospital
hr.: hair
ill.: Illiterate
Inf.: Infantry
KIA: killed in Action
LOA: leave of absence
LOC: Library of Congress
lt.: lieutenant
m.: married
MD: Maryland
MLCSH: Maryland Line Confederate Soldiers Home
mos.: months
MWIA: mortally wounded in action
NFR: no further record
OOA: Oath of Allegiance
OR: Official Records of the War of the Rebellion
Ord.: ordnance
PA: Pennsylvania
pd.: paid
pld.: paroled
PMG: Provost Marshall General
POW: prisoner of war
pres.: present
prom.: promoted
Pt.: Point
pvt.: private
QM: quartermaster
Regt.: Regiment
req.: requisition
res.: residence
RTD: returned to duty
s.: single
SANCSM: Society of the Army & Navy of the Confederate States of Maryland
sgt.: sergeant
SO: Special Orders
tnsfr.: transfer
UCV: United Confederate Veterans
US: United States
USAHEC: U.S. Army History and Education Center
UVA: University of Virginia
VA: Virginia
WIA: wounded in action

The Prisoner of War facilities referred to in the roster are as follows:

Camp Chase: Camp Chase POW Camp, Columbus, Ohio

Elmira: Elmira POW Camp, Elmira, New York

Ft. Delaware: Fort Delaware POW Prison, Delaware Bay, Delaware

Fortress Monroe: Fort Monroe POW Prison, Norfolk, Virginia

Hart Island: POW Prison at Hart Island, New York City, New York

Johnson's Island: POW Camp, near Sandusky, Ohio

Old Capitol Prison: POW Prison, Washington, DC

Pt. Lookout: Point Lookout POW Camp, St. Mary's County, Maryland

Roster of the Chesapeake Artillery, 4th Maryland Light Artillery Battery, CSA

Men Who Enlisted or Were Transferred into and Served with the Unit

ACTON, WASHINGTON ("WASH"): 1860 cen.: res. Charles County; age 29; farmhand; m. Enl. 8/5/1861, age 32, in the Stafford Light Artillery (VA), at Fredericksburg, VA, for 12 mos. Tnsfr. to 4th MD Art., SO 93/2, 4/21/1864. Pres. to 2/28/1865. Applied for disch. 3/18/1865, and it appears this was granted. NFR.

ALLSTON, FREDERICK JAMES ("FRED"): B. 1843 in St. Mary's County. 1860 cen: res. 15th Ward, Baltimore City, age 17, s., clerk, lived with parents and five siblings. Enl. 1/1/1862 as 3rd Corp., at Machodoc, VA, for war. Captured by Federal authorities 10/20/1862 "with a canoe load of goods" while ferrying supplies into Virginia. NFR. He lived in St. Mary's County following the war.

BAKER, HENRY ("DAD"): b. 4/3/1834. 1860 cen.: res. 8th Ward, Baltimore City; age 29; police officer; s., lived with mother and three siblings. Enl. Co. D, 1st MD Inf., 5/22/1861 for war at Harper's Ferry, VA. Present to 12/31/1861. Enl. 4th MD Art. 1/1/1861, Machodoc, VA, for war. Prom. Corp. before 5/1/1863. Present to 12/31/1864. NFR, appears to have been discharged.

BARCHUS, WILLIAM W.: 1860 cen.: res. Allegany County, age 26, laborer, s., lived with parents and three siblings. Enl. Co. K, 1st VA Art., 8/7/1862 for war at Petersburg, VA, as substitute for S.S. Carter. Tnsfr to 4th MD Art., SO 93/2, 4/21/1864. Adm. to Robertson Hospital 7/7/1864, "dysentery acute;" discharged 10/18/1864, for a 30-day furlough. Adm. again 11/11/1864, epilepsy. Detailed as hospital guard and messenger 11/8/1864 by SO 270/12. Appeared before Medical Examining Board 3/20/1865 and was discharged for disability. NFR.

BLUNT, JAMES ISAAC: 1860 cen.: res. Talbot County, age 21, b. in DEL, lived with father and two siblings; family owned 3 slaves. Enl. 2/6/1862, for war at Heathsville, VA. Adm. to hospital 4/18/1862, diarrhea. WIA 1st Fredericksburg 12/13/1862. Prom. to Corp. before 6/30/1863. Court martial 12/9/1863, with G.C. Phillips; charges unknown; reduced in rank to private. Present to 12/31/1864. Detailed 1/15/1865 to G.H. No. 9 thru 2/3/1865. Appears to have been discharged. NFR.

BOUCHET, MICHAEL: Lived in Baltimore, m. with grown children. Enl. 1/1/1862 for war at Machodoc, VA. Obtained James T. Cecil as a substitute 2/6/1862. NFR.

BRADY, MICHAEL H.: 1860 cen.: res. Gloucester County, VA, age 24, engineer, s. Enl. 1/1/1862 for war at Machodoc, VA, as an Artificer. Present to 6/30/1863. Adm. to G.H. in Staunton, VA, for debility 10/24/1863; RTD 10/31/1863. Extra duty as blacksmith, 3/1 to 6/6/1864. Absent on recruiting furlough 3/1/1865. Paroled at Richmond, VA, 5/8/1865 and returned home.

BROWN, JOHN WESLEY ("WES"): 1860 cen.: res. Monkton, Baltimore County, age 23, Methodist clergyman, s. Enl. 5/14/1862 for war at Richmond, VA. Adm. G.H. Richmond 6/8/1862, diarrhea and absent until after 7/15/1862. Present through 11/1/1863. LOA 1/1/1864–4/30/1864. Deserted 8/6/1864, took OOA 8/7/1864 and was released.

BROWN, PHILIP AULD HARRISON ("PHIL"): Brother of W. D. Brown. b. 1/3/1842 in Baltimore. Graduated from Dickinson College, Carlisle, PA, in 1860. Was a clerk in CSA QM Dept. in Goldsboro, NC, 1/15–5/29/1862. Enl. as 4th Sgt. 6/20/1862 for war at Richmond, VA. Furlough 3/1863. WIA Gettysburg, 7/2/1863. Cptd. at Hagerstown 7/7/1863 and sent to Ft. Delaware. Tnsfr. to Pt. Lookout 9/26/1863. Exch. 12/24/1863. Furlough 1/1864. Tnsfr. to CSA Signal Corps 2/9/1864, SO 31/10, and was signal officer on a blockade runner. OOA at Baltimore 5/15/1865. Ordained in the Episcopal Church in 1871; rector of Christ Church, Cooperstown, NY, 1872–74, vicar of Trinity Parish, NYC, 1875–1909. m. Jane Russell Averall Carter in 1879, seven children. d. 9/15/1909, age 67, bur. Christ Church Cem., Cooperstown, NY.

BROWN, WILLIAM DAWSON ("BILLY"): B. about 1831, res. 17th Ward, Baltimore City, s., lived at 23 Calvert St. He owned a shipyard at Hughes and Covington Sts. Prewar commanded the Lafayette Guards. Enl. 5/20/1861 as 3rd Lt., Co. E, Culpeper Court House Infantry. Apptd. Capt., 1st Co., 2nd MD Infantry Rgt. 8/1861, but the regiment was never formed. Enl. 1/1/1862 as 1st Lt. at Machodoc, VA. Elected Capt. 5/15/1862. Acting Chief of Artillery, Ewell's Division, 10/1862 to early 1863. Absent for battle of 1st Fredericksburg due to an unknown injury. MWIA at Gettysburg 7/2/1863, both legs fractured. First treated at the Daniel Lady farm, then the Elizabeth Weible farm; left leg amputated above knee at Weible's. d. 7/11/1863 and initially buried at the Weible farm. Obituary in the *Baltimore Sun* 7/14/1863. Removed by his family and re-buried 7/31/1863 Greenmount Cem., Baltimore. His funeral was interrupted by Federal soldiers who arrested all the men attending as Confederate sympathizers; see *Baltimore Gazette* 8/6/1863. Some of his wartime letters are in the Ward Family Papers, LOC.

BRYAN, ANDREW JOHN ("DOCTOR JACK"): 1860 cen.: res. Culpeper County, VA; age 31, doctor, m. with one child. Enl. 1/1/1862 for war at Machodoc, VA. POW 9/14/1862. Exch. at Aiken's Landing 9/27/1862. KIA Gettysburg 7/2/1863, bur. at the Daniel Benner farm.

BUCKMASTER, HENRY C.: 1860 cen.: res. 13th Ward, Baltimore City, age 25, clerk, s., b. in VA. Enl. in Richmond, VA as 5th Corp. 4/12/1862 for war. Furlough 2/1863. WIA Gettysburg 7/2/1863. Cptd. Gettysburg 7/4/1863. Adm. to G.H. West's Buildings, Baltimore 7/28/1863. Sent to Pt. Lookout 8/20/1863. Exch. 3/17/1864. Adm. to Robertson Hospital 8/25/1864, diarrhea; RTD 9/1/1864. Apptd. 4th Sgt. 12/1/1864. Apptd. 2nd Sgt. before 2/28/1865. Appears to have been discharged. Paroled at Baltimore 4/24/1865.

BURKE, WALTER L.: 1860 cen.: res. 20th Ward, Baltimore City, age 14, student, lived with mother and two sisters. Enl. for war with G. W. Goodhand and W. F. Holtzman 6/28/1863 at Dover, PA. Present to 12/31/1864. Deserted 2/22/1865. NFR. Ran a grocery store with W. F. Holtzman after the war, then became an advertising agent with his father.

CANFIELD, JOHN W.: Resident of Dorchester County. Enl. 11/18/1862 for war in Richmond, VA. Adm. to G. H. Staunton as convalescent 3/16/1863. Present 6/30/1863. Cptd. at Winchester 7/20/1863. Paroled until exchanged 8/16/1863 at Baltimore and forwarded to Pt. Lookout 8/17/1863. Took OOA on 1/26/1864 and was released. NFR. Postwar he moved to Kentucky, married, and had four children; was later a letter carrier in St. Louis, MO.

CARBERRY, THOMAS ALONZO ("TOM"): Resident of Baltimore City. Enl. 1/1/1862 for war at Machodoc, VA. Promoted to corporal before 5/1/1863. Received severe gunshot wound at 2nd Fredericksburg 5/2/1863, leg amputated below knee. Adm. Robertson Hospital 5/6/1863; transferred to Castle Thunder, Richmond, 5/10/1863. Convalescent at G. H. Staunton. Applied for artificial limb 4/27/1864 and was furloughed. Retired to Invalid Corps 8/31/1864 and was a clerk in Macon, GA. Promoted to QM Sgt. after 10/31/1864. Paroled at Albany, GA, 5/6/1865. 5'8", hr. black, eyes dark, cmplx. fair.

CECIL, JAMES T.: 1860 cen.: res. Harford County, age 24, miller, s. Lived with his mother and sister. Enl. 2/16/1862 for war at Heathsville, VA, as a substitute for Michael Bouchet. Present to 3/1/1862. Tnsfr. to 2nd Maryland Artillery, date unknown. Reported as AWOL on 1/1/1863. NFR. Lived in St. Mary's County after the war.

CECIL, JOHN T.: 1860 cen.: res. Queen Anne's County, age 25, laborer, s. Enl. 1/1/1862 for 1 year at Machodoc, VA. Absent 3/1/1862 on recruiting service to find a substitute. NFR.

CHEW, WALTER SCOTT: 1860 cen.: res. Georgetown, DC, age 19, clerk, s., lived with his parents and four siblings. Enl. as 1st Sgt. 1/1/1862 for war at Machodoc, VA. Elected 1st Lt. 5/15/1862. Commanded 4th MD Art. following the death of Capt. W. D. Brown at Gettysburg. Appt. Captain 6/6/1864. POW Fort Gregg, 4/2/1865. Committed to Old Capitol Prison, Washington, DC, and sent to Johnson's Island 4/9/1865. OOA 6/2/1865 and released. 5'6" cmplx. fair, hair light, eyes blue. Postwar married Marian Waters, no children; worked as a clerk in the US Capitol building in Washington. Died 2/19/1900, bur. Oak Hill Cemetery, Washington, DC.

COOK, JACOB F.: b. 5/19/1842. 1860 cen.: res. 12th Ward, Baltimore City, age 18, apprentice plumber, s., lived with his parents and five siblings. Enl. for war 1/1/1862 at Machodoc, VA. Present to 6/30/1863. Deserted 7/3/1863 at Gettysburg, PA. Sent to Ft. Delaware; forwarded to Pt. Lookout 9/26/1863 and presumably released. NFR. Postwar he was a reading clerk for the Baltimore City Council, a member of the Mt. Vernon chapter of the Grand Lodge of Maryland, and a member of the SANCSM; he married Sallie E. Cook and lived at 165 W. Fayette Street, Baltimore. Cook died 12/5/1898 and is buried at Loudon Park Cem. Cook wrote several lively articles about the Chesapeake Artillery in the *Baltimore Telegram* in 1879 and 1880 that were included in S. Z. Ammen's *Maryland Soldiers in the Confederate Army*.

CORRY, HENRY J.: enl. in Co. I, 1st Maryland Inf. Regt. for 1 year 7/27/1861. Adm. to G.H. No. 21, Richmond, VA, for pneumonia; returned to duty 5/29/1862. Disch. 6/15/1862, term of enlistment expired, age 17, 5'5" cmplx. light, eyes grey, hair light, occupation seaman. Enl. Co. B, 2nd Maryland Infantry Battalion 8/27/1862 in Richmond, VA. Present to 3/31/1864. Tnsfr. to 4th Maryland Art. before 7/1/1864. Present to 2/28/1865. Deserted sometime after that date; sent from City Point, VA, to the PMG in Washington, DC, 4/24/1865. NFR.

COTTRELL, EDWARD C.: b. in 1835, was a shoemaker prewar, res. Princess Anne, Somerset County. Cottrell was a noted secessionist before the war. Arrested 11/16/1861 and confined at Ft. McHenry for "Correspondence with rebels." Forwarded by command of Maj. Gen. John A. Dix to Ft. Lafayette in NYC, and so reported in the *New York Times* 12/4/1861. That same day the *Baltimore Sun* reported he had been offered his release upon taking OOA but refused. Dix finally recommended his discharge and he was released 2/22/1862. Enl. 6/13/1862 for war at Richmond, VA. Present through 11/1/1863. Wounded near Glendale, VA, 6/15/1864, flesh wound of upper left arm. Adm. to G.H. at Petersburg 6/23/1864 and tnsfr. to Chimborazo 6/24/1864. Furloughed for 40 days to Columbus, GA, 7/29/1864. Admitted for duty to G.H. No. 9 at Richmond, VA, 9/24/1864, and returned to active duty 11/2/1864. Present to 2/28/1865. Appmtx. Postwar he was a school teacher in Dranesville, VA, and married late in life, was widowed, and married again. Cottrell was a member of the John Q. Marr UCV Camp and wrote two articles in CV on the participation of the 4th MD Art. at Fort Gregg. D. 10/30/1910, aged 75; his death notice is in CV, 19, 9.

COVINGTON, ALLEN J.: 1860 cen.: res. Queen Anne's County, age 22, farmer, s., lived with his parents and two siblings. Enl. 11/1/1862 for war at Richmond, VA. Became an Artificer before 12/31/1864. Present through 2/28/1865. Appmtx. Reported to Provost Marshall, Washington, DC, 4/22/1865 on his way home.

CROWLEY, ROBERT A.: 1860 cen.: res. 3rd Ward, Baltimore City, age 18, a law student and clerk, s., lived with his father and two siblings. Enl. 1/1/1862 as 4th Sgt. for war at Machodoc, VA. WIA 5/3/1863 at 2nd Fredericksburg, gunshot wound to face. Adm. G.H. No. 9, 5/6/1863 Richmond, VA, tnsfr. to Chimborazo the next day. RTD and apptd. 2nd Sgt. before 6/30/1863. Furloughed 2/1864. Apptd. 1st Sgt. and present through 10/31/1864. Absent on sick furlough 12/31/1864. Appeared before the Medical Examining Board 3/8/1865, stating he had been sick for "8 months," and was sent to Robertson Hospital in Richmond 3/15/1865 with "chronic diarrhea"; RTD 4/2/1865, but could not reach the army; paroled there 4/18/1865, and given a pass to return home to Baltimore. Detained 5/4/1865 by the PMG, 8th A.C. USA; released 5/5/1865 "to go to New Jersey." NFR.

CULVER, EDWIN KENDALL ("E.K."): b. 9/23/1846 in KY. Enl. 4/5/1864 for war at Fredericks Hall, VA. Present through 2/28/1865. Deserted in 3/1865 and was detained at Pt. Lookout. OOA 3/29/1865 and released. He reported to the office of the PMG in Washington, DC, 6/24/1865, claiming to be a member of the 16th GA Inf., and secured transportation to Lincolntown, NC. Postwar he moved to Arkansas. He married Mary Osborne in 1868 and had three children with her before her death. Married Luella in 1886 and had six more children. D. 1/5/1915, bur. Thomas Cemetery in North Little Rock, AR. His obituary appeared in the *Little Rock Arkansas Gazette* 1/6/1915.

CULVER, WILLIAM H.: 1860 cen.: res. Worcester County, age 22, laborer, $0/$200, m. with one daughter. No record of enlistment or service in the NA, but listed in both of Lynch's rosters and included in Goldsborough's. Mentioned by Lynch in his casualty list and in Goldsborough's *Maryland Line* as having been killed at Fort Gregg. He does not appear in the 1870 Census and there are no Federal medical or capture records for him. KIA Fort Gregg 4/2/1865. Probably buried on Memorial Hill, Blandford Cemetery, Petersburg, VA.

CUSICK, FREDERICK ("FRED"): 1860 cen.: res. Charles County, age 18, clerk, s., lived with his parents and five siblings. Enl. for war 5/2/1861 in Co. B, 1st MD Inf. Regt. at Harper's Ferry, VA. Disch. 5/21/1862 at completion of term of service. Enl. for war in 4th MD Art. 6/13/1862 in Richmond, VA. KIA Gettysburg 7/2/1863 and bur. on the Daniel Benner farm. Removed to the Gettysburg Dead section of Hollywood Cem., Richmond, VA, on 7/4/1873 as an unknown.

DALLAM, CHARLES FRANCIS: B. in Baltimore 8/24/1834. 1860 cen.: res. 20th Ward, Baltimore City, age 27, s., lived with two sisters in a boarding house at the corner of Garden and Hoffman Sts. Attended the Maryland Institute for the Promotion of Mechanic Arts. Enl. for war 8/25/1862 at Gordonsville, VA. WIA at 2nd Fredericksburg and Gettysburg. Pres. through 11/1/1863. Furloughed 3/1864 and extended 4/3/1864 by SO 92/1. Present through 3/1/1865. POW 4/2/1865 at Fort Gregg and sent to Pt. Lookout. Signed the last morning report at Pt. Lookout as acting Sgt. Major 6/25/1865. Took OOA and released 6/26/1865, 5'5" cmplx. dark, hr. dark brown, eyes hazel. Reported to PMG, Washington, DC, 6/27/1865, and was furnished transportation to Baltimore. Postwar he was a partner in a wine and liquor importing firm at 114 Lombard St. in Baltimore, and later appointed as the city clerk. Married and had two daughters. He was a member of the ANSCSM and for 25 years was a member of the 5th MD Inf. Regt, Maryland National Guard. Resident of the MLCSH and died there 2/13/1913, aged 79.

DAWSON, LAMBDEN T.: b. 6/18/1842. 1860 cen: res. Talbot County, age 18, lived with his parents and two siblings; worked on his father's farm; the family owned 12 slaves. Enl. 1/1/1862 for war at Machodoc, VA. Present through 11/1/1863. Deserted 12/1863, cptd. 12/23/1863 and sent to Pt. Lookout. Took OOA and released 1/10/1864. NFR. Died in Chester, SC, of a cerebral hemorrhage 5/1/1926 at age 83, bur. there at Evergreen Cemetery.

DEAN, JAMES E.: 1860 cen.: res. Dorchester County, age 24, day laborer, m., $311/$81, illiterate. Enl. for war 1/1/1862 at Machodoc, VA. Adm. to G.H. No. 21, Richmond, VA, 4/13/1862, diarrhea, RTD 5/28/1862. Adm. again 9/6/1862 with rheumatism, declared unfit for field duty 10/18/1862 due to a hernia, ass. to duty there 10/21/1862 as a nurse. Returned to active duty 6/12/1863. Present through 11/1/1863. Court martial 3/7/1864, charges unknown; acquitted. WIA, shell fragment in the right thigh, 9/21/1864 at Petersburg, VA, and adm. to Robertson Hospital, Richmond, VA, 9/22/1864. Treated at several hospitals in Richmond and RTD 12/30/1864. Present 12/31/1864. Ass. to G.H. No. 9, Richmond, VA, for duty 1/30/1865. Paroled at Richmond 4/20/1865 and released.

DEAN, THOMAS L.: 1860 cen.: res. Caroline County, age 23, farm hand, s. Enl. 11/1/1862 for war at Richmond, VA. Present to 6/30/1863. Absent sick for May/June and September/October 1863 musters. Court martial 2/1/1864 with R.W. Webb, charges unknown, acquitted. NFR.

DOUGHERTY, DANIEL ("DAN"): 1860 cen.: res. 4th Ward, Baltimore City, age 23, moulder, s., lived with his mother and sister, all born in Ireland. Enl. as 5th Sgt. in Co. B, 1st Maryland Infantry Regiment on 5/21/1861. Discharged 5/21/1862 when term of enlistment ended. Enl. for war 6/13/1862 at Richmond, VA. Resent to 6/30/1863. MWIA Gettysburg, 7/2/1863, bur. on the Daniel Benner farm across the Hanover Road from the Daniel Lady farmhouse. Removed to Hollywood Cem., Richmond, VA, on 5/17/1873.

EGAN, ANDREW A. ("ANDY"): Lived at 88 Saratoga Street, Baltimore City. Enl. 1/1/1862 for war at Machodoc, VA. Severely WIA by a shell fragment in hip and thigh at 2nd Manassas 8/29/1862 and cptd. Paroled at Warrenton 9/29/1862. Treated in various hospitals in Richmond until 11/14/1863, when he was furloughed for 60 days. Applied for duty as a clerk in the CS QM Dept. 11/25/1863. Application forwarded by the Medical Examining Board after his appearance on 1/11/1864. Detailed as a clerk for Gen. Richard S. Ewell in Richmond, VA, by SO 15/2 1/16/1864. Paroled 4/10/1865 in Richmond and returned home.

EMBERT, JOHN R.H.: B. 3/13/1837 at Wye Neck, Queen Anne's County. Enl. for war 2/1/1862 at Heathsville, VA. Adm. to G.H. No. 21, Richmond, VA, 4/18/1862 for dysentery. Tnsfr. to Co. B, 1st MD Cavalry Regt. 11/5/1862. Adm. to G.H. No. 9 in Richmond, VA, 12/27/1863 for "camp itch." Deserted 3/10/1864. Arrested near Winchester, VA, 5/19/1864 as a bushwhacker: "was absent from his command when captured and evidence from letters found on his person and acknowledgements divulged to prisoner in guard house fully established the fact of his having volunteered to bushwhack the pickets at Winchester." He was sentenced to death along with two others, but the sentence was commuted on the scaffold to hard labor at the penitentiary at Albany, NY, by President Lincoln; transferred to Fortress Monroe for exchange, took OOA and was released 7/13/1865. His experiences are detailed in an article in CV 19, 382–383. Postwar he married and had three sons, one of whom lived to adulthood. D. 3/12/1904 aged 67, bur. at St. Peter's Cem., Queenstown.

ENNIS, JOSEPH H.: 1860 cen.: res. Worcester County, age 18, apprentice shoemaker, s. Enl. 1/1/1862 for war at Machodoc, VA. Apptd. 4th Corp. before 6/30/1863 and 3rd Corp. before 11/1/1863. Furloughed 2/1864. Apptd. 4th Sgt. before 10/31/1864. Promoted to 3rd Sgt. and present to 12/31/1864. Ass. to G.H. No. 9, Richmond, VA, for duty 2/1/1865. Paroled at Richmond, VA, 4/20/1865.

ENNIS, THOMAS H.: 1860 cen.: res. Talbot County, age 19, apprentice shoemaker, s. Enl. for war 8/1/1863 at Gordonsville,

VA. Present to 2/28/1865. Appears to have been discharged. NFR.

EVERNGAM, THOMAS JAMES: B. 4/1831 and a resident of Queen Anne's County; married with one son. Enl. 11/1/1862 for war at Richmond, VA. Present to 2/28/1865. KIA Fort Gregg 4/2/1865. Probably buried on Memorial Hill, Blandford Cemetery, Petersburg, VA. His brother was incarcerated in Ft. Delaware for burning the blockade ship *Hard Times* and died there 2/1/1863.

EWELL, GEORGE SHELDON ROSS: B. 2/13/1841 in DEL. No record of enlistment, but occurred after 3/1/1862 for war as Sgt. Detailed as a nurse to G.H. No. 18 in Richmond, VA, 9/13/1862, and as a hospital steward 1/8/1863. Ordered to First Arkansas Hospital, Ft. Gaines, GA, as a hospital steward by SO 126/4 on 1/18/1863, then to Wayside Hospital in Ft. Gaines by SO 32/3. Served in this capacity to 10/31/1864. NFR. It appears he was dropped from the rolls upon his appt. to hospital steward, as he does not appear on any of the unit's muster records, although his records do indicate he was a Sgt. in the 4th MD Art. He was married 12/29/1864 in Clay County, GA, and was a pharmacist postwar. D. 12/8/1914 age 73, bur. at Blakely City Cem., Early County, GA.

FAIRBANKS, FRANCIS M. ("FRANK"): 1860 cen.: res. Talbot County, age 19, clerk, s.. Enl. 1/1/1862 at Machodoc, VA. Present to 2/28/1865. Deserted 3/1865 and was taken to Pt. Lookout. OOA 3/29/1865 and released. NFR.

FORREST, JOSEPH: B. 9/5/1821 at Forrest Hall, St. Mary's County. 1860 cen.: res. St. Mary's County, age 38, plantation owner, m. with four children, $63,000/$51,650. He was the wealthiest man in St. Mary's County and owned 45 slaves and two plantations. Prewar he commanded the St. Mary's Rangers militia company. Signed a Special Requisition 9/30/1861 as Capt. of company in the 2nd Maryland Inf. Regt., but the unit was never formed. Enl. 1/1/1862 for war as Capt. of the Chesapeake Artillery at Machodoc, VA. Dropped at 5/15/1862 re-organization. His wife and children were banished from Maryland for being Southern sympathizers. He moved his family and slaves to Louisiana and then Texas. Took OOA 7/17/1865 at Galveston, TX, and returned to St. Mary's County, but his property had been declared "abandoned" and expropriated by the Federal government to operate "Government farms" for the Freedman's Bureau. He received a presidential pardon 10/9/1865, but his property was not returned to him until 3/1866. D. 3/8/1889 aged 67, bur. at Saint Francis Xavier Church Cem., St. Mary's County; his obituary appeared in the *St. Mary's Beacon* 3/14/1889, describing him as "a gentleman of the old school." The house on one of Forrest's estates, "Sandgates," has been restored and still stands near Oakville in St. Mary's County. See Ruffner for additional details on his life.

GARDNER, JOHN HENRY: 1860 cen.: res. Queen Anne's County, age 25, carpenter, s. Enl. 11/1/1862 for war at Richmond, VA. Present to 6/30/1863. Adm. to G.H. Hospital No. 9, Richmond, VA,10/10/1863 for "remittent fever." RTD 11/13/1863. POW 4/2/1865 at Fort Gregg and sent to Pt. Lookout 4/4/1865. Released 6/12/1865. D. in 1900; he was eulogized by Christopher Goodhand Lynch in the *Centreville Record* 5/3/1900.

GARRETT, CHARLES T.: 1860 cen.: res. Louisa County, VA, age 16, laborer, s., illiterate. Enl. 3/14/1864 at Fredericks

Hall, VA. Present to 11/1/1864. WIA in left arm at Cold Harbor 6/3/1864. Adm. to Stuart Hospital, Richmond, VA, 6/7/1864; ret. to duty 6/11/1864. He was Absent Sick and in and out of hospitals in Richmond, VA, 7/15/1864–2/16/1865 for impetigo, intermittent fever, and gonorrhea. Paroled in Richmond, VA, 5/5/1865.

GOLDSBOROUGH, ROBERT HENRY: B. 1/15/1841. 1860 cen.: res. Talbot County, age 19, s.; he and two of his brothers boarded with the wealthy Fedmann and Emory families, who owned eight slaves. No record of enlistment or service with the company, but he is listed on both of Lynch's rosters and included in Cook's. Appears to have enlisted in the battery after 3/1/1862 and left before enlisting in Co. B, 39th Battalion VA Cavalry on 10/29/1862. Apptd. 1st Lt. and ADC and transferred to the staff of Maj. Gen. Jeb Stuart 5/2/1863. POW Beverley Ford, VA, 6/9/1863, imprisoned at Old Capitol Prison and Johnson's Island. Exchanged 2/20/1865 and assigned to the staff of Maj. Gen. GWC Lee as ADC. KIA Sailor's Creek, 4/6/1865. Bur. Ashby-Goldsborough Family Cem., Easton.

GOODHAND, GEORGE W.: 1860 cen.: res. 18th Ward, Baltimore City, age 15, student, s. Enl. 6/28/1863 for war at Dover, PA, with W. L. Burke and W. F. Holtzman. Present through 2/28/1865. He became separated from the unit following the fall of Petersburg and was cptd. 4/12/1865 at Manchester, VA, took OOA and released same day.

GORE, JOHN W.: 1860 cen.: res. 10th Ward, City of Baltimore, age 39, clerk, s. Enl. 1/1/1862 for war at Machodoc, VA. Present through 6/30/1863. Cptd. 7/19/1863 in Berkeley County, VA (WVA), during the retreat from Gettysburg. Sent to Camp Chase, OH. OOA and released 1/16/1865. 5'11" tall, cmplx. fair, hair light, eyes blue.

GRAHAM, EDWARD (L.W. GRAHAM): 1860 cen.: res. 8th Ward, Baltimore City, age 25, carpenter, s., lived with his parents and two siblings. Enl. after 3/1/1862 and KIA 1st Fredericksburg 12/13/1862. No record of enlistment or service; listed in both of Lynch's rosters, and with no first name in both Goldsborough's and Cook's. Multiple references cite him as KIA at 1st Fredericksburg. He appears as KIA 12/13/1862 at 1st Fredericksburg on Capt. W. D. Brown's casualty list as L. W. Graham. There are no medical or Federal capture records for him, and he does not appear in the 1870 Census.

GRASON, JOHN: B. 12/22/1824. 1860 cen.: res. Queen Anne's County, age 36, farmer, s., lived with his parents and six siblings. Household wealth was $20,000/$20,000 and the family owned 32 slaves; his father was a former governor of Maryland. Enl. 2/9/1862 for war at Heathsville, VA. Detailed to procure horses 2/9–2/18/1862. El. 2nd Lt. 5/24/1862. KIA 1st Fredericksburg, 12/13/1862, and buried near Hamilton's Crossing. His obituary appeared in the *Baltimore Daily Gazette* 1/6/1863.

GREEN, ALEXANDER: 1860 cen.: res. Charles County, age 24, farmer, s., lived with his father and brother. Enl. in Co. E, 20th Battalion Virginia Heavy Artillery for war 4/23/1862. Adm. to G.H. Petersburg, VA, 4/3/1863 for duty until 6/15/1863. Adm. again 12/15/1863, RTD 1/12/1864. Tnsfr. to 4th MD Art. 5/3/1864 by SO 103/27. Present to 12/31/1864. Deserted 2/1/1865, took OOA and released. NFR.

GREEN, JOHN F. ("LITTLE"): B. 9/1842. 1860 cen.: res. Dorchester County, age 19, farmer laborer, s., boarded with another family. Enl. 1/1/1862 for war at Machodoc, VA. WIA, gunshot wound in left thigh, 1st Fredericksburg 12/13/1862. Adm. Chimborazo, Richmond, VA, 12/16/1862, and tnsfr. to Huegenot Springs Hospital 1/16/1862. Adm. Chimborazo on 4/26/1863 and left of his own accord 5/10/1863 to re-join the unit. WIA Gettysburg 7/2/1863. Present to 11/1/1863. WIA, flesh wound to forehead, at Petersburg 7/30/1864. Adm. to G.H. Petersburg 8/1/1864, tnsfr. to Chimborazo 8/14/1864, and again left of his own accord 9/1/1864 to re-join the unit. Present until 12/31/1864. It appears he was discharged. NFR. Postwar he worked as a stationary engineer and lived in Dorchester and Kent Counties. Resident of the MLCSH; d. 6/12/1928 age 86, bur. in Loudon Park Cem., Baltimore.

GREEN, VINCENT ("BIG"): B. 10/1841. 1860 cen.: res. Baltimore County, age 18, farm laborer, s. Enl. 1/1/1862 for war at Machodoc, VA. WIA, gunshot wound left leg above the knee at 1st Fredericksburg 12/13/1862. Adm. to 5th Div. Hospital, Camp Winder, 12/16/1862, and tnsfr. to G.H. Farmville, 1/15/1863. RTD 2/16/1863. Present to 12/31/1864. It appears he was discharged. NFR. Resident of MLCSH. D. 2/16/1919, age 77, bur. in Loudon Park Cem., Baltimore.

GRIMES, ROBERT J.: 1860 cen.: res. Hanover County, VA, age 17, farmer, s., lived with his parents and two siblings. Enl. for war 4/30/1864 in Hanover County. Adm. 6/7/1864 to G.H. No. 9, tnsfr. to Chimborazo 6/8/1864, diarrhea. RTD 6/10/1864. Adm. to G.H. No. 9 9/28/1864, remittent fever, tnsfr. to Chimborazo 9/29/1864. Ass. to duty there 10/7/1864. Marked as "Absent, sick" for musters of 11/1/1864 and 12/31/1864. Present 2/28/1865. Appmtx.

GWYNN, ALBERT W. ("WIZZIE"): 1860 cen.: res. 18th Ward, Baltimore City, age 15, s., lived with his parents and five siblings. Enl. 2/26/1862 for war at Machodoc, VA. Present to 3/1/1862. NFR; likely dropped from rolls because he was underage.

HARDESTY, JAMES RICHARD: 1860 cen.: res. 13th Ward, Baltimore City, age 25, clerk, m. with one son. Enl. 1/1/1862 for war at Machodoc, VA. WIA, 2nd Manassas 8/28/1862. Adm. G.H. Charlottesville, VA, 12/8/1862, smallpox, d. 12/21/1862. Buried in Virginia and removed to Loudon Park Cem., Baltimore, on 6/9/1874.

HARPER, JAMES KEMPER: 1860 cen.: res. Talbot County, age 15, s., lived with his parents and five siblings. Attended Georgetown University. Enl. 1/1/1862 for war at Machodoc, VA. WIA 1st Fredericksburg, 12/13/1862. Court martial 3/4/1863, charged with disobedience of orders; given company punishment. WIA 2nd Fredericksburg 5/2/1863. WIA Gettysburg 7/2/1863. Cptd. Gettysburg, PA, 7/4/1863. Sent to U.S.G.H. West's Buildings, Baltimore, sick, paroled for exchange there 9/25/1863, arrived at Camp Lee 9/29/1863. Furloughed 10/1863. Applied for detail as clerk 7/3/1864, but this was not approved. Absent sick at Robertson Hospital 11/1/1864. Present to 12/31/1864. Appears to have been discharged. NFR.

HARRISON, PHILIP LITTIG ("PHIL"): b. 1832 in Baltimore and worked as a clerk there before moving to Queenstown, Queen Anne's County. Enl. 2/10/1862 for war at Heathsville, VA. Detailed to procure horses 2/9/–2/18/1862. WIA 2nd Manassas 8/28/1862. In hospital until 3/24/1863. Adm. To G.H. No. 9 5/3/1863 for "acute dysentery." Detailed for hospital duty at Camp Winder 5/4/1863. Detailed as a clerk to Major J. B. Cary, Paymaster, Richmond, VA, 10/31/1863 by SO 269/7. Enl. Co. E, 3rd VA Local Defense Troops, 11/27/1863. Applied for a discharge 2/13/1865, which was granted effective 3/31/1865. Paroled at Lynchburg, VA, 4/13/1865.

HARVEY, MARTIN LUTHER: b. Charlotte County, VA, worked as a clerk. Enl. 4/21/1861 in 1st Co. Richmond Howitzers in Richmond, VA. Tnsfr. 9/11/1861 by SO 275/15 to 2nd Co. as drillmaster at Camp Lee, Richmond, VA. Tnsfr. to Chesapeake Artillery as Ordnance Sergeant 5/31/1862. Enl. as Private in 1st Co. Richmond Howitzers 1/26/1864, age 24 years, eyes hazel, hair dark, cmplx. dark, 5'10". Cptd. at Richmond, VA, and paroled 4/17/1865.

HERMANTROUT, WILLIAM H.F.: Enl. 5/14/1864 for war at Hanover Junction, VA. AWOL for September/October and November/December, 1864 musters, and dropped from the rolls.

HICKEY, JOHN P.: 1860 cen.: res. Kent County, age 25, school teacher, s., $135/$0; moved to Bowling Green, VA, before the war. Enl. for war as 2nd Corp. 1/1/1862 at Machodoc, VA. Adm. to G.H. No. 21, Richmond, VA, 5/1/1862, complaint unknown, RTD 5/9/1862. Prom. QM Sgt. before 5/1/1863, probably effective 8/9/1862 to replace J. S. Shafer, who was wounded at Cedar Mountain. Present to 3/1/1865. Paroled at Meridian, MS, 5/13/1865.

HILL, JOHN: 1860 cen.: res. Dorchester County, age 17, farm laborer, s., boarded with another family with his mother. Enl. for war 11/1/1862 at Richmond, VA. Present to 2/28/1865. Appmtx.

HOLTZMAN, WILLIAM FREDERICK ("BILLY"): b. 8/31/1843. 1860 cen.: res. 19th Ward, Baltimore City, age 16, s., lived with his parents at 25 Gilmore Street. Enl. 6/28/1863 at Dover, PA, with W. L. Burke and G. W. Goodhand. Ass. to Co. C, 5th VA Cav. Regt. Adm. to Chimborazo Hospital 8/4/1863 for an abcess, RTD 8/24/1863. Tnsfr. to 4th MD Art. 4/21/1864 by SO 93/2. Present to 2/28/1865. POW 4/2/1865 at Fort Gregg. Sent to Pt. Lookout 4/4/1865. OOA 6/9/1865 and released. Reported to PMG, Baltimore, 6/12/1865. Postwar he ran a retail store with Burke and later the two worked as advertising agents in Baltimore. He was a member of the SANCSM. D. 11/4/1901, aged 58.

HOOFF, JOHN JOHNSTON: b. 9/2/1844 in Alexandria, VA. Enl. for war 4/14/1862 at Richmond, VA. Adm. G.H. Charlottesville, VA, 11/18/1862 for "debility." RTD 1/8/1863. Adm. again for "neuralgia" 11/1/1864, RTD 1/5/1865. Appt. Capt. and ADC to Gen. William N. Pendleton before 2/28/1865 and dropped from rolls. OOA and paroled 5/25/1865 at Harper's Ferry, VA. Postwar he was a wholesale hardware dealer in Baltimore, married, was a member of the ANSCSM, the R. E. Lee UCV Camp, and a resident of the MLCSH. D. 5/7/1921 aged 76, bur. Saint Paul's Cem., Alexandria, VA. He was a nephew of Mary Ward; some of his wartime letters are in the Ward Family Papers at the LOC.

HOPKINS, ALEXANDER RIGBY ("BEY"): 1860 cen.: res. Talbot County, age 17, student, s., lived with his father and five siblings. The household's wealth was $23,000/$18,500; his father owned 12 slaves. Enl. as 1st Corp. for war 1/1/1862 at Machodoc, VA. KIA 2nd Fredericksburg, 5/3/1863. Buried near Hamilton's Crossing, Virginia, and removed to Loudon Park Cem., Baltimore, in 1874.

HUBER, PAUL F.: b. in 1843 in Wurtemburg, Germany. Enl. for war 8/25/1862 at Gordonsville, VA. WIA 1st Fredericksburg 12/13/1862. Cptd. Hagerstown, MD, 7/7/1863. Sent to Ft. Delaware 7/7/1863, and to Pt. Lookout 9/26/1863. Exch. 2/13/1865 and sent to Camp Lee, Richmond, VA, 2/27/1865. NFR. Postwar he was a house painter in Baltimore.

JACKSON, THOMAS G.: 1860 cen.: res. Cecil County, age 18, laborer, s., lived with his father and eight siblings. Enl. 1/1/1862 for war at Machodoc, VA. Present to 12/31/1864. Ass. to G.H. No. 9 1/31/1865 for duty, RTD 2/1/1865. Appears to have been discharged. NFR.

JONES, ROBERT CHEW: b. Kent Island, 12/20/43. 1860 cen.: res. Talbot County, age 16, farmer, s. He lived with two uncles and their wives, who owned 22 slaves. Enl. for war as 4th Corp. 1/1/1862 at Machodoc, VA. Lost his right arm in a training accident in February 1862, but returned to the company following his recovery. Present 3/1/1862. Served with the company for the remainder of that year. Granted a disability discharge 12/18/1862. Ass. as a clerk to the Provost Marshall Dept. in Richmond, VA, 1/7/1863. Apptd. 2nd Lt. and Enrolling Officer, 12th Congressional District, Reserve Forces of Virginia, CSA, 9/10/1863. Signed pay voucher 1/18/1865 for pay during the period 10/1–12/31/1864 and appears to have been discharged. NFR. Postwar he became a lawyer in Cumberland, married, and had two children. D. 10/31/1879, aged 35, bur. Rose Hill Cemetery in Cumberland. His obituary appeared in the *Cumberland Times* 11/1/1879.

KIRBY, FRANCIS M.: 1860 cen.: res. 19th Ward, Baltimore City, age 17, s. Enl. 6/1/1862 for war at Richmond, VA. Adm. to G.H. in Charlottesville, VA, 6/19/1863, scabies. RTD 7/13/1863. Present to 12/31/1864. AWOL 2/28/1865 NFR.

LANE, JOHN A.: 1860 cen.: res. Cecil County, age 24, laborer, s., lived with his parents and brother. Enl. 1/1/1862 at Machodoc, VA. Adm. to G.H. No. 21, Richmond, VA, 6/18/1862, typhoid fever. Treated in several hospitals; ret. to duty 3/30/1863. Adm. to Chimborazo 5/6/1863, debility. RTD 5/28/1863. Mistakenly arrested as a deserter in Richmond the next day and released. WIA Gettysburg 7/2/1863, shell laceration wound in head. Adm. G.H. No. 9 Richmond, VA, 7/21/1863. RTD 8/5/1863. Adm. to G.H. No. 9—again for scabies—8/7/1863. Treated at several hospitals for dysentery and gonorrhea. RTD 7/14/1864. Appmtx. OOA 5/31/1865 at Salisbury, NC. NFR.

LANGLEY, RICHARD E.: 1860 cen.: res. St. Mary's County, age 17, farmhand, s. Lived in his uncle's house with his brother; his uncle owned eleven slaves; orphaned at a young age. Enl. 1/1/1862 for war at Machodoc, VA. WIA severely in left shoulder at 2nd Fredericksburg, 5/3/1863. Adm. to G.H. No. 1, Richmond, VA, ret. to duty between 9/2/1863 and 11/1/1863. Adm. to G.H. No. 9, Richmond, VA, 6/7/1864, debility; RTD 7/17/1864. Adm. to Chimborazo 11/6/1864 for complications with his shoulder wound. Retired to the Invalid Corps 12/26/1864. Cptd. by Federal cavalry 3/15/1865 at Fredericks Hall, VA, sent to Pt. Lookout. Took OOA 6/14/1865 and released. 5'6" cmplx.

dark, hair brown, eyes blue. Postwar lived in St. Mary's County, worked as a carpenter and served as Judge of Elections. D. 1912, bur. Trinity Church Cemetery, Saint Mary's City.

LECOMPTE, THOMAS PRICE: b. 5/6/1841. 1860 cen.: res. Dorchester County, age 18, s., lived with his mother and four sisters; his mother owned one servant. Pvt. John Mowbray was a neighbor. Enl. for war as 2nd. Sgt. 1/1/1862 at Machodoc, VA. Adm. G.H. No. 21, Richmond, VA, 5/1/1862, syphilis, RTD 6/27/1862. Prom. Sgt. Major before 6/30/1863. WIA Gettysburg, 7/2/1863. Recommended for promotion to 1st Lt. for Valor & Skill by Col. Bradley J. Johnson 4/29/1864. Prom. to 1st Lt. 6/6/1864. Present to 2/28/1865 and it appears he was discharged. NFR. D. 3/21/1873 aged 31, bur. Christ Episcopal Church Cem., Cambridge.

LOND, JOHN S.: Res. Dorchester County. Enl. 11/1/1862 for war at Richmond, VA. Present to 11/1/1863, detailed to Ordnance Dept. Extra duty as teamster 1/1–2/28/1865. Appmtx. Reported to PMG, Baltimore, 4/22/1865 and returned home.

LYNCH, CHRISTOPHER GOODHAND ("CHRIS"): 1860 cen.: res. Queen Anne's County, age 18, farmer, s. Boarded with Pvt. William Tarbutton's family. Enl. 11/1/1862 for war at Richmond, VA. Adm. to G.H. No. 9 11/25/1863, remittent fever. Tnsfr. to Chimborazo the next day, RTD 1/25/1864. Absent, furlough 12/31/1864. Adm. 1/30/1865 to G.H. No. 9 for duty, RTD the next day. Present 2/28/1865. WIA and POW at Fort Gregg 4/2/1865 and sent to Pt. Lookout. Took OOA and released 6/14/1865. 5'10" cmplx. florid, hair brown, eyes grey. Reported to PMG, Washington, DC, 6/15/1865, transportation furnished to Baltimore. D. 1905 aged 63, bur. Spring Hill Cem. in Easton. He compiled two rosters of the company and published one with a brief history of the unit in the *Centreville Record* 5/3/1900; he also wrote the accounts of the unit at Gettysburg and Fort Gregg in Goldsborough's *The Maryland Line in the Confederate Army*. His papers are at the USAHEC in Carlisle, PA.

MACCUBBIN, GEORGE B.: 1860 cen.: res. Queen Anne's County, age 30, land agent, m. with four children, $0/$1,000. Enl. 2/1/1862 for war at Heathsville, VA. Detailed in 4/1862 to purchase horses and mules for the company. Present to 2/28/1865. Petitioned for a discharge 3/1/1865 and it was granted. Arrested by Federal authorities in Baltimore 3/31/1865 on a charge of piracy; he and several others had commandeered a boat to cross the Potomac on their way to Virginia in 1862. Acquitted 6/25/1865. Maccubbin was widowed after the war, moved to Mathews County, VA, and died there as the result of a homicide in 1870.

MASON, WILLIAM H. ("WILLIE"): 1860 cen.: res. Harford County, age 17, s., lived with his parents and six siblings. Enl. for 6 mos. 11/9/1861 in the Fredericksburg Artillery at Fredericksburg, VA, as a substitute for Charles Wallace. Enl. for war and received bounty 2/28/1862. Adm. Chimborazo 4/29/1862, diarrhea. Treated at several hospitals, RTD 8/2/1862. Enl. in 4th MD Art. for war 8/6/1862 at Gordonsville, VA. WIA 1st Fredericksburg 12/13/1862. Adm. Chimborazo 2/18/1863, "chronic bronchitis." RTD 3/30/1863. WIA Gettysburg 7/2/1863. Adm. to G.H. Staunton, VA, 8/2/1863, RTD 8/17/1863. Extra duty as teamster 4/18–5/31/1864. Absent on furlough 11/1/1864. Present to 2/28/1865. NFR and appears to have been discharged. Two of Willie's brothers served in the Federal 3rd Potomac Home Brigade of Maryland Infantry during the war, one of whom was mortally wounded near Frederick in 1864. Postwar he was a minister for the Southern Methodist Episcopal Church and died in 1879, age 41.

MCCLURE, GEORGE DOUGLAS ("DOUG"): B. at Bunker Hill, VA, 2/25/1840. 1860 cen.: res. 15th Ward, Baltimore City, age 20, clerk, s., lived with his parents and six siblings. Enl. 4/1/1862 for war at Fort Lowry, VA. Adm. to G.H. No. 21 5/14/1862, mumps. RTD 5/22/1862. Adm. to G.H. No. 21 7/18/1862, typhoid fever. RTD 7/25/1862. AWOL 11/1/1863. Cptd. at Payne's Farm 11/27/1863 and sent to Ft. Delaware. OOA 5/5/1865 and released. 5'10" cmplx. fair, hair light, eyes blue. Postwar he was a miller, a member of the SANCSM, and a resident of the MLCSH. D. 7/19/1905 at the Homeopathic Hospital in Baltimore, aged 65, bur. at Loudon Park Cem., Baltimore. His obituary appeared in the *Baltimore Sun* 7/20/1905.

MCCLURE, THOMAS: Enl. 6/1/1862 for war at Richmond, VA. Present to 6/30/1863. Absent deserted 11/1/1863. NFR.

MCCUMMINS, FRANCIS: 1860 cen.: res. Cecil County, age 15, s., lived with his parents and five siblings. Enl. 10/24/1861 for one year in Co. K, 9th VA Cav. at Fort Lowry, VA. Present to 1/1/1863. Enl. 4th MD Art., 7/21/1864 for war at Petersburg, VA. Present to 2/28/1865. Cptd. at Petersburg 4/3/1865 and sent to Hart Island, NY. OOA 6/20/1865 and released. 5'10" cmplx. light, hair dark, eyes gray. After the war he was a driver in Washington, DC. D. 1/24/1924 aged 68, bur. at Arlington National Cemetery, VA.

MCELWEE, ANDREW J. ("A.J."): 1860 cen.: res. 1st Ward, Baltimore City, age 22, laborer, s., lived with his mother and two siblings. Enl. for war 5/28/1862 at Richmond, VA. Present to 6/30/1863. Absent, deserted 11/1/1863. NFR.

METTEE, CHARLES H.: Enl. for war 8/15/1861 in Baltimore Light Artillery (2nd MD Artillery) at Richmond, VA. Present to 1/1/1862. Adm. to G.H. No. 7/2/1862, diarrhea; returned to duty 7/20/1862. Enl. for the war 7/17/1863 in Co. F, 1st Maryland Cavalry Battalion in Richmond, VA. Present to 1/1/1864 "In Brigade Guard House." Present to 3/31/1864. Tnsfr. to 4th MD Artillery "date unknown, papers lost," but before 6/16/1864 when he signed a receipt roll for clothing as a member of the company. Present to 12/31/1864. Deserted 2/22/1865. NFR. Postwar he lived in Baltimore working as a paperhanger, married, and had nine children, only three of whom lived to adulthood. Adjutant for the James R. Herbert UCV Camp 657 in Baltimore and a member of the SANCSM. D. 6/21/1916, aged 70; bur. Loudon Park Cem., Baltimore.

MONTGOMERY, JOHN C.: B. at Baltimore 7/20/1842. Enl. 1/1/1862 for 1 year at Machodoc, VA. NFR. Was a resident of the MLCSH.

MOORE, JAMES THOMPSON ("DELAWARE"): B. 11/15/1831. 1860 cen.: res. Newcastle County, DEL, age 30, millwright, lived with his brother's family. Enl. 1/1/1862 for war at Machodoc, VA. Extra duty as a blacksmith 3/1–6/8/1863. Present to 12/31/1864. Appears to have been discharged. NFR. Married after the war to Martha Horn, had seven children. D. 4/22/1920 aged 88; bur. Forest Oak Cem., Gaithersburg.

MOWBRAY, JOHN H.: 1860 cen.: res. Dorchester County, age 20, apprentice shoemaker, s. He was a neighbor of Thomas LeCompte. Enl. 11/1/1862 for war at Richmond, VA. Present to 2/28/1865. Appmtx. Reported to the PMG at Baltimore 4/22/1865 on his way home.

MUMMEY, THOMAS WORTHINGTON: 1860 cen.: res. Queen Anne's County, age 42, farmer, m. with four children. Enl. 6/13/1862 for war at Richmond, VA. Prom. to 2nd Corp. and present to 6/30/1863. Adm. to Chimborazo 6/3/1864, hemorrhoids. Applied for a clerkship in Richmond 6/27/1864. RTD 8/3/1864. Detailed as a clerk in Treasury Dept. before 11/1/1864. Paroled at Richmond, VA, 4/30/1865.

MYERS, JOHN: Enl. 6/1/1862 for war at Richmond, VA, present to 6/30/1863. Cptd. at Williamsport, PA, 7/7/1863 and sent to Ft. Delaware. Tnsfr. to Pt. Lookout 9/26/1863. Exchanged 10/30/1864. NFR.

OLDNER, PHILIP OCTAVIUS ("PHIL"): B. in Petersburg, VA 12/6/1842. Living in England at the start of the war. Enl. 6/13/1862 for war at Richmond, VA. WIA 1st Fredericksburg 12/13/1862. Adm. to G.H. No. 22, Richmond, VA, 12/19/1862. Tnsfr. to 5 Division G.H. at Camp Winder 2/1863. Ret. to duty 3/14/1863. Present 6/30/1863. MWIA in knee joint at Gettysburg 7/2/1863, d. at the David Stewart farm 7/20/1863 and buried there "east of the barn and near row of trees." Removed to Hollywood Cemetery, Richmond, VA, 5/17/1873, and re-buried at Loudon Park Cem., Baltimore, in 1874.

OLDSON, WILLIAM H.C.: 1860 cen.: res. 7th Ward, Baltimore City, age 34, clerk, \$0/\$200, married with four children. Enl. for war in Baltimore Light Artillery (2nd MD Art.) 8/15/1861 at Richmond, VA. Adm. to G.H. No. 21 3/31/1862, rheumatism; RTD 4/24/1862; adm. again 4/27/1862, acute rheumatism. Tnsfr. to G.H. Danville, 5/6/1862. RTD 6/1/1862. Enl. in 4th MD. Art. for war 8/30/1862 at Leesburg, VA. Cptd. 9/12/1862 at Frederick, sent to Ft. Delaware. Sent to Aikens Landing, VA, 10/2/1862 and exchanged 11/10/1862. Present to 11/1/1863. Adm. to G.H. No. 9, Richmond, VA, 5/23/1864 for organic disease of the heart and treated at several hospitals. Retired to Invalid Corps 11/2/1864, ass. to duty at G.H. No. 1, Lynchburg, VA, and detailed by SO 3/9 1/5/1865. Applied for discharge 2/1/1865, but no action taken. Reported to PMG, Washington, DC, 4/10/1865 on his way home.

PARKER, PETER HENRY: b. 4/7//1843. 1860 cen.: res. St. Mary's County, age 16, s., boarded and worked as a farm hand. He was Thad Parker's brother, and both worked on neighboring farms. Enl. 1/1/1862 for war at Machodoc, VA. Adm. to G.H. No. 21 6/22/1862, typhoid fever, tnsfr. to G.H. Danville, VA, 6/29/1862. RTD 8/13/1862. Pres. to 6/3/1863. WIA Gettysburg, 7/2/1863. Pres. to 11/1/1863. Extra duty as teamster 1/1–6/8/1864. Present to 12/31/1864. Ass. to G.H. No. 9, Richmond, VA, for duty for one day. Present to 2/28/1865. Appears to have been discharged. NFR. Married Martha Meador in 1868, eight children; lived and farmed in Amelia County, VA, postwar. D. 2/17/1917, aged 75.

PARKER, THADDEUS MARION ("THAD"): b. 2/8/1838. 1860 cen.: res. St. Mary's County, age 22, s., boarded and worked as a farm hand. He was Henry Parker's brother, and both worked on neighboring farms. Enl. 1/1/1862 for war at Machodoc, VA. Pres. to 6/30/1863. KIA Gettysburg 7/2/1863. Initially buried on the Daniel Benner farm, removed to Loudon Park Cemetery, Baltimore, 7/4/1873.

PERRY, JOHN GABRIEL ("GABE"): 1860 cen.: res. 4th Ward, Baltimore City, age 26, s. Enl. 1/1/1862 for war at Machodoc, VA. Detailed as a cook to 4th Div. G.H. at Camp Winder 5/24/1862 to after 11/1/1863, but returned to the company by 6/16/1864. Present to 12/31/1864. Detailed for duty to GH. No. 9, Richmond, VA, for one day (1/17/1865). Appears to have been discharged. NFR.

PETERS, JOSEPH L.: 1860 cen.: res. Queen Anne's County, age 20, farm hand, s., lived with his seven siblings. Enl. 11/1/1862 for war at Richmond, VA. Present to 2/28/1865. POW at Ft. Gregg and sent to Pt. Lookout. Appears to have taken the OOA and sent to PMG Washington, DC, 6/18/1865, where he registered and had transportation furnished to Baltimore.

PHILLIPS, GEORGE C.: Enl. as 8th Corp. 3/1/1862 for war at Richmond, VA. Prom. to 7th Corp. before 6/30/1863. Court martial 12/9/1863 with I. J. Blunt, charges unknown; reduced in rank to Private. Furloughed 5/1864. Promoted to 5th Corp. before 11/1/1864. AWOL 11/1 and 12/31/1864 and dropped from rolls. NFR.

PHILLIPS, SAMUEL W.: 1860 cen.: res. 18th Ward, Baltimore City, age 30, blacksmith, m. with two children, $0/$100. Enl. for war 11/9/1861 as a substitute in the Fredericksburg Artillery at Camp Clifton, VA. Adm. to Chimborazo 5/17/1862 with fractured arm, tnsfr. to G.H. Farmville, VA, 5/23/1862, RTD 8/2/1862. Enl. in 4th MD Art. 8/6/1862 at Gordonsville, VA, for war. Present to 11/1/1863. Furloughed 2/1864. Tnsfr. to CS Navy 4/6/1864 by SO 95/15. NFR.

PINDER, WILLIAM: 1860 cen.: res. Queen Anne's County, age 35, overseer, m. with four children, illiterate. Enl. 11/1/1862 for war at Richmond, VA. Present to 2/28/1865. Promoted to corporal sometime after 3/1/1865. WIA and POW at Fort Gregg 4/2/1865, and sent to Pt. Lookout. OOA 6/16/1865 and released. 5'8" cmplx. light, hair dark brown, eyes hazel. Sent to PMG, Washington, DC, and transportation furnished to Baltimore.

PLATER, JOHN EDWARD: B. near Sotterley Plantation, St. Mary's County, 6/10/1839; graduated from Georgetown University. His grandfather, George Plater, was a former governor of Maryland. Lived in Baltimore City and was a bookkeeper prewar. Member of the Maryland Guard Battalion and was a captain in the Lafayette Guards. Lt., 1st Co., 2nd MD Infantry Rgt. 8/1861 under Capt. W. D. Brown, but the regiment was never formed. Enl. 1/1/1862 as 2nd Lt. for war at Machodoc, VA. Elected 1st Lt. 6/30/1862. Absent sick for an undetermined period of time 9/1862. Commanded the battery at 1st Fredericksburg in Capt. W. D. Brown's absence. Present to 6/30/1863. Court martial 9/5/1863 for abandoning a caisson without permission at Gettysburg and dismissed from the service. RTD 2/20/1864 by SO 43/19 following the death of Lt. Benjamin G. Roberts the previous December, but it appears he never returned to the unit and was finally dropped from the rolls 6/6/1864 by SO 131/3. NFR. Postwar he moved west, married, and was a highly successful banker, first in Nevada and later president of the Los Angeles County Bank. D. 2/6/1926, aged 86; bur. Sacramento City Cemetery, Sacramento, CA. His obituary appears in the *St. Mary's Beacon*, 4/9/1926.

POISAL, JOHN, Jr.: B. in Baltimore in 1833. No record of enlistment or service, but mentioned in both of Lynch's rosters and included in Goldsborough's as having died in hospital during the war. He appears to have enlisted after 3/1/1862 and died sometime before 5/1/1863.

PORTER, GUSTAVUS: 1860 cen.: res. Queen Anne's County, age 23, farm laborer, s. He and his younger brother lived with his older brother's family on the latter's farm. Enl. 11/1/1862 for war at Richmond, VA. Present to 2/28/1865. POW at Fort Gregg 4/2/1865 and sent to Pt. Lookout. Took OOA 6/16/1865 and released, 5'7" cmplx. florid, hair brown, eyes gray. Sent to PMG at Washington, DC, 6/18/1865 and transportation furnished to Baltimore.

PRATT, JAMES P.: Res. of Queen Anne's County. Enl. 11/1/1862 for war at Richmond, VA. Present to 6/30/1863. Adm. to Robertson Hospital, Richmond, VA, 9/17/1863, "Debility from fever"; RTD 10/1/1863. Present to 2/28/1865. Appmtx.

RALEY, MICHAEL NORMAN: B. in 1843, res. of St. Mary's County. Enl. 1/1/1862 for war at Machodoc, VA. Detailed as driver of ordnance train before 6/30/1863 until 2/5/1864. Present to 12/31/1864. Appears to have been discharged. Took OOA and paroled at Winchester 4/26/1865. Arrested 5/2/1865 in Baltimore, released 5/11/1865 to "go to Northern Neck Va." NFR.

RANDILL, J.: 1860 cen.: res. Prince George County, VA, age 25, engineer, m.; he and his wife boarded with another family. Enl. 6/1/1864 for war in Hanover County, VA. Present to 12/31/1864. Appears to have been discharged. NFR.

RENSHAW, WILLIAM THOMAS: B. 1834 in Maryland. 1860 cen.: res. Somerset County, age 26, farm laborer, s. Enl. 6/14/1861 in Co. D, 40th Virginia Inf. Regt. for one year at March Camp, VA. Detailed as teamster 9/1/1861–1/1/1862. Re-enlisted for two years and received bounty 3/1/1862 at Heathsville, VA. Enl. in 4th MD Art. 5/22/1862 at Fredericksburg, VA. Detailed as driver of ordnance train before 6/30/1863 through 12/31/1864. NFR and appears to have been discharged. He was a farmer in Virginia and Wicomico County postwar, married, and had seven children. D. 11/24/1925 aged 91 in Danville, VA.

RICE, GEORGE T.: 1860 cen.: res. Talbot County, age 18, farm laborer, s. Enl. for war 1/1/1862 at Machodoc, VA. Attached to 2nd Corps Hospital at Guiney's Station, VA, as a nurse 12/13/1862–4/1/1863. Present to 11/1/1863. Cptd. 3/2/1864 near Spotsylvania, VA, during the Dahlgren Raid. Sent to Pt. Lookout 3/9/1864. Exchanged 3/15/1865 and arrived at Camp Lee, Richmond, VA, 3/19/1865. Paroled at Greensboro, NC, 5/9/1865; rank recorded as 3rd Lt., possibly a nominal rank assigned among the prisoner divisions at Pt. Lookout, as there is no record of his promotion in his service records and he was clearly a private when captured. Reported to PMG at Baltimore 5/13/1865 and took OOA. Lived in St. Mary's County after the war.

RICHARDSON, JOHN DUHAMEL: 1860 cen.: res. Worcester County, age 19, laborer, s., lived with his brother's family. Enl. 11/14/1862 for war at Richmond, VA. Pres. 6/30/1863. WIA Gettysburg 7/2/1863. Present to 11/1/1864. Furloughed 20 days 12/30/1864. Present to 12/31/1864. Furloughed 30 days 1/1/1865. Present 2/28/1865. Promoted to Sgt. after 3/1/1865, probably at the time T. P. LeCompte was discharged. Commanded the company at the Appomattox surrender. Registered with PMG, Baltimore, 4/22/1865. Postwar he lived at the MLCSH. D. 10/24/1925 aged 84, bur. Druid Ridge Cem., Pikesville.

RICHARDSON, NICHOLAS S. ("NICK"): 1860 cen.: res. Queen Anne's county, age 26, s. Enl. 1/1/1862 for war at Machodoc, VA. Detailed as a shoemaker at Staunton, VA, by SO 131/4 on 5/14/1863. Adm. G.H. No. 9 Richmond, VA, 6/15/1863 for "acute articular rheumatism." Furloughed 30 days 8/3/1863. Detailed as a shoemaker at the CS Clothing Depot, Richmond, VA, 9/1/1863–12/31/1864. NFR, appears to have been discharged.

ROBERTS, BENJAMIN G. ("BEN"): 1860 cen.: res. Queen Anne's County, age 22, farmer, s., $2,500/$1,000. Enlistment date unknown, presumably after 3/1/1862. Prom. 2nd Lt. upon death of Lt. J. Grason at Fredericksburg to date from 12/13/1862. Present to 6/30/1863. Severely wounded in the back and both arms at Gettysburg 7/2/1863. No medical records extant, but RTD before 9/2/1863. Present to 11/1/1863. Adm. to G.H., Charlottesville 11/18/1863, typhoid fever. D. 12/1/1863 aged 25. Buried in Virginia and removed to Loudon Park Cem., Baltimore, 6/9/1874. See Ruffner for additional details on his life.

RUSSELL, HENRY: 1860 cen.: res. 3rd Ward, Baltimore City, age 42, upholsterer, $0/$1,000, m. with seven children. Enl. 5/24/1862 for war at Richmond, VA. Under arrest for desertion 6/30/1863. Deserted before 11/1/1863 and dropped from rolls.

SCHAEFER, JOHN WILLIAM (a.k.a. JOHN WILLIAMS): Also spelled Shaefer, Shafer, and Schaffer. B. in Germany. Appears in the 1860 cen. as William Schaefer: res. 15th Ward, Baltimore City, age 21, music teacher, $0/$500, s., lived in a boarding house. A CSR for him as John W. Schaefer is included in the 4th Maryland Artillery's records; he does not appear in the company's muster rolls, but is listed on Lynch's first roster, as well as Goldsborough's and Cook's as William Schaefer. Enl. for war in 2nd Maryland Artillery 8/15/1861 as William Schaefer. POW, date unknown; paroled at Winchester 6/20/1862, sent to City Point for exchange 8/8/1862, exchanged 8/12/1862. AWOL 1/1/1863. Enl. in 4th Maryland Artillery as John W. Schaefer before 5/1/1863. POW at Williamsport 7/7/1863, 24 years old, 5'6". Sent from Harrisburg to Philadelphia as John Williams, Lee Artillery, possibly changing his name to hide his desertion from the 2nd Maryland Artillery; no soldier with the last name Williams or Schaefer served in the Lee Artillery. Received at Fort Delaware 7/23/1863 as John Williams, and also appears on a register of prisoners at Fort Delaware under that name. It appears he revealed his true identity at the opportunity for exchange; he was exchanged 2/27/1865 as John W. Schaefer, Chesapeake Artillery, "alias Jno. Williams, Lee's Va Batty." He also appears in a 5/6/1865 transcript from Fort Delaware as "Schaefer, John W. Pvt. Chesapeake Arty. Alias John Williams Lee's Va Batty." Admitted to GH No. 9 in Richmond as a paroled prisoner from Camp Lee 3/2/1865 as J. W. Schaefer, Pvt., 4th Maryland Battery. NFR.

SHAFER, JOHN S.: B. 12/17/1834 in Harford County, merchant. Listed in error as Henry Lynch's second roster, is listed twice in Goldsborough's roster as Henry Scheesler and Henry Shafer, and appears as Henry Shaeder in Cook's roster. Enl.

1/1/1862 as QM Sgt. for war at Machodoc, VA. WIA Cedar Mountain 8/9/1862, gunshot wound to left eye. Ass. as nurse to G.H. No. 3, Richmond, VA, 4/21/1863. Recommended for medical discharge 4/30/1863, loss of left eye and partial impairment of right eye. Discharged 6/5/1863. Postwar he moved to South Carolina, later to Charlotte, NC, where he was a farmer, married, and had three children. Was a member of UCV Camp No. 382. D. 8/21/1929 in Macon, GA, the last surviving member of the company. Bur. at Elmwood Cem., Charlotte, NC. His death notice appears in CV 10/1929, and his obituary in *The Bulletin* of the Catholic Laymen's Association of Georgia, 9/7/1929.

SHANNAHAN, JOHN HENRY KELLY, II: b. 11/28/1842. 1860 cen.: res. Talbot County, age 17, attended school and worked on his father's farm, s.; the family owned two slaves. Enl. for war 1/1/1862 at Machodoc, VA. WIA in thigh at Cedar Run 8/9/1862. Adm. to G.H. Charlottesville, VA, 8/11/1862, RTD 11/7/1862. WIA 2nd Fredericksburg. Present to 12/31/1864. NFR, appears to have been discharged. Postwar he was a highly successful businessman, married, and had three sons. D. 5/20/1916, aged 73, and bur. at Spring Hill Cemetery in Easton. His obituary appeared in CV, 24, 414.

SMITH, FRANCIS: 1860 cen.: res. 12th Ward, Baltimore City, age 30, tailor, s. Enl. 6/1/1862 for war at Richmond, VA. Present to 6/30/1863. NFR and no record of desertion, capture, or medical care; does not appear in 1870 Census. MWIA Gettysburg 7/2/1863, died at the Lady farm on the third or fourth, and buried across the road from the Lady house. Later removed as an Unknown in Box 1-V to the Gettysburg Dead section of Hollywood Cemetery, Richmond, VA, on 5/7/1873.

SMITH, GEORGE A.: 1860 cen.: res. Dorchester County, age 20, tailor, s. Enl. 1/1/1862 for war at Machodoc, VA. Adm. to G.H. No. 21, Richmond, VA, for mumps. Prom. to 3rd Corp. before 8/28/1862. WIA at 2nd Manassas 8/30/1862. Present to 12/31/1864. Ass. to G.H. No. 9, Richmond, VA, 1/29–1/31/1865 for duty. NFR, appears to have been discharged.

SMITH, WILLIAM: B. in 1812, res. of Baltimore City, a hatter, single. Enl. 1/1/1862 for war at Machodoc, VA. Present to 11/1/1863. Deserted 12/23/1863 and sent to Pt. Lookout. Took OOA and released 1/26/1864 to join US Service. Enl. for 3 yrs. in Co. C, 1st Regt. US Vol. Inf., age 51, 5'4" cmplx. light, eyes blue, hair dark. Present to 4/30/1865. Adm. to US G.H., St. Louis, MO, 6/29/1865, pneumonia. Mustered out 7/18/1865. NFR.

SPARKS, JAMES H.: 1860 cen.: res. Queen Anne's County, age 24, laborer, s. Enl. 11/14/1862 for war at Richmond, VA. WIA at 2nd Fredericksburg 5/3/1863, gunshot wound to right hip. Adm. to G.H. No. 9, Richmond, VA, 5/6/1863. Treated at several hospitals in Richmond. Absent wounded 6/30/1863. Present 11/1/1863 and through 2/28/1865. POW at Fort Gregg 4/2/1865, sent to Pt. Lookout 4/4/1865. Took OOA and released 6/19/1865. 5'10" cmplx. dark, hair dark brown, eyes light hazel. Registered with PMG at Washington, DC, 6/20/1865, and transportation furnished to Baltimore.

SPENCER, BEDINGFIELD HAND ("BEDNEY"): B. 6/6/1838 in Kent County. 1860 cen.: res. Anne Arundel

County, age 22, s., lived with and worked for his uncle, a wealthy lawyer who owned four slaves. Enl. 4/29/1862 for war at Richmond, VA. Present to 2/28/1865. Appmtx. Postwar he was a farmer in Church Hill, MD, and a resident of the MLCSH. D. 7/31/1900 aged 62, bur. Chesterfield Cem., Centreville. His obituary appeared in the *Chestertown Transcript* 8/14/1900.

STANSBURY, EDWARD O.N. : 1860 cen.: res. 8th Ward, Baltimore City, age 14, student, s. Enl. 1/1/1862 for war at Machodoc, VA. At age 15, he was the youngest member of the company. Present to 2/28/1862. Adm. to G.H. No. 21, Richmond, VA, 5/3/1862, typhoid fever. RTD 7/28/1862. Adm. to G.H. No. 9, Richmond, VA, 9/18/1862, debility, tnsfr. to G.H. Camp Winder, tuberculosis, and eventually to Robertson Hospital. Discharged from the service for disability 3/28/1863; he did not recover, dying in hospital on 4/16/1863. Bur. in Richmond and removed to Loudon Park Cem., Baltimore, in 1874.

STENET, WILLIAM J. ("WILLY"): Resident of Queen Anne's County. Enl. 10/1/1862 for war at Winchester, VA. Discharged before 6/30/1863, reason unknown.

STEPHENS, JAMES: 1860 cen.: res. 12th Ward, Baltimore City, age 29, merchant, m. with two children, $0/$500. Enl. 6/1/1862 for war at Richmond, VA. Present to 6/30/1863. NFR and no record of desertion, capture, or medical care; does not appear in 1870 Census. MWIA Gettysburg 7/2/1863, died at the Lady farm on the third or fourth, and buried across the road from the Lady house. Later removed as an Unknown in Box 1-V to the Gettysburg Dead section of Hollywood Cemetery, Richmond, VA, on 5/7/1873.

STEWART, FRANCIS M. ("FRANK"): 1860 cen.: res. Dorchester County, age 15, student, s., lived with his parents and ten siblings; his father was a wealthy farmer who owned two slaves. Enl. 10/1/1862 for war at Winchester, VA. Present to 12/31/1864. Absent on furlough 2/28/1865. NFR. Lived in Battle Mountain, NV, after the war.

STEWART, JAMES P.: 1860 cen.: res. Marshall County, VA, age 25, farmer, m., $0/$150. Enl. 1/1/1862 for war as 3rd Sgt. at Machodoc, VA. Present to 2/28/1862. Adm. to G.H. No. 21, Richmond, VA, typhoid fever. RTD 7/29/1862. Adm. to G.H. No. 9, Richmond, VA, 10/18/1862, complaint unknown, tnsfr. to 1st Div. G.H. Camp Winder 11/12/1862. Reduced to Pvt. before 6/30/1863. Present 6/30/1863 and through 2/28/1865. Discharged by order of Judge Haliburton of CS District Court, but did not leave the unit. POW 4/2/1865 at Fort Gregg, sent to Pt. Lookout. OOA and released 6/19/1865. 5'11" cmplx. fair, hair red, eyes hazel.

SUITE, NORRIS M.: 1860 cen.: res. St. Mary's County, age 24, farmer, m., $800/$200. Enl. 1/1/1862 for war at Machodoc, VA. Present to 11/1/1863. Extra duty as teamster 1/1–12/31/1864. Adm. to G.H. No. 9 for 48-hour furlough 1/16/1865. NFR and appears to have been discharged.

TARBUTTON, WILLIAM S.: 1860 cen.: res. Queen Anne's County, age 18, student; lived with his parents and five siblings; Pvt. C.G. Lynch was a boarder. His father was a wealthy farmer who owned ten slaves. Enl. 11/14/1862 for war at Richmond, VA. Present to 2/28/1865. Appmtx. Registered with PMG, Washington, DC, 4/22/1865 on his way home. Postwar he was a farmer in Kent County and had three children. D. in 1905, aged 63; his obituary is in the *Centreville Record*, 7/8/1905.

TINGES, CHARLES SEWALL: B. 6/23/1841 in Baltimore. Lived at 178 Garden St., Baltimore. Attended the College of St. James in Washington County. 1860 cen.: res. 20th Ward, Baltimore City, age 18, clerk, s., lived with his father and nine siblings. Attempted unsuccessfully to enlist in the 1st VA Cavalry 9/6/1862. Enl. 10/1/1862 for war at Winchester, VA. Adm. to G.H. Charlottesville, VA, 11/18/1862, "debility." RTD 1/8/1863. Present to 6/30/1863. WIA at Gettysburg 7/2/1863, cptd. at the David Stewart farm 7/5/1863. Sent to DeCamp G.H, Davids Island, NY, 7/17/1863 and paroled. RTD 1/26/1864. Present to 2/28/1865. Adm. to G.H. No. 9, 3/7/1865, and Robertson Hospital, Richmond, VA, "Rubiola"; RTD 4/2/1865. Paroled at Lynchburg, VA, 4/13/1865. Took OOA at Richmond, VA, 4/22/1865. Registered with PMG, Baltimore, 5/26/1865. Postwar he married, no children, and was employed as a clerk and insurance agent in Baltimore. D. in Baltimore 11/30/1918, aged 77.

TORRINGTON, JOHN: 1860 cen.: res. 6th Ward, Baltimore, City, age 19, wood turner, lived with his parents and three siblings. Enl. 3/30/1861 for three years in Child's Artillery Company (SC) at Castle Pinkney, SC, which became Co. C, 15th Battalion SC Heavy Art. Present to 4/30/1864. Tnsfr. to 4th MD Art. 6/1/1864 by SO 100/2. Present to 2/28/1865. Cptd. at Petersburg 4/3/1865, sent to Hart Island, NY. D. 6/10/1865 of chronic diarrhea. Bur. Grave #2971, Cypress Hills National Cemetery, Brooklyn, NY.

TOY, THOMAS B.: Res. of Baltimore, a bookkeeper. Enl. 10/1/1862 for war at Winchester, VA, age 25. WIA at 1st Fredericksburg 12/13/1862, severely in both legs. Adm. to hospital 12/16/1862, tnsfr. to G.H. Lynchburg 3/26/1863. Absent wounded 6/30/1863. Present 11/1/1863. Admitted again to Robertson Hospital, Richmond, VA, 2/3/1864, "Gunshot wound"; RTD 2/23/1864. Applied for a clerkship in the CS Treasury Dept. 1/24/1864; detailed as such 2/16/1864 by SO 45/2. Deserted in March 1865 and took OOA. Allowed to return to Baltimore for his father's funeral by the PMG. NFR. Settled in Castleton, NY, with his family and worked as a bookkeeper after the war. Died in the 1870s at about age 40.

TREGOE, JOHN ("JOHNNY TRIGGER"): 1860 cen.: res. Dorchester County, age 19, farm laborer, lived with his parents and seven siblings. Enl. 11/14/1862 for war at Richmond, VA. Cptd. at Front Royal, VA, 7/18/1863, paroled for exchange at Baltimore 8/1863, and sent to Pt. Lookout. Took OOA 1/26/1864 and volunteered for US service. Denied due to medical examination and requested a discharge 4/1/1864, which was presumably granted. NFR.

VALENTINE, JOHN CHARLES: Resident of New Orleans, LA, age 22, clerk, born in Ireland. Enl. as a 3rd Corp. for 12 months in Co. F, 2nd Louisiana Inf. Regt 5/11/1861. Promoted to 2nd Corp. 11/1/1861. Enl. as a seaman on the CSS *Virginia* (*Merrimac*) 3/21/1862, 5'7" cmplx. fair, hair black, eyes gray. Enl. 4th MD Art. 6/13/1862 for war at Richmond, VA. Adm. to G.H. No. 26, Richmond, VA, 12/28/1862, epilepsy. Granted a surgeon's certificate of disability and discharged from the service 1/30/1863. NFR.

VANSANT, JOHN B.: 1860 cen.: res. Queen Anne's County, age 19, farm hand, s., lived with his parents and four siblings. Enl. for war 11/14/1862. Present to 6/30/1863. Cptd. at Front Royal, VA, 7/23/1863 and sent to Old Capitol Prison, Washington, DC. Took OOA 12/20/1863, released and sent north. 5'5" cmplx. light, hair brown, eyes blue. NFR.

WALL, JAMES A.: Enl. 1/1/1862 for war at Machodoc, VA. Prom. to 3rd Sgt. 12/31/1862. Present to 6/30/1863. WIA 7/2/1863 at Gettysburg. On recruiting detail 8/1863. Prom. to 1st Sgt. before 11/1/1863, probably 7/2/1863, when Sgt. J. P. Williams transferred out. Present to 12/31/1864 and appears to have been discharged. NFR.

WARRINGTON, LEWIS: B. in Baltimore in 1838. Brother of S. Warrington. No record of enlistment or service, but he is listed on both of Lynch's rosters, as well as Goldsborough's and Cook's, and wrote a letter home from the company's camp in October 1862. Appears to have enlisted after 3/1/1862 and left the service before 5/1/1863. He is listed in the 1870 Census as a resident of Baltimore, age 32, a tobacco merchant, married with two children.

WARRINGTON, SMITH: Res. of Baltimore, age 7 in 1850 census. Brother of L. Warrington. Enl. 1/1/1862 for war at Machodoc, VA. Present to 6/30/1863. WIA at Gettysburg 7/2/1863, slightly in the face. Reported as Absent, Deserted on 11/1/1863, but it appears he was captured before that date. There are no Federal capture records for him explaining why his record was never amended, but he is listed on a roll of paroled and exchanged prisoners at Camp Lee, Richmond, VA, on 2/21/1865. NFR. He appears in the 1870 Census as a resident of Georgetown, DC, age 24, and a clerk at a lumberyard.

WEBB, RICHARD WATSON: B. 1841. Enl. 1/1/1862 for war at Machodoc, VA. Present to 11/1/1863. Court martial 2/1/1864 with J. T. Dean, charges unknown; acquitted. Furlough in 6/1864. Absent sick at field hospital 11/1/1864. Present 12/31/1864. Ass. to duty at G.H. No. 9 for one day on 1/30/1865 and 2/1/1865. Pres. 2/28/1865 and appears to have been discharged. NFR. Postwar he was a teacher and justice of the peace in Vienna, Dorchester County. Chairman of the 1898 Cambridge Democratic convention. Married and had four children, two of whom lived into adulthood. D. 1901, aged 60, bur. at Saint Paul's Cem., Vienna, Dorchester County.

WILKINSON, DANIEL A.: 1860 cen.: res. St. Mary's County, age 17, farmer, s.; lived with his parents and five siblings. Enl. as Bugler 1/1/1862 at Machodoc, VA. Pres. 2/28/1862. WIA 1st Fredericksburg 12/13/1862. Adm. G.H. No. 21, Richmond, VA, 6/22/1862, typhoid fever. Treated at several hospitals and RTD 8/1/1862. Pres. to 11/1/1863. WIA at Cold Harbor 6/3/1864, gunshot wound in right foot. Adm. to Chimborazo 6/9/1864, RTD 7/21/1864. Present to 12/31/1864. Absent on re-enlistment furlough 2/28/1865. Paroled at Ashland, VA, 5/2/1865. D. 12/12/1888, aged 46, in WVA; his obituary appears in the *St. Mary's Beacon*, 12/20/1888.

WILLIAMS, JAMES PETER: b. 1/28/1844 in Mt. Laurel, VA. 1860 cen.: res. 2nd Ward, Richmond City, VA, age 16, clerk, lived with his parents and one sibling. His father was a wealthy merchant and owned two slaves. Enl. in Co. K, 1st Virginia Art. (2nd Company Richmond Howitzers) 4/21/1861. Present to 3/30/1862. Served as an artillery instructor at Camp Lee, Richmond, VA. Tnsfr. to 4th MD Art. as 5th Sgt.

6/21/1862. Present to 6/30/1863. Tnsfr. to 1st Co. Richmond Howitzers as Corp. 7/1/1863. Appmtx. Postwar he was a freight agent and superintendent of the Lynchburg Division of the James River and Kanawha Canal. D. in Lynchburg, VA, 1/22/1893, aged 49. His wartime letters are at UVA.

WILLIAMS, WILLIAM M.: Res. of Queen Anne's County. Enl. 11/14/1862 for war at Richmond, VA. Present to 6/30/1863. WIA 7/2/1863 at Gettysburg, slightly to the face. Present to 2/28/1865. Appmtx. Reported to PMG, Washington, DC, 4/10/1865.

WILLSON, JAMES HENRY: Res. of Queen Anne's County. Enl. 3/1/1862 for war at Heathsville, VA. Adm. G.H. No. 9, Richmond, VA, 1/3/1863, complaint unknown. Present 6/30/1863. WIA Gettysburg 7/2/1863, shell wound in his right knee affecting the flexor tendons. Adm. to G.H. No. 9, Richmond, VA, and treated in several hospitals for ulcer of right leg and erysipelas. Granted 3-day furlough 2/20/1864 and RTD. Present 11/1/1864. Tnsfr. to Co. B, 1st MD Cav. 12/5/1864. NFR. Postwar resident of the MLCSH. D. 5/17/1923 aged 82, bur. Loudon Park Cem., Baltimore.

WILSON, WILLIAM: Enl. 1/1/1862 for 1 year at Machodoc, VA. Re-enl. for war 5/13/1862 and received $50 bounty. WIA Bristoe Station 8/27/1862. Tnsfr. as 1st Corp. to Co. A, 1st MD Cav. Regt. before 6/30/1863. Present to 12/31/1864 and appears to have been discharged. NFR.

YATES, WILLIAM FRANKLIN ("FRANK"): B. 12/13/1833. 1860 cen.: res. St. Mary's County, age 24, farmer and teacher, s., $0/$600. Enl. 6/15/1861 for 1 year in Walter's Maryland Company—the "Zarvona Zouaves"—at Tappahannock, VA, which became Co. H of the 47th Virginia Infantry Regiment and later part of the 2nd Arkansas Infantry Battalion. Present until 6/15/1862, when the company was disbanded. Enl. in the 4th Maryland Artillery 6/24/1862 for the war at Richmond, VA. Serving extra daily duty as teamster 11/1/1864 and 3/1/1865. Present to 2/28/1865. WIA, slightly on the head, date unknown. Appmtx. Reported to the PMG, Baltimore, on his way home. Married Mary Pauline Wathen 2/16/1890, later widowed. D. 5/2/1915, aged 81, bur. St. Aloysius Cem., Leonardtown; his obituary appeared in the *St. Mary's Beacon*, 5/6/1915.

YOUNG, BENJAMIN: B. 5/21/1819 in Prince George's County. Prewar residence Alexandria County, VA. Enl. 2/1/1862 for war at Heathsville, VA. Present to 2/28/1865. Applied for a discharge that was granted on 3/28/1865. Paroled at Richmond, VA, 3/28/1865, and took OOA 4/17/1865. Reported to PMG, Baltimore, 5/3/1865 on his way to Kent County. Postwar was a farmer in Kent County and a resident of the MLCSH. D. 3/31/1905 age 86, bur. Loudon Park Cem., Baltimore.

African-American Servant

COOPER, W.: The only CSR entry for Cooper is an inventory of the effects of "W. Cooper, late a Colored boy of the Ches. Artillery, who died at Guinea's Station on the 10th day of Jany, 1863." It is signed "H. Black, Surgeon in Charge" (Dr. Harvey Black was surgeon in charge of the field hospital of the 2nd Corps, Army of Northern Virginia). The effects consisted of "$6.00 cash in Confederate money." It is unknown whether Cooper was a freedman or a servant of one of the men; details of his history have yet to be discovered.

Other Names Associated with the Chesapeake Artillery

ADAMS, ANDREW: Enl. 1/1/1862 at Machodoc, VA. Bounty jumper who deserted on 1/6/1862 with Francis Bogue and William Jackson. Enl. 4/6/1862 at Richmond, VA, in Co. D, 1st Maryland Infantry Regt., and collected another bounty. He was discharged when that unit disbanded 8/16/1862 at Gordonsville, VA. NFR.

BOGUE, FRANCIS: Enl. 1/1/1862 at Machodoc, VA. Bounty jumper who deserted on 1/6/1862 with Andrew Adams and William Jackson. He next appears 3/12/1862 on a roster as a hospital guard in Richmond, VA. Cptd. near Washington, DC, 7/13/1864, and claimed to be a member of Co. C, 1st Maryland Cav. Regt.; there is no record of his enlistment or service in that unit. Sent to Elmira 7/25/1864. Paroled and sent to James River for exchange 2/20/1865. NFR.

CANE, THOMAS H.: No record of enlistment or service with the 4th Maryland Artillery. A CSR entry in his name, as well as that of H. Chester and J. P. Hooker, is included in the 4th Maryland Artillery records as a prisoner captured at Williamsport, MD, 7/6/1863. It is also indicated the capture record is an "error." NFR.

CASPER, W.: CSR in the records of the 4th Maryland Artillery. This is a transcription error for W. Cooper.

CHESTER, HARRY: No record of enlistment or service with the 4th Maryland Artillery. A CSR entry in his name, as well as that of T. H. Cane and J. P. Hooker, is included in the 4th Maryland Artillery records as a prisoner captured at Williamsport, MD, 7/6/1863. The capture record is listed in error.

COUBRAY, THOMAS: Appears in both of Lynch's rosters as well as Cook's. This is a transcription error for Thomas Carberry.

DEMPSEY, JOSEPH: Listed in error on both Lynch's and Goldsborough's rosters. He served in the 2nd Maryland Artillery.

GRASON, JAMES ("JIM"): Brother of John Grason. Enl. for 12 months 10/6/1861 in Co. H, 1st Maryland Infantry Regiment, discharged 6/18/1862 due to debility and absence due to illness. No record of enlistment or service in the 4th Maryland Artillery, but he is mentioned as being present with the company in letters written in October 1862 by Lt. John Grason and Pvt. Isaac Blunt; he is not listed in any of the historical rosters or other contemporary correspondence. It is possible he joined the battery sometime after 6/18/1862, but unlikely due to his poor health, and it is almost certain he was present with the company in some informal capacity. In the absence of being mentioned in any other contemporary or postwar accounts or rosters he is not listed as a company member.

HAAS, ISAAC C.: Listed in error on Lynch's and Goldsborough's rosters, likely because he lived in Baltimore after the war and was included in a list of members of the SANCSM published in 1883 as having served in "Chew's Battery." He served in R. Preston Chew's Virginia battery of Horse Artillery, not Walter S. Chew's 4th Maryland Artillery.

HOOKER, J. P.: No record of enlistment or service with the 4th Maryland Artillery. A CSR entry in his name, as well as that of T. H. Cane and H. Chester, is included in the 4th Maryland Artillery records as a prisoner captured at Williamsport, MD, 7/6/1863. The capture record is listed in error.

HOWARD, CHARLES: A CSR in his name is included in the 4th Maryland Artillery records as a deserter captured 2/22/1865 at Petersburg, VA, although there is no record of his enlistment or service in the battery. The capture record is in error; this is likely Charles Howard of Co. D, 1st Maryland Infantry Regt.; he enl. 5/22/1861 at Harper's Ferry, VA, and was discharged 10/26/1861. He applied to serve as a clerk in Richmond, VA, 11/28/1861. NFR.

IRVIN, JOHN: Listed in error on Lynch's (as John Irving) and Goldsborough's rosters. He served in the 2nd Maryland Artillery.

JACKSON, WILLIAM: Enl. 1/1/1862 at Machodoc, VA. Bounty jumper who deserted on 1/6/1862 with Andrew Adams and Francis Bogue. NFR.

LEWIS, WALTER: A CSR in his name is included in the 4th Maryland Artillery records as a deserter captured 2/22/1865 at Petersburg, VA, although there is no record of enlistment or service in the battery. The capture record is in error.

LUCAS, WILLIAM J.: Listed in error on Lynch's and Goldsborough's rosters. He served in the 2nd Maryland Artillery.

MALONEY, JAMES: Listed in error on Lynch's (as James Malsney) and Goldsborough's rosters. He served in the 2nd Maryland Artillery.

PIKE, SAMUEL or HENRY: Appears as Samuel in Lynch's roster and as Henry in Goldsborough's. Listed in error: there is no record of a soldier with either name having served in any Maryland Confederate unit, nor does either name appear in Maryland in the 1860 Census.

SHIELDS, ROBERT: Appears in Lynch's roster. Listed in error; there is no record of any soldier with that name having served in a Maryland Confederate unit, nor does the name appear in Maryland in the 1860 Census.

VALLANDIGHAM, J. L.: Records in his CSR relating to his capture at Romney, WVA, in 1864 cite the 4th Maryland Artillery in error. He served in Co. B, 1st Maryland Cav. Regt.

ENDNOTES

Chapter 1 Endnotes

1. Robert K. Krick, *Civil War Weather in Virginia* (Tuscaloosa: The University of Alabama Press, 2007), 45; Record Group 109 (RG 109), Compiled Service Records (CSRs) of Confederate Soldiers, National Archives Building, Washington, DC (NAB). Temperatures in the region that day were in the mid-50s Fahrenheit. The Northern Neck is the region within the peninsula formed by the Potomac and Rappahannock Rivers. It is unknown why Machodoc was selected as the unit's rendezvous point. Machodoc is near Nomini Bay, directly across the Potomac River from Saint Clements Bay and Breton Bay, and near Leonardtown in St. Mary's County, MD. Since Joseph Forrest was from St. Mary's County, it is probable he had crossed into Virginia at that point and was hoping to facilitate the recruitment of further enlistees from Maryland, many of whom crossed at Leonardtown. Additionally, Forrest had moved his family and slaves out of Maryland in 1861, and it is possible they were in the Northern Neck region (Evelyn Ward, *The Children of Bladensfield* [New York: The Viking Press, 1978], 78).
2. Captions and Records of Events (Captions and Records), Roll 294, Captain Forrest's Company Artillery (Chesapeake Artillery), CSRs of Confederate Soldiers from Virginia Units, RG 109, NAB; US War Department, *The War of the Rebellion: A Compilation of the Official Records ofthe Union and Confederate Armies,* 128 vols. (Washington, DC: US Government Printing Office, 1880–1901), 5, 1031 (hereafter cited as OR; all volumes are Series I unless otherwise specified); Joseph Forrest (Name), p. 218 [handwritten], line 32, Enumeration District 6, Page 218, Oakville, St. Mary's County, Maryland Census of Population, 8th Census of the United States, 1860 (Census year), National Archives Microfilm Publication M653, roll 479; Records of the Bureau of the Census, Record Group 29 (RG 29), NAB; Applications for pardon submitted to President Andrew Johnson by former Confederates excluded from earlier amnesty proclamations (Pardon Applications), RG 94, NAB; Joseph Forrest CSR, RG 109, NAB; Regina Combs Hammett, *History of St. Mary's County* (Ridge, Maryland: selfpublished, 1997), 126; Daniel D. Hartzler, *A Band of Brothers,* (Parker, CO: Bookcrafters, 1982), 29; E. Lewis Lowe to Hon. H. A. Corse, January 2, 1862, in John E. Plater CSR, RG 109, NAB. The 2nd Maryland Infantry Regiment was never formed. When the 1st Regiment's term of enlistment was over it was disbanded in August 1862. Using these soldiers as its nucleus, the 1st Maryland Battalion was formed in September; it was later redesignated the 2nd Maryland Battalion to distinguish it from the 1st Maryland Regiment [see Joseph H. Crute, *Units ofthe Confederate States Army* (Midlothian: Derwent Books, 1987), 61–2, and Robert J. Driver, *First and Second Maryland Infantry, CSA* (Bowie: Heritage Books, Inc., 2003)].
3. William Brown, 1850 Census, RG 29, NAB; William D. Brown CSR, RG 109, NAB; *Baltimore Sun,* July 14, 1863; John W. Woods, *Woods 'Baltimore City Directory Ending Year 1860,* Baltimore, MD: John W. Woods, 1860, 1877, 59, 553; Kevin Conley Ruffner, *Maryland's Blue and Gray* (Baton Rouge & London: Louisiana State University Press, 1997), 299; *Baltimore Sun*, May 4 and December 12, 1858.
4. *Saint Mary's Beacon*, April 9, 1926; John E. Plater CSR, RG 109, NAB; Isaac F. Nicholson, "The Maryland Guard Battalion," *Maryland Historical Magazine 6, no. 2 (1911)*: 119; Ruffner, *Maryland's Blue and Gray*, 320–321.

5. S. Z. Ammen, *Maryland Troops in the Confederate Army from Original Sources,* Maryland State Archives, 178 (hereafter cited as *Maryland Troops*); John E. Plater, *Invoice of Quartermaster Stores,* August 29, 1861, W. D. Brown, *Special Requisition,* August 29, 1861, Joseph Forrest, *Special Requisition,* October 2, 1861, in *Unfiled Papers* (Unfiled Papers) *and Slips Belonging in Confederate Compiled Service Records*, RG 109, NAB; *Richmond Daily Dispatch,* October 12, 1861. Pvt. Jacob F. Cook states in Ammen that the two companies consolidated while in Fredericksburg, and the requisitions signed by Forrest, Brown, and Plater place both companies there during August, September, and October 1861. It is unlikely the two companies consolidated at that time, as Forrest and Brown continued in their capacities as captains of separate companies at least as late as December 2, 1861. It is likely Cook is referring to the two companies consolidating at Machodoc, and that the initial planning for consolidation into an artillery unit began while they were still in Fredericksburg. A Norfolk native, John Selden Saunders was a USMA graduate and served as a lieutenant of ordnance in the regular army prewar. After enlisting in the Confederate Army, he served at the Richmond Arsenal before being assigned to the Department of Norfolk, commanded an artillery battalion at Sharpsburg, and acted as chief of artillery for Gen. R. H. Anderson's division as a lieutenant colonel. He later served in staff roles and surrendered at Appomattox. Postwar he lived in Baltimore, was active in the UCV, and died in 1904 at age sixty-seven (Robert K. Krick, *Lee's Colonels,* [Dayton, OH: Morningside, 1984], 286).
6. *Richmond Daily Dispatch,* October 12, 1861. The Huger Artillery was organized in Norfolk in June 1861, and was initially assigned to the Department of Norfolk before serving with the Army of Northern Virginia. Although the Louisiana Guard Artillery was formally organized in late October 1861, in New Orleans its precursor, Co. B, 1st Louisiana Volunteer Infantry Regiment, was serving in the Department of Norfolk at the time of the engagement at Cape Henry (Crute, *Units ofthe Confederate State Army,* 140, 401; F. Ray Sibley, ed., *Confederate Artillery Organizations* [El Dorado Hills, California: Savas Beatie, 2014], 110, 144).
7. OR, 4, 706; OR, 9, 38. The strength of the Department of Norfolk's field artillery battalion was 302 officers and men on November 30, 1861; by January 1862, this had been reduced to forty-seven effectives and no guns. Holmes, of North Carolina, was born in 1804 and was a West Point graduate. He served in the 8th US Infantry in Mexico before the war, was appointed a brigadier general in the Confederate Army in June 1861, and commanded a brigade at 1st Manassas. Holmes was promoted to major general commanding the Aquia District in October. He later commanded a division during the Seven Days campaign and still later the Trans-Mississippi Department. He was a farmer postwar and died in 1880 (Ezra J. Warner, *Generals in Gray* [Baton Rouge: Louisiana State University Press], 141).
8. OR, 51, pt. 2, 413; Unfiled Papers, RG 109, NAB.
9. James P. Williams to Pa, June 28, 1863, in Evelyn Cary Williams, ed., *Letters of James Peter Williams, 1861–1865,* Albert and Shirley Small Special Collections Library, University of Virginia (hereafter cited as Williams Letters, UVA).
10. See chapter 2 for a complete discussion of the battery's demographic composition.
11. Ruffner, *Maryland's Blue and Gray,* 34–40; Hammett, *History of St. Mary 's County,* 124.
12. W. D. Brown to Mrs. Ward, August 1, 1862, letter 691, box 4, Ward Family Papers, Library of Congress, hereafter LOC; Phil. Littig Harrison to Col. W H. Taylor, February 13, 1863, in Philip L. Harrison CSR, RG 109, NAB.
13. T. Worthington Mummey to Col. W. H. S. Taylor, June 27, 1864, in Thomas W. Mummey CSR, RG 109, NAB.
14. Jno J. Hooff to Aunt, September 17, 1862, letter 734, box 5, Ward Family Papers, LOC.

15. Andrew Egan to Hon. Jas M. Seddon, November 25, 1863, in Andrew A. Egan CSR, RG 109, NAB.
16. Edward C. Cottrell CSR, RG 109, NAB; *New York Times*, December 4, 1861; *Baltimore Sun,* December 4, 1861; OR, Series II, 1, pt. 1, 165–166, 738–739; OR, Series II, 2, pt. 1, 227.
17. Ammen, *Maryland Troops,* 9. Cook probably refers to Roderick Watson, a wealthy fifty-five-year-old farmer who lived across the Potomac from Mathias Point in Charles County, MD (Roderick Watson, *1860 Census,* RG 29, NAB).
18. Statement of George B. Maccubbin, in George B. Maccubbin CSR, RG 109, NAB.
19. OR, 5, 1032. The exact date the company moved to Heathsville is unknown, but it was before February 1, 1862; on that date John R. H. Embert, George Maccubbin, and Benjamin Young all enlisted in the battery at Heathsville (John R. H. Embert, George B. Maccubbin, and Benjamin Young CSRs, RG 109, NAB). The company's flag was probably presented in Heathsville; hand-stitched of wool bunting and inscribed with the date "Jan 23, 1862," it was carried by the battery for over two years and retired after the May 1864 Battle of North Anna. The names of all of the Chesapeake's unit and battalion commanders, as well as the battles the flag was carried in, are inscribed on it in various hands; it now resides in a private collection.
20. Ibid., 990, 1032; CSRs, Roll 13, RG 109, NAB; McPherson Kennedy, "The Baltimore Underground," *Richmond Times-Dispatch,* March 9, 1913. Presumably the other two captains recruiting in the area were Meriweather Lewis and John Tayloe for their cavalry companies. Both companies later became part of the 9th Virginia Cavalry Regiment: Lewis's as Company D and Tayloe's as Company I (Meriweather Lewis and John Tayloe CSRs, RG 109, NAB). Richard Lee Turberville Beale was born in Westmoreland County in 1819. A lawyer who served as a US Congressman and Virginia State Congressman before the war, he enlisted in the 9th Virginia Cavalry Regiment in 1861, eventually becoming its colonel. He later led a brigade in W. H. F. Lee's cavalry division, and was commissioned brigadier general in February 1865. Postwar he was a lawyer and served an additional term in the US Congress; he died in 1893 (Warner, *Generals in Gray,* 20).
21. Krick, *Civil War Weather in Virginia,* 46–47. Although these weather conditions were recorded for Richmond, those of Heathsville—only sixty miles away—would have been similar.
22. Joseph Forrest CSR, RG 109, NAB.
23. Dean S. Thomas, *Cannons* (Gettysburg; Thomas Publications, 1985), 28–29, 32.
24. Robert C. Jones and John Grason CSRs, RG 109, NAB. See Thomas, *Cannons,* 5–6. The most dangerous step in loading a Civil War-era cannon was ramming a new load into the barrel. If the barrel had not been properly sponged in the previous step it could leave sparks from the last round fired, potentially causing a premature discharge of the gun while the new load was still being rammed. This is likely the cause of Jones's injury. See chapter 8 for additional details of Jones's life.
25. OR, 5, 972.
26. Ibid., 994. Pickett, born in Richmond in 1825 and a West Point graduate, would go on to lead a brigade and division in the Army of Northern Virginia. He was an insurance agent in Norfolk postwar and died in 1875 (Warner, *Generals in Gray*, 239).
27. OR, 5, 972.
28. Ibid., 993–994.
29. Ibid., 1103; *Captions and Records,* Chesapeake Artillery, RG 109, NAB; Thomas, *Cannons*, 5. Lee also had a personal interest in the Northern Neck region: his birthplace and boyhood home, Stratford Hall, was on the Potomac River less than fifteen miles from Machodoc.
30. James B. Slaughter, *Settlers, Southerners, Americans* (Salem, WV: Don Mills, Inc., 1986) , 167; Carroll M. Garnett, "Tappahannock and Its Role in The War Between The States," *Essex County Historical Society Bulletin,* 19 (November, 1981), 1, (hereafter

cited as ECHSB); Carroll M. Garnett, "Fort Lowry-Camp Byron," *ECHSB,* 30, (May, 1987) , 1–3; Carroll M. Garnett, *Fort Lowry and Raiders on the Rappahannock* (New York: Vantage Press, 2002), 26, 43. The site of Fort Lowry is Lowry's Point on the Rappahannock River, near the intersection of Fort Lowry Lane and River Place, two miles northeast of Dunnsville, Virginia.

31. As listed in the 1860 Census, Ward was a wealthy fifty-three-year-old farmer and Episcopal minister; he lived at Bladensfield, in Richmond County, with his wife Mary and twelve children, who ranged in age from one month to twenty-three years; he owned three slaves. The family had moved temporarily to Tappahannock when Ward accepted a teaching position there. He had raised a local infantry company ("Essex Sharpshooters") before the war, as well as additional companies in 1861 that eventually became part of the 55th Virginia Infantry Regiment; he was the commander of the troops in Fort Lowry for several months. The Wards would lose two sons in the war: twenty-three-year-old Capt. William N. "Will" Ward Jr. of Company D, 47th Virginia Infantry Regiment, died in August 1862 of a shoulder wound received at the Battle of Gaines Mill; and eighteen-year-old Charles B. "Charley" Ward enlisted as a private in Company B of the 9th Virginia Cavalry Regiment on June 1, 1863, and was killed eight days later at the Battle of Brandy Station. Ward's daughter Evelyn wrote a memoir of her life at Bladensfield during the Civil War; the family's extensive papers, including several letters written by members of the Chesapeake Artillery, are at the Library of Congress, hereafter LOC (Ward family, 1860 Census, RG 29, NAB; Garnett, *Fort Lowry and Raiders on the Rappahannock,* 39; William N. Ward, Charles B. Ward, and William N. Ward Jr. CSRs, RG 109, NAB; *Slaughter, Settlers, Southerners*, Americans, 169; Ward, *The Children of Bladensfield,* 18).

32. Ward, *The Children of Bladensfield,* 46. Martha "Mattie" Ward would turn twenty-four in 1862, and her sister Mary, or "Mamie," 21.

33. W. D. Brown to Dear Madam, August 1, 1862, letter 691, box 4, Ward Family Papers, LOC.

34. OR, 5, 1100. Col. Francis Mallory was born in 1833 in Norfolk, Virginia. He graduated from VMI, was a civil engineer and officer in the US Army prewar, and enlisted in the Confederate Army as a lieutenant in March 1861, eventually becoming colonel of the 55th Virginia Infantry Regiment in September. He commanded Fort Lowry and its satellite installations as well, succeeding George Pickett in February 1862. Mallory was killed at the Battle of Chancellorsville May 2, 1863 (Bruce S. Allardice, *Confederate Colonels,* [Columbia and London: University of Missouri Press, 2008], 250; Francis Mallory CSR, RG 109, NAB; Garnett, *Fort Lowry and Raiders on the Rappahannock,* 104). Though not named specifically by Holmes, the battery he ordered placed at Fredericksburg could only have been the Chesapeake Artillery. All of the other four batteries in the Aquia District were on the Potomac River near Aquia Landing at this time: Braxton's Fredericksburg Artillery was at Camp Clifton (Captions and Records, Fredericksburg Artillery, Roll 330, RG 109, NAB); Andrews's Maryland Flying Artillery was at Shipping Point (Goldsborough, *Maryland Line,* 260; George L. Sherwood, *First Maryland Artillery and Second Maryland Artillery,* [Westminster, MD: Heritage Books, 2007], 13); Cooke's Stafford Light Artillery was at Brooke's Station (OR, 5, 1031); and Walker's Purcell Artillery was at Aquia and Potomac Creeks (OR, 5, 1032). Moreover, Capt. Joseph Forrest signed a receipt for supplies at Fredericksburg dated March 13, 1862, two days before Holmes informed Lee a battery had already been placed at Fredericksburg (Joseph Forest CSR, RG 109, NAB). Company B of the 55 th Virginia Infantry was serving as an artillery unit at Camp Ashby in Urbanna at that time; they were later reorganized as Fleet's Middlesex Artillery, but not until April 28, so it could not have been this unit. (Garnett, *Fort Lowry and Raiders on the Rappahannock,* p. 43;

Captions and Records, Capt. Fleet's Co. of Artillery, Roll 294, RG 109, NAB).

35. Joseph Forrest and George McClure CSRs, RG 109, NAB; Garnett, *Fort Lowry and Raiders on the Rappahannock,* 104–107; OR, 21, 550.

36. OR, 5, 1106; OR, 12, pt. 1, 36; OR, 12, pt. 3, 847. Fort Lowry and Tappahannock were attacked by a flotilla of Federal gunboats under Lt. R. H. Wyman on April 16, 1862. The barracks and installations at Fort Lowry were burned, but the town was not shelled (OR, 5, 37; Garnett, *Fort Lowry andRaiders on the Rappahannock,* 110; Slaughter, *Settlers, Southerners, Americans,* 169; Ward, *The Children of Bladensfield,* 50–53).

37. W. W. Goldsborough, *The Maryland Line in the Confederate Army, 1861–1865,* Baltimore, MD: Guggenheimer, Weil and Co., 1900, 319, (hereafter cited as Maryland Line); James P. Williams and Martin L. Harvey CSRs, RG 109, NAB; S. Z. Ammen, *Maryland Troops,* 178. Henry C. Buckmaster enlisted in the unit as a corporal on April 12 at Richmond (Henry C. Buckmaster CSR, RG 109, NAB).

38. Bradley T. Johnson, "The Maryland Line in the Confederate Army," in Brock, R. A., ed., *Southern Historical Society Papers.* 52 vols. (Wilmington, NC: Broadfoot Publishing Company, 1991), vol. 11, 23 (hereafter cited as SHSP). It is conjecture that the battery held their elections on May 15, but this was the most likely date. Capt. Joseph Forrest's final pay requisition was for pay up to May 15, presumably the last day he was captain and also the day of the elections (Joseph Forrest CSR, RG 109, NAB). None of the newly elected officers' commission dates are included in their service records, but it appears their commissions were approved for effective dates between May 15 and June 1, 1862. John Grason's records include a voucher he signed for pay as a 2nd lieutenant for May 24–July 1, 1862. Brown signed a pay voucher for pay as a captain for June 1–July 1, 1862. John Plater's commission occurred before August 29, 1861, when he signed a receipt for quartermaster's stores as a lieutenant with the unorganized 2nd Maryland Infantry Regiment; he signed a requisition for forage on June 2, 1862, as a 1st lieutenant of artillery (John S. Plater CSR, RG 109, NAB). Walter S. Chew's record indicates his commission date to lieutenant is "not known," and there are no requisitions or pay vouchers for this period in his records (Walter S. Chew CSR, RG 109, NAB). Sibley (ed.), *Confederate Artillery Organizations,* 157, originally published by the US War Department in 1898, incorrectly indicates these officers' commission date was July 23, 1862. This is not the date of their commissions, but that of an organization table for the Army of Northern Virginia in which the battery is first mentioned in the Official Records as part of that command (OR, 11, 648).

39. Goldsborough, *Maryland Line,* 319; William D. Brown, Walter S. Chew, John E. Plater, John Grason CSRs, RG 109, NAB. The battery continued to be almost universally referred to as the Chesapeake Artillery, the Chesapeake, or Brown's battery. The earliest use of the 4th Maryland Artillery designation in any of the company's records is not until December 8, 1862, and appears in a register when Pvt. Richard Hardesty was admitted to Robertson Hospital and gave that as his unit's designation (James R. Hardesty CSR, RG 109, NAB).

40. Jas. P. Williams to Aunt Mary, July 6, 1862, Williams Letters, UVA; OR, 27, pt. 3, 451; W. W. Goldsborough, "With Lee at Gettysburg," *Philadelphia Record,* July 10, 1900; Ammen, *Maryland Troops,* 181; Jno. J. Hooff to Dear Aunt, October 2, 1862, letter 741, box 5, Ward Family Papers, LOC.

41. W. D. Brown to Dear Madam, August 1, 1862, letter 691, box 4, Ward Family Papers, LOC. Brown refers to his brother, Sgt. Philip A. H. Brown, twenty years old on that date; John Hooff was nearly eighteen.

42. James P. Williams to Mama, June 19, 1862, Williams Letters, UVA; Williams refers to the command of Maj. Gen. Thomas J. "Stonewall" Jackson. Brig. Gen. William N. Pendleton was the chief of artillery for the Army of Northern Virginia.

43. CSRs, Roll 13, RG 109, NAB.
44. Jas. P. Williams to Aunt Mary, July 6, 1862, Williams Letters.
45. OR, 11, pt. 3, 539; *Richmond Daily Dispatch,* May 30, 1862.
46. James P. Williams to Mama, June 19, 1862, Williams Letters; *Richmond Examiner,* June 28, 1862. Battery No. 2 was on the east side of present-day Old Osborne Turnpike in Richmond, just north of its intersection with Long Street; Maj. Gen. James Longstreet commanded about one-half of Lee's army.
47. Jas. P. Williams to Aunt Mary, July 6, 1862, Williams Letters.
48. Jno. J. Hooff to Cousin Mary, September 30, 1862, letter 736, box 5, Ward Family Papers, LOC; Hooff is referring to Pvt. Philip L. "Phil" Harrison of the company; W. D. Brown [to Mary Ward], May 9, 1963, letter 910, box 5, Ward Family Papers, LOC; Lewis to Parents, October 16th, 1862, private collection.
49. Chew to Mother, October 2, 1862, private collection; I Jas Blunt to My dear Cousin, October 12, 1862, private collection; John Grason to Sallie Grason, October 16, 1862, private collection; Jno. J. Hooff to Cousin Mattie, no date, letter 737, box 5, Ward Family Papers, LOC; Jno. J. Hooff to Cousin Mary, September 30, 1862, letter 736, box 5, Ward Family Papers, LOC.
50. James P. Williams to Nannie, June 17, 1862, Williams Letters, UVA.
51. T. P. LeCompte to Mother, October 16, 1862, private collection.
52. OR, 51, pt. 2, 591; Stapleton Crutchfield was born in 1835 at Spring Forest, Virginia. He graduated from VMI and was a professor there before the war. Crutchfield enlisted as a captain of artillery in May 1861, eventually rising to colonel and chief of artillery for Jackson's command; he lost a leg at the battle of Chancellorsville. Crutchfield later commanded a brigade of heavy artillery; he was killed in action at Sailor's Creek in April 1865, and buried on the field (Allardice, *Confederate Colonels,* 117).
53. OR, 12, pt. 3, 964.

Chapter 2 Endnotes

1. Jas. P. Williams to Aunt Mary, July 6th, 1862, Williams Letters, UVA; Goldsborough, *Maryland Line,* p. 319; James P. Williams CSR, RG 109, NAB; Martin L. Harvey CSR, RG 109, NAB; James P Williams to Mama, June 19th 1862, Williams Letters, UVA.
2. The antebellum residences of 119 members of the company are known, or 88% of its total enrolment. The comparative data for the Army of Northern Virginia is drawn from Joseph T. Glatthaar's statistical analysis of the army and its branches, *Soldiering in the Army of Northern Virginia, a Statistical Portrait of the Troops Who Served under RobertE. Lee* (Chapel Hill: The University of North Carolina Press, 2011, hereafter cited as Soldicring In the Army of Northern Virginia). Using a stratified cluster sample of 600 soldiers (300 from infantry units and 150 each from the artillery and cavalry), Glatthaar applied statistical analysis methods to multiple features of the soldiers in the army, such as age, wealth, slaveholding status, and occupation. Glatthaar examined these elements in depth for the first time, and in so doing not only presented an accurate picture of the Army of Northern Virginia, but also eliminated a number of the army's myths. In this present study of the Chesapeake Artillery, census and other data was subjected to statistical analysis using a Chi-square test (chi^2) consistent with Glatthaar's practice that compares the statistical probabilities of differences between groups.
3. 1860 Census, RG 29, NAB. The company's higher proportion of urban dwelling men compared to the Army is statistically significant ($chi^2 = 57.211$, $p = .0001$). Although much higher than average, the Chesapeake Artillery would not have had the highest proportion of urban dwelling members among artillery units in the Army of Northern Virginia. Some units had membership almost exclusively from urban backgrounds, such as the Baltimore Light Artillery (2nd Maryland Artillery), Richmond Howitzers, and the Washington Artillery of New Orleans.

4. Glatthaar, *Soldiering in the Army of Northern Virginia,* 3, 5, 45–46; the difference in the company's average age compared to the army is statistically significant ($chi^2 = 64.730$, $p = .0001$), as is the difference in average age of the company compared to the artillery arm ($chi^2 = 18.063$, $p = .0012$). Ages for 111 of the unit's soldiers are known, or 83% of its total enrolment.
5. William Smith, 1860 Census, RG 29, NAB. William Smith CSR, RG 109, NAB.
6. Edward O.N. Stansbury CSR, RG 109, NAB; Edward Stansbury, 1860 Census, RG 29, NAB. Stansbury's exact date of birth is unknown; he was listed as fourteen years old in the 1860 Census taken for his family on July 9, sixteen years old on a Certificate of Disability for Discharge dated March 7, 1863, and seventeen years old in Judith Brockenbrough McGuire's diary entry for April 15, 1863. Therefore, he had to have turned seventeen at some point during the six weeks prior to his death on April 15.
7. E. K. Culver CSR, RG 109, NAB; E. K. Culver, 1860 Census, RG 29, NAB. There is no statistical difference between the proportion of teenaged soldiers among the unit's early enlisters and late enlisters ($chi^2 = .082$, $p = .7751$).
8. Glatthaar, *Soldiering in the Army of Northern Virginia,* 6. The difference in the distribution of occupations among the Chesapeake Artillery compared to the Army of Northern Virginia is statistically significant ($chi^2 = 95.805$, $p = .0001$). The antebellum occupations of ninety-one members of the company are known, or 68% of its total enrolment.
9. Ibid., 6, 47; Edward McPherson, *For Cause and Comrades: Why Men Fought in the Civil War* (New York: The Free Press, 1987), 11, hereafter cited as *For Cause and Comrades*. The difference in the battery's literacy rate compared to the Confederate Army is statistically significant ($chi^2 = 14.063$, $p = .0002$). The literacy of ninety-nine members of the battery is known, or 74% of total enrolment.
10. 1860 Census, RG 29, NAB. The economic status of 100 of the unit's members is known, or 75% of total enrolment. For comparative purposes, the same economic class definitions are used here as determined by Glatthaar in *Soldiering in the Army of Northern Virginia,* 8–9.
11. 1860 Census, RG 29, NAB; Glatthaar, *Soldiering in the Army of Northern Virginia,* 8–9. This is the method used by Glatthaar in his discussion of economic status, *Soldiering in the Army of Northern Virginia,* 7–8. The 85% of men in the unit who lived in other households compares to the rest of the Army at about 64%, a difference that is statistically significant ($chi^2 = 20.258$, $p < .0001$) and a further reflection of their youth. The household structure of 101 men of the unit is known, or 76% of total enrolment. The distribution of economic classes within the company was similar to that of the Army, but markedly different from the Artillery arm. Compared to the Artillery, the Chesapeake had about the same proportion of men in the lowest economic class, slightly over half the level of members in the middle class, and nearly one-third more in the highest economic class. This difference is statistically significant ($chi^2 = 749$, $p = 0.002$).
12. Daniel A. Wilkinson CSR, RG 109, NAB; Daniel Wilkinson, 1860 Census, RG 29, NAB.
13. Glatthaar, *Soldiering in the Army of Northern Virginia,* 6, 48; This difference is statistically significant ($chi^2 = 13.511$, $p = .0002$). The marital status of 100 of the unit's members is known, or 74% of its enrolment. The percentage of men in the Army of Northern Virginia who had children is calculated by taking the 37.5% of men who were married multiplied by the 82.2% of married men who had children. The difference in the company's lower level of married men compared to the Army is statistically significant ($chi^2 = 15.487$, $p = .0001$).
14. Individual and household slave ownership is known for 99 of the unit's members, or 74% of its total enrolment.
15. 1860 Census, RG 29, NAB; Glatthaar, *Soldiering in the Army of Northern Virginia,* 51, 154–165. One of Glatthaar's findings is that although only about 37% of the soldiers in the Army

of Northern Virginia owned slaves, over 44% came from slaveholding households, a rate 77% higher than the 25% of slaveholding households in the Confederate States as a whole; the lower level of household slave ownership for the men of the unit compared to the army is statistically significant (chi^2 = 50.478, p = .0001).

16. William Pinder, Gustavus Porter, William Tarbutton, Robert Goldsborough, 1860 Census, RG 29, NAB.
17. Joseph Forrest, William D. Brown, Walter Scott Chew, John E. Plater, John Grason, Benjamin G. Roberts CSRs, RG 109, NAB.
18. 1860 Census, RG 29, NAB. The difference in the distribution of officers in the company among economic classes compared to its enlisted men is statistically significant (chi^2 = 9.330, p = .0094). The difference in age between officers and enlisted men in the battery is statistically significant (chi^2 = 4.134, p = .0420). Because of the very small sample size for officers in the company, the age distribution used for the comparison of these two groups was men born in 1835 or before and men born in 1836 or after.
19. 1860 Census, RG 29, NAB. Since Chew was elected in 1862 and appointed in 1864, he is included in the calculations for both groups. It is important to note the officers elected in 1862 did not necessarily lack for skill or valor. Brown, Grason, and Chew were exceptional officers respected by their superiors and men.
20. See Kenneth W. Noe's thorough analysis of the differences in characteristics and motivations to serve of late enlisters in the Confederate Army compared to early enlisters in *Reluctant Rebels: The Confederates Who Joined the Army after 1861* (Chapel Hill: The University of North Carolina Press, 2010, hereafter cited as Reluctant Rebels). Noe defined early enlisters as those who enlisted before January 1, 1862. In this analysis of the Chesapeake Artillery, the definition of early enlisters has been revised to include men who enlisted on January 1, 1862, at Machodoc. There are two reasons for this. First, because the unit was formed later in the war, there would not be enough men in the sample of early enlisters to draw valid conclusions. Second, because Maryland soldiers who enlisted at Machodoc had to make their way across the Potomac River and then to a rendezvous point to enlist, the actual decision to enlist had to be made weeks or months prior to January 1, 1862, as well as requiring a physical presence with the intention to enlist before that date (Noe, *Reluctant Rebels,* 13). There were ninety-nine soldiers who served in the unit for whom enlistment dates were known and who were also found in the 1860 Census, or 74% of its total enrolment; fifty enlisted on or before January 1, 1862, and forty-nine after that date.
21. CSRs, Roll 13, RG 109, NAB; 1860 Census, RG 29, NAB; Noe, *Reluctant Rebels*, 15. The difference is statistically significant (chi^2 = 7.784, p = .0053). Although slaves were included as part of personal property valuation in the 1860 Census, slave ownership was not a factor affecting enlistment in the unit, since soldiers who came from slaveholding households were no more likely to enlist early than late; Joseph Forrest was the only individual slaveholder in the unit, and when he was dropped at the battery's reorganization there were no individual slave owners in its ranks for the remainder of the war. Further, there was no difference in the proportion of men from urban or rural residences and whether they enlisted early or late: late enlisters came from rural or urban residences in the same percentages as early enlisters, even though all of the men from slaveholding households came from rural counties. It appears members of the unit from wealthier households, regardless of where they lived or whether they came from slaveholding households or not, feared that Federal control of Maryland and the potential disruption of the Southern economy could affect the value of personal property and real estate and rushed to join the Confederate war effort.
22. The determination of the motivations of Confederate soldiers to enlist and serve is a large field of academic inquiry well beyond

the scope of this study. Other authors, notably Noe, *Reluctant Rebels*; McPherson, *For Cause and Comrades*; Joseph T. Glatthaar, *General Lee's Army* (New York: Free Press, 2008); and Bell Irvin Wiley, *The Life of Johnny Reb* (Baton Rouge and London: Louisiana State University Press, 1943), have examined these dynamics in depth and there is no full consensus. These authors based much of their research on hundreds of letters, and census data for sample sizes of Confederate soldiers also numbering in the hundreds. For the Chesapeake Artillery total enrolment was only 135 soldiers, and a mere twenty-eight letters are known that were written by members of the unit during the war. It appears from data analysis that protection of property was a strong motivation for men of the company to enlist early in the conflict, as was the sense of adventure suggested by the battery's youth and consistent rate of enlistment by teenaged unit members throughout the war. Several of the company's members (John H. Gardner, Thomas J. Everngam, and Francis Stewart of Queen Anne's County) enlisted in Richmond on November 1, 1862, after they had been drafted into the Federal army (John H. Gardner, Thomas J. Everngam, Francis Stewart CSRs, RG 109, NAB; *Baltimore Sun,* October 21, 1862). The battery's low desertion rate suggests a strong sense of unit cohesion and esprit de corps (see appendix F for an examination of desertion within the Chesapeake). Based on the limited volume of material mentioned by the men themselves, conclusions about other reasons for members of the battery to enlist and serve remain largely directional.

Chapter 3 Endnotes

1. Krick, *Civil War Weather in Virginia,* 68; Robert K. Krick, *Stonewall Jackson at Cedar Mountain* (Chapel Hill and London: The University of North Carolina Press, 1990), 17; John William Ford Hatton, "Memoir, John William Ford Hatton, First Maryland Battery C.S.A. 1861 to 1865," John William Ford Hatton Papers, LOC, 316, (hereafter cited as *Hatton Memoir*); Ammen, *Maryland Troops*, 179.
2. Jennings Cropper Wise, *The Long Arm of Lee,* vol. 1 (Lynchburg: J.P. Bell Company, Inc., 1915), 245. Alfred Ranson Courtney enlisted as a lieutenant in May 1861 at twenty-six. He was promoted to captain of the Henrico Artillery in July 1861, and to major and chief of artillery of Ewell's Division in July 1862. He later served in the A.I.G.O., and in 1863 reported to Gen. Simon B. Buckner. Postwar he served in the Virginia legislature and died November 4, 1914, at eighty (Alfred R. Courtney CSR, RG 109, NAB; Krick, *Lee's Colonels,* 86).
3. Krick, *Stonewall Jackson at Cedar Mountain,* 17, 32.
4. Ibid., 54.
5. OR, 12, pt. 2, 237.
6. Ibid., 238.
7. Ibid., 230. Early incorrectly indicated Dement moved forward with three pieces rather than the two deployed. Courtney had also positioned Latimer's battery on a shelf of Cedar Mountain to the right of the cedars and D'Aquin's battery and the remaining guns of Dement's to the right rear of the cedars on a ridge behind the Crittenden farmhouse.
8. Krick, *Civil War Weather in Virginia,* 68; Ammen, *Maryland Troops*, 179; OR, 12, pt. 2, 233; *Hatton Memoir*, 319.
9. Krick, *Stonewall Jackson at CedarMountain,* 134.
10. *Hatton Memoir*, 319; John H. K. Shannahan and John S. Shafer CSRs, RG 109, NAB; Krick, *Stonewall Jackson at Cedar Mountain,* 137. Shannahan would recover in hospital in Richmond and returned to duty three months later; Shafer lost sight in his left eye and much of that in his right eye and was subsequently given a medical discharge. Although the initial hospital admittance details are missing from Shafer's CSR, he could only have been wounded at Cedar Mountain; he is not listed in Brown's report of casualties for the Second Manassas campaign; there is no casualty report extant for the Chesapeake Artillery at Cedar Mountain. Shafer's records place him in a hospital in Richmond with a gunshot wound

to his left eye when he received pay on September 20, 1862.

11. OR, 12, pt. 2, 238.

12. Ibid., 183; John J. Hennessy, *Return to Bull Run* (New York: Simon & Schuster, 1993), 28.

13. OR, 12, pt. 2, 238, 233, 182; G. Campbell Brown, "Notes on Ewell's Division in the Campaign of 1862," *SHSP,* 10, 6, 260. The company could only have received the two Parrott guns at this time. Although it is conjecture that this was in recognition of their performance at Cedar Mountain, it is highly likely (see appendix A for a full discussion of the battery's acquisition of their Parrott rifles). The Parrott field rifle was a rifled cannon distinguished by a band of reinforcing iron wrapped around the breech to give it greater strength. It had an effective range of 2,000 yards (Bradley M. Gottfried, *The Artillery of Gettysburg*, [Nashville: Cumberland House Publishing, Inc., 2008], 259).

14. OR, 12, pt. 2, 705; Hennessy, *Return to Bull Run,* 71; Henry W. Thomas, *History of the Doles-CookBrigade* (Dayton: Morningside, 1981), 215.

15. OR, 12, pt. 2, 706; Tom Kelly, ed., *The Personal Memories of Thomas Jonathan Scharf* (Baltimore: Butternut and Blue, 1992), 36.

16. OR, 12, pt. 2, 707; Thomas, *History of the Doles-Cook Brigade,* 217; Kelly, ed., *The Personal Memoirs of Thomas Jonathan Scharf,* 37.

17. OR, 12, pt. 2, 707.

18. OR, 12, pt. 2, 708; Krick, *Civil War Weather in Virginia,* 66; Donald C. Pfanz, Richard S. Ewell: *A Soldier's Life* (Chapel Hill and London: The University of North Carolina Press, 1998), 249–251, hereafter cited as Pfanz, Ewell; Hennessy, *Return to Bull Run,* 106–107.

19. OR, 12, pt. 2, 709; Pfanz, Ewell, 252; map: "Plan and Battle of Kettle Run and Bristoe Station, August 27th, 1862," LOC. Robert C. Leachman was a wealthy fifty-year-old Baptist clergyman and owner of five slaves. He lived with his wife Elizabeth and one boarder (Robert C. Leachman, 1860 Census, RG 29, NAB).

20. OR, 12, pt. 2, 710; Capt. Samuel D. Buck, *With the Old Confeds* (Baltimore: H. E. Houck & Co., 1925), 52; "Report of Capt. W.D. Brown of Casualties in the Chesapeake Artillery, February 8, 1863," (Brown Casualty Report), Confederate States Army Casualty Lists and Narrative Reports, RG 109, NAB. Hennessy cites as an example of the casualties that day the 50% loss incurred by the 73rd New York as part of the Federals' 300 total casualties; Confederate casualties at Bristoe Station were about half that (Hennessy, *Return to Bull Run*, 134).

21. Hennessy, *Return to Bull Run,* 129–130; Pfanz, Ewell, 253; Buck, *With the Old Confeds,* 53.

22. Jno. J. Hooff to Cousin Mary, September 30th, 1862, letter 736, box 5, Ward Family Papers, LOC.

23. OR, 12, pt. 2, 710; Alan T. Gaff, *Brave Men's Tears: The Iron Brigade at Brawner's Farm* (Dayton: Morningside Press, 1996), 53–54, hereafter cited as *Brave Men's Tears*; *Rochester Daily Union and Advertiser,* September 11, 1862. See appendix B for an analysis of the battery's movements at Second Manassas.

24. Gaff, *Brave Men's Tears,* 61; Hennessy, *Return to Bull Run,* 169; *Richmond Times-Dispatch,* October 29, 1905; *Rochester Daily Union and Advertiser,* September 11, 1862. Garber was a twenty-five-year-old machinist from Augusta County, Virginia, and a prewar member of the Staunton Light Artillery, which was accepted into Confederate service in June 1861. He served with the unit through the entire war, eventually becoming its captain, was wounded three times, and was captured at Sailor's Creek April 6, 1865 (Asher Garber, 1860 Census, RG 29, NAB; Asher W. Garber CSR, RG 109, NAB; Crute, *Units of the Confederate States Army,* 414).

25. *Rochester Daily Union and Advertiser,* September 11, 1862.

26. Goldsborough, *Maryland Line,* 320.

27. James R. Hardesty and Philip L. Harrison CSRs, RG 109, NAB; T. P. LeCompte to

Mother, October 16th, 1862, private collection. Lawton, a West Point graduate from South Carolina, was appointed brigadier general on April 13, 1861, and served with the Army of Northern Virginia until seriously wounded at Sharpsburg on September 17, 1862. Upon his return to duty a year later he was placed in command of the Confederate quartermaster general's department until the end of the war (Warner, *Generals in Gray,* 176.).

28. Goldsborough, *Maryland Line,* 320. Goldsborough places this occurrence after the first day's fight, then continues to say the battery went back into action after dark to repel a night attack, although the fighting that day did not start again after breaking off. Not being present at the battle, he appears to have confused the nature of the fight at Groveton with a night attack; the battle started at dusk and continued until after dark. This incident could not have happened in the afternoon of August 28, before the battery went into action, as fires had been prohibited to prevent detection (Gaff, *Brave Men's Tears,* 59).
29. OR, 12, pt. 2, 652; Hennessy, *Return to Bull Run,* 208–209. This U-shaped depression with its flat floor is at the base of Stony Hill on its north side, about one mile directly behind the battery's position in the Confederate line (John J. Hennessy, *Second Manassas Battlefield Map Survey* [Lynchburg: H. E. Howard Inc., 2nd Ed., 1991], Troop Movement Map 1).
30. Ammen, *Maryland Troops*, 181; Goldsborough also cites this incident, *Maryland Line,* 320; Andrew Egan CSR, RG I09, NAB. Lynch, writing after the war and relying on memory, lists Baker, Pvt. Frederick Cusick, and Egan among the wounded at 2nd Manassas, rather than Harrison and Hardesty, and the error is repeated in Goldsborough's book. Brown's casualty report is clear that Baker and Cusick were not wounded there, and there are no medical records in either soldier's CSR indicating otherwise (Brown Casualty Report, RG I09, NAB).
31. OR, 12, pt. 2, 653; Brown's and Garber's batteries were most likely positioned on the rise immediately to the east of the intersection of the Warrenton Turnpike and Groveton-Sndley Road, in the vicinity of present-day Groveton Confederate Cemetery.
32. Goldsborough, *Maryland Line,* 320.
33. Ibid., 320.
34. Jno. J. Hooff to Cousin Mattie, n.d., letter 737, box 5, Ward Family Papers, LOC.
35. Hennessy, *Return to Bull Run,* 456–451; OR, 12, pt. 2, 653.
36. See D. Scott Hartwig, *To Antietam Creek* (Baltimore: The Johns Hopkins University Press, 2012), for the most complete modern treatment of the early phases of the Maryland Campaign.
37. OR, 19, pt. I, 966; Roll I3, RG I09, NAB.
38. OR, 19, pt. I, 966; William H. C. Oldson and Andrew J. Bryan CSRs, RG 109, NAB; Jno. J. Hooff to Aunt, September 17, 1862, letter 734, box 5, Ward Family Papers, LOC.
39. OR, 19, pt. I, 962.
40. Ibid., 962; Hartwig, *To Antietam Creek,* 539.
41. Jno. J. Hooff to Aunt, September 17th, 1862, letter 734, box 5, Ward Family Papers, LOC; Joseph A. Mason CSR, RG 94, NAB.
42. Ibid.
43. James P. Williams to Mama, October 31st, 1862, Williams Letters, UVA.
44. Jno. J. Hooff to Aunt, September 17th, 1862, letter 734, box 5, Ward Family Papers, LOC. To arrive at four days fighting at Manassas Hooff must have counted the three days of the battle of Second Manassas and the Battle of Chantilly, although the unit was not engaged there. He mentions the engagement of Bristoe Station separately.
45. T. P. LeCompte to Dear Mother, October 16th, 1862, private collection.
46. I Jas Blunt to My dear Cousin, October 12th, 1862, private collection.
47. Jno. J. Hooff to Aunt, October 2d, 1862, letter 741, box 5, Ward Family Papers, LOC; CSRs, Roll 13, RG 109, NAB. Following his court-martial for dereliction of duty for failing to advance with his battalion at the Battle of Sharpsburg, Courtney reported to Richmond after being relieved of duty with the ANV at his own request (Krick, *Lee's Colonels,* 86).

Chapter 4 Endnotes

1. James P. Williams to Mama, October 31st, 1862, Williams Letters, UVA; Jno. J. Hooff to Aunt, October 2, 1862, letter 741, box 5, Ward Family Papers, LOC; Jno. J. Hooff to Cousin Mary, September 30, 1862, letter 736, box 5, Ward Family Papers, LOC.
2. James P. Williams to Mama, October 31, 1862, Williams Letters, UVA.
3. Ward, *The Children of Bladensfield,* 78; Edwin W. Beitzell, *St. Mary's County Civil War Records,* St. Mary's County Historical Society (hereafter cited as SMCHS). Although Evelyn Ward is writing about events of autumn 1862, she refers to the Maryland soldiers as part of the Maryland Line, whose initial organization would not occur until twelve months later. For clarity, the words "soldier" and "soldiers" have been inserted here in place of her words "Liner" and "Liners."
4. *Hatton Memoir*, 251; James P. Williams to Mama, October 31, 1862, Williams Letters, UVA.
5. James P Williams to Mama, October 31, 1862, Williams Letters, UVA. In reality, the B&O was responsible for its own repairs, and took care of repairs with a high degree of efficiency. Of the destruction near Martinsburg, one of Jackson's staff officers later wrote, "when we left we were hardly beyond the sound of a steam whistle before the road was filling the air with the noise and smoke of countless trains..(Daniel Carroll Toomey, *The War Came by Train* [Baltimore: Baltimore & Ohio Railroad Museum, 2013], 67, 124).
6. Jno. J. Hooff to Aunt, September 17, 1862, letter 734, box 5, Ward Family Papers, LOC.
7. Jno. J. Hooff to Aunt, October 2, 1862, letter 741, box 5, Ward Family Papers, LOC.
8. I Jas Blunt to My dear Cousin, October 12th, 1862, private collection.
9. Jno. J. Hooff to Aunt, October 2, 1862, letter 741, box 5, Ward Family Papers, LOC. Brown already had a sweetheart, Maryjane Reid, a thirty-year-old schoolteacher who lived in Baltimore (Maryjane Reid, 1860 Census, RG 29, NAB).
10. Jno. J. Hooff to Cousin Mary, September 30, 1862, letter 736, box 5, Ward Family Papers, LOC.
11. Lewis to Parents, October 16, 1862, private collection; James P. Williams to Mama, October 31, 1862, Williams Letters, UVA; Jno. J. Hooff to Cousin Mattie, n.d., letter 737, box 5, Ward Family Papers, LOC.
12. *Hatton Memoir*, 352, 353–361; Francis Augustin O'Reilly, *The Fredericksburg Campaign* (Baton Rouge: Louisiana State University Press, 2003), 39, 42; Ammen, *Maryland Troops,* 183.
13. O'Reilly, *The Fredericksburg Campaign,* 46.
14. Krick, *Civil War Weather in Virginia,* 80; Keith S. Bohannon, *The Giles, Alleghany and Jackson Artillery* (Lynchburg, TN; H. E. Howard, 1990), 26; Ammen, *Maryland Troops,* 183. Cook's remembrance of the march over the Blue Ridge in winter weather and winter camp are placed sequentially after Gettysburg in his narrative, as if they occurred during winter 1863–64. He could only be describing the march from the Shenandoah Valley to Fredericksburg of November–December 1862. The events he describes in winter camp could only have taken place in winter 1862–63, as he mentions the names of soldiers in the unit who were later killed at Gettysburg in July 1863. It is possible Cook was trying to obscure the fact he had deserted at Gettysburg. See appendix H for further details on Cook's writing.
15. O'Reilly, *The Fredericksburg Campaign*, 55; Ammen, *Maryland Troops,* 180; John C. Montgomery CSR, RG 109, NAB. Cook collapses the events of the 1st and 2nd Fredericksburg battles into one, but because the battery's movements were markedly different in the two they can be readily separated.
16. O'Reilly, *The Fredericksburg Campaign,* 103, 127.
17. OR, 21, 636, 668.
18. Ibid., 636, 668.
19. Ibid., p. 636, 668. The nature of Brown's injury is unknown. There are no medical records for

him regarding this in his Compiled Service Records, likely because he recovered at the Wards' home Bladensfield over Christmas 1862. He returned to the battery before January 7, 1863, as on that date as Capt., Chesapeake Artillery and acting chief of artillery, Ewell's Division, he signed a personal recommendation for Cpl. Robert C. Jones (Robert C. Jones CSR, RG 109, NAB).

20. Ammen, *Maryland Troops,* 181; O'Reilly, *The Fredericksburg Campaign*, 151.
21. OR, 21, 637, 668–9.
22. O'Reilly, *The Fredericksburg Campaign,* 157.
23. James P. Williams to Uncle George, December 15, 1862, Williams Letters, UVA.
24. Ibid.; *Baltimore Gazette,* January 6, 1863; OR, 21, 637; Brown Casualty Report, RG 109, NAB; Isaac J. Blunt, James K. Harper, Paul Huber, William H. Mason, and Daniel Wilkinson CSRs, RG 109, NAB; Ammen, *Maryland Troops*, 180.
25. John W Turner, ed., *Captain Greenlee Davidson, CSA: Diary and Letters, 1851–1863* (Verona, VA: McClure Press, 1975), 64.
26. O'Reilly, *The Fredericksburg Campaign,* 157; John F. Green, Vincent Green, Philip O. Oldner, Thomas B. Toy CSRs, RG 109, NAB.
27. Ammen, *Maryland Troops,* 180.
28. OR, 21, 637.
29. Ibid., 669; James P. Williams to Uncle George, December 15, 1862, Williams Letters, UVA.
30. Ammen, *Maryland Troops,* 180.
31. Ibid., 180.
32. W. D. Brown [to Mary Ward], May 9, 1863, letter 910, box 5, Ward Family Papers, LOC; OR, 21, 669; Ammen, *Maryland Troops,* 180; James P. Williams to Uncle George, December 15, 1862, Williams Letters, UVA; Benjamin G. Roberts CSR, RG 109, NAB.
33. Ammen, *Maryland Troops,* 180–181. By "oven" Cook means a pot with a lid; "Goobers" are the Georgia soldiers from Anderson's brigade.
34. O'Reilly, *The Fredericksburg Campaign,* 461; James P Williams to Aunt Mary, January 1, 1863, Williams Letters, UVA.
35. Ward, *The Children of Bladensfield,* 78–79.
36. W. D. Brown [to Mary Ward], May 9, 1863, letter 910, box 5, Ward Family Papers, LOC. Brown is referring to Pvt. Phil Harrison. Based on the comments in his letter to Mary Ward, it appears Brown was at Bladensfield during Christmas 1862.
37. James P. Williams to Aunt Mary, January 1, 1863, Williams Letters, UVA.
38. James P. Williams to Aunt Mary, January 1, 1863, Williams Letters, UVA; Goldsborough, *Maryland Line,* 321. DeJarnette's Woods were on Spring Grove, the estate of Confederate congressman Daniel C. DeJarnette.
39. James P Williams to Aunt Mary, January 12, 1863, Williams Letters, UVA.
40. Ammen, *Maryland Troops,* 183. Cook lists Sgt. Philip Brown in error, rather than Sgt. Peter Williams; Williams's version is used here, as it was written during the war, and Cook was writing several years after the war.
41. Ibid., 183–184.
42. James P Williams to Aunt Mary, January 12, 1863, Williams Letters, UVA. Williams is referring to William Friend, at that time a widowed and wealthy fifty-seven-year-old minister living in nearby Port Royal, and his twenty-six-year-old daughter Anna, who Williams mistakenly took to be Friend's wife. Friend owned four slaves (William Friend and Anna Friend, 1860 Census, RG 29, NAB; William Friend, 1860 Census and Slave Schedules, RG 29, NAB).
43. Ammen, *Maryland Troops,* 183. Cook could only be referring to Sgt. Philip Brown, who at the time of Cook's writing was the vicar of the Episcopal Trinity Parish in New York City.
44. James P. Williams to Aunt Mary, January 1, 1863, Williams Letters, UVA.
45. James P Williams to Aunt Mary, January 12, 1863, Williams Letters, UVA.
46. James P. Williams to Aunt Mary, January 1 and 12, 1863, Williams Letters, UVA.
47. James R. Hardesty CSR, RG 109, NAB; James Hardesty, 1860 Census, RG 29, NAB.
48. Judith Brockenbrough McGuire, *Diary of a Southern Refugee During the War* (New York: E. J. Hale & Son, 1868), 207–208; Edward O. N. Stansbury CSR, RG 109, NAB; Edward Stansbury, *1860 Census*, RG 29, NAB;

Robertson Hospital Register entry for Edward Stansbury, Case Number 637, March 24, 1863, Virginia Commonwealth University Libraries (hereafter cited as VCU); Hollywood Memorial Association, *Register of the Confederate Dead, Interred in Hollywood Cemetery, Richmond, Va.* (Richmond: Gary, Clemmitt & Jones, Printers, 1869), 95.

49. OR, 25, pt. 2, 667; OR, 27, pt. 2, 505. Born in August 1843, Latimer attended the Virginia Military Institute and was a cadet drill instructor early in the war. He served as a lieutenant in the Courtney Artillery beginning September 1861, and was promoted to captain and that battery's commander in summer 1862 (Robert K. Krick, *Lee's Colonels,* 197–98).
50. Chris Mackowski & Kristopher D. White, *Chancellorsville's Forgotten Front* (California: Savas Beatie, 2013), 12–13.
51. Ibid., 47, 69.
52. James P. Williams to Pa, May 7, 1863, Williams Letters, UVA; *Hatton Memoir*, 406; Tunstall Smith, ed., Richard Snowden Andrews, *Lieutenant Colonel Commanding the First Maryland Artillery (Andrews' Battalion), Confederate States Army: A Memoir* (Baltimore: The Sun Job Printing Office, 1910), 81–82 (hereafter cited as Andrews Memoir).
53. Ammen, *Maryland Troops,* 179; James P. Williams to Sister, May 2, 1863, Williams Letters, UVA; *Hatton Memoir*, 406; Smith, ed., *Andrews Memoir,* 81–82.
54. James P. Williams to Pa, May 7, 1863, Williams Letters, UVA.
55. Mackowski & White, *Chancellorsville's Forgotten Front,* 133.
56. Smith, ed., *Andrews Memoir,* 83.
57. James P. Williams to Sister, May 2, 1863, Williams Letters, UVA. Williams is mistaken that the company went into action with only its two Parrotts; as Andrews reported, they went into action with all three rifled guns. It could only have been the 3-inch Ordnance rifle that had its vent damaged, as the battery went into action with its two Parrotts the next day, and the Ordnance rifle was replaced with two additional Parrotts a couple of weeks later.
58. James P. Williams to Pa, May 7, 1863, Williams Letters, UVA; Ammen, *Maryland Troops,* 179; "Report of operations and casualties in Lt. Col. R. Snowden Andrews's Battalion Artillery (Report of Casualties in Andrews's Battalion), in the 2nd Battle of Fredericksburg, VA. May 2 to 4, 1863," RG 109, *Confederate States Army Casualty Lists and Narrative Reports,* NAB.
59. Ammen, *Maryland Troops,* 179.
60. James P. Williams to Sister, May 2, 1863, Williams Letters, UVA.
61. Ibid. Williams is probably referring to Robert B. Corbin, a sixty-three-year-old farmer and resident of Caroline County. He had two daughters, Sally and Anna, who were twenty-two and eighteen, respectively, at the time of the battle (Robert Corbin, Sally Corbin, and Anna Corbin, 1860 Census, RG 29, NAB).
62. Ammen, *Maryland Troops,* 179.
63. James P. Williams to Sister, May 2, 1863, Williams Letters, UVA; Smith, ed., *Andrews Memoir*, 84.
64. OR, 25, 1001; Smith, ed., *Andrews Memoir,* 84.
65. Smith, ed., *Andrews Memoir,* 85; Mackowski & White, *Chancellorsville's Forgotten Front,* 174; Kelley, ed., *The Personal Memoirs of Jonathan Thomas Scharf of the First Maryland Artillery,* 68; *Hatton Memoir,* 409.
66. Smith, ed., *Andrews Memoir,* 86; James P. Williams to Pa, May 7, 1863, Williams Letters, UVA.
67. Smith, ed., *Andrews Memoir,* 87. The 1st Maryland Artillery lost three men killed and six wounded in the action of May 3 *(Report of Casualties in Andrews 'Battalion,* RG 109, NAB).
68. Christopher Goodhand Lynch, "The Chesapeake (4th Maryland Battery)," box 60, Civil War Miscellaneous Collection, US Army Heritage and Education Center (hereafter cited as USAHEC); Alexander Hopkins, Charles F. Dallam, James K. Harper, and John H. K. Shannahan CSRs, RG 109, NAB; Maryland Line Confederate Soldiers' Home Record Books, 1883–1932, MS 256, Special Collections Library, Maryland Historical

Society (hereafter cited as MLCSH Record Books, MS 256, MHS). Williams further stated that three men were slightly wounded in this movement and that no additional casualties occurred in the battle, but he was mistaken. Dallam, Harper, and Shannahan were slightly wounded by shell fire as the battery went into position, as recounted by Williams. Langley, Crowley, and Sparks all suffered gunshot wounds— Langley and Sparks severely—indicating they were wounded by the fire of Federal infantry of the 5th Maine, rather than the artillery fire the company encountered while going into position. Williams may not have been aware of the battery's casualties from rifle fire (Richard E. Langley, Robert A. Crowley, James H. Sparks CSRs, RG 109, NAB; James P. Williams to Pa, May 7, 1863, Williams Letters, UVA).

69. OR, 25, 584.
70. Ammen, *Maryland Troops,* 179.
71. Richard E. Langley, Robert A. Crowley, James H. Sparks CSRs, RG 109, NAB; Report of Casualties in Andrews's Battalion, RG 109, NAB. See chapter 8 for more details on Langley's wound.
72. Smith, ed., *Andrews Memoir,* 87; James P. Williams to Pa, May 7, 1863, Williams Letters, UVA; Mackowski & White, *Chancellorsville's Forgotten Front,* 176.
73. OR, 25, 1001; Mackowski & White, *Chancellorsville's Forgotten Front,* 231.
74. OR, 25, 1002; Smith, ed., *Andrews Memoir,* 87; Ammen, *Maryland Troops,* 180.
75. James P. Williams to Pa, May 7, 1863, Williams Letters, UVA.
76. Ibid.
77. Krick, *Civil War Weather in Virginia,* 95; Ammen, *Maryland Troops,* 181.
78. Ammen, *Maryland Troops,* 181.
79. Ibid., 181. Cook is referring to Quartermaster Sgt. John P Hickey, a twenty-seven-year-old teacher originally from Kent County (John Hickey, 1860 Census, RG 29, NAB).
80. W. D. Brown [to Mary Ward], May 9, 1863, letter 910, box 5, Ward Family Papers, LOC.
81. *Richmond Daily Dispatch,* May 6, 1863.
82. *Richmond Examiner,* May 7, 1863.

Chapter 5 Endnotes

1. James P. Williams to Aunt Mary, May 21, 1863, Williams Letters, UVA.
2. Ibid.
3. Johnson was born in Virginia in 1816 and was a graduate of West Point. He served in the Seminole and Mexican Wars, resigning from the US Army in 1861 to become colonel of the 12th Georgia Infantry Regiment. He was promoted to brigadier general in late 1861, and led a brigade in Jackson's command during the Valley Campaign; he was seriously wounded in the foot at the Battle of McDowell. Upon his return to duty, Johnson was promoted to major general in February 1863, and given command of Jackson's old division (Warner, *Generals in Gray,* 158–159).
4. *Hatton Memoir*, 434; Edwin B. Coddington, *The Gettysburg Campaign: A Study in Command* (Dayton: Morningside Press, 1968), 51; Bradley M. Gottfried, *Roads to Gettysburg: Lee's Invasion of the North, 1863* (Shippensburg: White Mane Books, 2001), 17 (hereafter cited as *Roads to Gettysburg*).
5. *Hatton Memoir*, 437; OR, 27, pt. 2, 499; Gottfried, *Roads to Gettysburg*, 40.
6. OR, 27, pt. 2, 442, 450.
7. *Hatton Memoir*, 442; James P. Williams to Pa, June 28th, 1863, Williams Letters, UVA.
8. James P. Williams to Pa, June 28, 1863, Williams Letters, UVA. Williams is referring to Lee's General Orders No. 72, prohibiting the destruction of private property and authorizing the commissary, quartermaster, ordnance, and medical departments to acquire needed supplies (see Coddington, *The Gettysburg Campaign,* 154–155).
9. Ibid.
10. Ibid.
11. Coddington, *The Gettysburg Campaign*, 197, 220; Bradley M. Gottfried, *The Maps of Gettysburg: An Atlas of the Gettysburg Campaign, June 3–July 13, 1863* (New York and California: Savas Beatie, 2007), 35.
12. OR, 27, pt. 2, 503; Captions and Records, Roll 13, RG 109, NAB; James P. Williams to Pa, June 28, 1863, Williams Letters, UVA; W. W

Goldsborough, "With Lee at Gettysburg," *Philadelphia Record,* July 10, 1900.

13. *Hatton Memoir,* 451; OR, 27, pt. 2, 504; James P. Williams to Pa, July 7, 1863, Williams Letters, UVA; W. W. Goldsborough, "With Lee at Gettysburg," *Philadelphia Record,* July 10, 1900; James A. Wall CSR, RG 109, NAB; Ammen, *Maryland Troops,* 178. Williams incurred a rank reduction to corporal to join the Richmond Howitzers' 1st Company; he had previously served in the 2nd Company, where he did not get along with his officers. Although he seems to have been motivated to leave the unit so he could serve with his friends from home, he also had strong friendships in the Chesapeake, and he may have regretted his decision. In the same letter he continued, "I hated very much to leave the Chesapeake, but Henry Williams kept working at it, until he got the transfer & I was obliged to go." Henry S. Williams, Peter's cousin, enlisted in the Howitzers' 1st Company as a 4th sergeant in Richmond in April 1861, and was elected to Jr. 2nd lieutenant in December 1862. Following the Gettysburg campaign he suffered from chronic hepatitis, entering the hospital July 23, 1863, and did not return to active duty; in 1864, he was assigned to the enrolling service (Henry S. Williams CSR, RG 109, NAB).
14. *Hatton Memoir,* 452.
15. OR, 27, pt. 2, 504, 543; Edward A. Moore, *The Story of a Cannoneer Under Stonewall Jackson* (New York and Washington: The Neale Publishing Company, 1907), 189; *Hatton Memoir*, 452; Randolph H. McKim, *A Soldier's Recollections: Leaves from the Diary of a Young Confederate* (New York: Longmans, Green, and Co., 1910), 194; David Shultz, "Benner's Hill: What Value? Andrews' Artillery Battalion and the Heights East of Town," *Gettysburg Magazine*, 44, 56–57. It could be interpreted that Latimer's battalion spent the night of July 1 near Stevens's Run, about a third of a mile northeast of Gettysburg and west of Rock Creek, consistent with Johnson's report the division "moved along the Gettysburg and York Railroad to the northeast of the town, and formed line of battle in a ravine in an open field." Contemporary accounts by members of Johnson's artillery units make it clear Latimer's battalion stayed with the division, crossed Rock Creek with it after dark on July 1, and camped that night in the fields south of the Wolf farm south of the York Pike, a mile or so directly east of the town. The ravine and open fields Johnson refers to are almost certainly the area around Benner's Run, which flows south between Benner's Hill and Brinkerhoff's Ridge from north of the Hanover Road, and skirts the south end of Benner's Hill before reaching Rock Creek (Capt. Calvin D. Cowles, 23d US Infantry, comp., *The Official Military Atlas of the Civil War* [New York: The Fairfax Press, 1978], Plate 95). The battalion's march along the York Pike would have taken them out of Gettysburg in a northeasterly direction from the town. Andrews reported their location that night on "the extreme left of Gettysburg, between the York and [Hanover] roads, facing the Cemetery Hill, when the command was parked, and encamped for the night." This places the battalion in the fields east of Gettysburg and south of the York Pike. Moore, of the 1st Rockbridge Artillery, which had been attached to Johnson's division, recalled his battery had been posted "a mile east of the town," which also places them south of the York Pike in the vicinity of the Wolf farm. Hatton recalled that on the night of July 1st the battalion "parked at night in a wheat field east of the town," and McKim, a member of Johnson's staff, described the division's position that night as "east and southeast of the town." None of the contemporary accounts indicate the battalion moved after daylight, or separately from the rest of the division, during the night from a position along Stevens's Run.
16. Albert A. Nofi, *The Gettysburg Campaign: June–July 1863* (Cambridge: De Capo Press, 1996) , 169; *Hatton Memoir,* 452; OR, 27, pt. 2, 504, 518, 531, 536; Harry W. Pfanz, *Gettysburg: Culp's Hill and Cemetery Hill* (Chapel Hill and London: The University of

North Carolina Press), 1993, 130; Moore, *The Story of a Cannoneer Under Stonewall Jackson,* 189.

17. Pfanz, *Culp's Hill and Cemetery Hill,* 170.

18. OR, 27, pt. 2, 543; Schultz, "Benner's Hill: What Value? Andrews's Artillery Battalion and the Heights East of Town," *Gettysburg Magazine* 44, 70.

19. Shultz, "Benner's Hill: What Value? Andrews's Artillery Battalion and the Heights East of Town," *Gettysburg Magazine* 44, 76.

20. Ibid., 69; Ammen, *Maryland Troops,* 181; Goldsborough, *Maryland Line,* 324.

21. W. W. Goldsborough, *The Chesapeake Artillery at Gettysburg,* David E. Cronin Papers, MS 670.9, New York Historical Society, hereafter NYHS; Goldsborough's reconnaissance was also described by a soldier of the 1st Maryland Infantry Battalion in Ammen, *Maryland Troops,* 131. Goldsborough likely followed a farm lane that ran west up Benner's Hill from the Lady farm to a shelf along the east side midway up the hill, then north before curving west again and on to the northern crest. This would allow him to be out of sight of the Federals on Cemetery Hill until he emerged at the crest.

22. Shultz, "Benner's Hill: What Value? Andrews's Artillery Battalion and the Heights East of Town," *Gettysburg Magazine,* 44, 75. Almost all contemporary sources describe the field south of Hanover Road as being in wheat; Pvt. Clarence Fonerden of Carpenter's battery described it as rye (Clarence A. Fonerden, *A Brief History of the Military Career of Carpenter's Battery* [New Market, VA: Henkel & Company, 1911], 43).

23. OR, 27, pt. 1, 358, 749, 870; Bert H. Barnett, "Our Position Was Finely Adapted to Its Use," *The Guns of Cemetery Hill,* GNMP Library and Research Center, 242.

24. Christopher Goodhand Lynch, "Visit to His Battle Field," box 60, Civil War Miscellaneous Collection, USAHEC; Ammen, *Maryland Troops*, 181; David L. Ladd and Audrey J. Ladd, *The Bachelder Papers: Gettysburg in Their Own Words* (Dayton: Morningside House, Inc., 1994), vol. 2, 981, and vol. 3, 1616 (hereafter cited as The Bachelder Papers).

25. Ammen, *Maryland Troops,* 132.

26. Moore, *The Story of a Cannoneer Under Stonewall Jackson,* 190–191.

27. Christopher Goodhand Lynch, "Visit to His Battle Field," box 60, Civil War Miscellaneous Collection, USAHEC; Ammen, *Maryland Troops*, 181.

28. Ammen, *Maryland Troops,* 182.

29. Christopher Goodhand Lynch, "Visit to His Battle Field," box 60, Civil War Miscellaneous Collection, USAHEC; Ammen, *Maryland Troops,* 182. Both Andrews, in his report, and Hatton, in his memoirs, indicate Federal gunners had the correct range on Benner's Hill immediately. However, Lynch and Cook clearly state the Federals' initial shots went high. It is likely Federal gunners had already established the correct range on parts of the hill but not all, initially excluding the area occupied by the Chesapeake at the Hanover Road (OR, 27, pt. 2, 543; *Hatton Memoir,* 452).

30. OR, 27, pt. 1, 358; Moore, *The Story of a Cannoneer Under Stonewall Jackson,* 191.

31. Christopher Goodhand Lynch, "Visit to His Battle Field," box 60, Civil War Miscellaneous Collection, USAHEC; W. W. Goldsborough, "The Chesapeake Artillery at Gettysburg," David E. Cronin Papers, MS 670.9, NYHS; Ammen, *Maryland Troops,* 182. Solid shot consisted of iron bolts or balls used against cannon to disable them and destroy equipment and caissons. Case shot was a hollow iron shell or ball filled with lead balls that exploded and scattered its contents; it was a highly effective anti-personnel projectile.

32. Ammen,*Maryland Troops,* 182; Goldsborough, *Maryland Line,* 324; W. W. Goldsborough, *The Chesapeake Artillery at Gettysburg,* David E. Cronin Papers, MS 670.9, NYHS; William A. Frassanito and Elwood Christ, *The Daniel Lady Farm and the Battle of Gettysburg.* Gettysburg, PA: Gettysburg Battlefield Preservation Association, 1999

33. Washington Hands, *Washington Hands Civil War Notebook*, MS 2468, MHS, 95. Brown's

father, John S. Brown, was sixty-three years old at the time of the battle (John S. Brown, 1850 Census, RG 29, NAB). Hands was twenty-seven years old when he enlisted in the 1st Maryland Infantry Regiment in May 1861, and then reenlisted when that unit became the 1st Battalion in fall 1862. He transferred to the 2nd Maryland Artillery in August 1864, and was paroled at Lynchburg, Virginia, on April 15, 1865 (Washington Hands CSR, RG 109, NAB). John W Torsch was a twenty-seven-year-old wood engraver from Baltimore when he enlisted in July 1861 as 2nd lieutenant in the "Maryland Zouaves," which became part of the 2nd Arkansas Battalion and then the 47th Virginia Infantry. When the company was disbanded in June 1862, he enlisted as captain of Company E in the 1st Maryland Battalion, which later became known as the 2nd Maryland Battalion. Torsch was wounded in the neck at Cold Harbor June 4, 1864, returned to duty by September, and commanded the unit at Appomattox. Postwar he was active in several veterans organizations, married, and had one daughter. He died October 1, 1898, at sixty-five, and is buried in Loudon Park Cemetery in Baltimore (John W. Torsch, 1860 Census and 1880 Census, RG 29, NAB; John W. Torsch CSR, RG 109, NAB; *Baltimore Sun,* October 5, 1898).

34. William M. Williams and Peter Parker CSRs, RG 109, NAB; Goldsborough, *Maryland Line,* 324; Ammen, *Maryland Troops,* 182; OR, 27, pt. 2, 458.
35. W. W. Goldsborough, *The Chesapeake Artillery at Gettysburg,* David E. Cronin Papers, MS 670.9, NYHS; William M. Williams and Peter Parker CSRs, RG 109, NAB; Goldsborough, *Maryland Line,* 324; Ammen, *Maryland Troops*, 182; OR, 27, pt. 2, 458.
36. Pfanz, *Culp's Hill and Cemetery Hill,* 180; Entry for July 2, 1863, Samuel Thomas McCullough Diary, Hotchkiss-McCullough Manuscripts, 1846–1912, Library of Congress (hereafter cited as McCullough Diary).
37. Ammen, *Maryland Troops,* 182.
38. Frederick Cusick, Andrew J. Bryan, Daniel Dougherty, 1860 Census, RG 29, NAB; Frederick Cusick, Andrew J. Bryan, Daniel Dougherty CSRs, RG 109, NAB; Ammen, *Maryland Troops*, 182.
39. Ammen, *Maryland Troops,* 182.
40. Philip Oldner, Thaddeus Parker, Smith Warrington, 1860 Census, RG 29, NAB; Philip O. Oldner, Thaddeus M. Parker, Smith Warrington, James H. Willson CSRs, RG 109, NAB; Smith, ed., *Andrews Memoir,* 121.
41. OR, 27, pt. 2, 544; Charles Tinges, 1860 Census, RG 29, NAB; Charles S. Tinges CSR, RG 109, NAB.
42. W. W. Goldsborough, *The Chesapeake Artillery at Gettysburg*, David E. Cronin Papers, MS 670.9, NYHS; Goldsborough, *Maryland Line,* 325. Cook and Lynch wrote that three of the unit's four guns had been silenced, while in his official report Andrews stated the battery could only fire two pieces. It is evident both were correct, as the company had only one piece still in action after that of Sgt. James Wall's detachment was disabled: Sgt. Robert Crowley's gun had already been abandoned because of casualties, and Sgt. Phil Brown's had a wheel broken. Once Sgt. Brown repaired the damaged wheel of his piece he resumed firing, so the battery finished the engagement with two pieces in action (Ammen, *Maryland Troops*, 182; Goldsborough, *Maryland Line,* 325; OR, 27, pt. 2, 544).
43. OR, 27, pt. 1, 870; Bert H. Barnett, "Our Position Was Finely Adapted to Its Use:" *The Guns of Cemetery Hill,* GNMP Library and Research Center, 243. Capt. James H. Rigby, commanding Federal Battery A, Maryland Light Artillery, was in position on Powers Hill on the Baltimore Pike about 2,500 yards to Latimer's left and slight rear. Rigby opened fire on Graham's and Raine's 20-pounders on Benner's Hill at about 1400, but finding the range too great ceased firing (OR, 27, pt. 1, 899).
44. W. W. Goldsborough, *The Chesapeake Artillery at Gettysburg,* David E. Cronin Papers, MS 670.9, NYHS; OR, 27, pt. 2, 544; *Hatton*

Memoir, 454. In his report Andrews only referred to the casualties of Carpenter's battery as a result of this crossfire. However, it is apparent the crossfire also encompassed the position of the Chesapeake, which suffered accordingly. Using reported casualties as a basis for comparison, Carpenter's battery incurred a casualty rate of 26.4% and the Chesapeake 22.4%. Since the Federal guns on Culp's Hill had been placed there for the purpose of reducing the range to the right flank of Latimer's position, Raine's and Dement's batteries on the battalion left, closest to Culp's Hill, suffered much lower casualty rates (5.7% and 7.1%, respectively). Stated another way, Carpenter's and Brown's batteries accounted for less than 50% of the personnel of the four batteries of Latimer's battalion, but suffered over 80% of its casualties. An officer of Ricketts' Federal battery in position on Cemetery Hill observed from his vantage point that "these two batteries (Brown and Carpenter I take it) suffered greatly." This crossfire did not extend to Hardwicke's section of Raine's battery or Graham's 1st Rockbridge Artillery, both in position on Benner's Hill north of Hanover Road to the Chesapeake's right. Graham's battery also reported a high casualty rate at Gettysburg (23.5%), but almost all of these were incurred on July 3, during the artillery bombardment preceding Longstreet's assault. Hardwicke's and Graham's casualties on July 2 were minimal (Ladd and Ladd, *The Bachelder Papers,* vol. 3, 1621; David A. Petruzzi and Steven A. Stanley, *The Gettysburg Campaign in Numbers and Losses* [El Dorado Hills, CA: Savas Beattie LLC, 2012], 129, 130; Moore, *The Charlottesville, Lee Lynchburg and Johnson's Bedford Artillery,* 96; Moore, *The Story of a Cannoneer Under Stonewall Jackson,* 191–193).

45. OR, 27, pt. 1, 870; OR, 27, pt. 2, 544.

46. Benjamin G. Roberts, Thomas P LeCompte, John A. Lane, Henry C. Buckmaster, James K. Harper, John F. Green, Charles F. Dallam, John D. Richardson CSRs, RG 109, NAB; Daniel Carroll Toomey, *The Maryland Line Confederate Soldiers 'Home, and Confederate Veterans ' Organizations in Maryland* (Baltimore: Toomey Press, 2001), 48, hereafter cited as *The Maryland Line Confederate Soldiers' Home.*

47. OR, 27, pt. 2, 544; *Hatton Memoir,* 453; Ladd and Ladd, *The Bachelder Papers,* vol. 3, 1616.

48. Ammen, *Maryland Troops,* 182; OR, 27, pt. 1, 358; Robert Stiles, *Four Years Under Marse Robert* (New York and Washington: The Neale Publishing Company, 1903), 218.

49. OR, 27, pt. 1, 358; Ladd and Ladd, *The Bachelder Papers,* vol. 3, 1621; Christopher Goodhand Lynch, "Visit to His Battle Field," box 60, Civil War Miscellaneous Collection, USAHEC; Unidentified museum description record, ca. 1920, private collection. Brown's box is now part of a private collection.

50. Stiles, *Four Years Under Marse Robert,* 218.

51. Smith, ed., *Andrews Memoir,* 119; *Hatton Memoir*, 458.

52. Ammen, *Maryland Troops,* 182; Gregory A. Coco, *A Vast Sea of Misery: A History and Guide to the Union and Confederate Field Hospitals at Gettysburg, July 1–November 20,1863* (Gettysburg: Thomas Publications, 1988), 116; Kathleen R. Georg, transc., *Record of Confederate Burials: The Journal of Dr. J. W. C. O'Neal,* Gettysburg National Military Park Library and Research Center, 1982 (hereafter cited as O'Neal Journal, GNMP); Ronald L. Waddell, *The Daniel Lady Farm Historical Survey,* Special Collections Library, University of Arkansas, 2003 (hereafter cited as Lady Farm Survey); William D. Brown CSR, RG 109, NAB. Brown was initially buried at the Weible farm; his family later had his body disinterred and sent to Baltimore for burial at Greenmount Cemetery (O'Neal Journal, GNMP; *Baltimore Sun,* July 31, 1863).

53. OR, 27, pt. 2, 505; *Hatton Memoir,* 458.

54. OR, 27, pt. 2, 505; Henry C. Buckmaster, James K. Harper, Francis Smith, James Stephens CSRs, RG 109, NAB; Rufus B. Weaver, M.D., Paper No. 3, 3rd and 4th Shipments, Rufus B. Weaver, M.D. Disinterment and Shipment Records, GNMP (hereafter cited as Weaver, Paper No. 3,

GNMP); Daniel Lady Claim, Quartermaster's Claims, RG 92, NAB. For a complete discussion of the disposition of the company's dead and wounded at Gettysburg see appendix C.

55. Charles S. Tinges, Philip O. Oldner CSRs, RG 109, NAB; Kent Masters Brown, *Retreat from Gettysburg* (Chapel Hill and London: University of North Carolina Press, 2005), 76; Gregory A. Coco, *A Strange and Blighted Land, Gettysburg: The Aftermath of a Battle* (Gettysburg: Thomas Publications, 1995), 219; Weaver, Paper No. 3, GNMP; Mary H. Mitchell, *Hollywood Cemetery: The History of a Southern Shrine* (Richmond: The William Byrd Press, 1985), 155 (hereafter cited as Hollywood Cemetery).

56. Jacob F. Cook CSR, RG 1Q9, NAB (see a further discussion of Cook's desertion in appendix H); Bunch, *Roster of the Courts-Martial in the Confederate States Armies* (Shippensburg: White Mane Books, 2001), 275; Ruffner, *Maryland's Blue and Gray,* 321; Unsigned report of Lt. Col. R. Snowden Andrews, August 6, 1863, in Charles I. Raine CSR, RG 109, NAB; John E. Plater CSR, RG 109, NAB.

57. *Hatton Memoir,* 459.

58. OR, 27, pt. 2, 44S; Philip A. H. Brown, Panl H. Huber, Smith Warrington, John Myers, John W. Schaefer CSRs, RG 109, NAB.

59. OR, 27, pt. 2, 45Q; John Tregoe, John W. Gore, John W. Canfield, John B. Vansant CSRs, RG 109, NAB. The two other men who deserted were Pvts. Thomas McClure and Andrew J. McElwee (Thomas McClure and Andrew J. McElwee CSRs, RG 109, NAB).

60. McHenry Howard, *Recollections of a Maryland Confederate Soldier and Staff Officer Under Johnston, Jackson, and Lee* (Baltimore: Williams & Wilkins Co., 1914), 221; *Richmond Examiner,* Jnly 30, 1863.

61. James P. Williams to Pa, Jnly 7/1S63, Williams Letters, UVA.

62. Nannie to Dearest Brother, July 22, 1863, Williams Letters, UVA.

Chapter 6 Endnotes

1. Unsigned report of Lt. Col. R. Snowden Andrews, August 6, 1863, in Charles I. Raine CSR, RG 109, NAB. Contee enlisted at twenty-five as a 1st lieutenant in the 1st Maryland Artillery in July 1861; he came from a wealthy farm family in Anne Arundel County. He was seriously wounded at Stephenson's Depot on June 15, 1863, and declared unfit for field duty a year later. Contee subsequently served as an enrolling officer in Wythe County, Virginia (Ruffner, *Maryland's Blue and Gray,* 302–303).

2. Ruffner, *Maryland's Blue and Gray,* 302–303; John Plater CSR, RG 109, NAB; Bunch, *Roster of the Courts-Martial in the Confederate States Armies,* 275; Benjamin G. Roberts CSR, RG 109, NAB.

3. John A. Lane, William H. Mason, W. L. Burke, George W. Goodhand CSRs, RG 109, NAB; Scott L. Mingus, Sr., *Flames Beyond Gettysburg: The Confederate Expedition to the Susquehanna River, June, 1863* (New York and California: Savas Beatie, 2012), 295.

4. *Richmond Examiner,* July 30, 1863; Thomas H. Ennis CSR, RG 109, NAB.

5. OR, 29, pt. 1, 424; OR, 36, pt. 2, 988; OR, 36, pt. 3, 861. The Chesapeake's battle flag is now part of a private collection.

6. Adrian G. Tighe, *The Bristoe Campaign: General Lee's Last Strategic Offensive with the Army of Northern Virginia, October 1863 (Self-published, 2011)*, 70; OR, 29, pt. 1, 417, 424; *Krick, Lee's Colonels,* 30.

7. OR, 29, pt. 1, 417; *Hatton Memoir,* 460.

8. *Hatton Memoir,* 461; OR, 29, pt. 1, 424.

9. OR, 29, pt. 1, 424.

10. Ibid., 428, 424.

11. Ruffner, *Maryland's Blue and Gray,* 295; *Hatton Memoir*, 462. Braxton was born in 1836 and lived in Fredericksburg before the war. He enlisted in April 1861, and became captain of the Fredericksburg Artillery the next month. Braxton was promoted to major in March 1863, and to lieutenant colonel in February 1864. Postwar he was a civil engineer for the RF&P and C&O Railroads (Krick, *Lee's Colonels,* 56).

12. *Hatton Memoir*, 465; OR, 29, pt. 1, 425; Captions and Records, Roll 13, RG 109, NAB.
13. Martin F. Graham and George F. Skoch, *Mine Run: A Campaign of Lost Opportunities* (Lynchburg, TN: H. E. Howard, 1987), 31 (hereafter cited as Mine Run); OR, 29, pt. 1, 425.
14. Krick, *Civil War Weather in Virginia,* 111; Graham & Skoch, *Mine Run,* 37; James K. Harper and Benjamin G. Roberts CSRs, RG 109, NAB.
15. Graham & Skoch, *Mine Run,* 46.
16. OR, 29, pt. 1, 425.
17. George D. McClure CSR, RG 109, NAB.
18. OR, 29, pt. 1, 425.
19. Graham & Skoch, *Mine Run,* 80; Fonerden, *A Brief History of the Military Career of Carpenter 's Battery,* 44.
20. OR, 33, 210; Sherwood, *First Maryland Artillery and Second Maryland Artillery,* 37; Howard, *Recollections of a Maryland Confederate Soldier,* 252; Benjamin G. Roberts, Lambden Dawson, William Smith CSRs, RG 109, NAB. During October–December 1863, the Army of Northern Virginia experienced the second highest number of total desertions of the entire war (Glatthaar, *Soldiering in the Army of Northern Virginia,* 15). Long was born in 1825 and a graduate of West Point. He served with the artillery of the US Army until he resigned in June 1861, and entered Confederate service as a major of artillery. Appointed brigadier general in September 1863, he became commander of the artillery of the 2nd Corps until the end of the war, surrendering at Appomattox. Postwar he wrote a biography of Robert E. Lee and other articles despite the onset of blindness. He died in 1891 (Warner, *Generals in Gray,* 191–2).
21. Henry Buckmaster, Charles Tinges, Henry Willson, John E. Plater CSRs, RG 109, NAB; Ruffner, *Maryland 's Blue and Gray,* 320–321. Although Plater's records state he was "returned to duty," it appears he did not return to the company. There are no records for him February 20–June 6, 1864, when he was dropped from the rolls, and he signed no requisitions for pay or supplies. Lt. Walter Chew continued to sign requisitions during this period as "Lieutenant, Commanding Battery," even though Plater outranked him by virtue of his earlier commission date and would have been placed in command had he been with the unit. Moreover, the tri-monthly returns for the unit during the first few months of 1864 include only one officer present, who could only have been Chew (OR, 36, pt. 3, 861).
22. OR, 33, 210.
23. Ibid., 194.
24. George Rice CSR, RG 109, NAB. Ultimately the Kilpatrick-Dahlgren raid was a failure, called off after achieving very few of its objectives, and Dahlgren was killed (George E. Pond, "Kilpatrick's and Dahlgren's Raid to Richmond," in Robert Underwood Johnson and Clarence Clough Buell, eds., *Battles and Leaders of the Civil War* [New York: Thomas Yoseloff, 1956], vol. 4, 95–96).
25. Warner, *Generals in Gray,* 156–157; Bradley T. Johnson, "The Maryland Line in the Confederate Army," SHSP, 11, 23–26.
26. Bradley T. Johnson, "The Maryland Line in the Confederate Army," SHSP, 11, 23–26.
27. Ibid., 23–26; Ruffner, *Maryland's Blue and Gray,* 184–185; Ammen, *Maryland Troops,* 125; Yr Husband [to Jane Claudia Saunders Johnson], April 1, 1864, and April 18, 1864, Bradley T. Johnson Papers Collection, David M. Rubenstein Rare Book & Manuscript Library, Duke University. Johnson had sent Capt. John Torsch of the 2nd Maryland Infantry Battalion to South Carolina to recruit Maryland soldiers serving there who had enlisted early in the war. In his letter April 1 Johnson wrote of the South Carolina soldiers: "The Charleston men are humbug Torsch says—there are 150 there that 18 deserted in one night to the Yanks, and they generally are the hardest sort of cases. He thinks they mainly want to get here to desert. There were Swedes, Dutch, French, Irish and Yankees, all claiming to be Marylanders because they were enlisted in Baltimore. They are unwilling to go in again, unless as Artillery or Cavalry, both of which are impossible I think, as they cant get horses for the last + the government had none to give

them for the first." Only one soldier from a South Carolina unit transferred to the 4th Maryland Artillery—Pvt. John Torrington of the 15th Battalion South Carolina Heavy Artillery on June 2, 1864; he served without absence until captured at Fort Gregg on April 2, 1865 (John Torrington CSR, RG 109, NAB).

28. Captions and Records, Roll 13, RG 109, NAB; Walter S. Chew CSR, RG 109, NAB; Ruffner, *Maryland's Blue and Gray,* 304–5; Thomas LeCompte, Walter Chew, 1860 Census, RG 29, NAB; OR, 36, pt. 1, 1054.

29. George W. Booth, *Personal Reminiscences of a Maryland Soldier,* 101; Ammen, *Maryland Troops,* 143. The first time the battery is referred to in the Official Records as the 4th Maryland Artillery rather than the Chesapeake Artillery is in an organization table of forces in the Richmond and Petersburg lines dated May 5–10, 1864 (OR, 36, pt. 2, 207). The company continued to be referred to as the Chesapeake Artillery and its men as the Chesapeakes in contemporary accounts.

30. Ammen, *Maryland Troops,* 125; OR, 36, pt. 2, 209; Entry for April 23, 1864, McCullough Diary.

31. Gordon C. Rhea, *To the North Anna River* (Baton Rouge: Louisiana State University Press, 2000), 229, 264, 287; Entry for May 20, 1864, McCullough Diary; *Hatton Memoir,* 563, 564.

32. Rhea, *To the North Anna River,* 348; *Hatton Memoir,* 565; Entry for May 24, 1864, McCullough Diary.

33. Entry for May 25, 1864, McCullough Diary; Rhea, *To the North Anna River*, 361; Ernest B. Furgurson, *Cold Harbor 1864: Not War But Murder* (New York: Alfred A. Knopf, 2000), 47.

34. Entries for May 28–30, 1864, McCullough Diary; Ammen, *Maryland Troops,* 143.

35. See Ruffner's discussion of the Maryland Line in *Maryland's Blue and Gray,* 179–188; Bradley T. Johnson, "The Maryland Line in the Confederate Army," SHSP, 11, 26; OR, 36, pt. 1, 1045, 1050; Warner, *Generals in Gray*, 157. Wise, in *The Long Arm of Lee,* vol. 1, 822, mistakenly states the battery was assigned to Pegram's battalion, likely because of the turgid writing style of William Pendleton's report of the Battle of Cold Harbor. Pendleton's report reads, with emphasis added for greater clarity, "Pegram's battalion occupying Turkey Ridge, *McIntosh's* on Pegram's left [*Dement's and Chew's batteries having been here added to this battalion*], Richardson's battalion on McIntosh's left, Lane's on Richardson's left." OR, 36, pt. 2, 984. David G. McIntosh, born in 1836 and a lawyer from South Carolina, enlisted as captain with the Pee Dee Artillery in March 1862. He was promoted to major a year later, and to lieutenant colonel on February 27, 1864. By the end of the war he was the acting 2nd Corps chief of artillery. Postwar he settled in Towson, Maryland, and was the president of the Maryland Bar Association. He died in 1916 at age eighty (Krick, *Lee's Colonels*, 218).

36. OR, 42, pt. 3, 1193; *Hatton Memoir,* 568.

37. OR, 36, pt. 1, 1049; Furgurson, *Cold Harbor,* 137–138; *Hatton Memoir,* 579. The exact positions of the 4th Maryland Artillery and the other batteries in McIntosh's battalion on Turkey Hill relative to each other are unknown. The 1st Maryland Artillery had to have been in position immediately to the right of the 2nd Maryland Infantry Battalion on the higher ground east of the Watt house, as in the battle of June 3, the Battalion fired the captured and retaken guns of Caskie's battery under the direction of members of the 1st Artillery following the Federal breakthrough at Boatswain's Creek. Since both casualties of the 4th Maryland at Cold Harbor were the result of gunshot wounds and not artillery fire, the battery had to have been in close enough proximity to Federal infantry to be directly engaged with them. Presumably, this means the 4th Maryland was in the very near vicinity of the 1st Maryland Artillery during the Federal breakthrough; both units having just been assigned to McIntosh's battalion, they were most likely adjacent to each other, with the 4th Artillery to the 1st's immediate right.

38. *Hatton Memoir,* 580–81; Furgurson, *Cold Harbor,* 144–148.
39. Daniel A. Wilkinson, Charles T. Garrett CSRs, RG 109, NAB; OR, 36, pt. 1, 1050–1051.
40. *Hatton Memoir,* 589; Furgurson, *Cold Harbor*, 213.
41. OR, 36, pt. 1, 1050–1052; *Richmond Daily Dispatch,* June 14, 1864; Edward C. Cottrell CSR, RG 109, NAB.
42. *Hatton Memoir,* 593; Walter S. Chew CSR, RG 109, NAB.
43. *Hatton Memoir,* 593–96.
44. OR, 40, pt. 1, 757; Pendleton's description of the position of Chew's and Clutter's batteries would place them on a shelf near the west end of present-day Archer Avenue, on the left bank of the Appomattox River in Colonial Heights, Virginia. Marmaduke Johnson, born in 1826 in Virginia and a lawyer prewar, enlisted as captain of the Jackson Flying Artillery in March 1862. He was promoted to major and assigned to McIntosh's battalion in February 1864, and promoted to lieutenant colonel a year later; he surrendered at Appomattox. Postwar he ran a hotel in Richmond and died there in 1871, age forty-five (Krick, *Lee's Colonels,* 180).

Chapter 7 Endnotes

1. OR, 40, pt. 1, 757; OR, 42, pt. 3, 1339–42; James L. Speicher, *The Sumter Flying Artillery: A Civil War History of the 11th Battalion Georgia Light Artillery* (Gretna: Pelican Publishing Company Inc., 2009), 226, hereafter cited as The Sumter Flying Artillery.
2. Speicher, *The Sumter Flying Artillery,* 228; Lt. P. C. Hoy, "Some Interesting Recollections of an Officer of Bradford's Battery," in Hampton Newsome, John Horn, and John G. Selby, eds., *Civil War Talks: Further Reminiscences of George S. Bernard and His Fellow Veterans* (Charlottesville: University of Virginia Press, 2012), 226; "Hughes Military map of Richmond & Petersburgh Va.," LOC.
3. Eugene H. Levy, "Donaldsonville Cannoniers at the Siege of Petersburg," *New Orleans Times-Picayune*, June 16, 1902.
4. Speicher, *Sumter Flying Artillery,* 226; OR, 40, pt. 1, 758.
5. OR, 40, pt. 1, 759–60.
6. Krick, *Civil War Weather in Virginia,* 133; John F. Green CSR, RG 109, NAB. Green had also been wounded at 1st Fredericksburg and Gettysburg.
7. Krick, *Civil War Weather in Virginia,* 134–9; Brett Schulte, transc., Confederate Inspection Report: Corps Artillery, Third Corps, Army of Northern Virginia, www.behondthecrater.com.
8. James E. Dean CSR, RG 109, NAB; Richard J. Sommers, *Richmond Redeemed: The Siege at Petersburg* (Garden City: Doubleday & Company, Inc., 1981), 211, 583.
9. See Ruffner's discussion of this incident, *Maryland's Blue and Gray,* 186–187, as well as the *Hatton Memoir*, 675–679; OR, 42, pt. 3, 1341.
10. John J. Fox III, *The Confederate Alamo: Bloodbath at Petersburg's Fort Gregg on April 2,1865* (Winchester, VA: Angle Valley Press, 2010), 16–17, 87, hereafter cited as *The Confederate Alamo*.
11. The exact date the company occupied Fort Gregg is unknown. The battalion record of the Washington Artillery for October 12, 1864, states "One-half of our artillery drivers are armed with muskets to put on duty at Fort Gregg." (Napier Bartlett, *Military Record of Louisiana* [Baton Rouge: Louisiana State University Press, 1964], 210). A soldier of Cutts's battalion who volunteered for the same duty arrived at Fort Gregg "about December 1, 1864," and found Chew already in command of the fort with two guns (A. E. Strother, "Battle and Capture of Fort Gregg," CV, 29, 425). Presumably, the battery was moved to Fort Gregg in late October, after the earthwork was finished and having already received the horses from the disbanded 1st Maryland Artillery.
12. Contemporary and postwar accounts provide a bewildering variety of descriptions of the battery's armament in Fort Gregg: "two twelve-pound napolean brass guns" (A. E.

Strother, "Battle and Capture of Fort Gregg," CV, 29, 425), "two six-pound guns" (Lt. F. B. Craige to Gen. James H. Lane in SHSP, 3, 25), "three pieces of artillery" (Lt. A. B. Howard to Gen. Lane in SHSP, 3, 26), "two three-inch Parrott guns" (" The Battle at Fort Gregg," SHSP, 28, 265), and "two pieces of artillery.. .six-pound rifle pieces" (Lt. D. M. Rigler to Gen. James H. Lane in SHSP, 3, 26), among others. The published recollections of Confederate soldiers were all made years or even decades after the war, rely on memory, and are not consistently reliable. In a tabular report of the armament of batteries in the Army of Northern Virginia dated December 28, 1864, while the company was positioned at Fort Gregg, the 4th Maryland Artillery's armament is listed as including two Ordnance rifles (OR, 42, 3, 1341). It is clear the two 3-inch Ordnance rifles were placed in position in Fort Gregg, and in the veterans' memories these sleeker guns were confused with 6-pound field guns. The later disposition of the 10-pound Parrott rifle is unknown. It is probable this gun was removed from the battery's armament in March 1865 because of reduced unit strength.

13. Pvt. Edward Cottrell recalled he was on a cooking detail that worked in "the yard of an unoccupied dwelling house about four hundred yards in the rear of the fort"; this is the same location as the Gregg house (E. C. Cottrell, "The Fight at Fort Gregg," CV, 7, 308; Fox, *The Confederate Alamo,* 18). It is almost certain the company established a camp at the Gregg house, with its cooking utensils, forge, battery wagon, and other equipment there. Several soldiers would also have been located there by the nature of their duties, including Commissary Sgt. John Hickey and Quartermaster Sgt. George Maccubbin, a thirty-four-year-old land agent from Queen Anne's County, as well as the company's artificers, Pvts. Allen Covington, a twenty-six-year-old farmer from Queen Anne's County; and Michael Brady, a twenty-eight-year-old engineer from Gloucester County, Virginia, among others (John P. Hickey, George B. Maccubbin, Allen J. Covington, Michael H. Brady CSRs, RG 109, NAB).

14. Fox, *The Confederate Alamo,* 19; E. C. Cottrell, "The Fight at Fort Gregg," CV, 7, 308.

15. Captions and Records, Roll 13, RG 109, NAB; CSRs, Roll 13, RG 109, NAB; Krick, *Civil War Weather in Virginia,* 142–143; Glatthaar, *Soldiering in the Army of Northern Virginia,* 15. Pvt. "Wes" Brown deserted on August 6, 1864, and took the OOA the next day; Pvt. William Hermantrout deserted sometime after September 1 (John W Brown and William Hermantrout CSRs, RG 109, NAB). The battery's unweighted desertion rate was lower than 2% during 1864, compared to an average unweighted desertion rate of nearly 9% for the Army of Northern Virginia during the same year.

16. A. E. Strother, "Battle and Capture of Fort Gregg," CV, 29, 425; R. B. Thetford, "Commands Holding Fort Gregg," CV, 29, 335.

17. Captions and Records, Roll 13, RG 109, NAB; CSRs, Roll 13, RG 109, NAB; OR, 42, 3, 1341

18. Krick, *Civil War Weather in Virginia,* 147–154; Captions and Records, Roll 13, RG 109, NAB; CSRs, Roll 13, RG 109, NAB; Phil Littig Harrison to Col. W. H. Taylor, 13 February 1865, in Philip L. Harrison CSR, RG 109, NAB. See the introduction to the roster for a complete discussion of the determination of which soldiers received discharges within the unit.

19. CSRs, Roll 13, RG 109, NAB.

20. OR, 46, pt. 2, 1320.

21. Ibid., 1329, 1333–1334. Owen, born in 1840, had been a member of the Washington Artillery of New Orleans before the war and enlisted with the battalion as its adjutant in May 1861. He was promoted to major in August 1863, and was wounded at the Battle of the Crater July 30, 1864. Owen was promoted to lieutenant colonel in March 1865 (Krick, *Lee's Colonels,* 253).

22. Wm. Miller Owen, *In Camp and Battle with the Washington Artillery* (Boston: Ticknor

and Company, 1885), 368; Bradley T. Johnson, "Maryland in the Civil War," in Clement A. Evans, ed., *Confederate Military History* (Atlanta: Confederate Publishing Company, 1899), vol. 2, 131. Several participant accounts mention the removal of the company's guns from Fort Gregg: "A few days before the battle of April 2 our two.. .guns were taken from Fort Gregg and sent down on our lines south.. .Captain Chew was still left in command," (Strother, CV, 29, 425); "There being no artillery in the fort," (Francis McElroy to W. M. Owen, CV, 8, 487); a Virginia soldier of the supernumerary artillerists described the 4th Maryland the morning of April 2 as "horseless and gunless," (George W. Kennedy to George W. Koontz, March, 1907, in David Gregg McIntosh papers, VHS 1862–1916, Virginia Historical Society, Richmond).

23. Captions and Records, Roll 13, RG 109, NAB; CSRs, Roll 13, RG 109, NAB. The only mention of Pinder as a corporal is by Jacob F. Cook in CV, 7, 200. Cook was not present at Fort Gregg, but collected anecdotes from members of the company after the war for his series of articles in the *Baltimore Telegram.* It is likely Pinder was promoted after the company's last muster on March 1, 1865, as was John Richardson, to Sergeant; neither promotion was recorded in these soldiers' CSRs at that late date, although Richardson was listed as a sergeant in the final roll at the Appomattox surrender. Chew would have needed a sergeant and a corporal in Fort Gregg, in addition to Hickey being in command of the battery's camp at the Gregg house. The total of twenty-nine men present for duty at the end of March is derived from the individual CSRs of the men in the company, comprising the twelve killed or captured at Fort Gregg on April 2, 1865, three captured during the Appomattox campaign, thirteen who surrendered at Appomattox, and one who managed to escape during the Appomattox campaign and surrender at another location.

24. "The Battle at Fort Gregg," SHSP, 28, 265; Owen, *In Camp and Battle with the Washington Artillery,* 368; Krick, *Lee's Colonels*, 218; Frank McElroy and Henry A. Battles CSRs, RG 109, NAB. Owen mistakenly identified Battles as belonging to the 1st Company of the Washington Artillery rather than the 4th, although the detachment Battles led had to come from the battalion's 1st Company, as stated by Owen. The 1st Company was the only company of the Washington Artillery battalion that had 3-inch Ordnance rifles as part of its armament (OR, 42, pt. 3, 1341).

25. Edwin C. Bearss, *The Petersburg Campaign* (El Dorado Hills, CA: Savas Beatie, 2014), vol. 2, 516; A. Wilson Greene, *Breaking the Backbone ofthe Rebellion* (Mason City, IA: Savas Publishing Company, 2000), 364; Owen, *In Camp and Battle with the Washington Artillery,* 368–369.

26. Entry for April 1, 1865, David Gregg McIntosh diary, David Gregg McIntosh papers, VHS 1862–1916, Virginia Historical Society, Richmond (hereafter cited as David Gregg McIntosh diary, David Gregg McIntosh papers, VHS); E. C. Cottrell, "The Fight at Fort Gregg," CV, 7, 308; Bearss, *The Petersburg Campaign,* vol. 2, xv.

27. OR, 46, pt. 1, 932; Bearss, *The Petersburg Campaign,* vol. 2, 540. Multiple participant accounts state Chew was in command of Fort Gregg the morning of April 2: "Defenders of Fort Gregg," CV, 25, 23; F. B. Craige to Gen. James H. Lane in SHSP, 25, 25; A. E. Strother, "Battle and Capture of Fort Gregg," CV, 29, 425; E. C. Cottrell, "The Fight at Fort Gregg," CV, 7, 308.

28. OR, 46, pt. 1, 932; Fox, *The Confederate Alamo,* 78; Owen, *In Camp and Battle with the Washington Artillery*, 371.

29. OR, 46, pt. 1, 932; Fox, *The Confederate Alamo,* 59; James H. Lane, "Defence of Fort Gregg," SHSP, 3, 20; "Chesapeake Battery at Fort Gregg," CV, 7, 200; Gen. N. H. Harris, "Defence of Battery Gregg," SHSP, 8, 475; Francis McElroy to S. M. Owen in SHSP, 8, 487.

30. E. C. Cottrell, "The Fight at Fort Gregg," CV, 7, 308; CSRs, Roll 13, RG 109, NAB.

31. Bartlett, Military Record of Louisiana, 218; Fox, *The Confederate Alamo,* 79–80; Greene, *Breaking the Backbone of the Rebellion,* 391.
32. George W. Kennedy to George W. Koontz, March 1907, David Gregg McIntosh papers, VHS; James H. Lane to Dear General [Wilcox] in SHSP, 3, 23; Greene, *Breaking the Backbone of the Rebellion,* 386; "The Battle at Fort Gregg," SHSP, 28, 265. Multiple additional witness accounts refer to the two guns during the attack on Fort Gregg as "Chew's battery" and to Chew as the commander, indicating he was in command of the artillery at this time ("Defenders of Fort Gregg," CV, 25, 23; George W. Richards, "Fort Gregg Again," SHSP, 31, 370; J. E. Gaskell, "Last Engagement of Lee's Army," CV, 29, 261; John O'Connell, *Four Years Campaigning with the Army of the Potomac & James,* Box 87, Foldcr 6, Civil War Document Collection, USAHEC, n.d).
33. Fox, *The Confederate Alamo,* 80; A. K. Jones to Dear General [Harris] in SHSP, 8, 484.
34. George W. Richards, "A Surgeon's Defense of the Garrison," SHSP, 31, 371; "Defenders of Fort Gregg," CV, 25, 23.
35. James H. Lane, "The Defence of Battery Gregg—General Lane's Reply to General Harris," SHSP, 9, 106; Christopher G. Lynch, "Roster of Queen Anne's Confederates," *Centreville Record,* May 3, 1900; Christopher Lynch, 1860 Census, NAB; Entry for April 1, 1865, David Gregg McIntosh diary, VHS.
36. Fox, *The Confederate Alamo,* 99; Greene, *Breaking the Backbone of the Rebellion,* 412; E. C. Cottrell, "The Fight at Fort Gregg," CV, 7, 308.
37. OR, 46, pt. 1, 1195.
38. Christopher G. Lynch, "Roster of Queen Anne's Confederates," *Centreville Record,* May 3, 1900.
39. "Defenders of Fort Gregg," CV, 25, 23; Entry for April 1, 1865, David Gregg, McIntosh diary, VHS.
40. Michael Wetzel, "Fort Gregg: A One-Armed Comrade's Descriptions of its Capture," *National Tribune,* August 21, 1890; Robert Davison, "How Fort Gregg Was Taken," *National Tribune,* March 10, 1904; J. E. Gaskell, "Last Engagement of Lee's Army, CV, 29, 261.
41. Fox, *The Confederate Alamo*, 140; Maj. Gen. C. M. Wilcox, "Defense of Batteries Gregg and Whitworth, and the Evacuation of Petersburg," SHSP, 4, 29; Owen, *In Camp and Battle with the Washington Artillery*, 372.
42. Greene, *Breaking the Backbone of the Rebellion,* 398; Goldsborough, *Maryland Line*, 325.
43. A. E. Strother, "Battle and Capture of Fort Gregg," CV, 29, 426; OR, 46, 1, 1179; "Defenders of Fort Gregg," CV, 25, 23; George H. Snow to Gen. James H. Lane SHSP, 3, 24; Entry for April 1, 1865, David Gregg McIntosh diary, David Gregg McIntosh papers, VHS; John O'Connell, *Four Years Campaigning with the Army of the Potomac & James,* Box 87, Folder 6, Civil War Document Collection, USAHEC, n.d. O'Connell also stated, "the Commander was laying killed just at the salleyport sword in hand. A young Reb laying up against the magazine badly wounded to whom I gave a drink of water from my canteen told me in a whispering voice that the Capts name was Chew. I took a good look at him he... had on a new gray [uniform] with Broad Red Stripes down the seam of the Pants..." However, O'Connell and the wounded young Confederate soldier were mistaken on both counts; the prostrate artillery officer was not dead, nor was it Capt. Walter Chew. As the only other artillery officer in Fort Gregg, the officer seen by O'Connell could only have been Lt. Frank McElroy. Although neither Chew nor McElroy have any medical records of wounds received at Fort Gregg, Powell A. Casey's extensive research on the Washington Artillery found it was McElroy who was wounded there, probably knocked unconscious during the melee, with an injury from which he soon recovered without requiring medical treatment. Moreover, Chew's coat had been used as wadding during the attack when ammunition ran low, so at the end of the battle he was dressed in shirtsleeves, not a uniform (Powell A. Casey, *An Outline ofthe Civil War Campaigns and Engagements of the Washington Artillery of New Orleans* [Baton Rouge:

Claitor's Publishing, 1986], 47; Frank McElroy and Walter S. Chew CSRs, RG 109, NAB; Goldsborough, *Maryland Line,* 325).

44. Goldsborough, *Maryland Line,* 325; entry for April 1, 1865, David Gregg McIntosh diary, VHS.

45. Fox, *The Confederate Alamo,* 229. See Fox's discussion (249–250) of a pointless war of words that raged several decades after the war in the pages of the Southern Historical Society Papers, *Confederate Veteran,* and the *National Tribune.* In a debate that did credit to few of the participants, regional bias, fading memory, or both contributed to soldiers from North Carolina and Maryland denying credit for fighting at Fort Gregg to those from Louisiana and Mississippi, and vice versa. In the confusing, fluid battle at Fort Gregg, with a loose organization of soldiers from multiple units not under any unified command, it is likely limited vision or knowledge prevented many of the participants, if not all, from having a full understanding of what occurred during the fighting there.

46. The other nine soldiers of the unit captured at Fort Gregg in addition to Chew were Cpl. William Pinder and Pvts. Christopher Lynch, Charles F. Dallam, John H. Gardner, Billy Holtzman, Joseph Peters, Gustavus Porter, James Sparks, and James Stewart (CSRs, Roll 13, RG 109, NAB).

47. Entry for April 1, 1865, David Gregg McIntosh diary, David Gregg McIntosh papers, VHS; James H. Lane to Dear Gen. [Wilcox] in SHSP, 3, 23; George H. Snow to Gen. James H. Lane in SHSP, 3, 23–24.

48. Bearss, *The Petersburg Campaign,* vol. 2, 548; Chris M. Calkins, *The Appomattox Campaign* (Pennsylvania: Combined Books, 1997) , 58; Owen, *In Camp and Battle with the Washington Artillery,* 373–74; Entry for April 1, 1865, David Gregg McIntosh diary, David Gregg McIntosh papers, VHS. By "Baltimore piece" McIntosh could only have been referring to the 4th Maryland Artillery, as it was the only unit from Maryland in the battalion.

49. OR, 46, pt. 1, 1180; Francis McCummins and John Torrington CSRs, RG 109, NAB.

50. Calkins, *The Appomattox Campaign,* 58; Fox, *The Confederate Alamo*, 78; OR, 46, pt. 1, 1273. There is disagreement among historians as to which batteries composed McIntosh's battalion during the Appomattox campaign, and even who commanded it. The units composing the battalion have been taken from Brock's *The Appomattox Roster* as the most pertinent contemporary record. McIntosh was not present at the Appomattox surrender, so Owen was assigned the responsibility of paroling and surrendering McIntosh's battalion in addition to other units. These included Capt. Edward Owen's battalion of the Washington Artillery, remnants of the 13 th and 38th Battalions of Virginia Artillery, and the Donaldsonville Artillery battery (Owen, *In Camp and Battle With the Washington Artillery*, 389; R. A. Brock, *The Appomattox Roster* [New York: Antiquarian Press, Ltd., 1962], 58).

51. Owen, *In Camp and Battle with the Washington Artillery,* 374; Entry for April 1, 1865, David Gregg McIntosh diary, David Gregg McIntosh papers, VHS; OR, 46, 1, 1281; Calkins, *The Appomattox Campaign,* 59; George W. Goodhand CSR, RG 109, NAB.

52. Owen, *In Camp and Battle with the Washington Artillery,* 374; Calkins, *The Appomattox Campaign*, 59; William Marvel, *Lee's Last Retreat* (Chapel Hill & London: The University of North Carolina Press, 2002), 50; Entries for April 4 and 7, 1865, David Gregg McIntosh diary, David Gregg McIntosh papers, VHS. The journeys of Tinges, Harrison, and Rice are conjecture, but the most likely sequence of events. All three men were in Richmond on April 2 when the evacuation order for the city was given: Tinges was released from Robertson Hospital that same day; Rice had arrived at Camp Lee on March 19; and Harrison had been detailed as a clerk in the paymaster's office and was serving with Ewell's Richmond Local Defense Troops. They almost certainly left with Ewell's force, as otherwise they would have been captured when Federal troops moved in to the city on April 3. It is apparent all three kept up with the column as far as

Amelia Court House; had they straggled they would have been captured by the ever-present Federal cavalry. Amelia Court House is the most likely place they re-joined the unit; this is where Ewell's column joined the rest of the army on April 4, and the point at which the elements of the Army of Northern Virginia were at their closest proximity during the Appomattox campaign. Clearly none were with Ewell's column when it was captured almost in its entirety on April 6 at the Battle of Sailor's Creek. Moreover, they had to have been with the lead element of the army and in company with the battery to make their way to other locations, where they finally surrendered. (Robertson Hospital Register entry for C. S. Tinges, Case Number 1318, March 9, 1863, VCU; Robertson Hospital release pass for Charles S. Tinges, April 2, 1865, author's collection; OR, 46, 1, 1293; Pfanz, *Ewell,* 439; Philip L. Harrison, George T. Rice and Charles S. Tinges CSRs, RG 109, NAB).

53. OR, 46, pt. 1, 1281; Owen, *In Camp and Battle with the Washington Artillery*, 391; Marvel, *Lee's Last Retreat*, 54. Pendleton reported, "I reached Amelia courthouse on the morning of the 4th, and immediately proceeded to make arrangements for reducing the artillery with the troops to a proportionate quantity, and properly to dispose of the surplus." Owen wrote that at Appomattox he surrendered three batteries with twelve guns, as enumerated by McIntosh; 251 officers and men in the battalion exclusive of staff were listed on the rolls at Appomattox, nearly the full complement of 300 men for three batteries of four guns each. It is apparent Owen consolidated Chew's, Donald's, and Chamberlayne's batteries into one. Both Price's and Hurt's batteries were near full strength at the Appomattox surrender: Price's had four officers and eighty enlisted men for a total of eighty-four, and Hurt's had two officers and eighty-one enlisted men for a total of eighty-three. It was recorded Hurt's battery also surrendered four guns and three caissons at Appomattox, and presumably Price's battery did as well . Combined, the three consolidated batteries contained a comparable number: one officer and eighty-six enlisted men for a total of eighty-seven to work the remaining four guns. Of these Chamberlayne's was the largest, with forty-five men present at Appomattox, followed by Donald's with one officer and twenty-six men, and the 4th Maryland Artillery with seventeen men. The consolidated battery was probably under the command of Lt. William T. Wilson of Donald's battery, the only commissioned officer present with any of the three consolidated batteries. It is possible Chamberlayne's battery had responsibility for two guns, Donald's for one, and the 4th Maryland battery continued to manage their one piece, since Richardson stated the Chesapeakes surrendered one gun at Appomattox. It appears each of these consolidated batteries continued to maintain their identity as separate units: each surrendered as a separate unit at Appomattox, and in describing the action of April 7 at Cumberland Church, Owen refers directly to Chamberlayne's battery by name as accompanying an infantry charge with one gun, rather than as part of a consolidated battery. At some point the few survivors of Latham's battery (most of whom had been captured at Rice's Station on April 6) were added, as they surrendered at Appomattox as part of McIntosh's battalion (Brock, *The Appomattox Roster,* 55–62; Owen, *In Camp and Battle with the Washington Artillery*, 378; entry for April 4, 1865, David Gregg McIntosh diary, David Gregg McIntosh papers, VHS; Crute, *Units of the Confederate States Army*, 402).

54. OR, 46, pt. 1, 1265; Owen, *In Camp and Battle with the Washington Artillery*, 376.

55. Owen, *In Camp and Battle with the Washington Artillery,* 377; Bearss, *The Petersburg Campaign*, vol. 2, 553.

56. Owen, *In Camp andBattle with the Washington Artillery,* 378; Calkins, *The Appomattox Campaign,* 134; Christopher M. Calkins, "Battle Cumberland Church," *Thirty-Six Hours Before Appomattox: April 6 And 7, 1865* (privately published, 1980); Entry for April

7, 1865, David Gregg McIntosh diary, David Gregg McIntosh papers, VHS.

57. Entry for April 7, 1865, David Gregg McIntosh diary, David Gregg McIntosh papers, VHS; Owen, *In Camp and Battle with the Washington Artillery,* 379; Calkins, "Cavalry Battle Near Farmville," *Thirty-Six Hours Before Appomattox*.

58. Owen, *In Camp and Battle with the Washington Artillery,* 382–383; Calkins, *The Appomattox Campaign*, 174–175.

59. Owen, *In Camp and Battle with the Washington Artillery,* 382–383; Entry for April 9, 1865, David Gregg McIntosh diary, David Gregg McIntosh papers, VHS.

60. Entries for April 9 and 15, 1865, David Gregg McIntosh diary, David Gregg McIntosh papers, VHS ; John P. Hickey, George T. Rice, Philip L. Harrison, and Charles S. Tinges CSRs, RG 109, NAB; Mark L. Bradley, *This Astounding Close: The Road to Bennett Place* (Chapel Hill & London: The University of North Carolina Press, 2000), 168; Marvel, *Lee's Last Retreat*, 179.

61. Krick, *Civil War Weather in Virginia*, 155; Owen, *In Camp and Battle with the Washington Artillery,* 388–389; Calkins, *The Appomattox Campaign,* 188. One of the soldiers absent when the roll was called was Pvt. John Lond of the 4th Maryland Artillery. He likely fell behind the battalion on the march and was absent on April 9, but present for the final surrender; the parole record in his CSR clearly states he was surrendered at Appomattox with the Army of Northern Virginia and that his parole was dated April 10 (John S. Lond CSR, RG 109, NAB). This is why a total of only twelve men of the unit, Lond excluded, are listed on the parole list for the surrender at Appomattox, even though Sgt. John Richardson stated after the war he surrendered twelve men not including himself (Brock, *The Appomattox Roster,* 55–56; Toomey, *The Maryland Line Confederate Soldiers' Home*, 77).

62. Krick, *Civil War Weather in Virginia*, 155; Owen, *In Camp and Battle with the Washington Artillery,* 388–389; Toomey, *The Maryland Line Confederate Soldiers' Home,* 77; CSRs, Roll 13, RG 109, NAB; Mary Worth-Grover to Mrs. Ellis, ca. 1910, author's collection.

63. Owen, *In Camp and Battle with the Washington Artillery*, 392; OR, 46, pt. 1, 1267.

64. Owen, *In Camp and Battle with the Washington Artillery,* 393.

Chapter 8 Endnotes

1. John Richardson, 1860 Census, RG 29, NAB; W. D. Brown [to Mary Ward], May 9, 1863, letter 910, box 5, Ward Family Papers, LOC; Jones, *History of Dorchester County, Maryland* (Baltimore: Williams & Wilkins, 1902), 261.

2. Krick, *Civil War Weather in Virginia*, 155; John D. Richardson, John Hill, John H. Mowbray, John S. Lond, James Pratt, Allen J. Covington CSRs, RG 109, NAB; John Richardson, John Hill, John Mowbray, John Lond, James Pratt, Allen Covington, 1850 Census, 1860 Census, 1870 Census, 1920 Census, RG 29, NAB; Toomey, *The Maryland Line Confederate Soldiers' Home*, 76–77; MLCSH Record Books, MHS.

3. Edward C. Cottrell, William F. Yates CSRs, RG 109, NAB; Edward C. Cottrell, William Yates, 1870 Census, 1880 Census, and 1900 Census, RG 29, NAB; E. C. Cottrell, "Chesapeake Battery at Fort Gregg" and "The Fight at Fort Gregg," CV, 7, 200 and 308; "Members of Mark Camp, Fairfax, Va.," CV, 19, 9.

4. William M. Williams CSR, RG 109, NAB; Smith, ed., *Andrews Memoir,* 122; 1870 United States Federal Census [database online], Provo, UT, USA: Ancestry.com Operations, Inc., 2009, accessed September 21, 2014.

5. George B. Maccubbin CSR, RG 109, NAB; George Maccubbbin, 1860 Census and 1870 Census, Non-population Census Schedules for Virginia, 1850–1880, RG 29, NAB.

6. John H. Gardner, Thomas J. Everngam, William Tarbutton CSRs, RG 109, NAB; John Gardner, Thomas Everngam, William Tarbutton, 1860 Census and 1880 Census, RG 29, NAB; *Baltimore Sun,* October 21, 1862; *Centreville Record,* May 3, 1900.

7. John Torrington, 1860 Census, RG 29, NAB; John Torrington CSR, RG 109, NAB; Frances

Ingmire and Carolyn Ericson, *Register of Confederate Soldiers and Sailor who Died in Federal Prisons and Military Hospitals in the North* (Nacogdoches: Ericson Books, 1984), 41.

8. Walter S. Chew CSR, RG 109, NAB; Walter Chew, 1880 Census, RG 29, NAB.

9. Bedingfield H. Spencer Admission Application, MLCSH Record Books, MS 286, MHS; Mary Worth-Grover to Mrs. Ellis, ca. 1910, author's collection.

10. William Miller Owen, "The Artillery Defenders of Fort Gregg," SHSP, 19, 71; William Miller Owen, "The Artillery Defenders of Fort Gregg: A Correction," SHSP, 20, 33. Owen appears to have forgotten that the 4th Maryland Artillery was in position in Fort Gregg awaiting their consolidation with the 2nd Maryland Artillery when he took command of McIntosh's battalion. On April 2, 1865, Owen ordered Lt. Frank McElroy to retake the section of guns that had been captured from Battle's command of the Washington Artillery at Fort Owen, advance along the Boydton Plank Road to engage Hamblin's Federal brigade, and retire to Fort Gregg. At that point Owen repaired to his headquarters at the Gregg House, so he was not present when Chew took command of the gun section, nor was he a witness to the participation of the soldiers of the 4th Maryland Artillery during the subsequent attack on Fort Gregg.

11. Joseph Forrest CSR, RG 109, NAB; Joseph Forrest, 1860 Census, RG 29, NAB; Joseph Forrest, Pardon applications, RG 94, NAB; Ruffner, *Maryland's Blue and Gray,* 308; Forrest Family History File, SMCHS; Chronicles of St. Mary's 12, no. 3 (March 1964), 20; 16, no. 12 (December, 1968), 243–244; Margaret K. Fresco, *Marriages and Deaths, St. Mary 's County, Maryland, 1634–1900* (privately published, 1982), 380; *St. Mary 's Beacon,* March 14, 1889; Beitzell, St. Mary's County Civil War Records, SMCHS; Edwin W. Beitzell, *Point Lookout Prison Camp for Confederates,* privately published, 1972, 120. The house on one of Forrest's estates, "Sandgates," has been restored and still stands near Oakville, in St. Mary's County (National Register of Historic Places, NRIS Number 78003179, Sandgates on Cat Creek, LOC).

12. Philip A. H. Brown CSR, RG 109, NAB.

13. O'Neal Journal, GNMP; *Baltimore Daily Gazette,* August 3, 1863; Col. J. Thomas Scharf, *The Chronicles of Baltimore: Being a Complete History of "Baltimore Town" and Baltimore City from the Earliest Period to the Present Time* (Baltimore: Turnbull Brothers, 1874), 628; *The Baltimore Sun,* August 4, 1863.

14. Alumni biographies, Archives, and Special Collections, Dickinson College; Ammen, *Maryland Troops*, 183; Cooperstown Glimmerglass, September 16, 1909.

15. Jacob F. Cook CSR, RG 109, NAB; John W. Woods, *Woods 'Baltimore City Directory for 1877* (Baltimore: John W. Woods, 1877), 956; Jacob F. Cook, 1860 Census, 1870 Census, and 1880 Census, RG 29, NAB; Record books, *Society of the Army & Navy of the Confederate States of Maryland Collection 1871–1926,* MS 2825, Maryland Historical Society (hereafter cited as SANCSM Records, MS 2825, MHS); Charles F. Dallam Admission Application, MLCSH Record Books, MS 256, MHS; Ammen, *Maryland Troops,* 178–184. Ironically, Cook was not eligible for residence in The Maryland Line Confederate Soldiers' Home because he had deserted. See appendix H for more information on Cook postwar.

16. Christopher G. Lynch CSR, RG 109, NAB; Christopher Lynch, 1860 Census, 1870 Census, 1880 Census, RG 29, NAB; Goldsborough, *Maryland Line,* 324–328; Christopher G. Lynch Papers, box 60, Civil War Miscellaneous Collection, USAHEC; *Centreville Record,* May 3, 1900.

17. John J. Hooff CSR, RG 109, NAB; John Hooff, 1860 Census, 1870 Census, 1880 Census, 1900 Census, 1910 Census, 1920 Census, RG 29, NAB; Geo. A. Meekins, *Fifth Regiment, Infantry, Md. Nat. Guard, US Volunteers: A History of the Regiment from its First Organization to the Present Time,* Illustrated (Baltimore: A. Hoen & Co., 1899), 13,

(hereafter cited as Fifth Regiment); MLCSH Record Books, MS 256, MHS; Interment records, Loudon Park Cemetery.

18. James P. Williams CSR, RG 109, NAB; Williams Letters; James P. Williams, 1860 Census, 1880 Census, RG 29, NAB.
19. Smith Warrington CSR, RG 109, NAB; Ammen, *Maryland Troops,* 180–181; Smith Warrington, 1870 Census, RG 29, NAB.
20. Francis McCummins, 1860 Census, RG 29, NAB; Francis McCummins CSR, RG 109, NAB; Mrs. Wm. H. Boyd, *Boyd's Directory ofthe District ofColumbia, 1888* (Washington, DC: Elizabeth S. Boyd, 1887), 601.
21. E. K. Culver CSR, RG 109, NAB; E.K. Culver, 1870 Census, 1880 Census, 1900 Census, 1910 Census, RG 29, NAB; R. L. Polk and Company, *Polk's Little Rock City Directory, 1893–1913* (Little Rock: R. L. Polk & Company, 1894, 1896, and 1898); *Arkansas Gazette,* January 6, 1915; E. K. Culver, *Applications for Headstones for US Military Veterans, 1776–1970,* RG 92, NAB.
22. Peter H. Parker CSR, RG 109, NAB; Peter Parker, 1860, 1880, 1900, 1910 Censuses, RG 29, NAB; Peter H. Parker Death Certificate, Division of Vital Records, Department of Health, Richmond, VA.
23. W. L. Burke, William F. Holtzman, George W. Goodhand CSRs, RG 109, NAB; Walter L. Burke, William F. Holtzman, George Goodhand, 1860, 1880, 1900 Censuses, RG 29, NAB; Baltimore County & Baltimore City Equity Papers, MSA.
24. G. S. R. Ewell CSR, RG 109, NBA; George Ewell, 1880 and 1910 Censuses, RG 29, NAB. For a thorough treatment of Confederate veterans organizations in Maryland, see Toomey, *The Maryland Line Confederate Soldiers' Home,* 89–109.
25. Thomas Toy, 1860 Census, RG 29, NAB; Thomas B. Toy CSR, RG 109, NAB; Robertson Hospital Register entry for T. B. Toy, Case Number 882, February 3, 1864, VCU.
26. J. Bettenton to The Honble C.G. Memminger, Secy of Treasurey, January 20, 1864, in Thomas B. Toy CSR, RG 109, NAB.
27. Jackson Douglas to Hon C. G. Memminger, Secty of the Treasury, January 22, 1864, in Thomas B. Toy CSR, RG 109, NAB.
28. Thomas B. Toy CSR, RG 109, NAB; Thomas Toy, 1870, 1880 Censuses, RG 29, NAB.
29. J. B. Cary to Brig. Genl. A. R. Lawton, Oct. 11, 1864, in Philip L Harrison CSR, RG 109, NAB; Philip Harrison, 1850 Census, RG 29, NAB; Robert J. Driver, *Richmond Local Defense Troops, CSA* (Appomattox: H. E. Howard, 2011), 422.
30. Philip L. Harrison CSR, RG 109, NAB; Philip Harrison, 1880 Census and 1900 Census, RG 29, NAB.
31. John E. Plater, 1870 Census and 1900 Census, RG 29, NAB; *Los Angeles Herald,* October 4, 1893; *Los Angeles Times,* February 24, 1936; *St. Mary's Beacon,* April 9, 1926.
32. John E. Plater, 1900 Census and 1920 Census, RG 109, NAB; St. Mary's Beacon, April 9, 1926.
33. Robert Jones, 1860 Census, RG 29, NAB; Robert C. Jones CSR, RG 109, NAB; *Cumberland Times,* November 1, 1879; Chew to Mother, October 2, 1862, private collection.
34. Robert C. Jones CSR, RG 109, NAB; *Cumberland Times*, November 1, 1879.
35 John Shannahan, 1860 Census, RG 29, NAB; John H. K. Shannahan CSR, RG 109, NAB; CV, 24, 414.
36. CV, 24, 414; Robert Caulk, "Pvt. John Henry Kelly Shannahan II," copy in possession of author, 29; *The Easton Gazette,* September 7, 1901.
37. CV, 24, 414.
38. Thomas A. Carberry CSR, RG 109, NAB; James P. Williams to Pa, May 7, 1863, Williams Letters, UVA; Ammen, *Maryland Troops,* 179; Report of Casualties in Andrews's Battalion, RG 109, NAB.
39. Richard E. Langley, 1850 Census and 1860 Census, RG 29, NAB; James L. Langley, 1860 Census, 1860 Slave Schedule, RG 29, NAB; Richard E. Langley CSR, RG 109, NAB.
40. Richard E. Langley, 1900 Census and 1910 Census, RG 29, NAB; *St. Mary's Beacon,* October 8, 1896, July 19, 1900.

41. James T. Moore CSR, RG 109, NAB; Ammen, *Maryland Troops,* 180–181; James T. Moore, 1860 Census, 1880 Census, 1900 Census, 1910 Census, RG 29, NAB.
42. Charles S. Tinges, 1860 Census, RG 29, NAB; Charles S. Tinges CSR, RG 109, NAB; College of St. James Register, 1854, 13.
43. Charles S. Tinges CSR, RG 109, NAB.
44. Charles S. Tinges, 1870 Census, 1880 Census, 1900 Census, 1910 Census, RG 29, NAB; R.L. Polk and Company, *Polk's Baltimore City Directory* (Baltimore: Nichols, Killam & Maffitt, 1860–1918); *Baltimore City Death Record Index,* MSA.
45. *Baltimore Sun,* November 20, 1883.
46. Records of the ANSCSM, MHS; William F. Holtzman, W. L. Burke, and George W. Goodhand CSRs, RG 109, NAB; Goldsborough, *MarylandLine,* 325; William Holtzman, Walter L. Burke, 1860 Census, 1870 Census, 1880 Census, 1900 Census, RG 29, NAB; *Baltimore County and City Equity Papers,* MSA.
47. Records of the ANSCSM MHS; *Baltimore Sun,* June 10, 1874; Toomey, *The Maryland Line Confederate Soldiers' Home,* 98–99; Interment records, Loudon Park Cemetery; Weaver, Paper No. 3, GNMP; Georg, transc., *O'Neal Journal,* GNMP. By 1873, the grave markers of Cpl. Dan Dougherty and Pvts. Fred Cusick and Jack Bryan at Gettysburg had been lost or were illegible; both men were recorded by Weaver as unknowns when the remains of Parker and Oldner were shipped to Baltimore. These soldiers' remains were re-interred in the Gettysburg Dead section of Hollywood Cemetery in Richmond, as were the unknown remains of Pvts. James Stephens and Francis Smith, who had also been buried next to Dougherty at Gettysburg. For a complete discussion of the disposition of the Chesapeake's dead at Gettysburg see appendix C. The same fate must have befallen the grave marker and remains of Pvt. Edward Graham at Fredericksburg; he was likely re-interred at Hollywood Cemetery as an unknown. The disposition of the remains of Lt. John Grason, also initially buried near Hamilton's Crossing at Fredericksburg, is unknown. Neither Graham nor Grason have marked graves at Hollywood Cemetery (see Chris Ferguson, *Southerners at Rest: Confederate Dead at Hollywood Cemetery* [Winchester, VA: Angle Valley Press, 2008]).
48. Charles F. Dallam, 1860 Census, RG 29, NAB; Charles F. Dallam CSR, RG 109, NAB; Toomey, *The War Came by Train,* 240; F. G. Duffield, "The Merchants' Cards and Tokens of Baltimore," *The Numismatist* 20, no. 3 (March, 1907), 68; Polk, *Polk's Baltimore City Directory for 1892, 298;* Meekins, Fifth Regiment, 11; SANCSM Records, MS 2825, MHS; Certificate of Eligibility for Cross of Honor Application to United Daughters of Confederacy, Charles F. Dallam papers, author's collection.
49. Charles F. Dallam Admission Application, MLCSH Record Books, MS 256, MHS; Toomey, *The Maryland Line Confederate Soldiers' Home*, 47–48.
50. Toomey, *The Maryland Line Confederate Soldiers' Home,* 15–17. The records of the home are incomplete, so the actual number of former members of the company who lived there is unknown. Those of the home's records still extant indicate the following ten men did live there: Charles F. Dallam, John F. Green, Vincent Green, John J. Hoof, G. Douglas McClure, John C. Montgomery, John D. Richardson, Bedingfield H. Spencer, J. Henry Willson, and Benjamin Young (Death Records, box 8, MLCSH Record Books, 1882–1932, MSA256, MHS; Toomey, *The Maryland Line Confederate Soldiers 'Home,* 47–87).
51. Benjamin Young CSR, RG 109, NAB; Toomey, *The Maryland Line Confederate Soldiers' Home,* 87; Benjamin Young Admission Application, MLCSH Record Books, MS 256, MHS.
52. MLCSH Record Books, MS 256, MHS.
53. Beddingfield H. Spencer CSR, RG 109, NAB; Bedingfield Spencer, 1860 Census, RG 29, NAB; Toomey, *The Maryland Line Confederate Soldiers'Home,* 79; Bedingfield H. Spencer Admission Application, MLCSH Record Books, MS 286, MHS; *Chestertown Transcript,* August 4, 1900.

54. George D. McClure CSR, RG 109, NAB; George McClure, 1860 Census, RG 29, NAB; Ammen, *Maryland Troops,* 179; Toomey, *The Maryland Line Confederate Soldiers' Home*, 70.
55. George D. McClure Admission Application, MLCSH Record Books, MS 286, MHS. See appendix H for more details on McClure's application to the MLCSH.
56. James H. Willson CSR, RG 109, NAB; James Willson, 1920 Census, RG 29, NAB; Toomey, *The Maryland Line Confederate Soldiers ' Home*, 85; MLCSH Record Books, MS 256, MHS; Interment records, Loudon Park Cemetery.
57. Jones, *History of Dorchester County, Maryland,* 261; John F. and Vincent Green CSRs, RG 109, NAB; John F Green, Vincent Green, 1860 Census, 1870 Census, 1900 Census, and 1910 Census; RG 29, NAB; Toomey, *The Maryland Line Confederate Soldiers' Home,* 53; MLCSH Record Books, MS 256, MHS; interment records, Loudon Park Cemetery.
58. John S. Shafer CSR, RG 109, NAB.
59. John Shafer, 1870 Census, 1880 Census, 1900 Census, 1910 Census, and 1920 Census, RG 29, NAB; CV, 37, 387; *The Bulletin of the Catholic Laymen's Association of Georgia,* September 7, 1929.
60. *Confederate Veteran*, 37, 387; *The Bulletin of the Catholic Laymen's Association of Georgia,* September 7, 1929; Civil War Service Records, www.fold3.com, accessed September 29, 2014.
61. *The Bulletin of the Catholic Laymen's Association of Georgia,* September 7, 1929.
62. Ammen, *Maryland Troops*, 182; *Centreville Record,* May 3, 1900; T. Worthington Mummey to Col. W. H. S. Taylor, June 27, 1864, in Thomas W. Mummey CSR, RG 109, NAB; W. D. Brown to unaddressed [Mary Ward], May 9, 1863, letter 910, book 5, Ward Family Papers, LOC.

Appendix A Endnotes

1. Ammen, *Maryland Troops,* 179.
2. Goldsborough, *Maryland Line,* 319.
3. OR, 12, pt. 2, 237–238.
4. OR, 12, pt. 2, 162.
5. OR, 12, pt. 2, 187; Booth, *Personal Reminiscences of a Maryland Soldier*, 59.
6. OR, 12, pt. 2, 707.
7. OR, 19, pt. 1, 837, 963.
8. James P. Williams to Aunt Mary, May 21, 1863, Williams Letters, UVA.
9. Kelley, ed., *The Personal Memoirs of Jonathan Thomas Scharf,* 34. Capt. Clermont L. Best was the chief of artillery for Banks's corps at Cedar Mountain. Missing reports on the actions of the Federal artillery at Cedar Mountain prevent the identification of which battery lost the Napoleon referred to. Best's report of the battle was lost and is not included in the Official Records (I, 12, p. 148). So, too, is a special report to Best on the operations of Knap's, Roemer's, and Muhlenberg's batteries by Brig. Gen. Samuel W. Crawford, commander of the 1st Brigade of Brig. Gen. A. S. Williams's division, which these batteries were attached to during the battle (OR, 12, pt. 2, 152). The captured gun may have been one of the Napoleons of Lt. Edward D. Muhlenberg's Battery F, 4th US Artillery.
10. Goldsborough, *Maryland Line,* 261.
11. *Hatton Memoir,* 317–319; Augustus James Albert, account of service in the Civil War, MS 1860, Special Collections Library, MHS, 12.
12. Ammen, *Maryland Troops,* 182.
13. Goldsborough, *Maryland Line*, 321
14. Goldsborough, *Maryland Line,* 321; Hartwig, *To Antietam Creek,* 560; Jno. J. Hooff to Aunt, September 17, 1862, letter 734, book 5, Ward Family Papers, LOC.
15. Jno. J. Hooff to Aunt, September 17, 1862, letter 734, book 5, Ward Family Papers, LOC.
16. Fonerden, *A Brief History of the Military Career of Carpenter's Battery,* 37; Moore, *The Story of a Cannoneer Under Stonewall Jackson,* 139.
17. Kelley, ed., *The Personal Memoirs ofJonathan Thomas Scharf,* 51. Cpl. George F. Scott enlisted in the 1st Maryland Artillery July 16, 1861, at Richmond, Virginia. He was killed in action at the battle of Payne's Farm on November 27, 1863 (George F. Scott CSR,

RG 109, NAB); Hartwig, *To Antietam Creek*, 561.

Appendix B Endnotes

1. Brown Casualty Report, RG 109, NAB; OR, 12, pt. 2, 651–654. The only mentions of the Chesapeake Artillery during the Second Manassas battle in the Official Records is their inclusion in an organization table for the Army of Northern Virginia (OR, 12, pt. 2, 550) and in a casualty list compiled for Ewell's division (OR, 12, pt. 2, 811–813).
2. OR, 12, pt. 2, 651; Pfanz, *Ewell*, 254.
3. Gaff, *Brave Men 's Tears,* 61–64; Hennessy, *Second Manassas Battlefield Map Study,* 36, Troop Movement Map 1; Asher W. Garber, "Staunton's Brave Artillery Boys," *Richmond Times-Dispatch,* October 29, 1905; Goldsborough, *Maryland Line,* 320.
4. Brown Casualty Report, RG 109, NAB.
5. OR, 12, pt. 2, 652. Only three batteries are mentioned by Crutchfield as having changed position at some point during the battle: Braxton's, Garber's (Balthis'), and Wooding's. Every other battery he mentions remained stationary.
6. Ibid., 653.
7. Ammen, *Maryland Troops,* 181; Hennessy, *Second Manassas Battlefield Map Study,* Troop Movement Map 4; Brown Casualty Report, RG 109, NAB.
8. OR, 12, pt. 2, 653.
9. Goldsborough, *Maryland Line,* 320; Jno. J. Hooff to Cousin Mary, September 30, 1862, letter 736, box 5, Ward Family Papers, LOC. Goldsborough confuses the timing and sequence of events at Bristoe Station and Second Manassas. He mistakenly places Andy Egan's wounding at Bristoe Station on August 27, as well as Dad Baker's close call; the actual timing of these events occurring on August 29 is confirmed by Brown's day-by-day casualty report. Goldsborough does place the Stonewall Jackson incident during the first day 's battle on August 28, however, and this is the most likely time this event occurred. Goldsborough does not say when Grason encountered the wounded Federal officer, but this could only have happened on August 30, when the Federal presence in Jackson's center ended.
10. Brown Casualty Report, RG 109, NAB.

Appendix C Endnotes

1. James Peter Williams to Pa, July 7, 1863, Williams Letters, UVA; Smith, ed., *Andrews Memoir,* 122.
2. James Peter Williams to Nannie, June 6, 1863, James Peter Williams to Pa, July 7, 1863, Williams Letters, UVA; Smith, ed., *Andrews Memoir,* 122; OR, 27, pt. 2, 341, 544. In a supplemental report recommending replacements for officers killed in the battle dated August 6, Andrews stated, "Whilst there is no official information of the fact, I have no reason to doubt that Capt. Brown has died of his wounds." (Charles I. Raine CSR, RG 109, NAB).
3. Lynch, "The Chesapeake (4th Maryland Battery)," box 60, Civil War Document Collection, USAHEC; Ammen, *Maryland Troops,* 182; Benjamin J. Roberts and James R. Hardesty CSRs, RG 109, NAB; Goldsborough, *Maryland Line,* 182; Christopher Lynch, "Roster of Queen Anne's Confederates," *The Centreville Record*, May 3, 1900.
4. Gregory A. Coco, *Gettysburg's Confederate Dead* (Gettysburg: Thomas Publications, 2003), 14–15; *O'Neal Journal,* GNMP.
5. Coco, *Gettysburg's Confederate Dead,* 20–24; *O'Neal Journal,* GNMP; Richter, Edward G. , "The Removal of the Confederate Dead from Gettysburg," *Gettysburg Magazine* 2, (January, 1990), 113.
6. Ammen, *Maryland Troops,* 182; Smith, ed., *Andrews Memoir,* 124; Hands, *Washington Hands Civil War Notebook,* MHS, 95; William D. Brown CSR, RG 109, NAB; *Richmond Examiner,* July 30, 1863.
7. *Baltimore Sun,* July 14, 1863; William D. Brown CSR, RG 109; NAB.
8. *Baltimore Sun,* July 14, 1863; William D. Brown CSR, RG 109; NAB.
9. Hands, *Washington Hands Civil Notebook, 1860–1865,* MS 2468, MHS, 95.

10. *O'Neal Journal,* GNMP; Coco, *A Vast Sea of Misery,* 116; Site visit and discussion with Greg Coco on Confederate 2nd Corps hospitals May 8, 2003; Telephone discussion with Ron Waddell October 18, 2002; Email message to author from Ron Waddell May 23, 2003; Waddell, *The Daniel Lady Farm Historical Survey,* Special Collections Library, University of Arkansas, 2003 (hereafter cited as Lady Farm Survey). Waddell's historical survey of the Daniel L ady farm exceeded 10,000 pages, yet he found no reference to the use of the Lady farm as a field hospital. He concluded the farm was utilized as an aid station only because of its proximity to the action on Benner's Hill. This is further supported by the abandonment of the farm by the Confederates as a medical facility immediately upon their withdrawal. Waddell determined that Maj. Joseph W. Latimer's arm was amputated at the Weible farm by Latimer's brother, who was a surgeon with the army; since Brown was initially buried there, it is almost certain his leg was amputated there as well.
11. The arrangements were made through the United States Christian Commission; a note pinned to Brown's uniform resides in a private collection and reads, "Uniform and effects of Capt. W. D. Brown of Baltimore MD. J.Y. Foster, U.S.C.C" (author's collection). Foster was a delegate of the US Christian Commission from Philadelphia who worked to alleviate the suffering of wounded at Gettysburg. See his article, "Four Days at Gettysburg," *Harper 's New Monthly Magazine,* 28, no. 165 (February, 1864).
12. In an earlier notation O'Neal had mistakenly recorded the marking as "Corp. W.B.," but no soldier in Ewell's entire 2nd Corps with the rank of corporal and the initials "W.B" was killed at Gettysburg; the captain designation is correct (O'Neal Journal, GNMP, 25; Robert K. Krick and Chris L. Ferguson, *Gettysburg's Confederate Dead: An Honor Roll from America's Greatest Battle* [Winchester: Angle Valley Press, 2014], 6–22 [hereafter cited as *Gettysburg's Confederate Dead*]). See Robert K. Krick and Chris L. Ferguson, *Gettysburg 's Confederate Dead: An Honor Roll from America 's Greatest Battle* (Winchester, VA: Angle Valley Press, 2014), 6–22 (hereafter cited as Krick and Ferguson).
13. *O'Neal Journal,* GNMP; Waddell, *Lady Farm Survey;* Jay Jorgenson, "Joseph W. Latimer, the 'Boy Major,' at Gettysburg, *Gettysburg Magazine,* 10, (January, 1994), 33. William R. Bissell was forty-nine years old when he enlisted as a drill master in the 8th Virginia Infantry Regiment in April 1861. Born in Virginia, he was a wealthy hotel keeper in Bel Air, Maryland, at the start of the war, married with five daughters and two sons ranging in age from two to twenty-two. He was wounded in the side at the Battle of 1st Manassas and was elected captain of Company A in April 1862. As a member of Garnett's Brigade of Pickett's Division, Bissell received a gunshot wound in the shoulder at Gettysburg during Longstreet's assault of July 3, 1863. His arm was amputated; he died on July 16 at the age of fifty-three. His wife had made her way to Gettysburg and was at his side at the time of his death. Bissell was originally buried at the Presbyterian Graveyard on High Street in Gettysburg, and later removed to the Churchville Presbyterian Church Cemetery in Harford County (William Bissell, 1860 Census, RG 29, NAB; William R. Bissell CSR, RG 109, NAB; James E. Crismer, "A Saga of the Civil War: William and Margaret Bissell," *Harford Historical Bulletin,* 60, [Spring, 1994], 51–94).
14. Philip O. Oldner CSR, RG 109, NAB; Brown, *Retreat from Gettysburg,* 76; Coco, *A Strange and Blighted Land,* 219; Samuel B. Weaver, MD, Paper No. 3, 3rd and 4th Shipments, GNMP; Mitchell, *Hollywood Cemetery*, 155.
15. Frederick Cusick, Thaddeus M. Parker, and Andrew J. Bryan CSRs, RG 109, NAB; Ammen, *Maryland Troops,* 182; Samuel Weaver Disinterment and Shipment Records, GNMP. Some modern historians place their burial on the Christian Benner farm, but O'Neal's journal notation is very specific,

listing their names and unit together under the underlined heading, "Daniel Benner Farm." Moreover, the Daniel Benner farm consisted of 150 acres fronting the south side of the Hanover Road bordered on the west by Rock Creek, with the Christian Benner farm immediately to the south of it; to reach the Christian Benner farm would have necessitated transporting the bodies an additional 600 yards or so—highly unlikely on the same evening following the gruelling action at Benner's Hill, as well as a march of twenty-five miles the day before (*O'Neal Journal,* GNMP; Harrison, *Benner 's Hill and Tract No. 04–101,* GNMP).

16. Ammen, *Maryland Troops,* 182; Smith, ed., *Andrews Memoir,* 122; *O'Neal Journal,* GNMP.
17. *O'Neal Journal,* GNMP; Pinckney W. Hatrick CSR, RG 109, NAB; Krick and Ferguson, 59–72; Rufus B. Weaver, MD, List of Confederate Dead Exhumed on Battlefield at Gettysburg Pa, Rufus B. Weaver, MD Exhumation and Shipment Records, GNMP (hereafter cited as Weaver, List of Confederate Dead, GNMP). Pinckney Hatrick was a twenty-five-year-old schoolteacher in Greensboro, North Carolina, when he enlisted as a 1st lieutenant in Co. A, 53 rd North Carolina Infantry Regiment, at Guilford on March 3, 1862. He also served with the regiment while it was stationed in the Department of North Carolina prior to the Gettysburg campaign.
18. James Stephens and Francis Smith CSRs, RG 109, NAB. This is the same methodology used by Harrison and Busey to determine battle deaths of soldiers in Pickett's Division during Longstreet's assault of July 3 (Kathy Georg Harrison and John W. Busey, *Nothing But Glory: Pickett's Division at Gettysburg* [Gettysburg: Thomas Publications, 1993], 451).
19. Daniel Lady Claim, Quartermaster's Claims, RG 92, NAB; Samuel B. Weaver, MD, Paper No. 3, 3rd and 4th Shipments, GNMP. O'Neal also recorded several burials "back of the barn" at the Lady farm, but these are likely wounded men who died in the barn and were thus buried close by.
20. Ammen, *Maryland Troops*, 182.
21. Smith, ed., *Andrews Memoir,* 122; Lynch, "The Chesapeake (4th Maryland Battery)," box 60, Civil War Miscellaneous Collection, USAHEC; Ammen, *Maryland Troops,* 182; Goldsborough, *Maryland Line,* 328; Lynch, "Roster of Queen Anne's Confederates," *Centreville Record,* May 3, 1900.
22. Henry C. Buckmaster and James K. Harper CSR's, RG 109, NAB. Another less likely possibility is that Buckmaster and Harper were captured at the Daniel Lady farm; used as an aid station during the battle, it was abandoned by the Confederates when Johnson's division left the area on July 3rd (Daniel Lady Claim, Quartermaster's Claims, RG 92, NAB).
23. Toomey, *The Maryland Line Confederate Soldiers Home*, 48.
24. Lynch, "The Chesapeake (4th Maryland Battery)," box 60, Civil War Miscellaneous Collection, USAHEC; Goldsborough, *Maryland Line,* 328; Lynch, "Roster of Queen Anne's Confederates," *Centreville Record,* May 3, 1900.
25. James K. Harper CSR, RG 109, NAB.
26. John A. Lane CSR, RG 109, NAB; Smith, ed., *Andrews Memoir,* 122.
27. Lynch, "The Chesapeake (4th Maryland Battery)," box 60, Civil War Miscellaneous Collection, USAHEC; Goldsborough, *Maryland Line*, 328; Lynch, "Roster of Queen Anne's Confederates," *Centreville Record,* May 3, 1900.
28. William H. Mason CSR, RG 109, NAB.
29. Lynch, "The Chesapeake (4th Maryland Battery)," box 60, Civil War Miscellaneous Collection, USAHEC; Goldsborough, *Maryland Line*, 328; Lynch, "Roster of Queen Anne's Confederates," *Centreville Record,* May 3, 1900.
30. Lynch, "The Chesapeake (4th Maryland Battery)," box 60, Civil War Miscellaneous Collection, USAHEC (incorrectly listed as Nicholas Richardson); Goldsborough, *Maryland Line,* 328 (incorrectly listed as

Nicholas Richardson); Lynch, "Roster of Queen Anne's Confederates," *Centreville Record,* May 3, 1900 (incorrectly listed as Nicholas Richard).

31. Smith, ed., *Andrews Memoir,* 122; Benjamin G. Roberts CSR, RG 109, NAB.
32. Charles S. Tinges CSR, RG 109, NAB.
33. Goldsborough, *Maryland Line,* 328.
34. Smith Warrington CSR, RG 109, NAB; Lynch, "The Chesapeake (4th Maryland Battery)," box 60, Civil War Miscellaneous Collection, USAHEC; Goldsborough, *Maryland Line*, 328; Lynch, "Roster of Queen Anne's Confederates," *Centreville Record,* May 3, 1900.
35. Smith, ed., *Andrews Memoir,* 122.
36. James Henry Wilson CSR, RG 109, NAB; Lynch, "The Chesapeake (4th Maryland Battery)," box 60, Civil War Miscellaneous Collection, USAHEC; Toomey, *The Maryland Line Confederate Soldiers' Home,* 85.
37. CSRs for Paul H. Huber, John Myers, John Tregoe, John W. Gore, John W. Canfield, John Vansant, RG 109, NAB.
38. Bunch, *Roster of the Courts-Martial,* 275; Ruffner, *Maryland's Blue and Gray,* 321; Unsigned report of W. Snowden Andrews, August 6, 1863, in Charles I. Raine CSR, RG 109, NAB; John E. Plater, Jacob F. Cook, Thomas McClure, and Andrew J. McElwee CSRs, RG 109, NAB. Plater appeared before a court-martial on September 5 and was dismissed from the service. His sentence was amended to a four-month suspension and loss of pay by Jefferson Davis, and he was "returned to duty" on February 20, 1864. It appears he did not return to the unit. Plater was finally dropped from the rolls on June 6 when Lt. Walter S. Chew was appointed captain to replace Brown, and Sgt. Maj. Thomas P. LeCompte was promoted to 1st lieutenant in Plater's stead.
39. See Petruzzi and Stanley, *The Gettysburg Campaign,* for a complete listing of casualties for all units in the Army of Northern Virginia during the Gettysburg campaign.

Appendix D Endnotes

1. CSRs; Roll 13, RG 109, NAB. Brown's advertisement ran as follows: "THE CHESAPEAKE ARTILLERY, of Maryland, is now with the army of Gen. Jackson. Marylanders desiring to join the same will receive all necessary information by applying to Maj. GEO. W. KYLE, No. 14, Pearl street. Absentees from the company will report immediately for duty. W.D. BROWN, Capt. Comd'g" *(Richmond Dispatch,* August 6, 1862).
2. OR, 36, pt. 3, 861; OR, 46, pt. 3, 1320, 1333.

Appendix E Endnotes

1. Brown Casualty Report, RG 109, NAB; Smith, ed., *Andrews Memoir,* 81, 122; OR, 27, pt. 2, 544; Casualties in Andrews's Battalion, RG 109, NAB.
2. Goldsborough, *Maryland Line*, 328; Lynch, "The Chesapeake (4th Maryland Battery)," box 60, Civil War Miscellaneous Collection, USAHEC; Lynch, "Roster of Queen Anne's Confederates," The *Centreville Record*, May 3, 1900; Ammen, *Maryland Troops,* 182; *Richmond Examiner,* June 29, 1864.
3. Glatthaar, *Soldiering in the Army of Northern Virginia*, 55. This difference is significant ($chi^2 = 7.539$, $p = .0060$). Glatthaar also includes accidental deaths in his discussion of losses in the army and its branches, but the Chesapeake Artillery incurred no deaths due to accidents.
4. Glatthaar, *Soldiering in the Army of Northern Virginia*, 55. This difference is significant ($chi^2 = 6.092$, $p = .0136$).
5. The percentage wounded of the battery was statistically similar to that of the ANV artillery as a whole. Former Pvt. Frank Yates reported in the 1890 Special Census for Veterans that he had suffered "slight wounds on head" during the war, but it is unknown when these wounds occurred. There are no medical records in his service record, indicating he did not require hospitalization, and his name does not appear on any casualty lists, consistent

with the practice in the Army of Northern Virginia of not reporting slight wounds (L. Tilden Moore, *1890 Special Census of the Civil War Veterans of Maryland* [Westminster: Willow Bend Books, 2001], vol. 2, 185; William F. Yates CSR, RG 109, NAB).

6. Glatthaar, *Soldiering in the Army of Northern Virginia,* 55. Both differences are significant: compared to the ANV Infantry, $chi^2 = 4.570$; $p = .0325$, while compared to the Artillery, $chi^2 = 9.767$; $p = .0018$.

7. Pvt. Edward Stansbury died of disease in April 1862; he had been discharged for disability the month before but never recovered, the only member of the battery to have been discharged for disability and also dying of disease while still in military medical care. Because he was in military medical care at the time of his discharge and also died in the same military hospital, he is included for the purposes of this analysis in the group Died of Disease, rather than Discharged for Disability. Pvt. Willy Stenet was discharged, but is not included in this total because it is unlikely he was discharged for disability; there are no medical records in his CSR. Likewise, Pvt. Benjamin Young is also excluded from the Discharged for Disability totals. He stated he was discharged because he was "disabled by wounds" in his application for residency at the Maryland Line Confederate Soldiers Home in 1891. There is no mention of his being wounded anywhere in the historical record, nor are there any medical records in his CSR. He served until after March 1, 1865, and it appears he was discharged because he had served for over three years and was therefore eligible, not because of disability.

8. Alfred C. Young, III, *Lee's Army During the Overland Campaign* (Baton Rouge: Louisiana State University Press, 2013), 12. Young applied a correction factor of 94% to Present for Duty totals on muster rolls to determine the troop strength of units in the Army of Northern Virginia during the Overland Campaign battles of 1864. This correction accounts for men who became ill or detached from their units immediately before a battle. The same correction factor has been applied to muster roll totals here. This factor compares well to the Chesapeake Artillery at Gettysburg, for example. The unit had eighty men present for duty on June 30 when mustered near Chambersburg, Pennsylvania; 94% of this total is between seventy-five and seventy-six men. Two days later, in the action on Benner's Hill, two men are known to have been absent; Sergeant Peter Williams transferred to the Richmond Howitzers on July 1, and Henry Russell was under arrest for desertion, for a total of seventy-eight. Adding men whose duties would have kept them in the rear, the total men engaged at Gettysburg could very reasonably total seventy-five or seventy-six. This is supported by Busey and Martin's study of troop strengths at Gettysburg; these authors determined that the Chesapeake Artillery had seventy-six men present during the engagement on Benner's Hill (John W. Busey and David G. Martin, *Regimental Strengths at Gettysburg* [Baltimore: Gateway Press, Inc, 1982], 156).

Appendix F Endnotes

1. Glatthaar, *Soldiering in the Army of Northern Virginia,* 13, 53.
2. See Glatthaar, *Soldiering in the Army of Northern Virginia,* 3–16 for a thorough analysis of desertions in the Army of Northern Virginia.
3. Glatthaar, *Soldiering in the Army of Northern Virginia,* 13; This difference is significant ($chi^2 = 14.846$, $p = .0050$).
4. Glatthaar, *Soldiering in the Army of Northern Virginia*, 14; This difference is significant ($chi^2 = 21.799$, $p = .0001$).
5. Glatthaar, *Soldiering in the Army of Northern Virginia,* 13; This difference is significant ($chi^2 = 10.980$, $p = .0009$). The cumulative desertion figures for the Army of Northern Virginia were determined by adding the monthly desertion totals up until January 1, 1865; See Glatthaar, 15.
6. These were Pvts. Jacob F. Cook, Thomas McClure, Andrew J. McElwee, and Henry Russell. Russell had attempted to desert during the army's advance into Pennsylvania and was under arrest at the time of the company's

muster on June 30, 1863. It is unlikely he participated in the action at Gettysburg on July 2 (Jacob F. Cook, Thomas McClure, Andrew J. McElwee, Henry Russell CSRs, RG 109, NAB).

7. OR, 44, pt. 3, 1329. The deserters at this time were Pvts. Alexander Green, Francis Kirby, Walter L. Burke, Charles Mettee, Henry Corry, and Edwin K. Culver (Alexander Green, Francis Kirby, W. L. Burke, Charles Mettee, Henry Corry, Edwin K. Culver CSRs, RG 109, NAB). Sixty-one officers and enlisted men were present for duty with the battery at its muster on December 31, 1864, at Petersburg (CSRs, Roll 13, RG 109, NAB; OR, 46, pt. 3, 1333).
8. Compared to the Army of Northern Virginia, the Chesapeake's adjusted desertion rate is lower to a significant degree ($chi^2 = 6.750$, $p = .0094$), and even weakly significant compared to the lower desertion rate of the ANV's artillery arm ($chi^2 = 2.599$, $p = .1069$).

Appendix G Endnotes

1. Joseph Forrest CSR, RG 109, NAB.
2. OR, 12, pt. 2, 238, 233, 183.
3. James P. Williams to Aunt Mary, May 21, 1863, Williams Letters, UVA.
4. OR, 29, pt. 1, 424; OR, 36, pt. 2, 988; OR, 36, pt. 3, 861.
5. OR, 42, pt. 3, 1341; OR, 36, pt. 1, 1054; Walter S. Chew CSR, RG 109, NAB.
6. OR, 42, pt. 3, 1341.
7. OR, 46, pt. 2, 1329; Strother, CV, 29, 425.
8. OR, 46, pt. 1, 1281; Owen, *In Camp and Battle with the Washington Artillery,* 391.
9. Toomey, *The Maryland Line Confederate Soldiers' Home,* 76–77.

Appendix H Endnotes

1. George D. McClure CSR, RG 109, NAB.
2. A. C. Trippe to James R. Wheeler Esq, June 19, 1905, in Geo. D. McClure Admission Application, MLCSH Record Books, MSA 256, MHS. Trippe enlisted as a private in Company A of the 2nd Maryland Infantry Battalion. He was wounded in the shoulder at Gettysburg in the assault on Culp's Hill, promoted to lieutenant in the CS Ordnance Department in November 1863, and paroled at Burkesville, Virginia, in May 1865. Postwar he played a prominent role in several fraternal and charitable organizations in Baltimore. He died in 1918; his death notice is in the *Washington Post,* July 18, 1918, and his obituary is in CV, 26, 404.
3. Geo. D. McClure Admission Application, MLCSH Record Books, MS 256, MHS.
4. Toomey, *Maryland Line Confederate Soldiers' Home*, 70.
5. Jacob F. Cook CSR, RG 109, NAB.
6. Paul H. Huber, John Myers, John Tregoe, John W. Canfield, John B. Vansant, and John W. Gore CSRs, RG 109, NAB.
7. Ammen, *Maryland Troops*, 178. There is no mention of Cook residing at the home in any of the home's records, and if he did apply for residency, his application has been lost. See appendix A for a discussion of myths promulgated by veterans after the war.
8. Ammen, *Maryland Troops,* 178; SANCSM Records, MS 2825, MHS; Charles F. Dallam Admission Application, MLCSH Record Books, MSA 256, MHS.

Introduction to the Roster Endnotes

1. Record Group 94, Applications for Pardon Submitted to President Andrew Johnson by Former Confederates, NAB; Record Group 94, Compiled Service Records of former Confederate soldiers (Galvanized Yankees) who served in the 1st through 6th US Volunteer Infantry Regiments 1864–1866, NAB; Record Group 109, Confederate States Army Casualty Lists and Narrative Reports, NAB; Record Group 109, Compiled Service Records of Confederate Soldiers, NAB; Record Group 249, Selected Records of the War Department Relating to Confederate Prisoners of War, 1861–1865, NAB.
2. Christopher Goodhand Lynch Papers, box 60, Civil War Miscellaneous Collection, USAHEC.
3. Ammen, *Maryland Troops*, 178; J. Thomas Scharf, *History of Western Maryland,* (Philadelphia: L. H. Everts, 1882), 338.

4. Captain George W. Booth, *Illustrated Souvenir: Maryland Line Confederate Soldiers 'Home* (Pikesville: Board of Governors, 1894), 90.
5. L. [Christopher Goodhand Lynch], "Roster of Queen Anne's Confederates," the *Centreville Record,* May 3, 1900.
6. Goldsborough, *Maryland Line,* 319–328.
7. Census of the United States, 1850, 1860, 1870, 1900, 1910, 1920, RG 29, NAB; Interment records, Loudon Park Cemetery.
8. William Culver is mentioned in Goldsborough's roster, and also as killed at Fort Gregg in the narrative written by Christopher Goodhand Lynch in Goldsborough, *Maryland Line*. He is also listed in both of Lynch's rosters compiled in 1865 and 1900, as well as Lynch's 1865 casualty list. Although Lynch appears to be the only source for Culver's service in the unit, Lynch was present at Fort Gregg, so he is a credible witness. Culver appears in the 1860 Census but not the 1870 Census, further supporting Lynch's information.
9. Robert Goldsborough is listed in W. W. Goldsborongh's roster with no first name or initials (implying that the two were not related), in both of Lynch's 1865 and 1900 rosters, and in Cook's roster with no first name or initials. See also Robert Goldsborough, 1860 Census, RG 29, NAB, and Robert H. Goldsborough CSR, RG I09, NAB.
10. Edward Graham is listed in Goldsborough's roster as "Edward Grahame" and on Goldsborough's casualty list for 1st Fredericksburg as " Graham," with no first name or initials. Graham is also listed in Lynch's 1865 and 1900 rosters, as well as Lynch's casualty list for 1st Fredericksburg, and on Cook's roster as " Grahame" with no first name or initials. Graham appears in the 1860 Census but not the 1870 Census.
11. John Poisal, Jr. is listed in Goldsborongh's roster as "John Poisel," and on Goldsborough's casualty list as "John Poisal," having died in a hospital. Lynch spells his name "John Poisel" on his 1865 and 1900 rosters, as well as the 1865 casualty list as having died in a hospital. Cook's roster includes him as "John Poisel." He does not appear in the 1870 Census.
12. Lewis Warrington is listed on the rosters of Goldsborough and on both of Lynch's, as well as on Cook's. He appears in the 1870 Census.
13. Brown Casualty Report, RG 109, NAB. Although it may seem odd that Brown would misspell the names of the men under his command, these types of reporting errors were common. In the same report Brown gave Pvt. William H. Mason's initials as "J. C."
14. Benjamin Young CSR, RG 109, NAB; Toomey, *The Maryland Line Confederate Soldiers Home,* 87.

BIBLIOGRAPHY

Albert, Augustus James. *Account of Service in the Civil War, 1861.* MS 1860, Special Collections Library, Maryland Historical Society.

Allardice, Bruce S. *Confederate Colonels: A Biographical Register.* Columbia and London: University of Missouri Press, 2008.

Ammen, S. Z. *Maryland Troops in the Confederate Army from Original Sources.* Maryland State Archives, Annapolis, MD, 1879.

Barnett, Bert H. "Our Position Was Finely Adapted to Its Use." In *The Guns of Cemetery Hill,* [231–259] Gettysburg, PA: Gettysburg National Military Park Library and Research Center, 2006.

Bartlett, Napier. *Military Record of Louisiana.* Baton Rouge: Louisiana State University Press, 1964.

Bearss, Edwin C. *The Petersburg Campaign.* 2 vols. California: Savas Beatie, 2014.

Beitzell, Edwin W. *Point Lookout Prison Camp for Confederates.* Privately published, 1972.

Beitzell, Edwin W. *St. Mary's County Civil War Records.* Leonardtown, MD: St. Mary's County Historical Society, , n.d.

Bohannon, Keith S. *The Giles, Alleghany and Jackson Artillery.* Lynchburg, TN: H.E. Howard, 1990.

Booth, George W. *Illustrated Souvenir: Maryland Line Confederate Soldiers' Home.* Pikesville, MD: Board of Governors, 1894.

Booth, George W. *Personal Reminiscences of a Maryland Soldier in the War Between the States, 1861–1865.* Gaithersburg, MD: Butternut Press Inc., 1986.

Boyd, Elizabeth S. *Wm. H. Boyd's Directory of the District of Columbia, 1888.* Washington, DC: Elizabeth S. Boyd, 1887.

Bradley, Mark L. *This Astounding Close: The Road to Bennett Place.* Chapel Hill & London: The University of North Carolina Press, 2000.

Brock, R. A., ed. *Southern Historical Society Papers.* 52 vols. Wilmington, NC: Broadfoot Publishing Company, 1991.

Brock, R. A. *The Appomattox Roster.* New York: Antiquarian Press, Ltd., 1962.

Brown, Kent Masters. *Retreat From Gettysburg: Lee, Logistics, and the Pennsylvania Campaign.* Chapel Hill and London: University of North Carolina Press, 2005.

Buck, Samuel D. *With the Old Confeds: Actual Experiences of a Captain in the Line.* Baltimore, MD: H. E. Houck & Co., 1925.

Bunch, Jack A. *Roster of the Courts-Martial in the Confederate States Armies.* Shippensburg, PA: White Mane Books, 2001.

Busey, John W. and David G. Martin. *Regimental Strengths at Gettysburg.* Baltimore: Gateway Press, Inc., 1982.

Calkins, Christopher M. *Thirty-Six Hours Before Appomattox: April 6 and 7, 1865.* Privately published, 1980.

Calkins, Christopher M. *The Appomattox Campaign.* Pennsylvania: Combined Books, 1997.

Caulk, Robert. "Pvt. John Henry Kelly Shannahan II, CSA (1842–1916)." Copy in author's possession, 2000.

Casey, Powell A. *An Outline of the Civil War Campaigns and Engagements of the Washington Artillery of New Orleans.* Baton Rouge, LA: Claitor's Publishing, 1986.

Chrismer, James E. "A Saga of the Civil War: William and Margaret Bissell." Harford Historical Bulletin 60 (Spring 1994): 51–94.

Coco, Gregory A. *A Vast Sea of Misery: A History and Guide to the Union and Confederate Field Hospitals at Gettysburg, July 1–November 20, 1863.* Gettysburg, PA: Thomas Publications, 1988.

Coco, Gregory A. *A Strange and Blighted Land. Gettysburg: The Aftermath of a Battle.* Gettysburg, PA: Thomas Publications, 1995.

Coco, Gregory A. *Gettysburg's Confederate Dead.* Gettysburg, PA: Thomas Publications, 2003.

Coddington, Edwin B. *The Gettysburg Campaign: A Study in Command.* Dayton, OH: Morningside Press, 1968.

Cowles, Capt. Calvin D., 23rd U.S. Infantry, comp. *The Official Military Atlas of the Civil War.* New York: The Fairfax Press, 1978.

Crute, Joseph H., Jr. *Units of the Confederate States Army*. Midlothian, VA: Derwent Books, 1987.

Cunningham, S. A., ed. *Confederate Veteran*. 40 vols. Wilmington, NC: Broadfoot Publishing, 1986.

Dallam, Charles Francis. Papers. Author's collection.

Davis, George B., Leslie J. Perry, and Joseph W. Kirkley. *The Official Military Atlas of the Civil War*. New York: The Fairfax Press, 1978.

Driver, Robert J., Jr. *First and Second Maryland Infantry, CSA*. Bowie, MD: Heritage Books, Inc., 2003.

Driver, Robert J., Jr. *Richmond Local Defense Troops, CSA*. Appomattox, VA: H. E. Howard, 2011.

Evans, Clement A., ed. *Confederate Military History*. Atlanta: Confederate Publishing Company, 1899.

Ferguson, Chris. *Southerners at Rest: Confederate Dead at Hollywood Cemetery*. Winchester, VA: Angle Valley Press, 2008.

Fonerden, Clarence A. *A Brief History of the Military Career of Carpenter's Battery*. New Market, VA: Henkel & Company, 1911.

Fox, John J., III. *The Confederate Alamo*: *Bloodbath at Petersburg's Fort Greg on April 2, 1865*. Winchester, VA: Angle Valley Press, 2010.

Frassanito, William A., and Elwood Christ. *The Daniel Lady Farm and the Battle of Gettysburg*. Gettysburg, PA: Gettysburg Battlefield Preservation Association, 1999.

Fresco, Margaret K. *Marriages and Deaths, St. Mary's County, Maryland, 1634–1900*. Privately published, 1982.

Furgurson, Earnest B. *Not War But Murder: Cold Harbor, 1864*. New York: Alfred A. Knopf, 2000.

Gaff, Alan T. *Brave Men's Tears*: *The Iron Brigade at Brawner's Farm*. Dayton, OH: Morningside Press, 1996.

Garnett, Carroll M. *Fort Lowry and Raiders on the Rappahannock*. New York: Vantage Press, 2002.

Georg, Kathleen R., transc. *Record of Confederate Burials: The Journal of Doctor John W. C. O'Neal, M. D.* Gettysburg, PA: Gettysburg National Military Park Library and Research Center, 1982.

Glatthaar, Joseph T. *General Lee's Army From Victory to Collapse*. New York: Free Press, 2008.

Glatthaar, Joseph T. *Soldiering in the Army of Northern Virginia, A Statistical Portrait of the Troops Who Served under Robert E. Lee*. Chapel Hill: The University of North Carolina Press, 2011.

Goldsborough, W. W. *The Chesapeake Artillery at Gettysburg*. Edward Cronin Papers, New York Historical Society, n.d.

Goldsborough, W. W. *The Maryland Line in the Confederate Army*. Baltimore, MD: Kelly, Piet, and Company, 1869.

Goldsborough, W. W. *The Maryland Line in the Confederate Army, 1861–1865*. Baltimore, MD: Guggenheimer, Weil and Co., 1900.

Gottfried, Bradley M. *Roads to Gettysburg: Lee's Invasion of the North, 1863*. Shippensburg: White Mane Books, 2001.

Gottfried, Bradley M. *The Maps of Gettysburg: An Atlas of the Gettysburg Campaign, June 3–July 13, 1863*. New York and California: Savas Beatie, 2007.

Gottfried, Bradley M. *The Artillery of Gettysburg*. Nashville, TN: Cumberland House Publishing, Inc., 2008.

Graham, Martin F., and George F. Skoch. *Mine Run: A Campaign of Lost Opportunities*. Lynchburg, TN: H. E. Howard, 1987.

Greene, A. Wilson. *Breaking the Backbone of the Rebellion: The Final Battles of the Petersburg Campaign*. Mason City, IA: Savas Publishing Company, 2000.

Hammett, Regina Combs. *History of St. Mary's County, Maryland, 1634–1990*. Ridge, MD: Self-published, 1997.

Hands, Washington. *Washington Hands Civil War Notebook, 1860–1865*. MS 2468, Special Collections Library, Maryland Historical Society.

Harrison, Kathy Georg. *Benner's Hill and Tract No. 04-101: History of Site and Recommendations for Site*. Gettysburg, PA: Gettysburg National Military Park Library and Research Center, n.d..

Harrison, Kathy Georg, and John W. Busey. *Nothing But Glory: Pickett's Division at Gettysburg*. Gettysburg, PA: Thomas Publications, 1993.

Hartwig, D. Scott. *To Antietam Creek: The Maryland Campaign of September 1862*. Baltimore, MD: The Johns Hopkins University Press, 2012.

Hartzler, Daniel D. *A Band of Brothers: Photographic Epilogue to Marylanders in the Confederacy*. Colorado: Bookcrafters, 1982.

Hartzler, Daniel D. *Marylanders in the Confederacy*. Silver Spring, MD: Family Line Publications, 1986.

Hatton, John William Ford. *Memoir, John William Ford Hatton, First Maryland Battery C.S.A., 1861 to 1865*. John William Ford Hatton Papers. Library of Congress.

Hennessy, John J. *Second Manassas Battlefield Map Study*. 2nd ed. Lynchburg, TN: H. E. Howard, Inc., 1991.

Hennessy, John J. *Return to Bull Run: the Campaign and Battle of Second Manassas*. New York: Simon & Schuster, 1993.

Hollywood Memorial Association. *Register of the Confederate Dead, Interred in Hollywood Cemetery, Richmond, Va*. Richmond: Gary, Clemmitt & Jones, Printers, 1869.

Howard, McHenry. *Recollections of a Maryland Confederate Soldier and Staff Officer Under Johnston, Jackson, and Lee*. Baltimore, MD: Williams & Wilkins Co., 1914.

Ingmire, Frances, and Carolyn Ericson. *Register of Confederate Soldiers and Sailors Who Died in Federal Prisons and Military Hospitals in the North*. Nacogdoches, TX: Ericson Books, 1984.

Johnson, Bradley T. *Bradley T. Johnson Papers Collection*. David M. Rubenstein Rare Book and Manuscript Library, Duke University.

Johnson, Robert Underwood, and Clarence Clough Buell, eds. *Battle and Leaders of the Civil War*. 4 vols. New York: Thomas Yoseloff, 1956.

Jones, Elias. *History of Dorchester County, Maryland*. Baltimore, MD: Williams & Wilkins, 1902.

Jorgenson, Jay. "Joseph W. Latimer, the 'Boy Major,' at Gettysburg." *Gettysburg Magazine* 10 (January, 1994): 33.

Kelley, Tom, ed. *The Personal Memoirs of Jonathan Thomas Scharf of the First Maryland Artillery*. Baltimore, MD: Butternut and Blue, 1992.

Krick, Robert K. *Lee's Colonels: A Biographical Register of the Field Officers of the Army of Northern Virginia*, 2nd ed. Dayton: Morningside, 1984.

Krick, Robert K. *Stonewall Jackson at Cedar Mountain*. Chapel Hill and London: The University of North Carolina Press, 1990.

Krick, Robert K., and Chris L. Ferguson. *Gettysburg's Confederate Dead: An Honor Roll from America's Greatest Battle*. Winchester, VA: Angle Valley Press, 2014.

Krick, Robert K. *Civil War Weather in Virginia*. Tuscaloosa: The University of Alabama Press, 2007.

Ladd, David L., and Audrey J. Ladd, eds. *The Bachelder Papers: Gettysburg in Their Own Words*. Dayton, OH: Morningside House, Inc., 1994.

Long, Robert L. *Valor in a Border State: Confederate Soldiers of St. Mary's County, Maryland*. Privately published, 2012.

Lynch, Christopher Goodhand. Papers. Civil War Miscellaneous Collection, US Army Heritage and Education Center, Carlisle, PA.

Mackowski, Chris, and Kristopher D. White. *Chancellorsville's Forgotten Front*. El Dorado Hills, CA: Savas Beatie, 2013.

Manakee, Harold R. *Maryland in the Civil War*. Baltimore: Maryland Historical Society, 1961.

Marvel, William. *Lee's Last Retreat*. Chapel Hill & London: The University of North Carolina Press, 2002.

Maryland Line Confederate Soldiers' Home Record Books. 1883–1932. MS 256, Special Collections Library, Maryland Historical Society.

McCullough, Samuel Thomas. Diary. Hotchkiss-McCullough Manuscripts, 1846–1912, Library of Congress.

McIntosh, David Gregg. David Gregg McIntosh Papers, 1862–1916. Virginia Historical Society, Richmond, VA.

McPherson, Edward. *For Cause and Comrades: Why Men Fought in the Civil War*. New York: The Free Press, 1987.

McGuire, Judith Brockenbrough. *Diary of a Southern Refugee During the War*. 2nd ed. New York: E.J. Hale & Son, 1868.

Meekins, Geo. A. *Fifth Regiment, Infantry, Md. Nat. Guard, U.S. Volunteers: A History of the*

Regiment from Its First Organization to the Present Time, Illustrated. Baltimore, MD: A. Hoen & Co., 1899.

Mingus, Scott L., Sr. *Flames Beyond Gettysburg: The Confederate Expedition to the Susquehanna River, June, 1863*. New York and El Dorado Hills, CA: Savas Beatie, 2012.

Mitchell, Mary H. *Hollywood Cemetery: The History of a Southern Shrine*. Richmond, VA: The William Byrd Press, 1985.

Moore, Edward A. *The Story of a Cannoneer Under Stonewall Jackson*. New York and Washington: The Neale Publishing Company, 1907.

Moore, L. Tilden. *1890 Special Census of the Civil War Veterans of the State of Maryland*. Westminster, MD: Willow Bend Books, 2001.

Moore, Robert H., II. *The Charlottesville, Lee Lynchburg and Johnson's Bedford Artillery*. Lynchburg, VA: H.E. Howard, Inc., 1990.

Newman, Harry Wright. *Maryland and the Confederacy*. Annapolis, MD: Author, 1976.

Newsome, Hampton, John Horn, and John G. Selby, eds. *Civil War Talks: Further Reminiscences of George S. Bernard and His Fellow Veterans*. Charlottesville: University of Virginia Press, 2012.

Noe, Kenneth W. *Reluctant Rebels: The Confederates Who Joined the Army after 1861*. Chapel Hill: The University of North Carolina Press, 2010.

Nofi, Albert A. *The Gettysburg Campaign: June–July 1863*. Cambridge, MA: De Capo Press, 1996.

O'Connell, John. *Four Years Campaigning with the Army of the Potomac & James*. Civil War Document Collection, US Army Heritage and Education Center, Carlisle, PA, n.d.

O'Reilly, Francis Augustin. *The Fredericksburg Campaign: Winter War on the Rappahannock*. Baton Rouge: Louisiana State University Press, 2003.

Owen, Wm. Miller. *In Camp and Battle with the Washington Artillery*. Boston: Ticknor and Company, 1885.

Petruzzi, J. David, and Steven A. Stanley. *The Gettysburg Campaign in Numbers and Losses*. El Dorado Hills, CA: Savas Beattie LLC, 2012.

Pfanz, Donald C. *Richard S. Ewell: A Soldier's Life*. Chapel Hill and London: The University of North Carolina Press, 1998.

Pfanz, Harry W. *Gettysburg: Culp's Hill and Cemetery Hill*. Chapel Hill and London: The University of North Carolina Press, 1993.

Rhea, Gordon C. *To the North Anna River*. Baton Rouge: Louisiana State University Press, 2000.

Richter, Edward G. J. "The Removal of the Confederate Dead from Gettysburg," *Gettysburg Magazine* 2, (January, 1990): 113.

R.L. Polk and Company. *Polk's Baltimore City Directory*. Baltimore, MD: Nichols, Killam & Maffitt, 1860–1918.

R.L. Polk and Company. *Polk's Little Rock Directory*. Little Rock, AR: R.L. Polk & Company, 1894, 1896, 1898.

Ruffner, Kevin Conley. *Maryland's Blue & Gray*. Baton Rouge & London: Louisiana State University Press, 1997.

Scharf, J. Thomas. *The Chronicles of Baltimore: Being a Complete History of "Baltimore Town" and Baltimore City from the Earliest Period to the Present Time*. Baltimore, MD: Turnbull Brothers, 1874.

Scharf, J. Thomas. *History of Maryland*. Baltimore, MD: John B. Piet, 1879.

Scharf, J. Thomas. *History of Baltimore City and County From the Earliest Period to the Present Day: Including Biographical Sketches of their Representative Men*. Philadelphia: Louis H. Everts, 1881.

Scharf, J. Thomas. *History of Western Maryland*. Philadelphia: L. H. Everts, 1882.

Schulte, Brett, transc. Confederate Inspection Reports: Corps Artillery, Third Corps, Army of Northern Virginia. www.beyondthecrater.com.

Shultz, David. "Benner's Hill: What Value? Andrews' Artillery Battalion and the Heights East of Town." *Gettysburg Magazine* 44 (January, 2011): 56–60.

Sheads, Scott Sumpter, and Daniel Carroll Toomey. *Baltimore During the Civil War*. Baltimore, MD: Toomey Press, 1997.

Sherwood, George L. *First Maryland Artillery and Second Maryland Artillery*. Westminster, MD: Heritage Books, 2007.

Sibley, F. Ray, ed. *Confederate Artillery Organizations*. El Dorado Hills, California: Savas Beatie LLC, 2014.

Sifakis, Stewart. *Compendium of the Confederate Armies: Kentucky, Maryland, Missouri, the Confederate Units, and the Indian Units*. Berwyn Heights, MD: Heritage Books, 2009.

Slaughter, James B. *Settlers, Southerners, Americans: The History of Essex County, Va*. Salem, WV: Don Mills, Inc., 1986.

Smith, Tunstall, ed. *Richard Snowden Andrews, Lieutenant Colonel Commanding the First Maryland Artillery (Andrews's Battalion), Confederate States Army: A Memoir*. Baltimore, MD: The Sun Job Printing Office, 1910.

Society of the Army & Navy of the Confederate States of Maryland Collection. 1871–1926. MS 2825, Special Collections Library, Maryland Historical Society.

Sommers, Richard J. *Richmond Redeemed: The Siege at Petersburg*. Garden City, NY: Doubleday & Company, Inc., 1981.

Speicher, James L. *The Sumter Flying Artillery: A Civil War History of the 11th Battalion Georgia Light Artillery*. Gretna, LA: Pelican Publishing Company Inc., 2009.

Stiles, Robert. *Four Years Under Marse Robert*. New York and Washington, DC: The Neale Publishing Company, 1903.

Strickler, Theodore D. *When and Where We Met Each Other On Shore and Afloat: Battles, Engagements, Actions, Skirmishes, and Expeditions During the Civil War 1861–1866*. Washington, DC: The *National Tribune*, 1899.

Thomas, Dean S. *Cannons: An Introduction to Civil War Artillery*. Gettysburg, PA: Thomas Publications, 1985.

Thomas, Henry W. *History of the Doles-Cook Brigade*, Army of Northern Virginia, C.S.A. Dayton, OH: Morningside, 1981.

Tighe, Adrian G. *The Bristoe Campaign: General Lee's Last Strategic Offensive with the Army of Northern Virginia*, October 1863. Self-published, 2011.

Tinges, Charles Sewall. Papers. Author's collection.

Toomey, Daniel Carroll. *The Civil War in Maryland*. Baltimore, MD: Toomey Press, 1983.

Toomey, Daniel Carroll. *Marylanders at Gettysburg*. Baltimore, MD: Toomey Press, 1994.

Toomey, Daniel Carroll. *The Maryland Line Confederate Soldiers' Home and Confederate Veterans' Organizations in Maryland*. Baltimore, MD: Toomey Press, 2001.

Toomey, Daniel Carroll. *The War Came by Train: The Baltimore & Ohio Railroad During the Civil War*. Baltimore, MD: Baltimore & Ohio Railroad Museum, 2013.

Turner, John W., ed. *Captain Greenlee Davidson, CSA: Diary and Letters, 1851–1863*. Verona, VA: McClure Press, 1975.

US War Department. *The War of the Rebellion: A Compilation of the Official Records of the Union and Confederate Armies*. 128 vols. Washington, DC: US Government Printing Office, 1880–1901.

Waddell, Ronald L. *The Daniel Lady Farm Historical Survey*. Special Collections Library, University of Arkansas, 2003.

Wallace, Lee A., Jr. *The Richmond Howitzers*. Lynchburg, TN: H. E. Howard Inc., 1993.

Ward, Evelyn. *The Children of Bladensfield*. New York: The Viking Press, 1978.

Ward Family. Papers. Library of Congress.

Warner, Ezra J. *Generals in Gray: Lives of the Confederate Commanders*. Baton Rouge and London: Louisiana State University Press, 1959.

Weaver, Rufus B., MD. Exhumation and Shipment Records. Gettysburg National Military Park Library and Research Center.

Wiley, Bell Irvin. *The Life of Johnny Reb*. Baton Rouge and London: Louisiana State University Press, 1943.

Williams, Evelyn Cary, ed. *Letters of James Peter Williams, 1861–1865*. Albert and Shirley Small Special Collections Library, University of Virginia, Lynchburg, 1937.

Wise, Jennings Cropper. *The Long Arm of Lee, or The History of the Artillery of the Army of Northern Virginia*. 2 vols. Lynchburg, VA: J.P. Bell Company, Inc., 1915.

Woods, John W. John W. *Woods' Baltimore City Directory*. Baltimore, MD: John W. Woods, 1860, 1877.

Young, Alfred C., III. *Lee's Army During the Overland Campaign*. Baton Rouge: Louisiana State University Press, 2013.

INDEX